Popular Politics and the English Reformation

This book is a study of popular responses to the English Reformation. It takes as its subject not the conversion of English subjects to a new religion but rather their political responses to a Reformation perceived as an act of state and hence, like all early modern acts of state, negotiated between government and people.

These responses included not only resistance but also significant levels of accommodation, cooperation and collaboration as people attempted to co-opt state power for their own purposes. This study argues, then, that the English Reformation was not done *to* people, it was done *with* them in a dynamic process of engagement between government and people. As such, it answers the twenty-year-old scholarly dilemma of how the English Reformation could have succeeded despite the inherent conservatism of the English people, and it presents the first genuinely post-revisionist account of one of the central events of English history.

ETHAN H. SHAGAN is Assistant Professor of History at Northwestern University. He received his Ph.D. from Princeton University in 2000 and was a Junior Fellow of the Harvard University Society of Fellows. He has published articles in the *English Historical Review*, the *Journal of British Studies*, the *Journal of Ecclesiastical History*, and in numerous edited collections. This is his first book.

Cambridge Studies in Early Modern British History

Series editors

ANTHONY FLETCHER
Victoria County History, Institute of Historical Research, University of London

JOHN GUY
Professor of Modern History, University of St. Andrews

JOHN MORRILL
Professor of British and Irish History, University of Cambridge,
and Vice-Master of Selwyn College

This is a series of monographs and studies covering many aspects of the history of the British Isles between the late fifteenth century and the early eighteenth century. It includes the work of established scholars and pioneering work by a new generation of scholars. It includes both reviews and revisions of major topics and books, which open up new historical terrain or which reveal startling new perspectives on familiar subjects. All the volumes set detailed research into our broader perspectives and the books are intended for the use of students as well as of their teachers.

For a list of titles in the series, see end of book.

POPULAR POLITICS
AND THE ENGLISH
REFORMATION

ETHAN H. SHAGAN

Assistant Professor, Department of History, Northwestern University

CAMBRIDGE
UNIVERSITY PRESS

PUBLISHED BY THE PRESS SYNDICATE OF THE UNIVERSITY OF CAMBRIDGE
The Pitt Building, Trumpington Street, Cambridge, United Kingdom

CAMBRIDGE UNIVERSITY PRESS
The Edinburgh Building, Cambridge CB2 2RU, UK
40 West 20th Street, New York, NY 10011-4211, USA
477 Williamstown Road, Port Melbourne, VIC 3207, Australia
Ruiz de Alarcón 13, 28014 Madrid, Spain
Dock House, The Waterfront, Cape Town 8001, South Africa

http://www.cambridge.org

© Ethan Shagan 2003

First published 2003
Reprinted 2004

Printed in the United Kingdom at the University Press, Cambridge

Typeface Sabon 10/12pt.   *System* LATEX 2$_\varepsilon$ [TB]

A catalogue record for this book is available from the British Library

Library of Congress Cataloguing in Publication data
Shagan, Ethan H., 1971–
Popular Politics and the English Reformation / Ethan H. Shagan
p.   cm. – (Cambridge Studies in Early Modern British History)
Includes bibliographical references and index.
ISBN 0 521 80846 4 (hardback) – ISBN 0 521 52555 1 (paperback)
1. Great Britain – Politics and government – 1509–1547.   2. Christianity and
politics – Great Britain – History – 16th century.   3. Great Britain – Politics and
government – 1547–1553.   4. Public opinion – England – History – 16th century.
5. Populism – England – History – 16th century.   6. Reformation – England.
I. Title.   II. Series
DA332 S48   2002   2002025672
942.05 – dc21

ISBN 0 521 80846 4 hardback
ISBN 0 521 52555 1 paperback

CONTENTS

PART III
Sites of Reformation: collaboration and popular politics under Edward VI

ACKNOWLEDGEMENTS

This seeds of this book were first planted in my mind in 1994 during a typically thought-provoking coffee break with Peter Lake. To attempt to acknowledge all of the help that I have received during the intervening years seems a hopeless task, and even at my most self-indulgent I could not possibly express here the gratitude that I owe to so many wonderful people. So let me begin by offering a pre-emptive pint of ale to all those friends, family and colleagues whose names do not appear here but who have supported me over the years; you know who you are, and I look forward to making good my debts.

My most profound thanks go to the three mentors who have trained me as a scholar: Peter Lake and Diarmaid MacCulloch saw this project through from beginning to end, while Tim Harris gave me the confidence to undertake so daunting a project in the first place. Any readers familiar with Tudor–Stuart historiography will see their fingerprints throughout this volume, but what readers will not see is that my occasional ability to transcend their interpretations and find my own voice is itself the greatest testament to their skill and generosity as teachers.

I also owe enormous thanks to the scholars and friends who read and commented upon various versions of the text. Entire drafts, either as thesis or typescript, were read by Tim Breen, Tony Grafton, Bill Heyck, Bill Jordan, Peter Lake, Diarmaid MacCulloch and Peter Marshall. Drafts of individual chapters or sections were read by Margaret Aston, Tom Freeman, Tim Harris, Amanda Jones, Michael Questier, Nicholas Tyacke and Diane Watt. Over the years, I have also benefited from countless conversations with colleagues (both in British history and in other fields) who pushed my thoughts in new directions. While I cannot express my gratitude here for all these conversations, I am especially grateful to Bernard Bailyn, Alastair Bellany, Philip Benedict, Brian Cowan, Natalie Davis, Jeff Dolven, Ken Fincham, Ben Frommer, Eric Klinenberg, Greg Lyon, Ian McNeely, Judith Maltby, Ed Muir, Richard Rex, Margaret Sena and Lisa Wolverton. The late Lawrence Stone provided both intellectual stimulation and personal encouragement for which I will always be grateful. Simon Healy saved me from my own para-noia by checking a key reference for me at the eleventh hour. I also received enormously helpful guidance from the editors of this series and from William Davies at Cambridge University Press; most especially, I am grateful for the boundless generosity of John Morrill.

This book also would not have been possible without financial support from a variety of institutions. Particular thanks go to Princeton University and Northwestern University for numerous grants and extensive relief from the more onerous responsibilities of academia. Research in London was supported by a dissertation year fellowship from the North American Con-ference on British Studies. Much of the writing was done in the uniquely supportive atmosphere of the Harvard University Society of Fellows. And, of course, the Michael and Rena Shagan Scholarship Fund made contribu-tions over the years too numerous to mention.

I have had the privilege of presenting various portions of this book to a wide range of scholarly groups. My particular thanks go to the history faculty at Cambridge University, members of the British religious history seminar at the Institute of Historical Research in London, and the University of Chicago Renaissance Colloquium for their helpful comments. I also owe thanks to various audiences at the Sixteenth Century Studies Conference, the North American Conference on British Studies, and the British Studies Colloquium at Princeton University.

It is a pleasure to thank the personnel at numerous libraries and archives. The staffs of the record offices in Worcester, Gloucester, Kent, Oxford and Stratford-upon-Avon were particularly helpful, as were the staffs of the Dr Williams Library, the Bodleian Library, the Parker Library at Corpus Christi College, Cambridge, and the Institute of Historical Research. I also want to thank the staff of the British Library manuscript students room, both at the British Museum and at St Pancras, and the staff of the Public Record Office, both at Chancery Lane and at Kew. In particular, the staff of the Map and Large Documents Room at Kew went above and beyond the call of duty to make me happy and comfortable in a place where I feel like I have spent more waking hours during the last decade than I have in my own home.

The one debt which must be acknowledged beyond all others, however, is to Sarah Paul. For eight years she has put up with, if not 'a *ménage à trois* with a dead archbishop', then at least an extended roll in the hay with some revolting peasants. With love and friendship, this book is for her.

ABBREVIATIONS

APC	*Acts of the Privy Council of England.* Ed. J. R. Dasent. 32 vols. London, 1890–1907.
BIHR	*Bulletin of the Institute of Historical Research*
BL	British Library
CCCC	Parker Library, Corpus Christi College, Cambridge
CSP Spanish	*Calendar of Letters, Despatches, and State Papers, Relating to the Negotiation between England and Spain.* Ed. Martin A. S. Hume *et al.* 13 vols. London, 1862–1954.
CUL	Cambridge University Library
DNB	*The Dictionary of National Biography*
EETS	*Early English Texts Society*
EHR	*English Historical Review*
Foxe	*The Acts and Monuments of John Foxe.* Eds. G. Townshend and S. R. Cattley. 8 vols. London, 1837–41.
GRO	Gloucestershire Record Office
HJ	*Historical Journal*
HMC Bath	*Calendar of the Manuscripts of the Marquis of Bath, Preserved at Longleat, Wiltshire.* 5 vols. Historical Manuscripts Commission. London, 1904–80.
JBS	*Journal of British Studies*
JEH	*Journal of Ecclesiastical History*
LP	*Letters and Papers, Foreign and Domestic, of the Reign of Henry VIII, 1509–47.* Ed. J. S. Brewer *et al.* 21 vols. and 2 vols. Addenda. London, 1862–1932.
Original Letters	*Original Letters Illustrative of English History.* Ed. Henry Ellis. 11 vols. in 3 series. London, 1824–46.
P&P	*Past and Present*
PRO	Public Record Office, London
SCJ	*The Sixteenth Century Journal*

Statutes	*The Statutes of the Realm.* Eds. A. Luders *et al.* 11 vols. London, 1810–28.
St.P.	*State Papers Published under the Authority of His Majesty's Commission, King Henry VIII.* 11 vols. London, 1830–52.
TBGAS	*Transactions of the Bristol and Gloucestershire Archaeological Society*
TRHS	*Transactions of the Royal Historical Society*
TRP	*Tudor Royal Proclamations.* Eds. Paul L. Hughes and James F. Larkin. 3 vols. New Haven, 1964–9.
VCH Gloucester	*A History of the County of Gloucester.* Eds. William Page *et al.* The Victoria History of the Counties of England. 11 vols. London, 1907– .
Wriothesley	*A Chronicle of England during the Reigns of the Tudors, A.D. 1485–1559. By Charles Wriothesley, Windsor Herald.* Ed. W. D. Hamilton. 2 vols. Camden Society new series vols. 11 and 20. New York, 1965.
WRO	Worcestershire Record Office

NOTE ON THE TEXT

Throughout this text, spelling and punctuation have been modernised in all quotations except for the titles of books and places where the intended meaning is unclear. Parts of chapter 2 were previously published in my 'Print, Orality and Communications in the Maid of Kent Affair', *JEH*, 52 (2001), 21–33, used here with kind permission of Cambridge University Press.

Introduction

Europe's sixteenth century was an age of faith. Religion could be found everywhere, not only in churches and liturgies but in financial transactions, legal proceedings and scientific treatises. Spirituality structured the intimacy of family life no less than the conduct of foreign wars. Even time was reckoned according to sacred rhythms: so many hours to matins, so many weeks to Michaelmas, so many years since the incarnation of Christ. So pervasive was religion, in fact, that the great revolution of the early modern world was not a conflict over political philosophy or economic resources but rather a dispute over the path to Christian salvation. By destabilising traditional religion, the Protestant Reformation sent violent shock waves through even the most seemingly stable communities and institutions. As old certainties were questioned, old loyalties tested and old practices undermined, the Reformation seemed to dissolve the glue that held together the familiar coherence of the social world.

Yet if the centrality of religion for sixteenth-century experience underscores the importance of the Reformation, it also makes the Reformation very difficult to explain. For how could radically divisive ideologies have developed so swiftly within an intellectual framework so fundamental to contemporary society? Why would a revolution have been accepted or embraced by a population so heavily invested in the very belief system that the revolutionaries sought to disturb? These questions have been pondered for centuries, and they constitute the highest peaks that a Reformation historian might hope to climb; given their inherent complexity, it is unlikely that any scholar could scale them in a lifetime. This book suggests, however, that one possible approach to these peaks – from a base-camp, as it were, within the comparatively manageable subfield of Tudor England – might be to turn the questions themselves inside out and approach the issue of religious change indirectly. For, if religion permeated every aspect of sixteenth-century experience, that implies that religion itself was not a rigid or self-contained sphere but rather was structured through its interactions with the culture in which it was imbedded. Paradoxically, then, the very pervasiveness of religion in

1

the early modern world obliges us to explore the process of religious change not only in formal spiritual settings but also in more mundane sites where the social meanings of religion were constructed and contested.[1]

This book thus suggests that an analysis of popular politics allows us to understand the English Reformation – and, *mutatis mutandis*, the European Reformation more generally – in fundamentally new and more satisfying ways. Approaching the Reformation through a study of popular politics may seem peculiar, not only because it appears open to charges of reductionism, but because an influential revisionist movement among Tudor historians would purport to render the whole project redundant. English people, we have been told, were almost uniformly conservative, stubbornly resisting a Reformation foisted upon them by a 'predatory Crown on the prowl', as J. J. Scarisbrick has eloquently termed the Tudor regime.[2] Yet, twenty years after Scarisbrick challenged the notion of a 'popular Reformation' in England, the remarkable penetration of England's 'Reformation from above' remains largely unexplained. After all, the Tudor government possessed no bureaucracy, no police force, no standing army, and was utterly reliant upon local collaboration – from the haughtiest justice of the peace to the lowliest village constable – for the maintenance of ordinary administration. For whatever reasons, these local officials, as well as the peasants who were all-too-capable of unseating them when their duties conflicted with popular expectations, accommodated some aspects of the Reformation, embraced others and only occasionally reacted with unambiguous opposition. Only by exploring these conflicting responses can we hope to transcend the intractable revisionist paradox that the English Reformation produced a 'Protestant nation, but not a nation of Protestants'.[3]

I

In the western tradition, the archetypal narrative of religious conversion is St Paul on the road to Damascus: a blinding light, the voice of the Lord, 'and immediately there fell from his eyes as it had been scales: and he received sight forthwith, and arose, and was baptized' (Acts 9:18). A no less remarkable conversion can be read in Augustine's *Confessions*, where a disembodied

---

[1] Similarly broad conceptions of the Reformation and its cultural consequences can be found in, e.g., Alexandra Walsham, *Providence in Early Modern England* (Oxford, 1999); Susan Karant-Nunn, *Zwickau in Transition, 1500–1547: The Reformation as an Agent of Change* (Columbus, Ohio, 1987); David Sabean, *Power in the Blood: Popular Culture and Village Discourse in Early Modern Germany* (Cambridge, 1984); Robert Scribner, *Popular Culture and Popular Movements in Reformation Germany* (London, 1987).

[2] J. J. Scarisbrick, *The Reformation and the English People* (Oxford, 1984), p. 135.

[3] Christopher Haigh, *English Reformations: Religion, Politics, and Society under the Tudors* (Oxford, 1993), pp. 279–81 and Conclusion *passim*.

voice tells the narrator to open the Scriptures and read whatever passage he falls upon. When Augustine reads the admonition in Romans 13:13 to 'put on the Lord Jesus Christ, and make no provision for the flesh, to gratify its desires', he finds that he needs no further study: 'For instantly even with the end of this sentence, by a light, as it were, of confidence now darted into my heart, all the darkness of doubting vanished away.'[4] These epiphanies, moved by the workings of the Holy Spirit in humble and receptive vessels, were conversions simultaneously of mind, soul and heart, the sorts of absolute breaks from the past that the later evangelical John Bunyan represented through his allegorical Christian, abandoning home and family in favour of 'life, life, eternal life'.[5] Such conversions were, in a word, revolutionary. They represented the liberation of the divine within souls crushed by sin and the subsequent creation of new men out of the ashes of the old, not unlike eighteenth-century French 'citizens' or twentieth-century Russian 'comrades' working, as they believed, to liberate the untapped potential of oppressed human beings.

It should perhaps be obvious that, in reality, such remarkable and total conversions are extremely rare in any human society; continuity always pulls heartlessly at the seams of revolution. Moreover, if these absolute conversions are rare among individuals, they are virtually unthinkable on a wider, national scale; for a society to 'become Christian' or 'become Protestant' in the manner of Saul becoming Paul, too many of the threads that tie together thought, history and culture would necessarily have to be severed. Yet historians of the English Reformation, working in the tradition of such eminent sixteenth-century scholar–divines as John Bale and John Foxe, have until recently held remarkably tightly to the revolutionary ideal in their discussions of how England broke from the Roman yoke and embraced a new religion. The expulsion of the pope and the translation of the Bible cleared a path for the Holy Spirit to enter English hearts; the sermons of Hugh Latimer and the liturgies of Thomas Cranmer gave England a True Church; and Bloody Mary's terrible fires cauterised England's ragged amputation from Rome, bringing all but the hardest hearts into the fold just as surely as did the martyrdoms of the early Church. By 1559, then, the nation's conversion was over and something called the Church of England had been born, leaving the new dilemma of over-zealous puritanism, rather than the old dilemma of irascible Catholicism, as the principal threat to English religious unity. Scales had fallen from their eyes indeed.[6]

---

[4] St Augustine, *St. Augustine's Confessions*, ed. W. H. D. Rouse, 2 vols. (Cambridge, Mass., 1912), I, p. 465.
[5] John Bunyan, *The Pilgrim's Progress*, ed. Roger Sharrock (London, 1965), p. 53.
[6] The traditional interpretation of the English Reformation can be found in such classic works as Gilbert Burnet, *History of the Reformation of the Church of England*, ed. Nicholas Pocock,

This narrative, while always opposed by a Catholic counter-narrative, has only recently been challenged from within and systematically dismantled by a revisionist movement among English Reformation scholars. The agenda for revisionism was first established in 1975 with Christopher Haigh's *Reformation and Resistance in Tudor Lancashire*.[7] Haigh's classic study of one of the realm's 'dark corners' explored the difficulties faced by a government attempting to import an extrinsic Reformation into a fundamentally conservative culture. First, he showed that, far from being disenchanted with medieval Catholicism and hankering for reform, most Lancastrians were satisfied with their Church and the spiritual nourishment it provided. Second, he traced the enforcement of the Reformation upon a largely unwilling public, painting a picture of reluctant and disingenuous rather than enthusiastic Reformation. Third, he explored the deep divisions that arose in Elizabethan Lancashire as a result of the Reformation, concluding that, as the population settled into a conservative, hybrid form of worship, it remained the task of Protestant preachers to evangelise and convert the common people.

Haigh's attempts to undermine commonplace assumptions about the success of Protestantism were echoed by a variety of other historians, most notably J. J. Scarisbrick and Eamon Duffy. These scholars expanded Haigh's ideas into new narratives of the Reformation in which religious change was an aggressive and destructive process, not a movement of liberation but a violent attack on traditional society by an avaricious government. For Scarisbrick, the centrepiece of Reformation history became the resistance strategies employed by English subjects to counter the Tudor juggernaut. The Reformation, in this view, accomplished only negative goals like the destruction of church fabric; it erected nothing in place of the old religion, which thus remained the most potent and 'popular' belief system in England throughout the sixteenth century.[8] Duffy had a somewhat darker view, suggesting that, because late-medieval Catholicism was a religion built around communal solidarity and outward ceremony, the regime's elimination of the external trappings of traditional religion had enormous effects. For Duffy, the breathtaking beauty of traditional worship could not be re-erected once its foundation was undermined, so the failure of Protestants to convert the masses was, for conservatives, at best a pyrrhic victory.[9]

7 vols. (Oxford, 1865) and John Strype, *Ecclesiastical Memorials*, 3 vols. (Oxford, 1822). This model is most famously exemplified in recent historiography, although perhaps with more subtlety than the revisionists allow, in A. G. Dickens, *The English Reformation*, 2nd edn (London, 1989).

[7] Christopher Haigh, *Reformation and Resistance in Tudor Lancashire* (Cambridge, 1975).
[8] Scarisbrick, *The Reformation and the English People*.
[9] Eamon Duffy, *The Stripping of the Altars: Traditional Religion in England 1400–1580* (New Haven, 1992). Other important contributions to the revisionist critique, by no means in complete agreement with one another, are in Haigh, *English Reformations*; Christopher Haigh (ed.), *The English Reformation Revised* (Cambridge, 1987); Eamon Duffy, *The*

As Haigh noted, two sets of questions were implicit in the revisionist critique.[10] First was whether the Reformation was energised from above or below, in other words whether religious change was an expression of popular aspirations or an act of state enforced upon the populace. Second was whether the Reformation occurred quickly or slowly, that is whether the traditional demarcation point in Tudor history, the Elizabethan religious settlement of 1559, marked the end of the English Reformation or simply one stage in a much longer struggle for ideological control of the nation. The revisionist position, then, was a response to studies like A. G. Dickens's *English Reformation* that had described the Reformation as rapid and from below. Haigh and his fellow travellers instead suggested it was slow and from above, not being completed, if indeed it ever was, until the middle of Elizabeth's reign at the earliest.

Revisionism, in all its different formulations, has had a tremendous and largely beneficial influence on our understanding of the English Reformation, and few historians today would deny that in a simple contest between A. G. Dickens's interpretation on the one hand, and Haigh's or Duffy's interpretation on the other, Haigh and Duffy win hands down. The anti-Catholic prejudices embedded in the traditional model have rightfully been overthrown, and the newer interpretations have forced us to appreciate the coherence and vitality of the religious system that was so violently ripped apart in the middle decades of the sixteenth century. Yet, for all its benefits, the revisionist model remains no less imprisoned than its predecessor in a paradigm defined by the phantasmagoric goal of 'national conversion'. 'Success' for the Reformation remains a composite of individual religious conversions, each heaped upon the next, until the mass of Protestants in England tips some notional interpretive scales and the nation itself becomes Protestant. Listen, for instance, to Haigh trying to count the number of Protestants in Queen Mary's England:

We do not know about all mid-Tudor Protestants, or even all the Protestant cells. The Protestant iceberg certainly had a submerged section, but how large was it? What proportion of all Protestants were the 3,000 possibles discovered by combing the records from 1525 to 1558, or the 280 known to have been burned between 1555 and 1558? One in ten? One in a hundred? One in a thousand? We cannot

Voices of Morebath: Reformation and Rebellion in an English Village (New Haven, 2001); Margaret Bowker, *The Henrician Reformation: The Diocese of Lincoln under John Longland 1521–1547* (Cambridge, 1981); Sharon Jansen, *Dangerous Talk and Strange Behaviour: Women and Popular Resistance to the Reforms of Henry VIII* (New York, 1996); Ian Green, *Print and Protestantism in Early Modern England* (Oxford, 2000); Ian Green, *The Christian's ABC: Catechism and Catechizing in England c.1530–1740* (Oxford, 1996); Ronald Hutton, *The Rise and Fall of Merry England: The Ritual Year 1400–1700* (Oxford, 1994).
[10] Christopher Haigh, 'The Recent Historiography of the English Reformation', *HJ*, 25 (1982), 995–1007.

tell, but even the biggest multiplier would create only a small fraction of the total population ... Is it likely, given the shortage of Protestant preaching and common hostility of popular response, that Protestants became even a large minority in only a short period? Could even a Latimer or a Bradford or a Knox shatter old loyalties and create a new consciousness by occasional evangelical forays?[11]

By focusing his understanding of the Reformation so narrowly on the small minority in whom was created 'a new consciousness', Haigh uncritically adopts the analytic categories of the most radical reformers, dividing the world into two rival camps no less starkly than Latimer, Bradford and Knox themselves. In assuming that the confessional lens is the only lens that matters, he neatly dismisses as irrelevant to the Reformation's 'success' such fundamental transformations as the undermining of the four-century-old papal primacy, the erosion of the purgatorial scheme of salvation at the centre of medieval worship, and the almost complete destruction of the physical infrastructure of traditional religion. Hence Haigh can argue that, despite the success of the government in achieving conformity to its 'political' Reformation, the Protestant Reformation – always defined in evangelical terms – remained largely a failure.[12] This is, in a sense, a theological argument masquerading as an historical one.

Of course, at an empirical level the revisionists are correct to say that few English people experienced Damascene conversions in the first half of the sixteenth century. Yet this observation might more usefully serve as the beginning of an analysis of the English Reformation rather than the end of one: if people did not convert en masse to Protestantism, what *did* they do? The whole notion of 'success' and 'failure', I would suggest, imposes severe limitations on the kinds of questions we can ask of the Reformation. By asking whether England 'became Protestant', we accept the notion, itself imbedded in a confessional understanding of the period, that the Reformation was essentially about religious conversion. Yet it is easy to show examples of people who did not 'become Protestant' none the less acting in ways that would have been unthinkable only a few years before. Some people plundered religious institutions, others denounced their priests in royal courts for their attachment to Rome, still others used English Bibles to construct arguments against the economic exploitation of the peasantry. These are all instances of 'Reformation', neatly traceable to Luther's revolt, yet none required an ideological commitment to *sola fide* or *sola scriptura*. Similarly, it is easy to show examples of conventionally pious Catholics arguing bitterly with one another over the nature of their Catholicism: what role did Rome play in True Religion? How could essential doctrine be distinguished from adiaphora? Did the unity of Christ's True Church depend upon the unity of the visible, institutional Church? Studying these fissures in traditional religion

---

[11] Haigh, *English Reformations*, p. 199.   [12] Ibid., pp. 285–95 and *passim*.

reveals a profound process of change; the ways people understood and legitimated even the most traditional beliefs altered dramatically. These changes represented an incursion of religious innovation into English culture without necessitating that the people who actualised them did so systematically, and without requiring the sorts of epiphanies that we associate with conversion narratives. We see in these phenomena neither the 'success' nor the 'failure' of the Reformation, but rather a process of cultural accommodation that is not easily mappable onto a simple, confessional axis.

In other words, the whole meta-narrative of conversion which historians have used to conceptualise the Reformation has impeded our ability to ask a different set of questions, to see the Reformation not in globalising terms but as a more piecemeal process in which politics and spiritual change were irrevocably intertwined. This perspective might be accused of reductionism, denying that the Reformation was motivated by genuine ideological commitment. Yet, on the contrary, it does not deny that evangelical conversion was possible, but simply asks what modes of analysis remain open to the historian once it is conceded that few such conversions in fact occurred. Rather than beginning and ending with the few sixteenth-century English people who experienced the Reformation as a coherent battle between two incommensurate worldviews, this analysis concentrates on the majority who neither wholly accepted nor wholly opposed the Reformation. For these people, ideas were not always solid objects stacked like bricks in coherent ideologies, but rather were rapidly shifting modalities that could have different meanings in different contexts. The ideas themselves are still central; no one is accused of acting disingenuously. But, in the practical world of political negotiation, ideas can be disassociated from their moorings and put to disparate uses. Far from being antithetical to the notion that ideas have power in history, this study argues that the amphibiousness and ambidexterity of new religious ideas is exactly what allowed them to penetrate English culture, seeping into the myriad crevices in the dominant belief system where ideas and practices were not fully aligned. Hence, sites of social friction like disputes between priests and their parishioners, or disputes between princes and their people, were exactly the places where new ideas were brought most forcibly to bear. It was at these sites that even subtle changes in beliefs could alter political dynamics in important and tangible ways, leading to significant changes in people's relationship to the sacred even if those people never imagined themselves as enemies of the old religion.

II

If, in the view of some revisionists, there were successful 'political Reformations' in Tudor England but not a successful Protestant Reformation, it immediately becomes incumbent upon us to examine the religious life of the people in terms divorced from the political. In other words, a history of sixteenth-century religion becomes a study of 'popular piety', a notional convergence of inward beliefs and outward ceremonial practices that forms, in an almost Durkheimian sense, a religious sphere within society. To this end, numerous historians in the past decade have made 'popular piety' their object of study, leading to an enormous growth in our knowledge of popular religious practices and the place of those practices in traditional society.

Revisionists, it should be noted, are far from agreed about the content of 'popular piety' in the early sixteenth century. The most comprehensive and convincing account is Duffy's *Stripping of the Altars*, which describes a richly complex religion based in communal solidarity and the outward, ceremonial forms of worship.[13] Christian piety consisted of participation in a vast structure of observance, from processing along the parish boundaries at Rogationtide to mortifying the flesh by 'creeping to the cross' on Good Friday. Every aspect of social life was constructed around the Church, from the cycles of feast and fast by which people measured time, to the great 'bede rolls' through which they remembered their dead. Duffy's analysis of the complexities of traditional religion, however, does not sit easily with Haigh's understanding of late-medieval Catholicism as an essentially *easy* religion that presented a less arduous alternative than the strict Biblicism and austerity of Protestantism. Haigh suggested that traditional Catholicism provided 'religious minimalists' with 'an undemanding scheme of salvation which rewarded decent living and participation in the sacraments; the Church would do the rest'. It was these 'minimalist' Christians, in Haigh's opinion, who rejected the new religion most forcefully, since 'the Protestant insistence that justification came from faith in Christ undercut the status and the prospects of the unthinking'.[14] While Duffy might grant the existence of these 'unthinking' Catholics, he would hardly ascribe to them the central role they play for Haigh; indeed, their presence undercuts Duffy's central claim that 'no substantial gulf existed between the religion of the clergy and the educated elite on the one hand and that of the people at large on the other'.[15]

The most important flowering of scholarship on 'popular piety', however, has come from historians following in the wake of the revisionists but not strictly adhering to their interpretations. The work of Beat Kümin, for instance, followed Duffy by focusing on the parish as the basic unit through which English people organised their religious experience. It was at the community level, in this analysis, that such important phenomena as prayers for the dead, the worship of saints and the rituals of prayer were all understood.

---

[13] Duffy, *Stripping of the Altars*; see also Duffy, *Voices of Morebath*.
[14] Haigh, *English Reformations*, p. 286.   [15] Duffy, *Stripping of the Altars*, p. 2.

Yet, diverging from Duffy, Kümin suggested that to understand religious change at the popular level we must look at how the economic organisation of the parish gradually shifted.[16] Historians such as Andrew Brown and Martha Skeeters have studied the contours of traditional religion in individual localities, adding encyclopedic knowledge of local customs to our general sense of late medieval and early modern Catholicism as a religious system.[17] Caroline Litzenberger has most recently focused this technique on one particular source, wills from the county of Gloucestershire, providing a far more careful treatment than was previously available and showing the wide range of language through which sixteenth-century testators could express their beliefs.[18] These and other studies are to be commended for their attempts to peer through the fog of religious conflict and analyse the thought-systems of the ordinary people to whom the various confessions would increasingly appeal. Kümin's study was particularly successful in capturing not just the theoretical contours of those thought-systems, but the fault lines that inevitably emerged in their practice, for instance the structural difficulties faced by parishes balancing the saving of souls with the investment of scarce resources.[19]

Within the concepts of 'popular piety' or 'popular religion' invoked by all these works, however, there lurk some rather formidable theoretical pitfalls. Most importantly, it is by no means clear that the delineation of a Durkheimian sphere of 'religious' belief and practice makes sense in a sixteenth-century context. This is not only because, as scholars habitually note, every aspect of early modern society was imbued with religion, but also because religious belief and practice was never understood solely as a private exercise reflecting the conscience of the practitioner. As Duffy has shown, worship was largely a communal activity; even salvation, which we might

---

[16] Beat Kümin, *The Shaping of a Community: The Rise and Reformation of the English Parish c. 1400–1560* (Aldershot, 1996). Duffy has since followed Kümin's approach in his *Voices of Morebath.*

[17] Andrew Brown, *Popular Piety in Late Medieval England: The Diocese of Salisbury 1250–1550* (Oxford, 1995); Martha Skeeters, *Community and Clergy: Bristol and the Reformation, c. 1530–c. 1570* (Oxford, 1993). A very different and more politicised local study of the Reformation is in Muriel McClendon, *The Quiet Reformation: Magistrates and the Emergence of Protestantism in Tudor Norwich* (Stanford, 1999).

[18] Caroline Litzenberger, *The English Reformation and the Laity: Gloucestershire, 1540–1580* (Cambridge, 1997).

[19] Other important, recent works on Tudor popular piety include Christopher Marsh, *Popular Religion in Sixteenth-Century England* (New York, 1998); Robert Whiting, *The Blind Devotion of the People: Popular Religion and the English Reformation* (Cambridge, 1989); Margaret Spufford (ed.), *The World of Rural Dissenters 1520–1725* (Cambridge, 1995); Hutton, *The Rise and Fall of Merry England*; Katherine French, Gary G. Gibbs and Beat A. Kümin (eds.), *The Parish in English Life, 1400–1600* (Manchester, 1997); Eric Carlson (ed.), *Religion and the English People, 1500–1640: New Voices, New Perspectives* (Kirksville, Mo., 1998).

assume to be a private matter between Christ and the individual Christian, was in practice mediated by the efforts of family, friends, priests and saints. As such, religious order depended to a large degree upon social cohesion, and the maintenance of a properly functioning Church was therefore a task shared by officials at all levels of government, both ecclesiastical and civil. For instance, while ecclesiastical courts had jurisdiction over offences against the Church, those courts were overseen by bishops who were themselves appointed by the Crown and held high offices of state. The resources of individual parishes were received and redistributed by lay churchwardens, who might also hold petty offices from the royal government or sit on manorial juries under the jurisdiction of local landlords. The 'advowsons' of clerical livings, the right to appoint priests to their positions as parsons, were often held by laymen, and at law the right of 'advowson' was treated as a piece of property that could be bought, sold or leased. Priests were maintained through tithes, but tithes were often farmed by laymen who leased the collection rights. When the church courts condemned heretics to death, the Church could not execute those heretics but rather had to hand them over to the royal government for burning. Many other examples could be given of the absolute dependence of traditional religion on the unity and univocality of Church and state.

Usually such nuances were irrelevant to the practical functioning of parish religion, and, indeed, many historians of European Catholicism have stressed the autonomy that communities traditionally exercised over their own religious lives.[20] The mid sixteenth century, however, was no ordinary time. The English Reformation, as an act of state intended to diminish the power and jurisdiction of the Church, energised exactly those fault lines in Christian society where piety collided with politics. Religious observance had always received much of its meaning from its invocation of properly constituted authority; going to church could not be divorced from what we might call its 'civil' functions – reinforcing community, hierarchy and obedience – any more than the state could function without divine sanction. But, if a properly functioning Church depended upon the invocation of an idealised social and political harmony, what were Christians to do when that harmony was fractured by a dispute between Church and Crown, especially a dispute played out in their own communities? If a radical priest altered the forms of local worship, for instance, was 'traditional religion' better maintained by obeying that priest or disobeying him? If a Catholic priest committed treason by defending the authority of the pope, did his conservative parishioners

[20] See, for instance, Jean Delumeau, *Catholicism between Luther and Voltaire: A New View of the Counter-Reformation* (London, 1977); Henry Kamen, *The Phoenix and the Flame: Catalonia and the Counter-Reformation* (New Haven, Conn., 1993); Philip Hoffman, *Church and Community in the Diocese of Lyon, 1500–1789* (New Haven, Conn., 1984).

better serve 'traditional religion' by hiding his words from the authorities or reporting him to a Justice of the Peace?

These questions point us towards the dangers of a decontextualised notion of 'popular piety' in which religious beliefs and practices are disassociated from notions of authority, legitimacy and power.[21] Even a wholly consistent religious practice, backed by a wholly consistent religious doctrine, could change its meaning dramatically in different political contexts. English people throughout the sixteenth century heard Catholic mass, for instance, but whether they heard mass in a church in 1533 or in a barn in 1553 radically changed the nature of that experience. English people throughout the sixteenth century went on pilgrimage to saints' shrines, but whether they did so openly in huge caravans or secretly in the dead of night changed their relationship to the divine. In both cases, even if practices remained unchanged, the bases of those practices, the sorts of authority that were invoked, the kind of community relationships that were defined, and the potential audiences to which the practices appealed, all shifted dramatically. Rather than reflecting divine order and invoking the victory won by Christ on the cross, they came to represent a struggle, invoking conflict and the failure of fallen humanity to resist temptation by the devil. Rather than representing the unity of Christendom, they played out a new casuistic calculus through which civil authority and religious authority were separated in people's minds, and the contradictory loyalties owed to them were carefully parsed and weighed.

The import of this discussion is that there was no 'popular piety' that existed prior to or independent of authority and obedience; all religious belief and practice necessarily depended upon *authorisation*, even if in most circumstances that dependence was unstated. When the Reformation forced to the forefront the issue of authority and obedience within the Church, every belief or practice, no matter how seemingly innocent, had to be interrogated: upon what basis, whether biblical, patristic, papal, royal or purely local, was that belief or practice held? If aspects of 'popular piety' were suddenly de-authorised, either by heretics in positions of power or, just as often, by Catholic reformers purging the Church of 'superstition', those de-authorised practices were torn loose from the edifice in which their meanings had been constructed. In confrontation with legitimate authorities like bishops or kings, these contested aspects of 'popular piety' might form the basis of nascent resistance, or they might be abandoned and quickly fade into distant memories. But they could not remain within a distinct religious sphere where conscience or inner piety existed independent of 'political Reformations'.

---

[21] See David Aers, 'Altars of Power: Reflections on Eamon Duffy's *The Stripping of the Altars: Traditional Religion in England 1400–1580*', *Literature and History*, third series, 3 (1994), 90–105. I would like to thank Judith Maltby for bringing this review to my attention.

III

Questions of authority and legitimacy naturally created moral dilemmas. As Haigh has described in fascinating detail, English people were never asked to embrace some overarching 'Reformation', but instead had change presented to them in a series of tiny bundles, rarely worth fighting over individually but insidiously adding up to substantial innovation. As such, they daily confronted issues of resistance and collaboration: was it ethical to disobey authority if obedience tended to further the growth of heresy? By what practices could an authority de-legitimise itself? At what point did passive obedience slip into active support for the regime's policies?[22]

Beginning with Haigh's *Reformation and Resistance in Tudor Lancashire*, the revisionist model has stressed the importance of resistance. This concept has been defined very liberally, in large part because of what is perceived as the totalising power of the Tudor regime: in an atmosphere saturated with coercion and brutal repression, any action (or inaction) short of absolute obedience can be glossed as resistance. So, for instance, when Henry VIII demanded in 1535 that priests erase the name of the pope from their service books, one priest 'resisted' simply by covering the word *papa* 'with small pieces of paper' that could later be removed, thus arguably complying with the letter of the law but subtly expressing his discontent.[23] This understanding of resistance, well attuned to recent theoretical literature of which James Scott's works are the most prominent exemplars, is a great improvement over earlier assumptions that silence or compliance were equivalent to consent.[24] We would not want for a moment to downplay the importance of even subtle attempts by English Catholics to retain their religious autonomy, whether through private prayers, the concealment of sacred objects, or that most flexible of responses to ecclesiastical visitations: '*omnia bene*'.[25]

If all is well in the revisionists' *theory* of resistance, however, their *practical* use of the concept is none the less problematic. In particular, a preoccupation with conversion narratives has led English Reformation scholars to ignore the very process of politicisation which scholars like Scott have suggested we should be looking for within the 'hidden transcripts' of peasant resistance.

---

[22] I owe thanks to Benjamin Frommer for numerous conversations on these issues.

[23] Haigh, *English Reformations*, p. 142.

[24] James Scott, *Weapons of the Weak: Everyday Forms of Peasant Resistance* (New Haven, Conn., 1985); James Scott, *Domination and the Arts of Resistance: Hidden Transcripts* (New Haven, Conn., 1990).

[25] Here, however, it is important to remember Hannah Arendt's proviso that in the political realm actions are de-coupled from motivations and become exterior and subjective, so that 'following orders' has very different connotations for public figures than it does for private citizens: 'Politics is not like the nursery; in politics obedience and support are the same.' See Hannah Arendt, *Eichmann in Jerusalem: A Report on the Banality of Evil* (New York, 1963), p. 255.

Let us take, for example, the Tudor regime's demands that subjects remove 'abused' images from their churches. Revisionist scholars have rightly noted a variety of responses to this government-sponsored iconoclasm that we might usefully characterise as 'resistance': some 'resistors' delicately hid away sacred images rather than destroying them, some 'resistors' refused to remove those images at all, and some 'resistors' took up arms against the regime that dared to order their removal in the first place. From a purely theological point of view, of course, these three groups shared something essential: a rejection of Protestant reinterpretations of 'idolatry'. But this theological perspective has obscured the fact that in a practical, political sense they were as likely to fight each other as to unite against a common enemy. To take another example, the priest described above, who finessed the demand to erase the name of the pope from his service books, may have 'resisted' in some sense, but he could hardly have won the approval of John Lyle, a Somerset priest who refused to erase the pope's name altogether and dared to erase the king's name instead![26]

While revisionist historians have stressed the concept of resistance, moreover, they have almost totally ignored the concept of collaboration.[27] In part this is because conformity can so easily be glossed as *mere* conformity – 'only following orders' – when demanded by a repressive regime, especially a regime widely considered legitimate. More importantly, however, this omission has been possible precisely because the Reformation is seen as a *theological* event, an inward spiritual process for which outward behaviour is merely an imperfect cipher. From this perspective, *real* collaboration could only exist where the motives of the collaborators matched the motives of reformers in the government, in other words only in the rare cases of genuine evangelical agitation in the countryside. Other cases of accommodation with the regime might result from fear or greed, but in these cases outward behaviour ceases to be an accurate gauge of religious sentiment and hence ceases to reflect a process of 'Reformation'. Certainly many English subjects bought the property of dissolved abbeys, for instance, but, since we know that Catholics could do so without injury to conscience, and since we assume that the Reformation was about conversion from Catholicism to

---

[26] PRO E 36/120, fol. 53r–v.

[27] The word 'collaboration' has almost uniformly negative connotations, just as the word 'propaganda' used to have, because it is most commonly applied to collaboration with the Nazis, where its association with mass murder flattens any moral ambiguity that might be attached to it. My goal here, however, is to suggest that the morality of collaboration with the Reformation was far from clear, and we have no business imposing moral judgments upon people who believed that the benefits of collaboration with the Reformation exceeded the liabilities. I therefore use the term 'collaboration' without opprobrium to refer to political actions in which subjects contributed to the effectiveness of controversial government policies.

Protestantism, we cannot consider these purchases examples of collaboration with the Reformation.

Needless to say, a fresh approach to collaboration is needed if we are to explore the political dynamics of Reformation. Thankfully, such an approach has been made available by a flood of theoretically sophisticated literature in modern European history which has thoroughly reassessed the relationships between repressive regimes and their people. As an increasing number of scholars have shown, the 'police state' paradigm, with its strict separation of state and society, does not make sense unless we believe that the 'police' do not go home to their families and communities at the end of the day; otherwise, the enforcers of state policy must be understood as imbedded members of the society to which they belong.[28] Within this new, society-centred approach – an approach all the more sensible for the early modern period, when there were no 'police' at all – various theoretical conclusions have emerged which can usefully be brought to bear on our understanding of the English Reformation.

One theoretical innovation – which undermines the notion that collaboration must be based on ideological unity – involves the ability of collaborators to form symbiotic relationships with authority and co-opt the state just as the state is co-opting the people.[29] This has been demonstrated most thoroughly in places like the Stalinist Soviet Union, where the regime's willingness to act upon denunciations from ordinary citizens put the state's formidable punitive powers into the hands of those citizens: the instruments of social control were essentially privatised and made available to anyone willing to use them.[30] So many people fabricated accusations against their room-mates to ease overcrowding in urban living quarters, for instance, that Russians coined a new term – 'apartment denunciations' – to describe the phenomenon.[31] Whether to score points in ongoing disputes or merely to prove their own loyalty, people make bargains with even the most odious regimes in more cases than we would usually care to admit. We will find

---

[28] I owe this formulation to Robert Crews. See also Sheila Fitzpatrick and Robert Gellately, 'Introduction to the Practices of Denunciation in Modern European History', in Sheila Fitzpatrick and Robert Gellately (eds.), *Accusatory Practices: Denunciation in Modern European History, 1789–1989* (Chicago, 1997), pp. 4–5.

[29] This idea has recently been brought to bear by Steve Hindle and Michael Braddick on the relationship between state and society in early modern England, but neither has explored how the Reformation itself, as an act of state, might fit within their models. See Steve Hindle, *The State and Social Change in Early Modern England, c.1550–1640* (Basingstoke, 2000); Michael Braddick, *State Formation in Early Modern England c.1550–1700* (Cambridge, 2000).

[30] Jan Gross, 'A Note on the Nature of Soviet Totalitarianism', *Soviet Studies*, 34 (1982), 367–76.

[31] Sheila Fitzpatrick, 'Signals from Below: Soviet Letters of Denunciation of the 1930s', in Fitzpatrick and Gellately (eds.), *Accusatory Practices*, p. 109.

these sorts of considerations time and again in the English Reformation, for instance in the case of the Yorkshireman Robert Jackson, whose denunciations led to two of his neighbours being executed for treason in 1538. We cannot know exactly why Jackson chose to play the role of government informant, but it was presumably no coincidence that he was simultaneously 'a suitor unto the king', and immediately after giving evidence against his neighbours he asked that the Council of the North write to Westminster to ensure 'the better speed in his said suit'.[32]

But symbiosis can also emerge in more complex and ideologically fruitful situations where the state and its citizens experience a 'convergence of interests' over certain policies; in Vichy France, for instance, many conservative citizens were reluctant to hand over their fellow Frenchmen to the Nazis but made exceptions for French communists because anti-communism was an area of overlap between the two ideologies.[33] These convergences – what we might call 'points of contact', to update Geoffrey Elton's term for the links between governors and the governed[34] – often had practical considerations as their heart, but that does not mean that ideas were irrelevant. As Stephen Kotkin has put it: 'The presence of coercion, subtle and unsubtle, does not mean the absence of a high degree of voluntarism any more than the holding of genuine ideals precludes the energetic pursuit of self-interest.'[35] Even small areas of overlap could have enormous consequences as people found themselves unintentionally committed to the logic of their own behaviour.

In the English Reformation context, we can see this phenomenon in the ways many people who had no apparent Protestant leanings none the less chose to act as mouthpieces for the regime. In 1538, for instance, an Essex ropemaker named John Luke overheard a visitor defend the authority of the pope at the 'vitelling house' that he operated out of his home. Luke's response was to denounce him to a Justice of the Peace, and while we can only guess at his motives – loyalism, concern for business, personal vendetta – certainly he could just as easily have kept the conversation to himself.[36] In 1535, parishioners from Halifax, Yorkshire, sued their vicar in the royal Court of Chancery for making them pay 'Peter's Pence', a traditional tax to Rome,

---

[32] PRO SP 1/242, fol. 116r [*LP* Add., 1377].

[33] Rab Bennett, *Under the Shadow of the Swastika: The Moral Dilemmas of Resistance and Collaboration in Hitler's Europe* (Basingstoke, 1999), p. 60.

[34] G. R. Elton, 'Tudor Government: The Points of Contact', in his *Studies in Tudor and Stuart Politics and Government*, 4 vols. (Cambridge, 1974–92), vol. 3. Steve Hindle has noted that the court, Privy Council and parliament were only the 'highest institutional expressions of state authority' and that in reality there was a great deal more 'social depth' to the 'points of contact' where governors secured consent for their authority: Hindle, *State and Social Change*, p. 21.

[35] Stephen Kotkin, *Magnetic Mountain: Stalinism as Civilization* (Berkeley, 1995), p. 358.

[36] PRO SP 1/130, fols. 151r–152r [*LP* XIII, i, 615].

before they could receive their Easter communion; they added to their bill of complaint an enthusiastic confirmation that 'the king our sovereign lord is the *supremum caput anglicanae ecclesiae*'.[37] In 1541, the king paid the Essex carpenter John Crowe 7d per day 'in taking down and breaking up the boards of the cloister' in the dissolved abbey of Barking, a commission which Crowe probably solicited and certainly could have refused.[38] These were all acts of collaboration in which ordinary English subjects furthered the project of state-sponsored Reformation in the process of co-opting state power for their own purposes. Though their actions may not have had unambiguous theological content, they contributed to government programmes that were clearly associated with religious reform, embedding those programmes within English society and rendering them increasingly quotidian.[39] When carpenters created rationales for participating in the destruction of monasteries, for instance, even if those rationales were consistent with Catholic orthodoxy, the mere fact of their casuistry represented a significant victory for the regime over those English subjects who actively resisted the dissolutions.

Another aspect of collaboration which we must bear in mind is that collaboration with the spirit of the law can be as important as collaboration with the letter, and in many cases the most significant forms of collaboration with a government's agenda in fact violate official policy. For example, Sheila Fitzpatrick has described the process of 'self-dekulakization' in the Soviet Union: the regime encouraged the ostracising of 'class enemies', and as a result many people forged new identities to avoid penalties for their social origins. This was strenuously opposed by the government, but despite its illegality this form of deception clearly functioned as a form of collaboration with the regime's broader ideological programme, leading people to internalise official categories of social relations.[40] Moreover, if illegality could sometimes function as collaboration, so, too, in some circumstances 'resistors' and 'collaborators' could be the same people. This has been described most thoroughly for well-placed public figures whose aid was essential to 'resistance' movements but who could only provide that aid if they

---

[37] PRO C 1/827, fol. 1r–v.   [38] Bodleian Rawlinson D. MS 782, fol. 2r.

[39] On this point, Václav Havel has offered a thought-experiment involving a greengrocer behind the Iron Curtain who puts in his shop window a government-issued sign reading, 'Workers of the world, unite!' In itself this action is insignificant, but when many greengrocers simultaneously display these signs 'they may create through their involvement a general norm and thus bring pressure to bear on their fellow citizens'. They may even 'learn to be comfortable with their involvement, to identify with it as though it were something natural and inevitable'. See Václav Havel, 'The Power of the Powerless', in his *Open Letters: Selected Writings 1965–1990*, ed. Paul Wilson (New York, 1992), quotes on pp. 132–3, 143.

[40] Sheila Fitzpatrick, *Everyday Stalinism: Ordinary Life in Extraordinary Times: Soviet Russia in the 1930s* (Oxford, 1999), pp. 132–8.

maintained their offices through vigorous collaboration. Thus the mayor of a small town in occupied France might resist the Nazis by night, but that did not make his collaboration during the day any less real.[41] Even Marshal Pétain, leader of Vichy France and collaborator *par excellence*, claimed to be a resistor in the sense that he embraced the Germans only in order to maintain his position and hence his ability to mitigate the effects of France's loss.[42]

In the English Reformation, as we will see, there were many parallels to this complexity. Since Henry VIII's Church was theoretically as opposed to Zurich as it was to Rome, there were any number of circumstances in which English Protestants contributed to the government-sponsored Reformation in ways that were technically illegal. Moreover, the Tudor government promulgated many policies, like the dissolutions of the chantries, in which the regime's financial interests and its spiritual interests might diverge. In these contexts, people often 'resisted' the Crown's economic predations and stole from the government in ways which, paradoxically, abetted the spiritual campaign of which those predations were a part.[43] And, of course, Edwardian priests who obeyed government orders and read to their congregations from the *Book of Homilies* and *Book of Common Prayer* every week did an incalculable service to the Protestant cause no matter how carefully they hid away the missals and antiphoners which those books had replaced.

We are thus in a position to revise considerably the revisionists' emphasis on 'resistance' as the dominant paradigm of popular responses to the English Reformation. In his 1993 textbook *English Reformations*, for instance, Haigh's understanding of resistance allowed him to make the remarkable claim that Elizabethan parishioners were 'resisting' the Reformation when they insisted that their ministers use Thomas Cranmer's *Book of Common Prayer!*[44] Their actions may have 'resisted' the sort of Reformation preached by the radical puritan Thomas Cartwright, but they just as effectively 'resisted' the sort of Counter-Reformation preached by the Jesuit Robert Parsons, and they collaborated with the sort of Reformation promulgated by Archbishop Whitgift.[45] Clearly, then, we need to analyse potential examples of resistance and collaboration within their political contexts rather than superimposing our own idealised conversion narratives upon them. Duffy, with somewhat more subtlety, suggested that the Reformation could be resisted through the 'evasion of the spirit' of the

---

[41] Bennett, *Under the Shadow of the Swastika*, pp. 48–9.

[42] Robert Paxton, *Vichy France: Old Guard and New Order 1940–1944* (New York, 1972), p. 358 and ch. 5 *passim*.

[43] See below, ch. 7.   [44] Haigh, *English Reformations*, pp. 289–90.

[45] On the different meanings attached to the Prayer Book, see Judith Maltby, *Prayer Book and People in Elizabethan and Early Stuart England* (Cambridge, 1998).

government's injunctions, for instance when people in 1538 obediently removed candles that had burned before images but then relit those candles in rood-lofts rather than destroying them.[46] 'Evasion of the spirit' is certainly an important concept and could constitute a form of resistance, but in context it could also partake of many other, sometimes conflicting impulses, and even Duffy's own example permits a more complex reading. Burning candles in the rood-loft instead of before images, after all, resisted the starkest versions of Reformed iconophobia but also implicated parishioners in a Lutheran-style emphasis on concentrating visual devotion on crucifixes rather than on other images.[47] Moreover, since this transformation resulted from a process of compromise, and hence allowed parishioners to continue worshipping without crises of conscience, it was far more insidious and potentially corrosive for traditional religion than more radical transformations against which parishioners might have been able to unite.

IV

All of these issues and contradictions arising from the current interpretive framework for the English Reformation – a framework defined by questions of national conversion, popular piety and resistance – suggest that new approaches are needed. We do not need to accept that the most interesting questions to be asked of the English Reformation are about conversions to Protestantism, nor do we need to accept that, bluntly put, Dickens's *The English Reformation* and Haigh's *English Reformations* are the two poles between which scholars of sixteenth-century religious change must forever oscillate. We can take as read the best work of revisionist scholars, accepting that English people did not, for the most part, embrace evangelical Protestantism; once this assumption is made, however, we can seek to understand just what English people did do and why.

This approach involves something that I call, for want of a better term, popular politics.[48] In using the adjective 'popular', I do not mean to imply

---

[46] Duffy, *Stripping of the Altars*, p. 419.
[47] I owe thanks to Diarmaid MacCulloch for correcting some of my earlier hyperbole on this issue.
[48] The best discussion of popular politics in early modern England is the introduction to Tim Harris (ed.), *The Politics of the Excluded, c.1500–1850* (Basingstoke, 2001), and the essays in that volume form an important new body of thought on the subject. An important recent discussion on a Europe-wide basis is Wayne Te Brake, *Shaping History: Ordinary People in European Politics, 1500–1700* (Berkeley, 1998). For theoretical discussions of popular politics in England before 1700, see I. M. W. Harvey, 'Was there Popular Politics in Fifteenth-Century England?' in R. H. Britnell and A. J. Pollard (eds.), *The McFarlane Legacy: Studies in Late Medieval Politics and Society* (New York, 1995); Clive Holmes, 'Drainers and Fenmen: The Problem of Popular Political Consciousness in the Seventeenth Century', in Anthony Fletcher and John Stevenson (eds.), *Order and Disorder in Early*

that 'popular politics' was somehow hermetically sealed from or antithetical to 'elite politics'. On the contrary, the two were irrevocably intertwined and in constant dialogue with one another, and popular politics could involve priests and gentlemen as often as peasants and artisans. Popular politics was also not necessarily or even commonly oppositional; the conservative imperative of loyalty to the monarch was often at the core of popular political activity. 'Popular politics' simply refers to *the presence of ordinary, non-elite subjects as the audience for or interlocutors with a political action*. Hence, in practice nearly any political action by peasants was 'popular', since even actions directed towards the king presumed auxiliary audiences who were asked to assent to and legitimate those actions. Political actions of the social elite, on the other hand, could sometimes be 'popular' and sometimes not, depending on their perceived audiences; a gentleman might try to accumulate power solely through machinations at court, for instance, or he might do so by bolstering his 'public' reputation and building a power base among his tenants. What defined popular politics, then, was not the social class of the people politicking, but rather the extent to which the governed played a role in their own governance. Popular politics presumed, in practice if not in theory, that issues of substantial importance to the life of the nation would be discussed and debated in public, and popular politics accepted, again in practice if not in theory, that those debates would significantly affect how the issues were decided.[49]

This dynamic was perfectly illustrated by the successful tax revolt in 1525 in which peasants, artisans, priests and gentlemen all played a significant role in forcing the government to withdraw its demand for a so-called 'Amicable Grant' to support proposed military adventures in France. The actions of these different social groups were all unequivocal examples of popular politics, since each appealed to the others for support and legitimation; none could have succeeded without the support of the whole. Perhaps less obviously, the king's demand for the Amicable Grant was itself a form of popular politics. In his instructions requiring bishops and nobles to collect the Grant, the king elaborately defended his claims to the French Crown, explained why he needed immediate funds for an invasion, and promised to return the money if circumstances changed and that invasion proved unnecessary. When the bishops and nobles tried to collect the tax,

Modern England (Cambridge, 1985); Keith Wrightson, 'The Politics of the Parish in Early Modern England', in Paul Griffiths, Adam Fox and Steve Hindle (eds.), *The Experience of Authority in Early Modern England* (New York, 1996); Keith Wrightson, 'Two Concepts of Order: Justices, Constables and Jurymen in Seventeenth-Century England', in John Brewer and John Styles (eds.), *An Ungovernable People: The English and Their Law in the Seventeenth and Eighteenth Centuries* (New Brunswick, N.J., 1980).
[49] See Ethan Shagan, '"Popularity" and the 1549 Rebellions Revisited', *EHR*, 115 (2000), pp. 121–33.

they gathered representatives of the commonalty and, in the words of the Bishop of Ely, '[declared] to the king's subjects there his grace's mind, intention, and pleasure, moving and persuading them by all the reasons and persuasions mentioned in the king's said instructions and as many more as I could devise'.[50] In other words, the king never assumed that revenues would be granted easily; his request, like the promulgation of many taxes in the pre-bureaucratic age, represented a self-conscious prologue to negotiation. This is certainly not to say that Henry VIII believed that the commonalty had a legitimate role in politics, but rather that he was not so naïve as to think he could coerce rather than persuade the population in matters of the purse.

By this definition, it is not hard to see that virtually any attempt to inculcate religious change at the local level constituted popular politics, since innovations were not merely promulgated by the regime but also explained, defended and glossed. The government not only told people in 1534 that they owed no more allegiance to the pope, for instance, but also told them *why*, defending the royal supremacy with an avalanche of tracts, sermons, statute preambles and so on. This was not because the commonalty were perceived by the regime as fitting interlocutors in the creation of policy, but because the Tudor regime lacked the power to govern without some degree of consent.

Responses to religious change, whether negative or positive, also constituted popular politics, since those responses were hardly ever mere affirmations or denials but rather were intended to win concessions, sway public opinion and influence policy. The Pilgrimage of Grace in 1536, for instance, was on one level an elaborate appeal to conservative courtiers like the Duke of Norfolk, and as such it was an elite political event. But on another level it was an enormous act of political theatre performed before the whole nation. When Robert Aske triumphantly rode into York at the head of four thousand rebel horsemen, for instance, his entry was mirrored by a procession of clerics who marched out of the cathedral to welcome him. This carefully staged event provided the citizens of York with powerful evidence that the pilgrims rather than the royal government now represented good order in Church and commonwealth.[51] A similar dynamic governed positive responses to religious change. One clerical supporter of the royal supremacy, for instance, sarcastically 'set forth and made an image of the bishop of Rome in snow . . . not only of him but also of other his adherents'. According to the priest, 'a great multitude of people to the number by estimation of 4,000' came to gawk at the spectacle.[52] This was a quintessentially 'popular' form

---

[50] BL Cotton MS Titus B. I., fol. 271r. See also BL Cotton MS Cleopatra F. VI, fols. 262r–65v and BL Cotton MS Cleopatra F. VI., fols. 267v–68r.
[51] See below, ch. 3.   [52] BL Harleian MS 283, fol. 127r [*LP* VIII, 1067].

of politics, adapting royal propaganda to a sub-literate, carnivalesque genre of satire in order to undermine belief in the holiness of the pope and his cardinals.

The interdependence of religious controversy and popular politics was exacerbated by the fact that Reformation battles were habitually fought over issues of *authority*. Debate over the theological merit of religious beliefs was, in the public arena, usually subjugated to quasi-secular issues of law and governance. Even in cases of heresy, the most inherently spiritual of offences, we find time and again that public debates centred on the practical and political questions of who had the power to define heresy and enforce the law. In the Essex town of Langham in 1534, for instance, a questman of the parish named John Vigorouse accused his neighbours of heresy for 'saying their matins together upon an English primer'. The accused parishioners, who seem to have had genuine evangelical sympathies, defended their actions not on theological grounds but rather on the grounds that the book in question had been printed with the king's 'royal privilege'. Vigorouse's response, likewise, was not to affirm the essential heresy of their actions but rather to question the efficacy of an appeal to so capricious an authority as Henry VIII: 'The king was never so glad to make them but he shall be so glad to pull them down again, and that within a short space.' This debate over the nature of royal policy, moreover, was mirrored by a remarkable mini-debate over the power to define heresy in the locality. One of Vigorouse's young servants, echoing the rhetoric of his master, 'did quarrel and brawl with other children... whom he called heretics'. The other children, echoing the rhetoric of their masters, called Vigorouse's servant a 'Pharisee'. With no royal authority available to enforce order in so mundane a conflict, Vigorouse decided to enforce it himself, instructing his servant to 'cut off their ears... if they so call thee hereafter'.[53]

When we look through the lens of popular politics, then, the question of national conversion quickly takes on a secondary significance in Tudor history, with other questions opening up far more fruitful avenues for exploring the process of religious change. When people said/did Protestant sounding/looking things, for what audiences did they perform those statements or actions? When people spoke seditious words against the Crown or heretical words against the Church, how did their neighbours decide whether to report them to the government? When people arose in armed rebellion against innovations in Church or commonwealth, what sorts of negotiated settlements were acceptable to them and why? These questions are not reductionist, since they do not deny the importance of religious ideas. But they differ from previous interpretive frameworks by accepting that the English Reformation, like every aspect of early modern governance, depended on the

---

[53] PRO E 36/120, fols. 59r–63v [*LP* VII, 145].

collaboration of the governed. People had far more choices available to them than either meek submission or violent resistance, and their choices formed an extended dialogue with the regime. Ideas associated with the Reformation could be adopted or adapted for a variety of purposes: as rhetorical strategies in appeals to the royal courts, as political strategies in local power struggles, as economic strategies in the acquisition of ecclesiastical wealth, or simply as coping strategies for making sense of the frightening implications of national schism. These strategies all contributed to a process of negotiation through which new ideas and practices took root in England.[54]

This does not imply that the Reformation was 'popular' in the sense of emanating from the will of the people, but rather that it was 'popular' in the sense that people played an important role in choosing what sort of Reformation they experienced and constructing the meanings of that Reformation in their communities. Most people felt religious change through the mediation of parish priests, local officials and other neighbours; religious debates were refracted through personal relationships and local power structures. In every town and village there were factions whose goals and priorities dovetailed with those of the regime, and often those factions could forge alliances with elements of central authority to gain ascendancy in their communities. Religious innovations were thus not forced on the population by an all-powerful government but rather were negotiated through layers of local agents and collaborators who were as much a part of local society as their more intransigent neighbours.[55]

This book, then, is an analysis of how ordinary English subjects received, interpreted, debated and influenced the process of religious change in the first quarter century of the English Reformation. It begins in the late 1520s, when ecclesiological issues first began to impact people's lives through Henry VIII's divorce, his attacks on the clergy, and the break with Rome. It concludes in 1553 with the death of Edward VI, the end-point of England's first

---

[54] It could be argued that this book overemphasises conflict in Tudor society by utilising court cases and other conflict-centred sources rather than the wills and churchwardens' accounts out of which the revisionists have constructed their more consensual narrative of the Reformation. Yet, even if the cases described in this book were atypical, they still allow us to access the wider assumptions, cultural fault lines, and complex agendas that underpinned and structured them. The people whose beliefs and actions are analysed here found themselves in extraordinary situations, which is why their views survive in the historical record, but that does not make those people any less ordinary.

[55] This is an antithetical argument to Christopher Marsh's suggestion that 'compliance' in the Reformation resulted from the 'emphasis people placed upon communal harmony and the maintenance of charity' (Marsh, *Popular Religion*, p. 203). It instead imagines a fundamentally contested process in which the Reformation could function as one component of the 'state' as Steve Hindle understands it: 'The state was a reservoir of authority on which the populace might draw, a series of institutions in which they could participate, in pursuit of their own interests.' This 'participation', as an essentially self-interested phenomenon, did not in any sense imply consensus (Hindle, *State and Social Change*, pp. 16 and 232).

experiment with Protestant government and Protestant worship.[56] The point is not to ask whether the Reformation had 'succeeded' by 1553, but rather to ask what sorts of changes had occurred through the *mediation* of the Reformation. The answer, it will be suggested, is that, while there were few conversions to Protestantism, there were none the less enormous changes in how English people imagined the Church, the relationship between Church and state, and the meanings of their own religious practices.[57] English religion, along with aspects of English culture only partially and in complex ways related to the divine, experienced a substantial revolution in the first half of the sixteenth century. This is not to say that the Catholic Queen Mary, who succeeded her Protestant brother in 1553, could not have re-established the hegemony of Roman Catholicism had she reigned long enough. But the religion she established was not, and could not have been, a mere 'conservative' return to the pre-Reformation Church. That religion was dead and buried.

This analysis, while proceeding in roughly chronological order, is divided into three broadly thematic sections. Part I concerns the first great *locus* of religious conflict in Tudor England: the break with Rome and the royal supremacy over the Church. The royal supremacy has been characterised by revisionists as a 'political Reformation', but, as we shall see, the very question of whether it was a religious issue or a purely political one was the subject of intense debate among contemporaries. Many Catholics could not accept the break with Rome as a simple dispute over jurisdiction, but rather interpreted it as a violent rending of Christ's mystical body (chapter 1). Indeed, at several crucial moments of conservative reaction against the Henrician Reformation, especially the maid of Kent's agitation (chapter 2) and the Pilgrimage of Grace (chapter 3), the people who most vocally condemned the royal supremacy took the lead in resisting the Tudor regime. The fact that many ostensibly traditionalist Catholics *supported* the royal supremacy, then, is not so natural and uninteresting as some historians would take it to be. These conformist Catholics, bound by the logic of the royal supremacy, formed political alliances with the regime and its heretical servants at crucial

---

[56] The decision to end this book in 1553 certainly does not imply that the English Reformation was somehow 'complete' by that date. Rather, I have chosen the death of Edward VI as an end-point in a conscious effort to reinvigorate early Tudor England as a subject of research. As this book will show, attempts to imagine the English Reformation as a slow process of attrition, and hence to push farther forward the date at which *real* change occurred, have obscured the dynamism and creative energy of the early sixteenth century.

[57] The book which comes closest to these conclusions is Whiting, *Blind Devotion of the People.* Yet, because Whiting was working very much within a confessional model, he could only conclude that commitment to traditional Catholicism declined without being replaced by anything substantive; for him politics was an explanation for religious change rather than a part of it.

moments rather than supporting their nonconformist, anti-Henrician neighbours. By dividing amongst themselves in the first, crucial battles over authority in the Church, Catholics made successful resistance to royal religious
policies nearly impossible.

If Part I deals with the contours of 'conservatism', Part II explores the
dynamics of change. In the years after the break with Rome, many people
who did not identify with the 'new learning' none the less adopted political
and economic strategies that savoured of Reformation rhetoric, setting them
apart from their more traditionalist neighbours and rendering them, at least
at certain times and places, allies of the Henrician regime. Section two analyses the activities of these people and the various 'points of contact' where
new religious ideas could enter their consciousness. One such 'point of contact' was the popular–political 'genre' of anticlericalism, especially the riots
and demonstrations through which communities disciplined or discharged
errant priests. When priests offended their communities, parishioners with
different religious beliefs could ally together against a common adversary,
often appealing to the regime's own perceived antipathy to the clergy. In this
context, new and old ways of imagining priestly abuses mixed promiscu-
ously, allowing new ideas to permeate popular culture (chapter 4). Another
'point of contact' was the dissolution of the monasteries, a context in which
not only wealthy landowners but people of all social classes had an opportunity to enrich themselves by claiming the spoils of dissolved religious houses.
In doing so, they contributed to a process of desacralisation that was central to the evangelical project and internalised the mentality of Scarisbrick's
'predatory Crown on the prowl' (chapter 5). Yet another 'point of contact'
was constituted by the theological debates raging in English churches in the
1540s, waged by the same parish priests and local officials through whom
ordinary subjects experienced governance. As the Reformation evolved from
a confusing aberration into the ordinary background of politics, English people increasingly conceived of local power structures in terms of confessional
divisions, and hence increasingly framed their own local disputes in confessional terms (chapter 6).

Part III explores how these 'points of contact' bore fruit during England's
first era of unabashedly Protestant government, the reign of Edward VI
(1547–53). The dissolution of the chantries, for instance, unlike the dissolution of the monasteries a decade before, was justified in bluntly evangelical
terms. Yet, despite this context, many English subjects found themselves
collaborating with the government's programme, while many others who
resisted the regime's depredations none the less contributed to the spiritual
project of abolishing belief in purgatory and intercessory prayer by enacting comparable depredations themselves (chapter 7). In the 1549 rebellions,
likewise, many English people made common cause with the government's

economic policies, providing a bridge to its more radical religious policies and creating a shared language of 'godly commonwealth' which the commons could co-opt and manipulate for their own ends. Perhaps most remarkably, the dynamics of accommodation and collaboration were so ingrained by the 1550s that even the Edwardian regime's most disruptive policies – the assault on parish churches and the abolition of the mass – found substantial support in the parishes among people looking for allies in their own local disputes (chapter 8). In all of these cases, we find English subjects accepting and contributing to the new religious order, using that new order as the basis for their economic activities, their community organisation, and their local politics. In doing so, they absorbed much of the language, priorities and interpretive framework of the government with whom they so profitably negotiated. The 'traditional religion' described so movingly by Eamon Duffy thus would have seemed far more alien to many English people in 1553 than Thomas Cranmer's new *Book of Common Prayer*, not because they believed that their souls would be saved only by faith, but because they had willingly performed such bluntly radical works.

This book thus describes neither the success nor the failure of the Reformation, at least to the extent that we measure the Reformation in terms of evangelical conversions. It does not help us understand whether England became a Protestant nation quickly or slowly, from above or below. It does not address the 'popularity' of the pre-Reformation Church, nor the process through which England acquired a 'Calvinist consensus'. What it does, however, is show that the English Reformation was not done *to* people, it was done *with* them. This dynamic process of engagement between government and people was, in some sense, itself the greatest success of the English Reformation.

PART I

The break with Rome and the crisis of conservatism

1

'Schismatics be now plain heretics': debating the royal supremacy over the Church of England

The centrepiece and actualising principle of the English Reformation was not a theological doctrine, like Luther's justification by faith alone, but an act of state: in November 1534, after years of extorting concessions from parliaments and clerical convocations, Henry VIII was endowed with the authority of 'supreme head of the Church of England'. This was far more than a mere ratification of the annulment of the king's marriage to Catherine of Aragon, the ostensible purpose for which he had challenged papal authority; it was a fundamental restructuring of power within the realm. For centuries, two governments, one royal and one ecclesiastical, had laid their overlapping claims to jurisdiction and sovereignty across the English polity. Two court systems had settled disputes, two tax systems had demanded revenues, and two rudimentary bureaucracies had maintained order. Now in a remarkable *coup d'état* the head of the Church government was overthrown, his legal authority eliminated, his political power outlawed, and his subordinates brought under the jurisdiction of the king of England.

One ironic result of this heavily politicised context is that, despite the significance of the royal supremacy for such diverse subjects as economic history, legal history and even the origins of the British Empire, one area in which its importance is not altogether clear is the study of religion. Earlier generations of scholars saw the overthrow of papal authority as promoting and enabling the concomitant growth of English Protestantism. Yet recently, historians have argued that 'in 1535 it was not inevitable – it was not even likely – that the break with Rome would be followed by changes in religious belief and practice'. Likewise, scholars have claimed that the break with Rome was not part of a radical religious programme – the king 'was always vigorously opposed to religious radicalism' – but rather contributed to the self-conscious creation of a Henrician *via media* between Rome and Geneva. Most recently, it has even been suggested that English Catholics were largely unaffected by the royal supremacy since most favoured a humanist and irenic style of piety – 'scriptural, reforming, and yet moderate' – more than obedience to Rome. On these views, the royal supremacy was a theologically indifferent policy, part of a 'political' rather than a spiritual Reformation.[1]

These revisions presume a great deal about the nature of English religiosity. Besides claiming that Church governance could easily be separated from 'religious belief and practice' and that there was general agreement about what constituted 'religious radicalism', they also imply that certain prominent elements of the medieval Church – notably monasticism and many outward forms of ceremonial observance – were inessential to traditional religion. With Henry VIII's eradication of these elements thus glossed as spiritually indifferent and largely peripheral to popular concerns, revisionists can claim that most English people shared a broad, irenic consensus – they were all Christians, weren't they? – which remained relatively immune to successive ecclesio-political onslaughts so long as people went to church, said their prayers and loved their neighbours. This is how historians can argue that English religion was in all *essentials* the same in 1590 as it had been in 1530: only fanatics on both sides who wanted to shove England off the middle path claimed that innovations like the overthrow of the pope were significant enough to alter the essence of English religion. It also explains how English Catholics could dutifully support the royal supremacy, the dissolution of the monasteries, vernacular Bibles and even salvation through faith alone, until Trent and the Jesuits imposed their foreign, dogmatic, unforgiving faith upon the intrinsic moderation of the English Church.[2]

While ostensibly concerned with the English Catholic tradition, lying just below the surface of these arguments is an unwavering belief in something called 'Anglicanism', a notional, indigenous English faith that developed organically in the Middle Ages, navigated the dangerous waters of the Reformation, and emerged unsullied in the Restoration settlement of 1662. Anglicanism, in this view, was a religion above the fray of confessional dispute, instinctively conservative yet happy to yield on outward matters so long as certain core elements of Christian piety survived. It was the default religion of the English people, intrinsically Catholic but not necessarily papal, based on community and tradition rather than doctrine, which linked ostensibly Catholic parishioners in the 1520s with ostensibly Protestant parishioners in the 1580s. The *via media* between Rome and Geneva, in other words, was religion with the ideology left out. Needless to say, this pollyannish view is in considerable tension with Eamon Duffy's sobering portrait of traditional

---

[1] Christopher Haigh, *English Reformations: Religion, Politics, and Society under the Tudors* (Oxford, 1993), p. 123; George Bernard, 'The Making of Religious Policy, 1533–1546: Henry VIII and the Search for the Middle Way', *HJ*, 41 (1998), 321–49, quotation at p. 325; Lucy Wooding, *Rethinking Catholicism in Reformation England* (Oxford, 2000), quotation at p. 89.

[2] Haigh, *English Reformations*; Wooding, *Rethinking Catholicism*.

religion being ripped apart at the seams in the middle decades of the sixteenth century. But, more importantly, this chapter will argue, the 'Anglican' ideal relies upon a dangerous teleology, isolating one strand of English religiosity, defining it as normative, and then projecting it backwards and forwards through time to illustrate the origins and development of English religious exceptionalism.

It cannot be denied that many English Catholics who supported Henry VIII's break with Rome saw themselves as the upholders of a conservative *via media*. Yet the fact that some people saw the royal supremacy as spiritually indifferent does not mean that the majority saw things that way, nor does it help us to understand how this view fitted into the larger debates of the time. The Act of Supremacy proclaimed that kings of England were supreme heads of the Church of England, yet for all the conciliarist and imperial bluster behind this claim, in practice no one knew in 1534 what a 'Church of England' was. Some contemporaries constructed narrow definitions which reduced the royal supremacy to a theologically indifferent claim to jurisdiction, while others defined the Church of England in highly radical terms as a grossly heretical assault on the one apostolic Church. These differences in interpretation were at the centre of the English Reformation, and they must be highlighted rather than elided. Rather than seeing the royal supremacy as either intrinsically radical or intrinsically indifferent, we need to appreciate that the very question of its spiritual significance was a crucial ground of contestation. It was along the fault lines created by this issue that the English Reformation at first largely operated, allowing people with a widely shared, traditionalist theology none the less to adopt vastly different and often violently antithetical responses to the government-sponsored Reformation of the 1530s.

This chapter will thus analyse Catholic reactions to the royal supremacy over the Church of England, focusing on evidence created before the summer of 1536, when the king first began to use his new authority for explicitly doctrinal experimentation.[3] Rather than seeing the nation's acceptance of the royal supremacy as a by-product of innate English moderation, I want instead to present that acceptance, to the extent that it occurred, as the result of a *political process*. This process splintered the traditionalist Catholic population, encouraging the rapid development of the least ideological strand

---

[3] For prior studies of responses to the royal supremacy, see e.g., G. R. Elton, *Policy and Police: The Enforcement of the Reformation in the Age of Thomas Cromwell* (Cambridge, 1972); Paul O'Grady, *Henry VIII and the Conforming Catholics* (Collegeville, Minn., 1990); Jean-Pierre Moreau, *Rome ou l'Angleterre? Les Reactions Politiques des Catholiques Anglais au Moment du Schisme, 1529–1553* (Paris, 1984); Glyn Redworth, *In Defence of the Church Catholic: The Life of Stephen Gardiner* (Cambridge, Mass., 1990); Anthony Shaw, 'Papal Loyalism in 1530s England', *Downside Review*, 117 (1999), 17–40; Ellen Macek, *The Loyal Opposition: Tudor Traditionalist Polemics, 1535–1558* (New York, 1996).

of medieval English Catholicism while dismantling or driving underground other, less ecumenical strands. The brand of Catholicism that survived and occasionally prospered in Henry VIII's England thus did so in active opposition to many other, equally viable modes of Catholic religiosity, in the process stripping English Catholicism of much that had made it a strong and vital faith to begin with.

I

Many English subjects would have been surprised to discover that the events of 1533–6 were inherently secular or political and did not constitute a spiritual Reformation. There were, of course, conciliarist arguments available within the late medieval Church that could be developed into strictly jurisdictional readings of the break with Rome, but the sheer volume of religiously motivated dissent against Henrician policies in these years belies the idea of a spiritually indifferent royal supremacy. To put the argument in its bluntest terms, Thomas More and John Fisher died protesting not a political dispute over sovereignty, but rather the nation's descent into heresy.

One barometer of the theological pressure generated by the royal supremacy was the large number of disaffected laymen who were prosecuted for accusing the king, either directly or obliquely, of heresy. In 1534, for instance, a Leicestershire servant called Henry Kylbre made the mistake of talking religion with the proprietor of the White Horse Inn in Cambridge, a hotbed of religious reform. When the proprietor told him, '[t]here is no pope but a bishop of Rome', Kylbre responded 'that he and whosoever held of his part were strong heretics'. When the proprietor countered that 'the king's grace held of his part', Kylbre carried his argument to its logical conclusion: 'then was both he an heretic and the king another'.[4] Another layman, called George Taylor, was accused at the Buckinghamshire sessions in February 1535 of saying: 'The king is but a knave and liveth in adultery, and is an heretic and liveth not after the laws of God.' Taylor was so outraged by the king's heresy that he said if he had the king's crown in his possession, he 'would play at football with it'.[5] Robert Augustyn said in the same year that if anyone wrote books against the pope 'otherwise than charity would require', he would 'take him and regard him no other ways than he would a schismatic, paynim, or Jew'. Augustyn also said that the chronicles of the realm were false when they accused the papacy of abusing King John, and that Rome had been so accused out of malice by 'false heretics'.[6] In August 1535, the elderly Worcestershire husbandman Edmund Brocke expressed

---

[4] PRO SP 1/84, fols. 111r–v [*LP* VII, 754].   [5] PRO SP 1/90, fol. 184r [*LP* VIII, 278].
[6] PRO SP 1/92, fol. 127r [*LP* VIII, 624].

similar ideas in a more rustic idiom; on a rainy day returning from market he told several of his neighbours: 'It is long of the king that this weather is so troublous or unstable, and I ween we shall never have better weather while the king reigneth, and therefore it maketh no matter if he were knocked or patted on the head.'[7] In July 1535 at the parish church of Gisburn, Yorkshire, when the priest read Archbishop Lee's articles on the royal supremacy 'as was directed from the king's grace' one parishioner became so angry that he 'came violently and took [the] book first of the priest's hands and pulled it in pieces'.[8]

Several women also denounced the king's apostasy. The eccentric prophetess Mrs Amadas, a minor court figure and widow of a keeper of the king's jewels, said in 1534 that 'there shall be a battle of priests, and that the king shall be destroyed, and there shall never [be] more kings in England, and the realm shall be called the land of conquest'. Her opinion of this eventuality is clear from other anti-Henrician statements, notably her insistence that 'the Lady Anne should be burnt' and her exclamation, 'I care not for the king a rush under my foot; it is the king of heaven that rules all.'[9] Another woman was among the most important early opponents of the regime: Elizabeth Barton, a prophetess and nun of St Sepulchre's, Canterbury, known as the maid of Kent. Chapter 2 will be devoted entirely to Barton's career; for now it is sufficient to show that her anti-government agitation explicitly treated the king's divorce and nascent supremacy as theological error. In one prophecy, for instance, 'an angel appeared and bade the nun go unto the king, that infidel prince of England, and say that I command him to amend his life, and that he leave three things which he loveth and purposeth upon, that is that he take none of the pope's right nor patrimony from him, the second that he destroy all those new folks of opinion and the works of their new learning, the third that if he married and took Anne to wife the vengeance of God should plague him'.[10]

Barton's quintessentially spiritual gloss on the royal divorce was most clearly visible in a vision following the king's controversial October 1532 trip to Calais in the company of Anne Boleyn. After the king's return, Barton

---

[7] PRO SP 1/95, fol. 76r [*LP* IX, 74]. Brocke was not alone in this interpretation of the weather. On 30 June 1535, Eustace Chapuys reported to Nicolas de Granvelle that 'many begin already to show discontent, saying that ever since these executions [of Fisher and the Carthusians] it has never ceased raining in England, and that is God's revenge': *CSP Spanish*, vol. 5, p. 506.

[8] PRO SP 1/94, fols. 22v–23r [*LP* VIII, 1024].

[9] BL Cotton MS Cleopatra E. IV, fols. 99r–100r. For Mrs Amadas's relation to Robert Amadas, see Elton, *Policy and Police*, pp. 59–60.

[10] *Three Chapters of Letters Relating to the Suppression of Monasteries. Edited from the Originals in the British Museum*, ed. Thomas Wright, Camden Society, 1st series vol. 26 (London, 1843), pp. 14–15.

described a remarkable event which she claimed had occurred when he attempted to receive the Eucharist: 'When the king's highness was at Calais in the interview between his majesty and the French king, and hearing mass in the church of Our Lady at Calais . . . God was so displeased with the king's highness that his grace saw not that time at the mass the blessed sacrament in the form of bread, for it was taken away from the priest (being at mass) by an angel, and ministered to the said Elizabeth then being there present and invisible.'[11] Within this vision was a bold and radical statement of the king's illegitimacy. By denying the body of Christ to the king in her vision, Barton symbolically imposed an interdict upon the regime; the blessed sacrament was deemed incompatible with the sacrilegious actions of the Henrician government. More remarkably, the Host was not merely denied to the king but transferred to Barton herself, the embodiment of spiritual purity and, as a nun, a metaphoric stand-in for that other Bride of Christ, the Catholic Church. In an important sense, then, Barton's vision represented the ritual transfer of authority from the monarch to the Church itself. And like all of Barton's revelations, this one was publicised to a remarkable degree through manuscripts, print, pulpit and word of mouth; indeed, the government made it a high priority, in the words of the Imperial ambassador, to 'blot out from people's minds the impression they have that the nun is a saint and a prophet'.[12]

Other evidence that the break with Rome was taken as heretical comes from the Catholic clergy. The parish priest of St Mary Woolchurch in London, for instance, announced that 'all those that preached at the king's commandment were heretics nowadays', and he added that 'if the king do follow such heretics . . . he shall not long continue'.[13] The popular Catholic preacher William Hubberdyne did not mention the king directly, but during his pulpit dispute with Hugh Latimer at Bristol in 1533 he announced 'that he or they whatsoever he or they be that speak against the pope or any point [of] his acts or ordinances is a heretic'.[14] In 1535, the vicar of Rye told a visitor from overseas that 'this realm was full of heretics and heresies, specially in that any corporal man should be supreme head of the Church'.[15] Sometime before the death of Anne Boleyn, Robert Wynter, parson of South Witham in Lincolnshire, called 'the king and the queen heretics and Lollards' and said he 'wished his knife in their bellies'.[16]

Another way to accuse Henry VIII of religious error was to condemn as heretical books published with the king's privilege. For instance, in 1534 John Fraunces, monk of Colchester, was accused of saying: 'There is a book

[11] *Statutes*, vol. 3, 25 Hen. VIII. c. 12, p. 448.   [12] *CSP Spanish*, vol. 4, part 2, no. 1154.
[13] PRO SP 1/94, fols. 1r–2r [*LP* VIII, 1000].   [14] PRO SP 2/O, fol. 31r [*LP* VI, 799].
[15] PRO SP 1/99, fol. 67r [*LP* IX, 846].   [16] PRO STAC 2/33/75.

called the nine articles lately come out in the king's name and his Council's, [and] where they that made it were before schismatics [they] be now plain heretics.'[17] The vicar of Newark, Master Lytherlande, preached on Quinquagesima Sunday 1534 that 'no man should suffer his servant or apprentice to have any of these new books against the pope, nor yet any man himself should have them', and he claimed that there were '23 books abroad in this country that the least of them was enough to make an heretic'.[18] Also at Newark, a 'Scottish friar' in 1534 used traditional 'evil counsellors' rhetoric to cloak his condemnation of early Reformation policies: 'Such books as were made *cum privilegio* . . . were heresies, and if the king and his Council and my lord of Canterbury do that which is agreed by parliament and contrary to the holy pope of Rome and the whole Church there, it is heresies. But I dare well say that the king's grace never knew of no such books, and I trust to see that such traitors as have made them that their heads shall have knocks.'[19]

It also should not be forgotten that a substantial number of English subjects fled the realm between 1534 and 1536 rather than acquiesce in the royal supremacy. On 30 June 1534, for instance, two observant friars from Newark called Hugh Payne and Thomas Hayfield were apprehended in secular garb while bargaining with a ship's captain to convey them to Brittany.[20] A clerk called William Dickinson was 'apprehended by the seaside in Sussex in journey to Rome'.[21] William Peryn, a Dominican friar who later became prior of St Bartholomew, Smithfield under Queen Mary, left England in self-imposed exile in 1534.[22] Friar Arthur of Canterbury gave a sermon at Herne, Kent on Easter 1535 in which he refused to pray for the king as supreme head and told his parishioners that it was sinful to disobey the established Church; by November of the same year he was residing in France.[23] Dr Richard Boorde of Sussex fled England in the same year, having allegedly said that he 'would rather be torn with wild horses than assent or consent to the diminishing of one iota of the bishop of Rome his authority'.[24]

There is thus copious evidence that among both clergy and commons there was a significant faction of traditionalist opinion that interpreted the royal supremacy in highly radical terms as not merely dubious political or ecclesiological policy, but as theological error.[25] The existence of such a powerful strand of opinion should not be a surprise, since surely Thomas More, John Fisher and the Carthusians executed in 1535 would not have developed such extraordinary reputations had their views not been shared

---

[17] PRO SP 2/P, fol. 152r [*LP* VII, 454].   [18] PRO E 36/120, fol. 5r.
[19] PRO SP 1/82, fol. 235r [*LP* VII, 261].   [20] PRO SP 1/85, fol. 93r [*LP* VII, 1020].
[21] *Original Letters*, vol. 3, series 3, p. 95.   [22] See *DNB* entry for William Peryn.
[23] Elton, *Policy and Police*, p. 16.   [24] Ibid., p. 84.
[25] Many more cases are noted in Shaw, 'Papal Loyalism in 1530s England', although I sometimes disagree with Shaw's interpretations.

by some sizeable portion of the populace. Yet by delineating this opinion and showing its importance before the beginning of the so-called 'radical' or 'Protestant' phase of the Henrician Reformation, we are forced to consider a new trajectory for that Reformation as a whole. Rather than beginning with an intrinsically conservative policy that was later hijacked by radicals, we instead see a deeply contested policy that could be interpreted as radical from the start. This implies that revisionist claims about the failure of the English Reformation must be reinterpreted from the beginning of our story; 'failure' was a relative term, and to some Catholics the mere acceptance of Henry VIII as supreme head of the Church implied a level of success for heresy that could not be tolerated.

II

To understand the basis of this nonconformist, anti-Henrician Catholicism, we must turn briefly away from the seditious words of disenchanted English subjects and towards the more fully developed arguments of theologians. Most importantly, we must consider the most elaborate statement of the nonconformist Catholic position, Reginald Pole's *Pro Ecclesiasticae Unitatis Defensione*, composed on the Continent between September 1535 and March 1536 in response to the executions of Fisher and More.[26] This text's unique-ness is owed to the author's unique circumstances: Pole was already in Italy when he wrote the tract, and in writing it he knowingly sentenced himself to exile. Yet we must not think of the *De Unitate* (as it was known) as any less central or any less authentically English than its great antithesis, Stephen Gardiner's *De Vera Obedientia*. Both tracts were written by prominent Englishmen as glosses on the same events, and both combined elements of political expediency with heartfelt views on the relationship between Church and state.

Much of Pole's tract was intended to show, ostensibly in response to Bishop Richard Sampson's defence of the royal supremacy, that the Roman Church was not an adiaphorous human construction but rather was coterminous in both form and doctrine with Christ's True Church on earth. Often this was

---

[26] On Pole's *De Unitate*, see Thomas Mayer, *Reginald Pole: Prince and Prophet* (Cambridge, 2000), ch. 1. My arguments here may seem opposed to Mayer's interpretations of Pole's views, especially in his ' "Heretics be Not in All Things Heretics": Cardinal Pole, His Circle, and the Potential for Toleration', in his *Cardinal Pole in European Context: A Via Media in the Reformation* (Aldershot, 2000). Yet, on the contrary, I agree with Mayer that even radical denunciations of Henry VIII were not incompatible with attempts to assert a prophetic voice and draw the errant king back into the fold. I would suggest only that Pole's belief that 'heretics be not in all things heretics', while perhaps in principle leaving room for toleration, in practice amounted to little more than an observation that even a broken clock is right twice a day.

accomplished through the familiar metaphor of the pope as head of the spiritual body of Christ; Pole wrote, for instance, that Fisher and More 'refused to admit that the head should be severed from the body of the Church', preferring to have 'their own heads severed from their bodies'.[27] Similarly, Pole argued that the Church of Rome, and by extension the pope himself, may speak for Christ: 'In rejecting the authority of the pontiff and demanding a king instead, you did not reject the pontiff. You rejected Christ.'[28] The rationale behind these arguments was one of history and precedent: Christ said, 'I shall never withdraw my spirit from you even to the consummation of the world', and hence those who doubt the validity of the Church 'injure Christ Himself' when they 'ignore the known fact that the spirit of Christ governs the Church' or suggest that 'for centuries the Church has been in ignorance concerning the question of the Church being governed by one or by many'.[29] Indeed, Pole marvelled that while 'in civil matters custom alone obtains the force of law after a space of a certain number of years, in the Church Sampson does not even admit the custom of a thousand years'.[30] Here Pole turns on its head the argument that governance of the Church is spiritually indifferent, suggesting that the successors of Peter could never have survived so long 'unless Rome, attacked as it so often was by heretics and so frequently plagued by barbarian peoples, had been supported by the Word of Christ'.[31]

Another strand of Pole's argument concerned not the legitimacy of papal authority but the illegitimacy of the king's authority. He noted, for instance, that in the Scriptures there were no Christian kings, and he mocked Sampson's attempts to prove 'on the authority of scriptures... that kings were appointed heads of the Churches, when you could not even show that

---

[27] Reginald Pole, *Pole's Defense of the Unity of the Church*, ed. Joseph E. Dwyer (Westminster, Md., 1965), p. 3; Reginald Pole, *Reginadi Poli Cardinalis Britanni, ad Henricum Octauum Britanniae Regem, pro Ecclesiasticae Unitatis Defensione* (Rome, 1536), fol. 2r: 'Pro qua causa tales uiri non dubitarunt, corpora sua ad supplicia offerre, cum capita sibi praecidi maluerunt, quam ei sententiae astipulari, quae a corpore ecclesiae, caput abscinderet'. I have generally used Dwyer's translation in the text, but, since his translation is often more interpretive than literal, I have included the original Latin in the footnotes. When necessary I have changed Dwyer's translation and noted the changes.
[28] Dwyer (ed.), *Pole's Defense*, p. 88; Pole, *Pro Ecclesiasticae Unitatis Defensione*, fol. 36r: 'Cum Pontificis authoritatem reiecistis, & Regem postulastis, non uos Pontificem, sed Christum reiecistis'.
[29] Dwyer (ed.), *Pole's Defense*, pp. 139 and 13–14; Pole, *Pro Ecclesiasticae Unitatis Defensione*, fol. 6r: 'Imo Christum ipsum afficias, quae cum spiritu Christi haud dubie docta sit, eam uelis tot seculis ignorasse, utrum ab uno, an a pluribus regeretur?'
[30] Dwyer (ed.), *Pole's Defense*, p. 107; Pole, *Pro Ecclesiasticae Unitatis Defensione*, fol. 43v: 'Cumque illic quod in sola consuetudine positum est, uel centum annorum spatio uim legis obtineat, hic ne mille quidem annos admittit'.
[31] Dwyer (ed.), *Pole's Defense*, p. 139; Pole, *Pro Ecclesiasticae Unitatis Defensione*, fol. 57v: 'Quod certe fieri non potuisset, nisi uerbo Christi Roma toties ab haereticis oppugnata, toties a barbaris gentibus infestata, niteretur'.

kings constituted any part of the body of the Church according to these same scriptures'.[32] The Bible, on the contrary, suggested that kings lacked spiritual authority: when Nebuchadnezzar ordered the Israelites to worship a golden idol, 'the best of the children of Israel considered it preferable to be thrown into a fiery furnace rather than obey the king in this respect'.[33] But more than arguments from scripture, Pole relied on Church history, asking: 'If the nature of the Church were such that it should be ruled by many heads, these supreme heads being kings, what kind of a Church, I ask you, are you making? Whose spirit would govern this Church if for many centuries it were ignorant of its own nature? . . . The Church has been illuminated for many years by a new light from heaven. Are you going to make it shine with your own paltry light?'[34]

The most extraordinary aspect of the tract, however, was its strong language against the king. Pole stated baldly that Henry VIII had been deserted by the spirit of God, and he launched a blistering assault on the king for his lusts, his hypocrisy in marrying Anne Boleyn, his manipulation of the universities, and his intimidation of advisors.[35] More pointedly, he wrote that 'Satan, prince of darkness, presided' at the judgment of Thomas More, and he asked the king: 'For how long do you hope to deceive God without punishment? Can you anticipate anything less than the greatest scourge of the wrath of God? Even now do you place your hope in those lies that fill the books containing a defence of your cause? Do you now place faith in threats of death and torture for those who dare to think the opposite?'[36] Finally, Pole denounced the king in absolute terms: 'To everyone you appear more cruel than any pirate, more bold than Satan himself. Truly, then, you were

---

[32] Dwyer (ed.), *Pole's Defense*, p. 35; Pole, *Pro Ecclesiasticae Unitatis Defensione*, fol. 14r–v: 'Tibi ne credi uis, scripturae authoritate capita ecclesiarum constitutos esse reges, prius quem ex scripturas ostendas, eos partem aliquam corporis ecclesiae fuisse?'

[33] Dwyer (ed.), *Pole's Defense*, p. 21; Pole, *Pro Ecclesiasticae Unitatis Defensione*, fol. 9r: 'qui optimi erant inter filios Israel, in fornacem ardentem coniici, quam ei praecepto Regis obedire'.

[34] Dwyer (ed.), *Pole's Defense*, p. 13; Pole, *Pro Ecclesiasticae Unitatis Defensione*, fol. 5v: 'Sed si hic tandem ecclesiae status sit, ut per plura capita regatur, horum autem capitum locum Reges teneant, quam quaeso eam facis, cuius spiritu regi, si tot saeculis statum suum ignorauit? Si nesciuit utrum ne ab uno an a pluribus regi deberet? Si plus homines, cum adhuc in tenebris uersarentur, de statu uniuersi cognouisse facis, quam ecclesiam noua de caelo luce illustratam, post tot secula, de suo?'

[35] Dwyer (ed.), *Pole's Defense*, pp. 180–96; Pole, *Pro Ecclesiasticae Unitatis Defensione*, fols. 72r–80v.

[36] Dwyer (ed.), *Pole's Defense*, p. 217; Pole, *Pro Ecclesiasticae Unitatis Defensione*, fol. 89r: 'Sathana . . . ipse profecto tenebrarum princeps prefuit'. Dwyer (ed.), *Pole's Defense*, p. 266; Pole, *Pro Ecclesiasticae Unitatis Defensione*, fol. 109r: 'Quousque te Deo impune illusurum esse speras? Quid potes nunc expectare, nisi maximum irae Dei flagellum? An in quibus spem adhuc habuisti, mendaciis, quibus libri causae tuae defensionem continentes sunt referti, & mortis ac cruciatuum minis in eos qui contra sentire audeant, iis etiam nunc fidis?'

such a terrible enemy to the Church that you can be compared with no one except Satan.'[37]

The underlying foundation of these arguments was a view of the Church in which all aspects of Christian history, theology and ecclesiology were wedded together by their common inspiration, the Holy Spirit. The mere idea of a 'Church of England' was in this view a monstrosity, a suggestion that Christ's Church might be beholden to national barriers erected by fallen man. Similarly, the conformist argument that the king would not alter doctrine while acting as supreme head was in this view irrelevant; to claim that the pope was not the successor of Peter, or that Peter was not prince of the apostles, was to challenge the veracity of the Holy Spirit that oversaw the Church.[38] Pole's position, like all Spirit-centred views of Christianity, left little room for adiaphora, assuming that the Holy Spirit would imbue all believers with the same truths; where there was disagreement in the Church there was almost certainly error. As such, Pole's theology was in some ways closer to the theology of puritanism than it was to the theology of his erstwhile friend Stephen Gardiner, who was willing to accept Church government as open to a broad range of interpretation.[39]

The *De Unitate* thus utterly rejected the idea of the break with Rome as compatible with Christ's faith, going so far as to compare Henry VIII to the devil almost a year before he began to use the supremacy for doctrinal experimentation. And, while Reginald Pole may have been far removed from popular politics, we can find similarly radical statements of nonconformist Catholicism in the words of preachers speaking directly to popular audiences. A young priest in Exeter cathedral, for instance, gave a sermon in 1534 in which he stated, cleverly but quite ambiguously, that since St Peter had denied Christ, 'therefore like loving people we deny Peter and take Christ's part'. His superiors, unsure of the spirit in which this comment was made, asked the priest to preach again, and in this second sermon the temptation to express his true feelings was evidently too strong. Preaching on 1 Corinthians 12, where Paul describes 'the parts of the natural body, and how that one member

---

[37] Dwyer (ed.), *Pole's Defence*, pp. 270–1; Pole, *Pro Ecclesiasticae Unitatis Defensione*, fol. 111r: 'Ut multo tu crudelior, quam ullus pirata, audacior, quam ipse Sathanas omnibus uideare; Tum uero ita ecclesiae infectus hostis, ut cum nemine nisi cum Sathana conferri possis'.

[38] It is striking how similar this defence of the papal supremacy was to John Fisher's defence of the unity of the Magdalene, with the same explicit references to the Holy Spirit as the author of Church authority and Christian unity. Indeed, Richard Rex has written that: 'Tradition was for Fisher, in effect, the record of the Holy Spirit's activity in leading the Church into all truth': Richard Rex, *The Theology of John Fisher* (Cambridge, 1991), p. 101 and *passim*.

[39] On 'Catholic puritanism' and its apocalyptic language in the Elizabethan and early Stuart periods, see Michael Questier, *Conversion, Politics and Religion in England, 1580–1625* (Cambridge, 1996). I would like to thank Dr Questier for discussing these issues with me.

dependeth on the goodness of the other', the priest 'referred in a likeness the mystical parts of Christ's body unto the parts of the natural body'. He described the clergy as the eyes of this mystical body, temporal rulers as the hands, and commoners as the feet. Finally reaching his crescendo, he told his audience: 'Masters, I fear me that the mystical body of Christ is made a monster. For that is called a monster, after the mind of the philosopher, when there lacketh a part of the natural body or else when there be too many parts, as two heads or three legs of a man, or else when the parts standeth out of order. And so the mystical body of Christ is or may be called a monster ... because there as the eyes should stand there standeth the hands.'[40] This was a wholly traditional metaphor, but it presented a view of Christianity in which virtually no aspect of ecclesiology could be considered spiritually indifferent; on this priest's logic, a man might no more alter the shape of the Church than he might alter the shape of his own body.

In 1535, Richard Crowley, curate of Broughton, Oxfordshire, was likewise accused of having 'maintained and upholden the power of the bishop of Rome, and called him pope'. In particular, one of his parishioners informed an assize justice that Crowley had preached that 'the sun is the head of the spirituality, [by] which he meaneth the pope, and the moon signifieth the king, and the stars the people of the world ... [and] the moon doth take her light of the sun, and now he sayth the light of the sun is taken from us and the world is dark and the people of the world be brought into blindness'. The moon allegory for the king suggested that royal power was a reflection of the power of the Church, while the sun allegory for the pope suggested that Rome was in some sense interchangeable with the 'light of the world', Christ himself. Crowley thus defended the pope's power and passionately declared that 'the bishop of Rochester and the father of Syon with Sir Thomas More and others died for the true faith and holding the true opinion, and so would I myself'.[41]

On Easter Sunday 1534, Gabriel Pecock, warden of the Observant Friars at Southampton, preached in St Swithun's church in Winchester, where a man called Robert Cooke was doing penance for sacramentarian heresy. The friar took advantage of the abjured heretic's presence to preach to his audience that they should 'live and die in their faith', telling a remarkable story as an exemplum:

Saint Maurice ... was a devout and holy man and a great captain under a noble prince, and had under him and at his commandment certain legions of knights ... Unto him, being among them in armor, was done a message from his prince and sovereign that

---

[40] BL Cotton MS Cleopatra E. VI, fol. 205r–v.
[41] PRO SP 1/95, fol. 49r [*LP* IX, 46]. This sun/moon metaphor was commonplace in papal literature and went back at least to the investiture controversy of the eleventh century.

he should do a certain thing which was against the law, under pain of death. He then considering that if he did his prince's commandment he should grievously displease God, and again on the other side if he did not he should suffer death, and although at that time he was of power and strength, able to have resisted his prince and so to have saved his own life...in the sight of all his soldiers [he] did cast his weapon out of his hand...exhorting his soldiers likewise to do, and there humbly offered himself to suffer for God's sake.

While ostensibly opposing resistance, the friar thus back-handedly accused the king of commanding his subjects contrary to God's law and urged them to refuse. He then made explicit which government policies he found so reprehensible, claiming that 'diverse hath preached and daily do preach that St Peter had never more power nor authority given unto him by God than any other of the apostles, and that the pope should have no more authority, power, or jurisdiction out of Rome than a bishop hath without of his diocese, nor a bishop no more than a simple priest, and so consequently the pope no more than a simple curate'. Here the friar had collapsed several different arguments together into a single, seamless manifesto, with the former positions coming from royal propaganda and the latter coming from evangelical theology; obviously the friar saw the overthrow of the pope as closely linked to more radical denials of clerical authority. All of these arguments, he preached, were 'grievous errors', and he 'took his book in his hand which lay upon the pulpit by him, and read therein five or six places approving *primatum Petri*, and Englished the same'.[42]

Perhaps the most extraordinary Romanist sermon from the early years of the royal supremacy was preached at Newark church by 'an observant friar, called Father Arte'. He first told the congregation that:

few did know the very Church of God, and therefore they did greatly err in their faith. But, sayth he, I shall put you out of all doubts, and show you plainly where is the faithful Church of Christ: the Church of Rome is the true and faithful Church of God, and none other. Whosoever is not of this Church is an infidel, and whosoever dieth out of this Church is damned to Hell. Neither is the Church of England the Church of God, nor the Church of France, nor any other Church in the world, but only the Church of Rome.

Arte then challenged the regime's scriptural rationale for the royal supremacy, arguing that, when Christ offered the keys to his kingdom, he was speaking 'only to Peter, and to none other of all the apostles, nor to no other man in the world. And whosoever said the contrary was an heretic, and that he would prove or die for it.' Having thus crossed the Rubicon, Arte launched into a remarkable tirade:

Therefore if the bishop of Canterbury do disobey the pope of Rome or the Church of Rome, as they say he doeth indeed, he is an heretic, a schismatic, and a member of

---

[42] PRO SP 2/P, fols. 149r–150r [*LP* VII, 449].

the devil. And whatsoever he be, king or lord, that doeth move you or teach you to disobey the pope of Rome, believe him no more than you would do the devil of hell, for all that so doeth teach you are the very members of the devil. Furthermore do not shrink, but rather suffer death though it be never so cruel, [before] you will receive any such doctrine either of king or lord, for they can but only slay your bodies, and if you follow their commandment and doctrine you shall lose both body and soul. And here he declared unto them the torments and deaths of diverse martyrs, to animate and courage the rude people rather to die than to believe anything that is said or written against the pope of Rome.[43]

Highly derogatory and decidedly spiritual glosses on the royal supremacy were thus being preached from English pulpits despite the likelihood that these sermons would significantly reduce the preachers' life expectancy. Given the evident vitality of this strain of opinion, we are faced with a discrepancy between standard historiographical views of the 'Henrician schism' and powerful contemporary conceptions of 'Henrician heresy'. The idea of 'schism' comes easily to historians who want to de-emphasise the importance of the Henrician Reformation, as indeed it did to sixteenth-century English Catholics who wanted to downplay the theological significance of their own conformity; hence in Mary's reign Stephen Gardiner and other Catholics were reconciled from their schismatic state rather than being forced to bear faggots, as a way of delineating them from Thomas Cranmer and the evangelicals, who were subjected to formal heresy proceedings. This firm distinction between schism and heresy, however, was something of a fiction, or at least a convenience, rather than an accurate depiction of the religious dynamics of the 1530s. Conformists like Gardiner did not consider themselves in the 1530s to be schismatics at all, but rather thought they were acting in accordance with legally constituted authority on matters that were spiritually indifferent; accepting their own actions as schismatic two decades after the fact was no less politic than their original conformity.

There was also a powerful strain of theological opinion that denied any significant distinction between schism and heresy. While, technically, schism was an ecclesiastical separation and heresy was an error of faith, such a neat division overlooked the centrality of unity in Catholic theology. Not only could the rending of Christ's body easily be seen as heretical in and of itself, but a large body of tradition recognised the difficulty of imagining a schism that was not at heart linked to error. In his writings against the Donatists, for instance, Augustine noted that in practice any schismatic Church inevitably drifted away from the mother Church in points of doctrine, and he thus reduced the distinction between schism and heresy to one merely of degree rather than of kind. In canon law, moreover, the penalties for schism and

---

[43] PRO E 36/120, fols. 5r–6r. This manuscript is undated, but its apparent fogginess over whether the Archbishop of Canterbury had really disobeyed the pope suggests that it comes from 1533 or very soon after.

heresy had long been identical, with schismatics judged to be merely exterior heretics.[44]

On 26 July 1535 this point was applied to the English situation by no less a person than Pope Paul III. While the papal excommunication of Henry VIII would not be promulgated for several more years, the pope wrote an open letter to Francis I of France accusing Henry VIII of 'heresy and schism, and the tearing of his realm from the universal Church' and suggesting that Henry, 'through rebellion, through heresy and schism, and other most enormous crimes, and now lately through the shameful slaughter of a cardinal of the Holy Roman Church . . . has deprived himself of his realm and royal dignity [and] should be declared of us to be thus deprived'.[45] It is never explained here what doctrinal 'heresy' Henry might have committed. Rather, the point is that the awesome sacrilege of rejecting Rome and beheading a cardinal could not in practice be lacking in fundamental error. The same Holy Spirit that oversaw the Church also directed fallen humanity towards the Truth, and a rejection of the Church thus entailed a loss of grace which inevitably produced a rejection of true faith.

A year later the same point was made more succinctly by Robert Aske, leader of the Pilgrimage of Grace, under interrogation by Thomas Cromwell's agents. Aske was questioned about Bishops Latimer and Cranmer, having allegedly described them as 'heretics and schismatics', and he was asked, 'For what causes ye noted them to be heretics?' and 'For what causes ye noted them to be schismatics?' He responded incisively: 'Aske sayeth [that] well he knoweth not the diversity betwixt a heretic and a schismatic, but he sayeth he can see they varied from the old usages of the Church, and because they preached contrary to the same.'[46] Here again the difference between the two offences is elided, with schism imagined as merely one stage in the life cycle of heresy.

These ideas were most fully elaborated in Pole's *De Unitate*. Pole, citing St Cyprian, argued that 'heresies do not arise nor are schisms born in any other way than through lack of submission to the priest of God'.[47] The point here was not to distinguish between schism and heresy but rather to equate

---

[44] Much of this paragraph summarises arguments and evidence in Questier, *Conversion, Politics and Religion in England*, pp. 69–70. In Mary's reign there remained a radical strand of Catholic opinion that rejected the regime's politic acceptance of former collaborators. John Standish, for instance, quoted Origen to prove that 'where be schisms there be heresies, there be dissentions, and finally utter destruction': John Standish, *The Triall of the Supremacy* (London, 1556), sig. T5v.

[45] Stephen Gardiner, *Obedience in Church and State: Three Political Tracts by Stephen Gardiner*, ed. Pierre Janelle (Cambridge, 1930), pp. 14–17.

[46] 'The Pilgrimage of Grace and Aske's Examination', ed. Mary Bateson, *EHR*, 5 (1890), pp. 330–48 and 550–78, quotations at pp. 552 and 567.

[47] Dwyer (ed.), *Pole's Defense*, p. 151, quoting St Cyprian's twelfth letter to St Cornelius; Pole, *Pro Ecclesiasticae Unitatis Defensione*, fol. 62r: 'Nec enim, inquit, aliunde haereses obortae sunt, aut nata sunt schismata, quam inde, quod sacerdoti Dei non obtemperatur'.

them: they are siblings, both born from the sins of pride and rebellion. Again citing St Cyprian, Pole argued that the Roman Church is the 'chair of Peter' and that 'this opinion has come down to us from that time to the present – about twelve hundred years. What doubt can there be about affirming that this was always the opinion of the Catholic Church? What doubt that all who dissent from this opinion are schismatics and heretics?'[48] Pole was even more precise in his condemnation of the rift between the king and the Holy Spirit, writing: 'What a great amount of pestilential sedition threatens us when you call into doubt whom one shall obey, whom one can trust, whose words one shall listen to! You snatch away knowledge of the cause of the Church of God, of the Church that is governed by the Holy Spirit, of the Church that cannot deceive or be deceived.'[49] Henry VIII was portrayed as leading his subjects out of the faith, with deadly consequences for their souls. As Pole put it:

No injury against the spouse of Christ can be slight. Everything done against the Church must be serious. The deed you perpetrated, however, so excels that it manifestly declares that you had in mind the overthrow of the foundations of the Church itself. For what else were you doing when you attempted to take away from the Church the Spirit of God, the pledge of love for the spouse, the pledge of life and eternal duration? What else but this were you attempting when you now called into doubt, after such a long period of time, so many of the decrees of the Church that had been established by the authority of the Spirit of God?[50]

III

Opposed to these Catholic nonconformist views, with all their nuance and variation, there was also a variety of conformist arguments available which

---

[48] Dwyer (ed.), *Pole's Defense*, p. 154. I have changed this quotation to 'twelve hundred years' from 'fifteen hundred years', which is *sic* in Dwyer's translation for 'annis mille & ducentis'. See Pole, *Pro Ecclesiasticae Unitatis Defensione*, fol. 63v: 'Romanam ecclesiam cathedram Petri esse, in petro fuisse fundatam ecclesiam; qui possumus aliter existimare, quam semper fuisse hanc sententiam ecclesiarum iam inde ab ipsis Apostolorum temporibus, cum ille pene aequa lis eorum temporum idem dicat? Quae sententia cum ab hinc annis mille & ducentis ad no peruenerit, quid est quod dubitemus affirmare hanc semper catholicae ecclesiae sententiam fuisse; & qui ab hac dissentiant, schismaticos omnes & haereticos esse?'

[49] Dwyer (ed.), *Pole's Defense*, pp. 199–200. Pole, *Pro Ecclesiasticae Unitatis Defensione*, fol. 81v: 'Quanta hinc pestiferae seditionis moles nobis impendet, quod indubium reuocas, cui quis obediat, cui credat, cuius verba audiat? Quod ecclesiae Dei, quae spiritu sancto regitur, quae nec falli potest, nec fallere, causae cognitionem eripis'.

[50] Dwyer (ed.), *Pole's Defense*, p. 268; Pole, *Pro Ecclesiasticae Unitatis Defensione*, fol. 110r: 'At quanta tandem haec in ecclesiam iniuria fuit? Nulla quidem in Christi sponsam tenuis esse potest. Quaecunque inferant, maximae sint oportet. Sed tamen haec abs te illata ita excellit, ut liquido declaret, in animo te habere ipsam funditus euertere. Nam quid aliud facis, cum spiritum Dei, pignus amoris in sponsam, pignus vitae, & sempiter nae durationis, asuferre ab ea conaris? Quid enim? Nonne hoc conaris, cum tot ab illa, spiritu Dei authore, constituta ac decreta, tot longissima & nunquam interrupta consuetudine confirmata, nunc denique tanto interuallo in dubium revocas?'

supported the royal supremacy and allowed Catholics to remain steadfastly loyal to Henry VIII.[51] For instance, a letter written by 'Father Fewterer, general confessor of the monastery of Syon' to the brethren of the Charterhouse of London began its defence of the king with an argument from Scripture: having much studied 'what the law of God will' for the authority of the bishop of Rome and the authority of the king, he discovered 'both in Old and New Testament great truths for our prince, and for the bishop of Rome nothing at all'. Particular scriptural precedents cited in the king's behalf were by now familiar to anyone involved in the debate over papal authority: Saul's power as 'head of the people and Church of God' was seen as a model for royal jurisdiction over the Church, while Paul's exhortation to 'all the Church to be obedient to his grace' was extended even to matters of faith. As Lucy Wooding has rightly noted, these appeals to scripture over and above the traditions of the Church represented an important strand of Catholic humanism that was available for appropriation by the king's Catholic allies.[52]

Yet we should be wary of asserting too strong a connection between humanism and support for the king; nonconformists like Reginald Pole and Thomas More were, of course, also humanists, while conformists could include alongside their humanism other arguments that were far more scholastic. Fewterer, for instance, followed his scriptural exegesis with a legal argument to prove that jurisdiction over cases in the church courts (like Henry VIII's divorce case) was adiaphorous and thus open to royal control. To make this argument, he posited that 'doctors do grant that the bishop of Rome may dispense and license a layman to be judge in a spiritual cause'. Given that such a dispensation was possible, he argued, it cannot be forbidden by God's law: there was neither scripture nor tradition that expressly forbade a layman from exercising authority over clerics, or else such a thing could never be licensed by Rome. But, the argument continued, if lay authority over the clergy was thus neither expressly ordered nor expressly forbidden in divine law, then it must be adiaphorous, and hence it might legitimately be enacted by the prince within the boundaries of his realm.[53] This was an extremely clever argument from canon law, but it assumed the authority of tradition

---

[51] Despite recent claims to the contrary (see Wooding, *Rethinking Catholicism*, pp. 72–3) there were also evangelical arguments available to support the royal supremacy, many of which interpreted it in heavily spiritual and even apocalyptic terms. I have considered some of these arguments in my 'Clement Armstrong and the Godly Commonwealth: Radical Religion in Early Tudor England', in Peter Marshall and Alec Ryrie (eds.), *The Beginnings of English Protestantism, 1490–1558* (forthcoming).

[52] Wooding, *Rethinking Catholicism*, chs. 2–3.

[53] BL Harleian MS 604, fols. 78r–80v. Since the surviving manuscript is a fair copy, and given its obvious propaganda value, it seems likely that this tract was intended for public consumption.

and the 'doctors' of the Church in ways that were largely antithetical to humanist formulations.

Another conformist Catholic was Simon Matthew, a prebendary of St Paul's who might serve as a model for the ideal of a Henrician *via media*. Matthew published a sermon in 1535 in which he explicitly attacked the primacy of St Peter, condemned the treason of Thomas More and John Fisher, and supported the succession of the infant princess Elizabeth. Most importantly, however, Matthew defended the Church of England against charges of schism and heresy, insisting that the unity of the Church consists not in allegiance to a single authority but rather in 'the knowledge of Christ and true belief in him'. In particular, the royal supremacy over the Church of England had no effect on the unity of the Church, since it was one of Christ's great miracles that 'the diversity of regions and countries maketh not the diversity of Churches, but the unity of faith maketh all regions one Church, although the same regions were unknown to us and us to them'. In Matthew's view, then, the real threat to the Church came from people on both sides of the nascent religious divide who interpreted the royal supremacy too broadly. On one side, More and Fisher were foolish to oppose their king over mere questions of jurisdiction; on the other side, Matthew attacked over-zealous 'defenders of the king's matter' who 'rage and rail...calling the bishop of Rome the harlot of Babylon or the beast of Rome' and were thus more fit 'to preach at Paul's Wharf than at Paul's Cross'.[54]

The Bishop of Lincoln, John Longland, supported the elimination of papal authority for altogether different reasons. For Longland, the key ecclesiological event of the 1530s was not the royal supremacy per se but rather the declaration that the Bishop of Rome had no more authority outside his diocese than any other bishop. The logical corollary of this position was not only that popes could not challenge the legal jurisdiction of monarchs, but also that popes could not challenge the spiritual jurisdiction of other bishops. Longland expanded this idea into an ecclesiology in which bishops were the ultimate spiritual authorities within their dioceses, just as kings were the ultimate secular authorities within their kingdoms. Thus rather than caesaropapism, Longland read into the royal supremacy a strict separation of Church and state, with bishops sovereign over all ecclesiastical affairs within their dioceses. Supremacy for the king implied only a figurehead position as father and first-Christian of the realm; spiritual power was held by

[54] Symon Matthewe, *A Sermon Made in the Cathedrall Churche of Saynt Paule at London, the XXVII. Day of June, Anno. 1535. by Symon Matthewe* (London, 1535), sigs. A7v–A8v, C7v–C8r, A5v, B6r, A7v, C7v–D1v. This sermon is discussed in Peter Marshall, 'Is the Pope a Catholic? Henry VIII and the Semantics of Schism', in Ethan Shagan and Margaret Sena (eds.), *Catholics and the 'Protestant Nation': Religious Politics in Early Modern England* (forthcoming).

the bishops, and Longland later opposed (though not always successfully) all attempts by the Crown, vicegerent or metropolitan to usurp that power within Lincoln.[55]

The quintessential conformist Catholic gloss on the royal supremacy, however, was Stephen Gardiner's *De Vera Obedientia*, one of the most influential tracts of the early Reformation and the great albatross that would hang around the necks of Gardiner and the Henrician conformists during the reign of Mary. For Gardiner, the allegiance of the Church to Rome was an historical accident rather than an expression of God's will, and he voiced his opposition to papal supremacy succinctly: 'This I utterly deny, that God ordained the bishop of Rome to be the chief as touching any absolute worldly power.' In particular, he expanded Pauline doctrines of Christ's covenant as a law of the spirit rather than of the flesh, arguing that the prerogatives given to Peter by Christ were 'not given unto flesh and blood, but to be a testimony of that excellent profession of his faith'. He admitted that in past times the Church of Rome had possessed great holiness and power, but he denied that this was grounds for worldly obedience; such power was *iure humano* rather than ordained by God. He concluded that all obedience within a given realm was rightfully due to the sovereign of that realm, and that the king of a Christian people might therefore be seen as head of the Church within his kingdom. Gardiner's interpretation of the 'Church' within a kingdom, however, was extremely narrow: 'The Church of England is nothing else but the congregation of men and women, of the clergy and the laity, united in Christ's profession. That is to say, it is justly to be called the Church because it is a communion of Christian people, and of the place it is to be named the Church of England.' Such a Church had no right to different doctrine than the rest of the universal Church, so the head of it had no prerogative to pronounce such doctrine; indeed, Gardiner's logic assumed that Christian doctrine is everywhere uniform and unambiguous. He imagined a world in which kings used the power of the sword to defend their realms against error; no king answers to a higher earthly authority, but all answer directly to Christ. In one sense this logic was quite radical in blurring the distinction between secular and ecclesiastical authority, but in another sense its truncated reading of Henry VIII's spiritual authority provided almost the ontological apex of conservatism. The king was given jurisdiction over the clergy within his realm, but otherwise the *status quo ante* remained unchanged. The 'Church of England' was merely the Church *in* England, and its head was merely the leader of the people who constituted that Church.[56]

---

[55] This paragraph summarises the argument in Margaret Bowker, *The Henrician Reformation: The Diocese of Lincoln Under John Longland 1521–1547* (Cambridge, 1981), pp. 65–88.

[56] Janelle (ed.), *Obedience in Church and State*, pp. 154–5, 126–7, 102–5 and 94–5.

Besides the carefully formulated responses of clerics, there is no doubt that many among the non-elite laity also supported the royal supremacy. Gardiner reported in 1535, for instance, that 'all sorts of people are agreed upon this point with most steadfast consent, learned and unlearned, both men and women: that no manner of person born and brought up in England hath ought to do with Rome'. John Tregonwell concurred in 1536, finding 'as much conformity among men, and as ready to obey the king's authority, injunctions, and other orders declared to them, as ever I saw any men obey the same'.[57] The grounds for this conformity, of course, are extremely difficult to discover; obedience to the law leaves few records. In some cases, however, we can get a sense of the variety of motivations behind support for the royal supremacy, and from these we can at least make some inferences about the structure of popular conformity.

To begin with, there clearly were reasons having nothing to do with ideology why subjects would have had an interest in supporting the royal supremacy. We must not underestimate the importance of fear; it took a particular kind of person to risk death for conscience' sake. Thus reluctant or passive conformity was an attractive option, and its contours occasionally became visible when someone whispered just a little too loudly that he or she was only going through the motions. John Pomfrey, for instance, told acquaintances at a Southwark alehouse in 1534 that they should 'take patience for a time', in other words conform to royal authority, since 'the day shall come that he that was called pope sometime shall be pope again'.[58] Pomfrey was evidently the one who should have been more patient, since his words were reported to the government. Sometimes these attitudes became apparent when otherwise-loyal subjects drank too much ale and inadvertently said or did things they later regretted. In February 1535, for instance, a Suffolk 'spinster' called Margaret Chanseler was brought before Sir Robert Drury for having said, among other things, that 'the queen's grace had one child by our said sovereign lord the king which she said was dead born, and she prayed God that he might never have another'. When Chanseler confessed to these words, her excuse was that 'she was drunken when she did speak them, and that the evil spirit did cause her to speak them, and she was very penitent for her offenses'.[59] Similarly, in Coventry in November 1535 a tailor and three yeomen became sickeningly drunk and then relieved themselves at the town cross in the marketplace; unfortunately for them, in their drunkenness they thought it would be amusing to 'pluck down part of diverse acts of parliament and other [of] the king's proclamations being fixed and nailed upon tables in the marketplace' and then use them to 'wipe their tails with'.[60]

Besides the proverbial 'stick' to assure compliance, there were also attractive 'carrots': there was money to be made through support of the king and opposition to Rome. For instance, one James Bacon, 'brewer of London', found himself involved in a contentious marriage suit in the diocesan courts in 1534. Rather than pursuing the case to its conclusion, Bacon made complaint directly to the Privy Council, arguing that his opponents had appealed their case to Rome. It is unclear whether Bacon had any ideological interest in the royal supremacy, but he was certainly not afraid to use it to his advantage.[61] Opposition to the papacy also obviated various payments, making the royal supremacy financially attractive and allowing supporters of the king to assume the role of crusaders for the economic rights of the people. At Northwater in Wales, for instance, Richard Gibbons, registrar to the Bishop of Bangor, complained in 1537 that one of the bishop's clerks had illegally reauthorised 'the feigned indulgence, pardon, and privileges of St Lazar...heretofore granted by the bishops of Rome then called popes'. According to Gibbons, this created 'great contention and variety of opinions amongst the inhabitants of Northwater' since 'by colour of the said feigned pardon' the local inhabitants were 'exacted and polled of their money contrary to the king's acts, ordinances, and provisions'.[62] Sometimes support for the king could be lucrative in more corrupt ways. When a Lincolnshire parson denounced the king and Anne Boleyn as 'heretics and lollards', two witnesses named Thomas Womburley and William Wake blackmailed him with the threat of a treason charge and made off with at least 40s in hush money.[63] And, of course, in a more general sense, anyone with even a token involvement in the Church or local government – from churchwardens to bailiffs to constables – stood to gain patronage by vociferously supporting the king's new title.

We should not assume, however, that all or even most conformity was merely expedient. There is ample evidence of principled motives behind support for the king's expanded powers, most importantly loyalism. The king had been given his supremacy through parliamentary process; in some people's opinions, opposition to the king thus represented opposition to the law. This loyalist dynamic can be seen in the village of Ashlower, Gloucestershire, where the constable was ordered by royal commissioners in 1534 to assemble the village to swear the oath of succession. The constable, being

---

[60] PRO SP 1/99, fols. 101v–102r [*LP* IX, 883].
[61] PRO SP 2/Q, fols. 108–12 [*LP* VII, 1605].
[62] BL Cotton MS Cleopatra E. VI, fol. 399r.   [63] PRO STAC 2/33/75.

'a man not learned', asked the vicar, one John Knolles, to read out the order, but Knolles utterly refused, replying 'that he would not publish it either for king nor queen'. After being pressured by a number of parishioners, Knolles finally agreed to read the order, but only so long as the people of Ashlower knew he was doing so for their sakes rather than the king's. This remark infuriated the constable, who refused to let the vicar read the order under such terms, since it represented a failure in his duty to the king. Here, even when the vicar proved willing to obey the letter of the law, the constable refused to allow reluctant conformity as a substitute for heart-felt loyalty to the sovereign.[64]

For another example, in 1534 the parson of Chesterton, Huntingdonshire, asked his curate, Thomas Arundell, to 'keep his counsel' concerning certain political prophecies in his possession. Arundell responded with loyalist language, saying he would keep the parson's counsel 'except against God and the king', and when he read the prophecies he flatly told the parson that they were unlawful. The parson answered by accusing Arundell of being one of Cromwell's 'disciples' and calling him a man of 'new laws', a strange reply given that the parson had trusted him with his secret in the first place. In response, Arundell informed the government of the parson's activities, sending Cromwell a copy of the seditious prophecies.[65] In a slightly later case from Aylsham, Norfolk, there were rumours in early 1537 that the king would confiscate the jewels of the parish church, leading a number of men to demand that the churchwardens give them the keys to the church's coffers so that they might 'defeat the king thereof'. The churchwardens refused to do so, however, 'saying that if it were the king's pleasure to have it, he was most worthy'.[66]

It is often difficult to know, of course, whether these protestations of loyalty were honest statements of belief or merely the politic responses of people telling the government what it wanted to hear. In the end we must fall back on the large number of cases in which loyalism was invoked and say with Geoffrey Elton that it would be 'quite pointlessly cynical to doubt that such feelings were often genuine'.[67] The conservative gentleman Sir John Gostwick, for instance, was clearly thinking of the sanctity of the law as much as the safety of his family when he advised his heir to report all disloyalty immediately to a justice or counsellor, 'for the longer you keep it, the worse it is for you, and the more danger toward God and the king's majesty'.[68] Loyalty to the sovereign was a powerful moral imperative in

---

[64] Elton, *Policy and Police*, pp. 120–1, citing PRO STAC 2/21/120. This manuscript is now missing from the PRO.

[65] PRO SP 1/88, fol. 56r [*LP* VII, 1624].   [66] PRO SP 1/120, fols. 247r–v [*LP* XIII, i, 1316].

[67] Elton, *Policy and Police*, p. 370.

[68] Whiting, *Local Responses to the English Reformation*, p. 136.

Tudor society, and it became all the more powerful when it dovetailed with political expediency.[69]

IV

There was therefore no single 'Catholic' position on the royal supremacy but rather a wide spectrum of opinions ranging from passionate loyalism to passionate opposition, with all shades of ambiguity and expediency in between. With the contours of these different positions now in place, we can examine the political process through which nonconformist positions, which would necessarily have been at the centre of any serious resistance to the Henrician Reformation, were in practice marginalised and driven underground. It was the peculiar genius of Henry VIII and his advisors that, despite the pleas of evangelicals and the pressures of Romanists, they sought throughout the 1530s to *politicise* their Reformation, keeping any questions of its legitimacy focused on loyalty rather than theology. In particular, by defining opposition to the royal supremacy as treason – 'papistry' rather than 'Catholicism' – the king linked the issue of ecclesiastical authority with the issue of worldly obedience, decoupling it from its theological roots.[70] With opposition to the royal supremacy defined as treason, the government could essentially ignore its religious content; the theological arguments of nonconformists did not have to be answered on their own terms so long as their crimes were against the state rather than the Church. This manoeuvre had the effect of splintering the Catholic nation, rendering the 'conservative' majority remarkably ineffective as a political force.

Two laws passed in parliament in 1534 and 1536 effectively defined opposition to the royal supremacy as a threat to national security and thus as a species of treason rather than a species of heresy. A law of November 1534 made it treason to attempt, whether through actions, writings or words, to deprive the king, queen or heir of their rightful titles and dignities. Since the king was from that same month given the title of 'supreme head of the Church of England', this gave the government a weapon for forcing compliance with the royal supremacy. The same law also made it treason to call the king a heretic, schismatic, tyrant, infidel or usurper of the Crown; obviously the government was aware that its innovations were often seen as spiritual

---

[69] For the importance of loyalism in early modern England, even in the context of popular protest, see Alison Wall, *Power and Protest in England 1525–1640* (London, 2000).

[70] Here I am changing the emphasis rather than disagreeing with the compelling argument in Richard Rex, 'The Crisis of Obedience: God's Word and Henry's Reformation', *HJ*, 39 (1996), 863–94. The exception that proves the rule that the government privileged loyalty over theology in its prosecutions is the case of Friar Forest: see Peter Marshall, 'Papist as Heretic: The Burning of John Forest, 1538', *HJ*, 41 (1998), 351–74.

and sought to silence this strand of opinion.[71] In 1536, the laws were expanded again, filling the gap in earlier legislation that had allowed people to defend the pope without explicitly attacking the king. The Act Extinguishing the Authority of the Bishop of Rome made it illegal to maintain the pope's authority through 'writing, ciphering, printing, preaching, or teaching', under pain of the penalties for praemunire: imprisonment at the king's pleasure and the confiscation of property. The use of praemunire rather than treason might be seen as a leniency, but it should rather be seen as a piece of propaganda aimed at politicising the Reformation further: praemunire referred to allegiance to a foreign monarch, exactly what Henry VIII defined Romanism to be.[72]

The effect of this legislation, and the elaborate propaganda that accompanied it, was to divide people who shared a common Catholic theology along political lines. The goal of the new laws was to leave no room for people to support the pope in words while conforming to the deeds required by the king, or to refuse compliance with the royal supremacy without actively rebelling against it. People either had to conform absolutely or else place themselves outside the political pale. Those who chose to conform, moreover, found themselves in a difficult position. To know of treason without reporting it was punishable by perpetual imprisonment and loss of goods, besides being a deadly sin, and anyone who accepted the royal supremacy had de facto accepted that opposition to the royal supremacy was treason. Even conformists who were uncomfortable with their new ecclesiastical allegiance thus found themselves duty-bound to denounce their Romanist neighbours.

In April 1535, for instance, one Thomas Smith, described as 'servant to the king's highness', sat at supper in the house of the London fishmonger Thomas Williamson, along with 'one Sir Roger, priest', a brewer called Laurence Oakson, and others. Their conversation turned to the clerics who were on that day transported from the Tower of London to Westminster, and when it was asked of what crime they were accused, Smith answered 'that as he heard reported, it was for their obstinacy and that they would not recognise and knowledge the king's highness (as most worthy) to be the supreme head of the Church of England'. The priest Sir Roger answered Smith with dangerous words: 'Tush, let men say what they will. God hath ordained here in earth a vicar general, which is the Bishop of Rome who hath power under God over all the world as well Christian as heathen, and all other bishops and priests be but ministers under him, and kings and princes executors

---

[71] The treason act of November 1534 is 26 Henry VIII, c. 13, printed in *Statutes*, III, pp. 508–9. It is discussed in Elton, *Policy and Police*, pp. 282–92.

[72] The act extinguishing the Bishop of Rome's authority is 28 Henry VIII, c. 10, printed in *Statutes*, III, pp. 663–6. It is discussed in Elton, *Policy and Police*, pp. 291–2.

of temporal justice unto their subjects.' When Smith replied that the priest had spoken 'untruly' according to 'statutes by parliament enacted, as also by plain Scripture', Sir Roger answered that he would 'live and die' by his words. Smith then threatened to denounce him to the authorities if he did not retract his statements, and the priest 'bade him do his worst'. It seems clear from the priest's recklessness that he did not think Smith could harm him; it took at least two witnesses to prove a capital crime, and Smith's scruples were not immediately seconded by anyone else in the room. Smith's next move, however, was to turn to the other guests at the table, 'requiring all and single the persons prementioned, upon their allegiance to the king's highness (as his true subjects) indifferently to report what at that time they heard'. Now the equation suddenly changed. The other witnesses, while perhaps reluctant in their own conformity, found themselves required to report the priest's conduct or else risk the law's fury themselves; theological positions notwithstanding, Sir Roger had committed a crime against the state. Realising his vulnerability, Sir Roger quickly changed his tune, and 'minding somewhat to colour his [remarks], partly changed his words'. This backsliding did not impress Thomas Smith, however, who, with his witnesses sworn to stand behind him, reported the priest to royal authorities.[73]

For another example, at Ordsall, Nottinghamshire, three gentlemen and a yeoman sued two local priests, Robert Nevyll and Edmund Webster, alleging that in 1534 they refused to offer parishioners communion unless they paid 'Peter's Pence', a traditional but now illegal tax to Rome. The two priests evidently continued in their Romanism for several years; the suit is undated, but internal evidence shows that it was brought in 1536 at the earliest. What is most interesting about this case is that not only the plaintiffs but also the *defendants* adopted the language of the royal supremacy: in their reply, the two priests denied having supported 'the whole usurped authority and jurisdiction of the Bishop of Rome'. What seems to have happened, then, is that two priests who flirted with nonconformity in 1534 were, by the end of 1536, convinced by the pressure of loyalist neighbours, as well as by new legislation threatening them with charges of treason, that they should accept the royal supremacy. Two potential opponents of the regime were forced to make themselves either conformists or traitors; they chose to remain within the pale.[74]

In the town of Loose in Kent, the vicar, Robert Fynnys, briefly forgot himself in a June 1536 sermon and referred to 'holy Urban, sometime pope of Rome'. Realising that this was unacceptable language, he quickly corrected

---

[73] PRO SP 1/92, fols. 72r–73v [*LP* VIII, 595]. The Thomas Smith discussed here is certainly not the author of *De Republica Anglorum*.

[74] PRO STAC 2/12, fols. 196r–197r. The suit must have come from 1536 or later, since it referred to the abrogation of holidays.

himself, saying: 'I should have said Bishop Urban.' Yet, despite his semantic alteration, the vicar preached that Urban had 'granted certain indulgence and pardon' to those who attended the feast of Corpus Christi and performed other rituals 'according to the old custom'. Two of his parishioners, Robert Arcles and Richard Burdon, confronted Fynnys in the churchyard after mass and asked him 'whether he would abide by the said words that he spoke in the pulpit or nay'? The priest said he would stand by his words, and with confirmation thus in hand Arcles and Burdon organised the parish to testify against Fynnys. The very next day, no less than ten different men gave nearly identical depositions denouncing the vicar in front of Henry Wyatt and Thomas Culpepper. It is possible, of course, that the townsmen had prior reasons to dislike their vicar, but none the less, for a community to attack their priest so unhesitatingly for saying something that would have been not only allowable but required of him a few years before is remarkable.[75]

Yet another example comes from Warwickshire, where over the Christmas holidays in 1535 the people of Oxhill allegedly visited 'diverse churches' outside their town and discovered, to their amazement, that the priests there regularly declared that the king was 'supreme head of the Church, and that the Bishop of Rome had been a long usurper'. The curate of Oxhill, it seems, had read the declaration of the king's supremacy only once, on the first Sunday after he had received it, after which his master the parson 'took away the same commandment with him, and would not suffer him in no wise to have it'. After their alleged 'discovery', the parishioners petitioned two local gentlemen for relief. The gentlemen investigated and found serious violations against the king's supremacy, including failure to erase the pope's name from service books and failure to pray for the king and queen at mass. It seems farfetched that the parishioners of Oxhill were really so naïve, and the whole event was almost certainly a staged protest, but their insistent support for the royal supremacy shows obedience to the law could be far from passive.[76]

It is very unlikely, of course, that most of these government informants were evangelicals. Far more often they had decidedly worldly motives for their collaboration with the regime, whether loyalty to the king, personal animosities or hope for material reward. The fundamental division engendered by the royal supremacy was thus between nonconformists and conformists rather than between Catholics and evangelicals. In local battles, it seems, collaborators who were willing to play their trump card enjoyed a considerable advantage. Romanism was defined as treason, and at law there could be no partial or mitigated treason; whatever ideological middle ground existed was quickly pushed outside the pale of acceptable public discourse.

[75] PRO SP 1/104, fols. 169r–170r [*LP* X, 1125].
[76] PRO SP 1/101, fol. 9r–v [*LP* X, 14]. The manuscript refers to Oxhill as 'Oxshulf'.

The result was that rather than uniting against Protestant heresy, Catholics of different political stripes fought one another, and the unified Catholic front envisioned by Reginald Pole from the safe distance of the Continent never had a chance to develop.

While the positions developed in response to the royal supremacy were not always theological per se, moreover, those positions did not cease to shape the political landscape when Henry VIII began more overt doctrinal experimentation. The broader implications of people's responses to the royal supremacy can be seen, for instance, in the nation's responses to the abrogation of saints' days. These abrogations, accepted by convocation in July 1536 and promulgated by royal injunction that August, abolished all holy days during harvest time and the law terms, with the exception of feasts of the Apostles, the Virgin and St George, plus the feasts of the Ascension, the Nativity of St John the Baptist, All Saints and Candlemas.[77] Much of parish life revolved around the feasts of the liturgical calendar and scheduled devotion to individual saints, so the elimination of so many holidays left communities devoid of much of their spiritual infrastructure. The abrogation of saints' days, moreover, raised the issue of the legitimacy of the royal supremacy in stark terms. On the one hand, the order was an unprecedented intrusion of the Crown into both ecclesiastical policy and local prerogatives, and the choices of saints' days to save (especially the focus on *scriptural* saints) reeked of doctrinal innovation. On the other hand, it was very difficult to claim that the institution of feasts was *iure divino*, so by the logic of adiaphora such activities might legitimately be banned by the king according to virtually anyone who had accepted the royal supremacy in the first place. Along such fault lines, battle lines were quickly drawn.

The most well-known reactions to the Henrician abrogation of saints' days come from Lincolnshire and the north, where dissent against the injunctions was closely associated with the Pilgrimage of Grace. The first rebel grievances in Lincolnshire, for instance, included the demand that holidays be kept as before, and the vicar of Louth, whose fiery sermon sparked the Lincolnshire rebellion, later claimed that the people had grudged against the putting down of holidays.[78] Margaret Bowker has even suggested that the timing of the outbreak of hostilities on 2 October was related to the fact that the previous day was the annual feast of the dedication of churches, which served as a flashpoint for resentment.[79] In the north there was similar trouble. At Watton in the East Riding of Yorkshire, for instance, the priest neglected on 8 October to announce the forthcoming holiday of St Wilfrid's Day; he was challenged by John Hallom, who only days later

[77] Bowker, *The Henrician Reformation*, p. 150; Diarmaid MacCulloch, *Thomas Cranmer: A Life* (New Haven, 1996), p. 166; J. D. Mackie, *The Earlier Tudors 1485–1558* (Oxford, 1994), p. 383.
[78] *LP* XI, 970 and *LP* XI, 553.   [79] Bowker, *The Henrician Reformation*, p. 151.

would be a leader of the Yorkshire rebellion, and the parish resolved over the priest's head that holy days would be bidden as before. On 15 October at Kirkby Stephen in Westmorland, the curate failed to announce the upcoming holiday of St Luke's Day; when pressured by the congregation, however, he rang the sacring bell and bade the holiday. John Dakyn, vicar general of the archdeaconry of Richmond, found that even after he had sworn the rebels' oath he was still physically threatened as a 'putter down of the holidays'.[80]

Much less well known but equally common, however, was the opposite scenario: priests who celebrated abrogated saints' days against the king's commandment faced opposition from loyalist factions in their parishes. In the villages of Stortford and Hadham in Hertfordshire, for instance, the curates and sextons 'made default' against the king's orders on Holy Rood Day in 1536 by keeping 'high and solemn, with ringing and singing'. According to Sir Henry Parker, their actions caused 'much dissension between them and other, which according to the king's commandment that day went to their bodily labor'.[81] At the church of St Nicholas in Warwick, the curate John Wetwod found himself jailed for commanding bells to be rung on St Lawrence Day in 1536. In this case, Wetwod had in fact told his parishioners the week before that they were to 'apply their occupations and work' on St Lawrence Day rather then celebrating, but he later yielded to pressure from the conservative prebendaries of the college to which his church was attached. Wetwod thus seems to have had a good excuse for breaking the law, but some of his parishioners complained to the local gentlemen William Lucy and John Coombs, both clients of Hugh Latimer, a man uninterested in excuses for 'superstition'. Thus, according to Wetwod, writing to Cromwell from Warwick jail, while 'the best justices in the shire of Warwick would gladly have bailed me, the said Master Lucy and Coombs will in no wise suffer me to go at large'.[82]

Another dispute arose in the Oxfordshire town of Thame in December 1536, where the vicar, one Dr Goodruge, illegally kept the feast of St Thomas 'the martyr'. When 'great ringing and clattering of bells' was made at the parish church on St Thomas's Day, one John Strebilhill allegedly confronted Goodruge and asked him, 'Master Doctor, ye have kept a solemn feast this day, where had ye such authority?' The vicar's response was that 'they would have it so', meaning that he kept the feast at the request of his parishioners. Strebilhill, however, disputed this view of popular sentiment, arguing that 'within a mile and a half of your church this day men did carry hay and went

[80] Michael Bush, *The Pilgrimage of Grace: A Study of the Rebel Armies of 1536* (Manchester, 1996), pp. 34, 293, 164.
[81] PRO SP 1/106, fol. 228r [*LP* XI, 514].
[82] PRO SP 1/106, fols. 153r–156r [*LP* XI, 431–2].

to the cart'. This claim raised the ire of a bystander, one Richard Childe, who injected harsher rhetoric into the discussion: 'He that went to the cart this day, I would his horse's neck had been to burst and his cart fettered.' Strebilhill responded: 'We have a king to whom of duty we ought to be obedient, but I think thou are of the northern sect, thou would rule the king's highness and not be ruled.' Childe answered: 'It was not I alone but it was the whole parish.'[83] Here we have two very different accounts of local sentiment, with a Henrician loyalist and an apparent opponent of the king's supremacy each claiming to speak for the community. It is not clear who was more correct, but once again the loyalist won the day by denouncing his Romanist neighbours to royal authorities.

Yet another dispute occurred in the environs of Glastonbury, where on St Mark's Day 1536 one Thomas Poole worked instead of keeping the holiday, arguing that he 'offended not therein because it was the king's commandment that men should so do'. One of Poole's neighbours, John Tutton, responded by calling Poole a heretic and suggesting that 'he was not bounden nor ought to keep the king's commandment if it were naught, as that was'. Tutton also railed against Cromwell, suggesting that he was a 'stark heretic' who 'ruleth the king' but would soon be put down. As a result, at least four local men came to Poole's aid and denounced Tutton to the authorities. It may be that these four men were already allies of Poole's, or they may honestly have been offended by Tutton's seditious words. Regardless, it is clear that those who tried to evade or oppose the king's commandments left themselves frighteningly vulnerable to collaborators in their midst.[84]

By far the most detailed and informative case of local disputes over abrogated saints' days comes from the town of Shirland, Derbyshire, where bells were rung on the feast of St Mark in April 1537.[85] James Aleyn, servant to his kinsman, the parson Thomas Aleyn, was at the parish church at procession time and heard the church bells ringing. After services were done, the servant 'spoke openly in the church, all the most part of the parishioners being then there . . . "Masters and friends, here I make answer for my master the parson here, that ye ring not solemnly of such days as be now forbidden."' This request met with a chilly reception from John Revell the elder, a seventy-two-year-old community leader, who told him bluntly that 'the parish might ring their bells and ask the parson no leave'. Indeed, according to the three men who actually rang the bells, they had been ordered to do so by the same John Revell, who ordered similar celebrations on other saints' days, telling the bell-ringers that 'he would bear them forth' if there were any trouble. Later in the evening of St Mark's Day, moreover, Revell confronted Parson

[83] PRO SP 1/123, fols. 120r–122v [*LP* XII, ii, 357].
[84] PRO SP 1/116, fols. 185r–186r [*LP* XII, i, 567].   [85] PRO STAC 2/26/194.

Thomas in the church, saying, 'Shall we neither ring nor sing? Then . . . the devil's turd in Tom Tinker's teeth!'

This altercation became the catalyst for a violent, year-long dispute over how to respond to the 1536 injunctions. On the side opposing the king's authority were John Revell the elder and his friends and kinsman, including the gentleman Robert Revell, Robert's son John Revell the younger, and the priest John Fernysworth. Supporting the king's authority were the parson Thomas Aleyn, the curate Sir Rauf Wyllat and a variety of laymen and lay-women. Defenders of the royal supremacy evidently endured serious abuse from the Revell family and their adherents. The curate, for instance, was in the process of reading the king's injunctions to the congregation when John Fernysworth told him, '"*fac finem*", and bade him come out of the pulpit'. John Revell the younger not only 'smote a priest in the head with a dagger' but also thrust a piece of pudding into the curate's mouth just as he was about to say mass, rendering him ritually unclean and preventing him from performing his duties. Robert Revell also went around the town asking shopkeepers and alewives not to provide 'meat nor drink' to the curate. Deep animosities were clearly at work in the dispute: in Lent 1536 the curate called Robert Revell a 'whoreson Jew heretic', while Revell countered by calling the curate a 'false whoreson whoremonger priest'.

Potentially more serious acts against the royal supremacy were also committed. When John Fernysworth received the king's writ, 'he nothing regarding it but despising it threw it to the wall before diverse persons and there leaving it where other men took it up'. The curate claimed that Robert Revell threatened to 'pluck the vestment over my head in the pulpit' if he read the king's commandments to the parish. The town constable, John Nowton, was also on the Revells' side; when the curate tried to force him to 'certify the king's grace' of events in the parish, the constable refused, instead seeking advice from 'his master' Robert Revell and coming back with the report that 'he would not meddle, for his master said that they were spiritual matters [and] the king had nothing to meddle thereof'.

Yet if one powerful faction in the town opposed the local implementation of the royal supremacy, there were plenty of other men and women who supported it. Besides the parson, the parson's servant and the curate, there was Edward Yeryng, a forty-eight-year-old townsman who was furious at the ringing of bells on St Chad's Day and demanded to know on whose authority the bells were rung; Yeryng was also the man who defiantly picked up the king's writ off the ground when Sir John Fernysworth threw it down. Moreover, despite the attempt of Robert Revell to prevent the curate from obtaining food or drink at local establishments, several witnesses reported that 'the alewives said . . . that the priest might have had meat or drink at their houses enough for anything that Revell said to the contrary'. Many other witnesses came forward to attack the Revells. Thomas Luddelam, for instance, was one of several townspeople who complained that the Revells had been responsible for the dismissal of large numbers of priests from the parish 'because they and the Revells were at variance and could not agree'. His kinsman Hugh Luddelam could not confirm first hand that John Revell the younger had 'put a pudding towards the priest's mouth', but he eagerly acknowledged it 'by report'. John Clerk told investigators that Robert Revell was 'a bearer and maintainer of Sir John Fernysworth', and avowed that the curate had been arrested 'by the command of the Revells' even though Robert Revell vociferously denied it.

In the town of Shirland, then, support for and opposition to the royal supremacy broke down along pre-existing fault lines in the community, with ideological differences over the king's authority filtered through the vagaries of personal feuds and local factions. It is clear that no one in this dispute was significantly influenced by Protestantism. It was the *opponents* of the royal supremacy who in this case engaged in anticlericalism, beating and humiliating local priests; the pro-Henrician curate, on the other hand, was traditionalist enough that he refused to say mass after food was stuffed into his mouth. Yet, despite the lack of overt doctrinal dispute, the Revells and their followers could not accept the implementation of the royal supremacy, while the curate and his followers could not accept the Revells' disloyalty. Emotions became so charged that local mechanisms of dispute-resolution broke down and the case ended up in Star Chamber, where witness after witness denounced their opponents as liars or enemies of the king. Even in the absence of overt Protestantism, it seems, the nation bitterly divided over the royal supremacy, and, with the resources of the Tudor state arrayed squarely behind the loyalist faction, opponents of the king's ecclesiastical authority were left frighteningly vulnerable.

v

Thus the politics of the royal supremacy, with its firm, bipartite division of the realm into conformists and traitors, hopelessly splintered the English Catholic majority. Those who should have been the leaders of a resisting faction instead were increasingly driven underground or into exile, fearful of condemnation not only by the regime but by their own neighbours. Those who might have applauded the intransigence of the nonconformists instead employed a spectrum of responses that were unhelpful, and sometimes antithetical, to the cause of resistance. Catholic supporters of the royal supremacy, whether out of expediency or loyalty, found themselves more in the business of creating new Catholic martyrs than of venerating old ones.

Yet the conformist versus Romanist division, while ostensibly political, was fuelled by ideology and was itself far from lacking in religious significance. At the centre of the Romanist movement were Catholics like Elizabeth

Barton, John Fisher and Thomas More, who had been the leaders of Catholic reform and renewal in the years before 1534. These ideologues, and the many ordinary men and women who marched to the beat of the same drummer, were widely considered at the time to be the vigorous and vital core of English religiosity, the leaven that leavened the whole lump of the English Church. Their elimination from the mainstream left a Church diminished. In a strange sort of selective cannibalism, those most committed to the propagation of the universal Church as John Colet would have understood it were gradually eaten away, leaving evangelicals as the most dynamic and aggressive voices in the English Church. Catholics, despite their majority, had no choice but to employ a highly defensive strategy to protect those aspects of traditional religion that they still enjoyed; those who would go on the offensive and present Catholicism as something more than the remnants of a shattered religious system risked placing themselves outside the boundaries of acceptable discourse.

Hence we have the odd spectacle that modern historians have attempted to define a peculiar style of moderate, conformable Christianity as the natural and normative religion of the English people. As has been shown, however, it was the political dynamics of the royal supremacy, rather than any natural moderation or belief in the *via media*, that rendered English Catholicism a force for conformity rather than a force for resistance in the 1530s. Such a transformation serves to illustrate just how much religious ground Catholics had already given away before the so-called 'Protestant' phase of the English Reformation even began.

2

The anatomy of opposition in early Reformation England: the case of Elizabeth Barton, the holy maid of Kent

On 20 April 1534, Elizabeth Barton and five of her associates died traitors' deaths at Tyburn, their heads afterwards displayed on pikes along London Bridge as a deterrent to other malcontents. According to the authorities, they had committed the most heinous of crimes. Not only had they promoted 'blasphemy of almighty God, whereby a great multitude of people of this realm were...induced to idolatry', but they had also 'brought in a murmur and grudge amongst themselves, to the great peril of the destruction of our said sovereign lord and his succession, and to the jeopardy of a great commotion, rebellion, and insurrection in this realm'.[1] In short, they had publicly manoeuvred to incite opposition against Henry VIII, his divorce from Catherine of Aragon, and the break with Rome. The government, fearful not only of Barton and her co-conspirators but also of the effect their agitation was having in the countryside, supplemented their executions with a remarkable propaganda blitz. Sermons against Barton and her associates were preached, proclamations against their activities were read throughout the realm, and subjects were given forty days to surrender any books concerning Barton in their possession or else face the law's fury themselves.[2]

What is so strange about this incident is not the execution of the traitors, nor the regime's obvious fear of their activities, but rather the identity of the main protagonist: Elizabeth Barton hardly fit the typical profile of Public Enemy Number One in sixteenth-century England. She was, first of all, a woman, and thus according to contemporary beliefs was virtually incapable of the sort of mental activity necessary to devise and hatch a rebellion. Moreover, she was a poor woman, first as a household servant and then as a nun, who died with virtually no possessions of her own.[3] She was less than twenty years old when her public 'career' began and she had a history of severe illness

---

[1] *Statutes*, vol. 3, 25 Hen. VIII. c. 12, p. 450.   [2] Ibid., p. 451.
[3] An inventory of Barton's possessions is in *Three Chapters of Letters Relating to the Suppression of Monasteries. Edited from the Originals in the British Museum*, ed. Thomas Wright, Camden Society 1st series, 26 (London, 1843), p. 26.

which often reduced her to delirium and at times left her close to death. Yet Barton had something that made her gender, physical condition and socio-economic background assets rather than liabilities, something which gave her enormous influence but also earned her the wrath of the royal government: she had regular, personal and direct access to God.

Elizabeth Barton, called the 'holy maid of Kent' or the 'nun of Kent' by contemporaries, was a prophetess, and for more than seven years she claimed – and was widely believed – to receive revelations from God and the Virgin Mary. This font of spiritual authority led Barton into the highest circles of power, offering advice to Thomas Wolsey, Thomas More, John Fisher and even Henry VIII himself. Several books were written supporting her claims to holiness, a pilgrimage was instituted to the shrine of the Virgin from which her visions derived, and people flocked to her convent of St Sepulchre's, Canterbury to confess their sins at her feet.

Little wonder, then, that when Barton's revelations took a decidedly political turn, declaring by divine authority that the king would be dethroned if he married Anne Boleyn, the regime took her words very seriously indeed.[4] After all, for a nun in an obscure convent to attack the regime was hardly newsworthy, but for God himself to challenge royal authority could easily provoke a rebellion. Barton had, it seemed, unearthed something which early modern regimes spent much of their time trying to bury: a source of political authority which was widely considered legitimate yet which was not under the control of royal authorities. It soon became clear, moreover, that this form of authority was well organised, well publicised and transcended theoretical boundaries between respectable political actors and the 'lewd' masses. The full fury of the Tudor propaganda machine was thus unleashed against the maid of Kent, challenging the very notion that the authority of inspiration might give the Church or its representatives a political voice in Henry VIII's England. By portraying Barton as morally and sexually corrupt, a pawn of lascivious and traitorous clerics attempting to undermine civil

---

[4] Much has been written on the politics of prophecy. In the continental context, the standard work is Ottavia Niccoli, *Prophecy and People in Renaissance Italy*, trans. Lydia Cochrane (Princeton, 1990). For England, see Sharon Jansen, *Political Protest and Prophecy under Henry VIII* (Woodbridge, 1991). Other useful works include: Sharon L. Jansen Jaech, 'The "Prophisies of Rymour, Beid, Marlyng": Henry VIII and a Sixteenth-Century Political Prophecy', *SCJ*, 16 (1985), 291–9; Alistair Fox, 'Prophecies and Politics in the Reign of Henry VIII', in Alistair Fox and John Guy (eds.), *Reassessing the Henrician Age: Humanism, Politics and Reform 1500–1550* (Oxford, 1986); Keith Thomas, *Religion and the Decline of Magic* (New York, 1971); Rupert Taylor, *The Political Prophecy in England* (New York, 1911); Madeleine Hope Dodds, 'Political Prophecies in the Reign of Henry VIII', *Modern Language Review* 11 (1916), 276–84; T. M. Smallwood, 'The Prophecy of the Six Kings', *Speculum*, 60 (July 1985), 571–92; Glanmor Williams, 'Prophecy, Poetry, and Politics in Medieval and Tudor Wales', in H. Hearder and H. R. Lyon (eds.), *British Government and Administration: Studies Presented to S. B. Chrimes* (Cardiff, 1974).

government, the regime comprehensively undermined her claims to legitimacy and left her supporters struggling to survive in a world which suddenly branded them, rather than the king, as the enemies of divinely sanctioned order.

Elizabeth Barton's eccentric career is hardly unknown to Tudor historians, who have often used it as a barometer of the discontent generated by Henry VIII's divorce.[5] Yet by shifting our frame of reference and considering the political dynamics behind Barton's spectacular rise and fall, we can gain new insights into the struggle for authority and legitimacy at the heart of the English Reformation. Barton's story may be seen as a case study of the phenomenon analysed in chapter 1: the ways in which radical Catholics in the early 1530s tried but ultimately failed to create a viable political challenge to Henry VIII. Barton's unassailable holiness provided both peasants and politicians with something approaching an acceptable alternative to royal authority with which they could 'legitimately' challenge the break with Rome. Thus for a brief moment Barton had the opportunity to unify the Catholic nation, allowing even the most ardent conformists to reimagine the Henrician Reformation not as a political event but as an offence against the universal Church. Once it realised the danger, however, even the relatively weak Tudor state found it remarkably easy to subvert Barton's claims. By using its own 'legitimate' authority to brand Barton a traitor, the regime shattered the Barton movement back into its constituent parts. In the process it exposed the near impossibility of the task facing any English Catholics who would try to translate popular piety into popular political opposition to Henry VIII.

---

[5] The best analysis of Barton's career is Diane Watt, *Secretaries of God: Women Prophets in Late Medieval and Early Modern England* (Cambridge, 1997), ch. 3. A more problematic account is Sharon Jansen, *Dangerous Talk and Strange Behavior: Women and Popular Resistance to the Reforms of Henry VIII* (New York, 1996), chs. 3–4. Jansen accepts many of the questionable assertions in the modern hagiography of Barton: Alan Neame, *The Holy Maid of Kent: The Life of Elizabeth Barton, 1506–1534* (London, 1971). Other useful works include: Diane Watt, 'The Prophet at Home: Elizabeth Barton and the Influence of Bridget of Sweden and Catherine of Siena', in Rosalynn Voaden (ed.), *Prophets Abroad: The Reception of Continental Holy Women in Late-Medieval England* (Cambridge, 1996); Diane Watt, 'Reconstructing the Word: The Prophecies of Elizabeth Barton', *Renaissance Quarterly*, 1 (1997), 132–59; Diane Watt, 'The Posthumous Reputation of the Holy Maid of Kent', *Recusant History*, 23 (1996), 148–58; Ethan Shagan, 'Print, Orality, and Communications in the Maid of Kent Affair', *JEH*, 52 (2001), 21–33; Richard Rex, 'The Execution of the Holy Maid of Kent', *BIHR*, 64 (1991), 216–20; Retha Warnicke, *Women of the English Renaissance and Reformation* (Westport, Conn., 1983); Patricia Crawford, *Women and Religion in England 1500–1720* (London, 1993); E. J. Devereux, 'Elizabeth Barton and Tudor Censorship', *Bulletin of the John Rylands Library*, 49 (1966–67), 91–106. Important older works include David Knowles, *The Religious Orders in England*, 3 vols. (Cambridge, 1959), III, ch. 15; A. Denton Cheney, 'The Holy Maid of Kent', *TRHS*, 18 (1904), 107–29; J. R. McKee, *Dame Elizabeth Barton O.S.B. The Holy Maid of Kent* (London, 1925).

I

Late medieval England experienced frequent, spontaneous eruptions of the divine. In a population devoted to the cult of the saints, a population which believed God to be so immanent that they regularly consumed his human incarnation, the appearance of mystics and prophets with concrete revelatory experiences was not only acceptable but expected. God could be found welling-up everywhere: in pilgrimage shrines associated with local miracles, in mystics who heard God's voice, and in the magical beliefs which regulated people's daily lives.[6]

The appearance of new miracles was therefore common enough that 'genres' developed to help contextualise them. One of the more elaborate of these genres featured prophetesses called 'holy maids', heirs to the long legacy of medieval female hagiography and the mystical tradition associated with Julian of Norwich and Margery Kempe.[7] The basic characteristics of this genre can be gleaned from the story of an early Tudor mystic whose career is unusually well documented: Anne Wentworth, daughter of Sir Roger Wentworth, known as the 'maid of Ipswich'. She apparently lived an ordinary childhood until at age twelve she was 'in marvellous manner vexed and tormented by our ghostly enemy the devil, her mind alienated and raving with despising and blasphemy of God, and hatred of all hallowed things'. Yet, despite these vexations, God gave young Anne Wentworth the strength to travel to the shrine of Our Lady of Ipswich, allowing her to prove her holiness along the way by prophesying and speaking from a trance words 'of such wisdom and learning that right cunning men highly marvelled'. When she arrived at the shrine, she fell into another trance, was briefly disfigured by the battle between God and the devil taking place within her body, then finally emerged, cured of all devilish influence. After her recovery, she took religious vows and entered a convent.[8] The salient characteristics here are

---

[6] Eamon Duffy has shown that such magical practices were compatible with the sort of Christianity taught by medieval theologians: see Eamon Duffy, *The Stripping of the Altars: Traditional Religion in England 1400–1580* (New Haven, 1992). Duffy's view has surpassed the older view which contrasted Christianity and magic, epitomised by Thomas, *Religion and the Decline of Magic* and Jean Delumeau, *Catholicism between Luther and Voltaire: A New View of the Counter-Reformation* (London, 1977).

[7] The fact that the role of the holy maid was paradigmatically female was not a coincidence; it seems clear that this was one area in which contemporary views of women left significant space for female power. See Elaine Huber, *Women and the Authority of Inspiration: A Reexamination of Two Prophetic Movements from a Contemporary Feminist Perspective* (Lanham, Md., 1985), esp. ch. 1; Caroline Walker Bynum, *Jesus as Mother: Studies in the Spirituality of the High Middle Ages* (Berkeley, 1982), p. 172; Gabriella Zarri, 'Living Saints: A Typology of Female Sanctity in the Early Sixteenth Century', trans. Margery Schneider, in Daniel Bornstein and Roberto Rusconi (eds.), *Women and Religion in Medieval and Renaissance Italy* (Chicago, 1996).

[8] Thomas More, *A dyaloge of syr Thomas More knyghte* (London, 1529), fol. 20r–v. Another contemporary account of the maid of Ipswich is in BL Harleian MS 651, fols. 194v–196v,

the young maid's gender and physical weakness (which proved that her evident wisdom and spiritual strength must be of divine rather than natural
origin), her prophesying, her association with a particular shrine (not surprisingly a shrine of the Virgin), and the ultimate containment of her disorderly
performance through her installation as a nun.

The holy maid genre was sufficiently well established by the sixteenth
century that several frauds appeared. The 'maid of Leominster', for instance,
began her 'career' when, apparently with the consent of the local prior, she
took up residence in the priory church and refused to leave for any reason.
It was widely believed that she 'lived without any meat or drink, only by
angels' food', an image promoted by the prior, who created tricks to fool the
populace into thinking she was 'a very quick saint'. People flocked to her
from all around the county, according to Thomas More, arriving in crowds
so thick that 'many that could not come near to her cried out aloud, "Holy
maiden Elizabeth, help me"', and were fain to throw their offering over their
fellows' heads'. Her hypocrisy was soon discovered, however, when it was
found that, despite claiming not to eat, she still created her own share of
excrement, and the material she voided 'had no saintly savour'.[9]

It is in this generic context that the early career of Elizabeth Barton must
be understood; there was no way to foresee at first that she would fly so far
beyond the traditional boundaries of a holy maid. In fact, it was the very
ordinariness of her revelations, her close fit with popular expectations, that
allowed her to gain credence in the first place. It was only years later, once
Barton's base of support was well established and her orthodox credentials
secure, that the king's revolutionary policies helped transform her into a
political figure of national reputation.

Barton's prophetic career began in 1525 when she was perhaps nineteen
years old and was working as a servant in the house of Thomas Cobb, a
steward on episcopal estates in Aldington, Kent.[10] While working for Cobb,
Barton suffered a terrible illness 'which did ascend at diverse times up into

---

while a brief, hostile account is in the sub-Cranmerian tract *A confutation of Unwritten
Verities*, printed in *The Works of Thomas Cranmer*, ed. J. E. Cox, 2 vols. (Cambridge,
1846), II, p. 65.

[9] More, *A dyaloge of syr Thomas More knyghte*, fols. 18v–19r. Another account is in
A confutation of Unwritten Verities, printed in Cox (ed.), *The Works of Thomas Cranmer*,
II, pp. 64–5, where another false holy woman in St Albans was also described. Thomas More
also mentioned another genuine holy maid called Helen of Tottenham and said that 'of her
trances and revelations there hath been much talking': Thomas More, *The Correspondence
of Sir Thomas More*, ed. E. F. Rogers (Princeton, 1947), pp. 484–5.

[10] The only contemporary indication of Barton's age is a manuscript introduction to a book
about her revelations, written by her confessor, Edward Bocking, which puts her birth in
1506. This would make her nineteen or twenty when her revelations began around Easter
1525. However, the Bocking manuscript contains numerous glaring errors, including the
claim that Barton had become a nun in 1524. The birthdate of 1506 must thus be seen as a
conjecture. See *LP* VI, 1468(6), translated in Neame, *The Holy Maid of Kent*, pp. 245–6.

her throat, and swelled greatly, during the time whereof she seemed to be in grievous pain, in so much as a man would have thought that she had suffered the pangs of death itself'.[11] According to hostile sources, as a result of her illness she 'was brought into such weakness and such idleness of her brain, that she often times trifled and spoke such words as she remembered not herself when she came to good advisement'.[12] Whether 'weakness' and 'idleness' are altogether fair terms is questionable, but it certainly seems that, as another hostile source put it, 'in the violence of her infirmity she seemed to be in trances' and spoke words that made little sense to those around her.[13]

At this point, according to the one sympathetic source at our disposal, her activities took on an extraordinary aspect. Seven months after her illness began, Barton lay sick in Cobb's house next to 'a young child of her master's [who] lay desperately sick in a cradle by her'. When Barton asked the child's nurse if it was dead and the nurse responded that it was not, Barton miraculously predicted that the child was about to die: '[Barton] replied that it should [die] anon, which word was no sooner uttered, but the child fetched a great sigh, and withal the soul departed out of her body.' It was this small miracle which 'first... moved her hearers to admiration' and indicated to those in the community that something potentially important was happening at Thomas Cobb's house.[14] Thereafter, with Barton still in the throes of her illness, more revelations came quickly. According to the same hagiographic source, she:

told plainly of diverse things done at the Church, and other places where she was not present, which nevertheless she seemed (by signs proceeding from her) most lively to behold (as it were) with her eye. She told also of heaven, hell, and purgatory, and of the joys and sorrows that sundry departed souls had and suffered there. She spoke frankly against the corruption of manners and evil life. She exhorted repair to the Church, hearing of mass, confession to priests, [and] prayer to Our Lady and saints.

She thus confirmed orthodox doctrine with such perfection that observers were convinced that Barton must have been inspired by God.[15]

For those living in the community of Aldington, therefore, something unusual was clearly happening, and news quickly filtered out into the country;

[11] William Lambarde, *A Perambulation of Kent: Conteining the description, Hystorie, and Customes of the Shyre* (London, 1576), p. 149. The portion of Lambarde's book cited here was, according to Lambarde, copied directly from a pamphlet from the 1520s entitled *A Marveilous Woorke of Late Done at Court of Streete in Kent*. There is no extant copy of this pamphlet, so its contents must be gleaned from Lambarde's long quotations. For more on this pamphlet, see Shagan, 'Print, Orality, and Communications in the Maid of Kent Affair'.
[12] 'The Sermon Against the Holy Maid of Kent and Her Adherents, Delivered at Paul's Cross, November the 23rd, 1533, and at Canterbury, December the 7th', ed. L. E. Whatmore, *EHR*, 58 (1943), 463–75, quotation at 464.
[13] *Statutes*, III, pp. 446–7.   [14] Lambarde, *Perambulation of Kent*, p. 149.
[15] Ibid., p. 150.

even hostile accounts admit that in those early days 'the fame' of Barton's revelations 'was greatly spread abroad in those parts of Kent'.[16] But it seems that the maid of Kent first came to the attention of the authorities not through rumour but through proper channels: the parson of Aldington, Richard Master, rode to Canterbury to inform his superiors that he had a possible saint on his hands. Archbishop Warham, however, was a cautious man. He ordered Master to listen carefully to Barton's supposed revelations, and 'if she had any more such speeches, he should be at them as nigh as he could, and mark them well'.[17] At the same time, Warham put together an investigating commission composed of seven monks and priests: Edward Bocking, William Hadleigh and a man called Barnes (all monks of Christ Church, Canterbury); two Observant friars (one named Father Lewis, the other unknown); Thomas Wall, comptroller to Archbishop Warham; and Richard Master, parson of Aldington.[18] This was no small group of men; Edward Bocking was a doctor of divinity and cellarer of Christ Church, while Master had been praised as 'learned in divinity, and of good and sober life' by no less a person than Erasmus.[19]

At roughly the same time, Barton's revelations began to take on a new tinge, becoming increasingly associated with a chapel of the Virgin at a place called Court at Street, a shrine near Aldington.[20] She predicted that Our Lady of Court at Street would cure her of her disease, and that the image of the Virgin there would perform miracles for all who worshipped it: 'Our blessed Lady will show more miracles there shortly, for if any depart this life suddenly, or by mischance, in deadly sin, if he be vowed to our Lady heartily he shall be restored to life again, to receive shrift and housel and after to depart this world with God's blessing.' She also miraculously described details of the shrine at Court at Street which she could not have known, including 'what meat the hermit of the chapel . . . had to his supper'.[21]

With the arrival of the episcopal commission and Barton's prophecy of her own cure coinciding so neatly, Barton's career was poised for a crescendo, and indeed it seems that an extraordinary event took place at the chapel at Court at Street in the early months of 1526. The commissioners from

---

[16] *Statutes*, III, p. 447.
[17] Whatmore (ed.), 'Sermon Against the Holy Maid of Kent', p. 464.
[18] Neame, *The Holy Maid of Kent*, pp. 62–3.   [19] Ibid., p. 29.
[20] There is no consensus about whether Court at Street was actually within the parish of Aldington, a question of some importance since Richard Master was later accused of faking the miracles there to increase pilgrimages to his parish. The act of attainder against Barton and her followers says that the shrine was in Aldington (*Statutes*, III, p. 447), while T. E. Bridgett claims that the shrine was in the neighbouring parish of Lympne (T. E. Bridgett, *Life of Blessed John Fisher* (London, 1888), p. 235), and Alan Neame claims that it enjoyed extra-parochial independence (Neame, *The Holy Maid of Kent*, p. 58).
[21] Lambarde, *Perambulation of Kent*, pp. 150–1.

Archbishop Warham pronounced Barton's holiness genuine, and 'at her next voyage to our Lady of Court of Street, she entered the chapel with *Ave Regina Caelorum*, in pricksong, accompanied with these commissioners, many ladies, gentlemen, and gentlewomen of the best degree, and three thousand persons besides, of the common sort of people'.[22] A crowd of three thousand may seem ridiculous for a small sixteenth-century community, but even government sources from Barton's prosecution allow that two thousand people were present.[23]

Inside the chapel, in front of all these witnesses, Barton put on a powerful performance, whether genuine or not. According to our hagiographic source: 'There fell she eftsoons into a marvellous passion before the image of our Lady, much like a body diseased of the falling evil, in the which she uttered sundry metrical and rhyming speeches, tending to the worship of Our Lady of Court of Street... [and] tending also to her own bestowing in some religious house, for such (said she) was Our Lady's pleasure.'[24] More than seven years later, the version of the story that Thomas Cranmer knew was even more elaborate. He wrote in a letter to Archdeacon Hawkins that 'when she was brought thither and laid before the image of Our Lady, her face was wonderfully disfigured, her tongue hanging out, and her eyes being in a manner plucked out and laid upon her cheeks, and so greatly disordered'. She then went into a three-hour trance in which she spoke from 'within her belly' about heaven, hell and pilgrimages, and then 'after she had lain there a long time, she came to herself again, and was perfectly whole'.[25] The extant sources disagree about whether Barton was permanently cured that day, but certainly her remarkable transfiguration in front of so many witnesses was the centrepiece of her career. Afterwards her prophetically stated need to enter 'some religious house' was granted; she became a novitiate of St Sepulchre's, Canterbury, and was professed a nun by 1528. Dr Edward Bocking of Christ Church, Canterbury, a member of the episcopal commission, became Barton's confessor with the consent of Archbishop Warham.[26]

With her experience at the chapel, her installation as a nun, and the beginning of her close relationship with Bocking and the monks of Christ Church, the formative stage of Elizabeth Barton's career can be said to have come to an end. She had achieved a great deal. In less than three years she had gone from being a poor, sickly and unknown maidservant to being a well-reputed holy woman and nun. She had attracted an enormous crowd

---

[22] Ibid., pp. 151–2.
[23] *Statutes*, III, p. 447; Whatmore (ed.), 'Sermon Against the Holy Maid of Kent', p. 465.
[24] Lambarde, *Perambulation of Kent*, p. 152.
[25] Thomas Cranmer, *The Remains of Thomas Cranmer* ed. Henry Jenkyns, 4 vols. (Oxford, 1833), I, p. 79.
[26] Wright (ed.), *Three Chapters of Letters Relating to the Suppression of Monasteries*, p. 19.

to watch her most prominent miracle, evidence of her personal charisma. And, perhaps most important, she had done all this with unimpeachable orthodoxy in both the form and content of her message. She had praised traditional practices such as pilgrimage and confession, lambasted the weak morals of the populace, and performed the expected prophetic functions of a holy maid, all without ever deviating onto controversial moral or political ground. She thus accomplished the considerable task of gaining widespread credence without making any enemies, with the notable exception of the heretic William Tyndale, whose enmity undoubtedly would have pleased her had she known of it.[27]

What we can see in the mid 1520s, then, is a woman who was eminently remarkable, but in almost totally unremarkable ways. She performed miracles, but exactly those miracles she was expected to perform. She pronounced learned doctrine, but doctrine with which no one might disagree. It should have been expected, then, that when she entered the convent at St Sepulchre's she would fade into relative obscurity as the maid of Ipswich had done. In reality, however, Barton played out her life in a wholly different fashion. Her reputation did not diminish with her entry into the convent but mushroomed into extraordinary dimensions. Her revelations and miracles, formerly so orthodox, became the bane of Henry VIII's government. It is to this extraordinary transformation that we now turn.

II

The phenomenon that precipitated the tidal shift in Elizabeth Barton's career was of course the Henrician Reformation. Barton had the misfortune of rising to prominence as an orthodox religious figure at just the time when definitions of orthodoxy were being flipped on their heads. Like the rest of England she faced the dilemma of whether to follow Church or Crown, and she chose to defend the beliefs and traditions at the centre of her new profession.

The first evidence of Elizabeth Barton's entrance into politics comes in a letter from Archbishop Warham to Cardinal Wolsey dated 1 October 1528. In it, Warham informed Wolsey that: 'Elizabeth Barton, being a religious woman professed in St. Sepulchre's in Canterbury, which had all the visions at our Lady of Court of Street, a very well disposed and virtuous woman (as I am informed by her sisters), is very desirous to speak with your grace personally. What she hath to say or whether it be good or ill I do not know.'[28]

---

[27] Tyndale excoriated Barton in his *Obedience of a Christian Man*, printed in William Tyndale, *Doctrinal Treatises and Introductions to Different Portions of the Holy Scriptures by William Tyndale, Martyr, 1536*, ed. Henry Walker (Cambridge, 1848), pp. 325–7.
[28] PRO SP 1/50, fol. 163r [*LP* IV, ii, 4806].

We do not know how well acquainted Warham was with Barton's prophetic activities; it is certainly possible that he had had no dealings with her since his commissioners had reported more than two years before. It seems much more likely, however, that Warham knew Barton well in 1528 and was lying to Wolsey about not knowing the reason for her request. Not only is it unlikely that he would have written a letter of introduction to the second most powerful man in England without some solid information, but we also know that soon afterwards he was firmly in Barton's camp. Thomas Goldwell, prior of Christ Church, Canterbury, for instance, said that Warham 'gave much credence unto her words in such things as she knew and surmised to know, that she did show unto him'.[29]

Wolsey's immediate reaction to meeting Barton is not known, but his general response is clear. Many observers reported him to have been impressed with her, and her enemies later credited her with turning Wolsey against the divorce: 'The said cardinal was as well minded and bent to go forth in the king's grace's said cause of matrimony and divorce as any man living (according to the law of God and the law of nature) till he was perverted by this nun and induced to believe that if he proceeded in the same God would sore strike him.'[30] Most importantly, Wolsey's reaction can be judged from the fact that, soon after meeting with him, Barton was allowed to meet with the king himself. Between 1528 and 1532, she apparently met with Henry VIII at least twice.[31] The dates of these meetings are unclear, and it is hard to be sure what was said when, but two important facts are certain. First, Barton told the king that if he proceeded with the planned divorce from Catherine of Aragon he would 'not be king of England' soon after.[32] Second, the king attempted to buy Barton's silence, offering to make her an abbess if she would support him; he was reportedly 'greatly displeased at her refusal'.[33]

What exactly was the content of Barton's prophecies that so impressed not only the masses but even these great lords? One crucial element in Barton's agenda was her defence of traditional Catholicism. Even before the experience at Court at Street, she had defended purgatory, the mass,

---

[29] Wright (ed.), *Three Chapters of Letters Relating to the Suppression of Monasteries*, p. 20.

[30] Whatmore (ed.), 'Sermon Against the Holy Maid of Kent', p. 467. For Cranmer's impressions, see Jenkyns (ed.), *The Remains of Thomas Cranmer*, I, p. 82.

[31] See Wright (ed.), *Three Chapters of Letters Relating to the Suppression of Monasteries*, p. 20, where Thomas Goldwell tells Thomas Cromwell that Barton told him she had been with the king 'two times at the least'. Sharon Jansen lists three occasions on which Barton and Henry VIII met, but this assumes that a meeting described as being 'in spirit' was in fact a real meeting: Jansen, *Dangerous Talk*, pp. 48–9 and 169; Wright (ed.), *Three Chapters of Letters Relating to the Suppression of Monasteries*, p. 15.

[32] Bridgett, *Life of Blessed John Fisher*, p. 253. See also *LP* VI, 1470.

[33] PRO SP 1/80, fol. 138r [*LP* VI, 1468(5)].

confession to priests and prayer to the saints, all orthodox beliefs and practices that were coming under attack from Germany.[34] Later, in the more mature phase of her revelations, these themes were still prominently displayed. For instance, one of her visions expressed resistance to vernacular bibles: an angel commanded her to tell a certain monk 'to burn the New Testament that he had in English'.[35] Another miracle associated with Barton was a letter, supposedly written in Mary Magdalene's hand and delivered by an angel, which informed a London widow 'that if she did diminish any part of certain gold hidden by her husband while he was alive, and bestowed it not entirely in the ornaments of the Church, she should do it to her husband's utter damnation and hers both'.[36]

These traditionalist Catholic themes thus provided the basis for much of Barton's political rhetoric as it became clear that Henry VIII would challenge papal authority in order to obtain his divorce. The most blunt of all Barton's political revelations stated, in several different forms depending upon the source, that the king would incur God's wrath, would become no king in the eyes of God, or would even be killed if he divorced Catherine of Aragon and married Anne Boleyn. One version of this prophecy which Barton supposedly 'showed . . . unto the king' shows a striking belief in the interpenetration of the royal supremacy and Protestant heresy: 'An angel appeared and bade the nun go unto the king, that infidel prince of England, and say that I command him to amend his life, and that he leave three things which he loveth and purposeth upon, that is that he take none of the pope's right nor patrimony from him, the second that he destroy all those new folks of opinion and the works of their new learning, the third that if he married and took Anne to wife the vengeance of God should plague him.'[37] According to a different version, Barton said 'that the king should not continue king a month after that he were married. And within six months after, God would strike the realm with such a plague as never was seen, and then the king should be destroyed'.[38] In yet another version, Barton said that if the king married Anne he would 'not reign king past one month afterward' and that even if God allowed him to remain on the thrown he would not be accepted as king 'in the reputation of God'.[39]

This was high treason. Only a decade before, the Duke of Buckingham, the highest peer in England, had been summarily tried and executed for merely

---

[34] Lambarde, *Perambulation of Kent*, p. 150.

[35] Wright (ed.), *Three Chapters of Letters Relating to the Suppression of Monasteries*, p. 16.

[36] 'Sermon Against the Holy Maid of Kent', p. 470.

[37] Wright (ed.), *Three Chapters of Letters Relating to the Suppression of Monasteries*, pp. 14–15.

[38] Jenkyns (ed.), *The Remains of Thomas Cranmer*, I, p. 82.

[39] Wright (ed.), *Three Chapters of Letters Relating to the Suppression of Monasteries*, p. 20.

listening to a prophecy that the king would die without issue and that he himself would take the throne. Yet Barton spoke these words with her own mouth, apparently to the king's face, and paid no penalty. From the moment that Barton uttered treason in the king's presence and was allowed to walk away unharmed, her career took on a new and potentially revolutionary dimension. This was, in a sense, the final act of legitimation: even the king did not dare to harm her. For those disaffected elements in the country who were looking for a way to oppose the break with Rome yet could not stomach open disloyalty, Barton now provided an answer. By latching onto this apparently untouchable prophetess, they could cobble together an apparently legitimate protest movement which might either persuade the king to change his policy, or else, in the final analysis, accept Barton's 'higher' authority over the king's. It should be stressed that this was not hypocrisy; Barton was a living saint by every contemporary definition. As such, she represented an almost unique potential link between the political aspirations of conformist and Romanist Catholics: conformists would not ordinarily give credence to a pope who opposed their anointed king, but they might be more than a little moved when a saint did so on direct orders from God and the Virgin.

Furthermore, Barton did not merely attack Henry VIII's blasphemy; she also gave stern warnings to Catholics that they must remain committed to papal authority or else face God's wrath. Barton had a vision concerning the pope himself in which 'it was showed unto her that if the pope did give sentence against the queen that then was, almighty God would be displeased with him, and send plagues to him for it'.[40] She apparently took this vision seriously enough to send letters to the pope in which she reminded him of his duty oppose the English king; the papal ambassadors Silvester Darius and John Anthony Pulleon were each dispatched to Rome bearing Barton's revelations, translated into Latin by Barton's adherents Thomas Laurence and Henry Gold.[41]

Besides the pope, Thomas Wolsey also received his share of attention in Barton's visions and was warned not to abandon his loyalty to Rome. According to an account recorded by Thomas More, Barton had personally told Wolsey of 'a revelation of hers, of three swords that God put in my lord legate's hand, which if he ordered not well, God would lay it sore to his charge. The first . . . was the ordering of the spirituality under the pope, as legate. The second, the rule that he bare in order of the temporality under the king, as his chancellor. And the third, she said, was the meddling he was put in trust with by the king, concerning the great matter of his marriage.'[42]

---

[40] Ibid., p. 20.
[41] Whatmore (ed.), 'Sermon Against the Holy Maid of Kent', pp. 467–8.
[42] Rogers (ed.), *Correspondence of Sir Thomas More*, p. 482.

In the end, Wolsey apparently did a passable job of juggling these conflicting duties; after Wolsey's death Barton claimed to witness the 'disputation of the devils for his soul' and then 'by her penance he was brought unto heaven'.[43]

Other political figures associated with Henry VIII also came under attack from Barton. She claimed, for instance, to have witnessed a devil whispering in Anne Boleyn's ear, asking her to influence the king's actions.[44] In another vision she claimed to have seen 'a root with three branches, and till they were plucked up it should never be merry in England, interpreting the root to be the late Lord Cardinal, and the first branch to be the king our sovereign lord, the second the duke of Norfolk, and the third the duke of Suffolk'.[45] Norfolk and Suffolk were among the highest peers in the realm and had made it their business to support the king's policies, but neither was believed to be an evangelical. Barton evidently wanted to make it clear that conformity to the king's religious policies, whatever its rationale, would provoke God's wrath.

The political meaning uniting these disparate revelations was encapsulated in one boldly symbolic vision, already cited in chapter 1, which Barton experienced in 1532. While Henry VIII was in Calais, on a trip which was rumoured (falsely) to be the occasion for him to marry Anne Boleyn, Barton had an out-of-body experience and believed that she accompanied the king. Her account of the event exists in several versions, of which the most detailed is in the act of attainder against her:

When the king's highness was at Calais in the interview between His majesty and the French king, and hearing mass in the church of Our Lady at Calais...God was so displeased with the king's highness that his grace saw not that time at the mass the blessed sacrament in the form of bread, for it was taken away from the priest (being at mass) by an angel, and ministered to the said Elizabeth then being there present and invisible, and suddenly conveyed and rapt thence again by the power of God into the said nunnery where she is professed.[46]

Here we have a bold and unambiguous statement that legitimate authority rested not with the Crown but with the Church. In this vision of the transfer of the sacrament, Barton imagined divine authority being passed from the hands of Henry VIII, who had forfeited his status as God's anointed, to Barton herself and the legitimate heads of the Church. It was precisely this rationale which provided a plausible ideology for opposition in a society as rigidly hierarchical as Tudor England. So long as the king could claim to be the sole repository of godly authority within his kingdom, rebellion against him could only with great difficulty be cloaked under the heading

---

[43] Wright (ed.), *Three Chapters of Letters Relating to the Suppression of Monasteries*, p. 16.
[44] Ibid., p. 15.   [45] *Statutes*, III, p. 449.   [46] Ibid., p. 448.

of conservatism. Barton's accretion of spiritual authority, however, opened a breach in the government's ideological walls that was large enough for both peasants and lords, waving Barton's flag, to march through.

III

Whether a revolt would really have emerged out of Barton's circle had she been left unhindered is an unanswerable question. But what made this possibility so real and frightening to the government was not merely Barton's message but the very public promulgation of that message. Barton not only spoke with a claim to legitimacy when she attacked government policies, she also spoke *loudly*. Building on her early career as a saint and the hagiographic momentum that had first propelled her to fame, Barton and her adherents were able to co-opt and manipulate the Church's propaganda machinery and turn it to explicitly political ends, a unique capability which allowed them to reach an enormous and variegated audience.

There can be little doubt that Barton achieved widespread acclaim despite the uncertainties of sixteenth-century communications. As already shown, even a hostile source admitted that in 1526, right at the beginning of her career and still living in a small village, she attracted more than two thousand people to see her at Court at Street. Another hostile source, a chronicle written in the late 1530s by a monk of St Augustine's, Canterbury, stated that 'a certain nun called Elizabeth Barton by marvelous hypocrisy mocked all Kent and almost all England'.[47] Christopher Warener, an anchorite with the Black Friars at Canterbury, admitted in 1533 that he had never actually seen Barton in a trance, but he accepted her reputation as a holy woman 'because of the common vulgar that went upon her'.[48] Eustace Chapuys, the Imperial ambassador, wrote to Charles V in 1533 that the government was taking extraordinarily public measures against Barton and her followers in order to 'blot out from people's minds the impression they have that the nun is a saint and a prophet'. He believed, furthermore, that the government would have to extend this propaganda not just locally but 'through the principal towns in the country'.[49]

At the base of any reputation in Tudor England was oral communication, and in Barton's case the circulation of news and gossip was inextricably tied to the mechanisms of popular hagiography. Barton's fame spread not only haphazardly but also through well-understood channels, particularly through the traditional practices of pilgrimage and the veneration of saints. In

[47] *Narratives of the Days of the Reformation, Chiefly from the Manuscripts of John Foxe*, ed. J. G. Nichols (Westminster, 1859), p. 280.
[48] PRO SP 1/80, fol. 21r [*LP* VI, 1336].   [49] *CSP Spanish*, vol. 4, part 2, no. 1154.

the aftermath of Barton's miracles at Court at Street, for instance, that shrine became the focus of a significant upwelling of popular devotion. Archbishop Cranmer wrote in 1533 that as a result of Barton's alleged miracles at the shrine 'there is established a great pilgrimage', and John Bale later claimed that Barton's revelations had been invented solely for the purpose of promoting the shrine.[50] While we certainly need not accept this cynical reading, it was entirely normal for shrines to advertise the miracles performed there, and advertising for Court at Street was tantamount to advertising for the maid of Kent.

There is also evidence that pilgrims flocked to see Barton herself at the convent of St Sepulchre's, Canterbury. In the aftermath of Barton's execution, for instance, the evangelical Richard Morison described how Barton and her monk associates had tricked vast numbers of gullible suppliants into believing that she had miraculous knowledge of their sins. Allegedly, pilgrims were made to confess to local monks and receive absolution before being allowed to meet with Barton, and the details of their sins were secretly passed to her so she could offer the pilgrims appropriately personalised warnings of hellfire when she saw them.[51] While Morison's account is clearly derogatory, the underlying phenomenon is confirmed in a letter from Thomas More, where he described a conversation he had with Hugh Rich, Warden of Richmond Priory, about 'strange things as concerned such folk as had come unto her, to whom, as she said, she had told the causes of their coming ere themselves spoke thereof'.[52]

Who were these people who came to visit Barton? We can never know in detail, but it seems likely that, since Barton lived in Canterbury, England's most popular pilgrimage destination, the people who came to see her were the same people who visited Becket's relics at Canterbury Cathedral. The existence of a local saint, publicised by the same priests and monks whom the pilgrims regularly encountered in their devotions, could easily have siphoned off some percentage of devotees and steered them towards a local convent before they returned home. This hypothesis is strengthened by the fact that Barton's leading backer in the locality was Edward Bocking, cellarer of Christ Church, the Cathedral priory; in other words, Barton had a public-relations man literally living and working within a stone's throw of Becket's bones. The implications of this assertion are significant. The coincidence of Barton's

---

[50] Cox (ed.), *Works of Thomas Cranmer*, II, p. 272; John Bale, *A Mysterye of Inyquyte Contayned within the Heretycall Genealogye of Ponce Pantolabus* (Geneva, 1545), fol. 30r.

[51] Richard Morison, *Apomaxis calumniarum convitiorumque* (London, 1537), sig. T3r–v, translated in Neame, *The Holy Maid of Kent*, pp. 141–2.

[52] Rogers (ed.), *The Correspondence of Sir Thomas More*, p. 486. This phenomenon is also confirmed in the register of Butley Priory, printed in A. G. Dickens, *Late Monasticism and the Reformation* (London, 1994), p. 66.

location at one of England's most popular tourist-traps gave her access to a national audience which she could not otherwise have reached. Moreover, the spread of Barton's fame through the mouths of pilgrims returning to their towns and villages from Canterbury imbued her with a powerful aura of holiness-by-association.

Besides oral communication, Barton's fame also spread through writing and print, and a variety of books described her early career and revelations well before she entered the controversy surrounding the king's divorce.[53] The most important of these, entitled *A Marveilous Woorke of Late Done at Court of Streete in Kent*, was printed by Robert Redman (apparently without attribution of authorship) and consisted of twenty-four folios; no copy now survives, but much of it was preserved in the *Perambulation of Kent* (1576), a history and geography of the county written by William Lambarde. This is the pro-Barton, hagiographic account cited above, containing a detailed description of Barton's first miracles. In addition to this pamphlet, there were probably other printed books describing the miracle at Court at Street,[54] and there were certainly manuscripts in circulation describing Barton's revelations. Thomas More, for instance, wrote that perhaps as early as 1526 the king had given him a 'roll of paper' which contained 'certain words of hers, that she had ... at sundry times spoken in trances'.[55]

That these written and oral communications had significant effects can be seen most clearly from the letters that Barton received from people seeking to benefit from her special access to the divine. One anonymous letter to Barton, for instance, explained that one of the writer's friends, a certain Mr White, was suffering from a terrible disease which he thought might be a 'plague of God'. White therefore asked Barton 'to make meekly petition to God for the knowledge hereof', for which service he sent her the considerable cash sum of four nobles. The writer of the letter also asked Barton if she had 'any knowledge of my brother's petitions, or my lady of Syon's', and he passed along to Barton the fond wishes of a certain Mr Wele and his wife, with whom he had dined that day.[56] Here, then, we have extraordinary evidence of a network of gentlemen and ladies who actually sent Barton money in return for solicited intercessions with God on their behalf.

---

[53] See Devereux, 'Elizabeth Barton and Tudor Censorship'.

[54] The authorship of *A Marveilous Woorke of Late Done at Court of Streete in Kent* and the likelihood that other printed accounts existed are discussed in Shagan, 'Print, Orality and Communications in the Maid of Kent Affair'.

[55] Rogers (ed.), *Correspondence of Sir Thomas More*, p. 481. More's statement in early 1534 that he was given the roll 'about 8 or 9 years ago' must be seen as an approximation, since nine years previously would have been before Barton's first trances.

[56] PRO SP 1/73, fol. 27v [*LP* V, 1698]. *LP* suggests that this letter may have been written by Henry Gold but does not explain this attribution.

In sum, even before Barton turned her attention to politics, a sophisticated machinery was in place to spread news of her holiness and provide access to her revelations. Again, the apolitical nature of this media apparatus is not coincidental, but was a prerequisite for its creation. Barton was famous in the 1520s exactly because she was uncontroversial, and contact with her, whether through post, press, or word of mouth, was contact with the divine. But, once Barton's fame was secure, and once her hagiographical apparatus was in place, that apparatus could be used to spread whatever message she chose to promulgate. And from late 1528 onwards, the Church's saint-making machinery was deftly redeployed against Henry VIII's divorce and England's break with Rome.

The written and printed side of Barton's hagiography, for instance, spilled inevitably into sedition as Barton's message became more politicised and controversial. Most importantly, Edward Bocking kept a 'great book [written] with his own hand' consisting of several 'quires' of paper which related Barton's revelations. No doubt at the beginning this 'great book' was more-or-less apolitical, intended to form the basis for later hagiography and perhaps eventual canonisation proceedings. After 1528, however, Bocking's book came to incorporate all of Barton's political prophecies, and, since it later provided the bulk of evidence on which Barton and her associates were attainted of treason, it evidently pulled no punches in its criticisms of Henry VIII. Moreover, this book did not merely sit unread in Christ Church priory. We know that it circulated, since Bocking was willing to lend out parts of the massive manuscript one 'quire' at a time.[57] More importantly, Thomas Laurence of Canterbury wrote out a copy of the 'great book...in a fair hand ready to be a copy to the printer when the said book should be put to stamp'.[58] This fair copy was in fact printed in a run of seven hundred copies, probably in 1533, by the printer John Scott, who sold five hundred copies to Bocking and kept two hundred for himself; unfortunately no copy survives today.[59]

Barton's oral communications networks were also expanded and restructured as her revelations took on a more political tone. In addition to the communications provided by the pilgrimage to St Sepulchre's, for instance,

---

[57] Whatmore (ed.), 'Sermon Against the Holy Maid of Kent', p. 468; Jenkyns (ed.), *The Remains of Thomas Cranmer*, I, p. 81; Wright (ed.), *Three Chapters of Letters Relating to the Suppression of Monasteries*, p. 21.

[58] *Statutes*, III, p. 448.

[59] *LP* VI, 1194; *LP* VI, 1589. Other books seem to have been written in Latin by Barton's supporters soon before her execution: there is an extant one-page introduction to Bocking's *Elizabethae virginis spiritualis gratiae libri secundi prologus*, and we know of a book by John Dering entitled *De Duplice Spiritu*. Neither of these works is known to have circulated. See Neame, *The Holy Maid of Kent*, pp. 245–6; Jenkyns (ed.), *The Remains of Thomas Cranmer*, I, pp. 88–9.

Barton's adherents began to travel throughout the country to spread news of her political pronouncements. At the centre of this operation were the five men who were later executed with her: Edward Bocking and John Dering, both monks of Christ Church; Hugh Rich and Richard Risby, both Observant Franciscans; and the secular priest Henry Gold, former chaplain to Archbishop Warham. It was these men who generally approached people outside the inner circle and told them that the saint about whom they had heard so much had received dire warnings that the king's divorce was against God's will. Thomas More, for instance, was first approached by Richard Risby around Christmas 1532, then by Hugh Rich some months later.[60] Thomas Goldwell, the prior of Christ Church, first met Barton in 1532, despite his policy 'not to be familiarly acquainted with women', because Risby assured him that she was 'a person much in the favour of God'.[61] The act of attainder against Barton claimed that 'Hugh Rich actually traveled to sundry places of this realm and made secret relation of the promises concerning the king's highness'.[62]

Besides these anecdotal references, there is overwhelming direct evidence of the scale of the communications network that was created. An anonymous government memorandum, apparently a compendium of various depositions, listed people to whom the ringleaders had told Barton's most seditious revelations. The lists are staggering. For example, we hear that:

Hugh Rich, friar Observant, hath showed the revelations concerning the king's grace and his reign to: my lady the Princess Dowager; my lady Mary her daughter; my lady of Salisbury; my lord Husse; my lady his wife; my lady marquis of Exeter; my lord of Rochester; my lady Darby; Sir Thomas More; Mr. Abell; item, to diverse priests in the country whose names he hath not yet showed; Mr. Whyte, Mr. Percy, Mr. Nele and his wife, merchants of London; Master Recorder of London; Hugh Fawkner and his wife; Mr. Semes and his wife; the confessor of Syon; my lady Kingston, and to some other ladies there; my lady abbess of Syon; prior of Sheen; the proctor; Brother William; the sexton; Father Vicar; to the brethren of their convent of Richmond and to diverse brethren of the holy religion whose names he hath not showed; Henry Gold, priest; Thomas Gold and his wife; a priest of Windsor; two priests of St. Alban's whose names he hath not showed; abbess of Burnham; to Mr. Dering, monk; my lady Belingham; Sir Thomas Arundell; Mr. John Arundell; Sir John Carew and his brother; Mrs. Katherine Champer; to his brother's wife and somewhat to his brother.[63]

---

[60] Rogers (ed.), *The Correspondence of Sir Thomas More*, pp. 481–2.

[61] Wright (ed.), *Three Chapters of Letters Relating to the Suppression of Monasteries*, pp. 19–20.

[62] *Statutes*, III, p. 450.

[63] PRO *SP* 1/80, fol. 126r–v [*LP* VI, 1468(1)]. There were multiple drafts of these lists, and in another version it is clear from Cromwell's marginalia that there was confusion about whether Thomas More really listened to the prophecy of the king's downfall: see *LP* VI, 1468(2).

Other lists exist for Barton, Risby, Dering, Bocking, Gold and Richard Master. They contain at least thirty more names of people who had been told directly of Barton's political revelations, not including numerous repeated names, plus a variety of collective references such as 'my lord Marquis of Exeter, and to diverse other of my lord marquis's servants'.[64] Three things should be noted about these lists. First, the lay people mentioned by name virtually all occupied the highest level of society. This is obviously a bias created by the fact that these are government sources, particularly concerned with elite rather than popular politics; there is no doubt that if Barton's adherents were telling their news to servants, they were telling others as well. Second, these lists record direct communication only. There is no way to know how many people were told the news second-hand by people on these lists, especially in and around monasteries like Sheen and Syon and the household of the marquis of Exeter, which were clearly becoming hotbeds of pro-Barton sentiment. Third, the large number of priests on these lists suggests that news travelled not only through ordinary word-of-mouth but through the pulpit as well.

The government, not surprisingly, was obsessed with this last possibility. The sermon preached against Barton at St Paul's Cross, for instance, said that among those 'infected' by Barton's prophecies were 'the whole number of friars observant, and by them a great number of the lay folk of all sorts'. It also stated that 'there were appointed certain elected persons by God (as the nun feigned in her revelations) who should preach, publish, and declare the wonderful works of God wrought by her. For diverse of these persons here present have confessed that, if the nun had sent them word that it had been the pleasure of God, that they should have preached to the people that the King's grace was no king afore God, they would have preached it.'[65] The act of attainder declared that all those indicted had 'agreed each with other secretly and set forth the said false and feigned revelations to their acquaintance and friends in this realm' and also had 'set forth in sermons and preachings the said revelations to the people of this realm'.[66]

Here, then, was the Church's latent political power come to fruition in an almost nightmarish inversion of the royal monopoly on authority and propaganda envisioned by Thomas Cromwell. In a sense, Barton was the living antithesis of the royal supremacy over the Church. While the government sought to define opposition to the royal supremacy as an offence against the state, Barton's intrinsic holiness instantly shifted it back to issues of spirituality and divine sanction. While the government sought to exploit popular

---

[64] PRO *SP* 1/80, fols. 126r–128r [*LP* VI, 1468(1)].
[65] 'Sermon Against the Holy Maid of Kent', pp. 467 and 468–9.
[66] *Statutes*, III, p. 449.

anticlerical sentiment, Barton was a living link between the laity and the clergy. While the government sought to extend their propaganda machinery into churches and pulpits, Barton reclaimed those churches and pulpits and expanded the Church's propaganda machinery into the great houses of the gentry and aristocracy. Thus, in the autumn of 1533, when they became aware of the full extent of Barton's movement, the king and his advisors decided that they had no choice but to flex their new ecclesiastical muscles for the first time. The government, as the new arbiters of the holy, made it their job to unmake a saint.

IV

The government's problem with Elizabeth Barton was not merely her treason but the whole idea that a young woman in the countryside could receive the same level of divine commission as the king himself. Regardless of the content of Barton's prophecies, their mere existence was fundamentally anathema to the Henrician Reformation, since they shattered the univocal and 'imperial' authority that Henry VIII was trying so hard to create. This viewpoint could not have been more neatly summarised than in the words of Thomas Cromwell, who in a scathing letter to Bishop Fisher asked: 'If credence should be given to every such lewd person as would affirm himself to have revelations from God, what readier way were there to subvert all commonwealths and good orders in the world?'[67] The idea that true prophesying had ended with the conclusion of the Scriptures was commonplace among evangelicals, and as early as 1528 William Tyndale had responded to 'the maids of Ipswich and of Kent' by arguing that 'when they cry, "miracles, miracles", remember that God hath made an everlasting testament with us in Christ's blood against which we may receive no miracles'.[68] But this position ran contrary to an enormous current of belief in the role of saints as mediators between the human and the divine, and it was against this current that the Henrician regime found itself swimming late in 1533.

Certainly one way to break the presumed connection between Elizabeth Barton's holiness and her political utterances was to discredit Barton herself. This would not end beliefs in miraculous prophecies altogether, but it could at least force people to admit that in this particular case they had been duped, which might, in turn, make them think more carefully the next time a prophetess came along. To this end, Barton and several of her adherents were arrested, a confession from Barton was either forced or fabricated, and

---

[67] Wright (ed.), *Three Chapters of Letters Relating to the Suppression of Monasteries*, p. 30.
[68] Walker (ed.), *Doctrinal Treatises and Introductions to Different Portions of the Holy Scriptures by William Tyndale*, pp. 325–7.

the peers of England were called together in an expanded Council meeting to hear the charges of treason against her.[69]

Even more important, however, the government set about systematically to subvert the linkage between divine inspiration and political engagement that was at the heart of the Barton movement. In two key texts, a St Paul's Cross sermon preached against Barton and the act of attainder against her, the regime retold Barton's story in such detail that they in effect reinvented her in the popular imagination. Both of these texts, moreover, were intended for mass transmission, counteracting the publicness that made Barton's holiness so potentially dangerous. The act of attainder circulated widely in both full and edited forms and was required to be proclaimed throughout the country, while the sermon was preached not only to an enormous crowd at St Paul's but also in Canterbury and perhaps other places as well.[70] These were the centrepieces of the government's propaganda campaign, not only exposing Barton as a fraud but arguing that any claim to holiness that derived its legitimacy from the Roman Catholic Church was necessarily corrupted by the avarice and carnality at the heart of that Church.

The sermon at St Paul's Cross began by admitting that, while living in Aldington, Barton really had suffered from a disease that made her delirious. While in her delirium, she muttered words about the seven deadly sins and the ten commandments which seemed holy, and thus Richard Master rode to Canterbury to inform the archbishop. It was at this point, however, that the sermon's narrative diverged from the hagiographic account in *A Marveilous Woorke*, alleging that while Master was away Barton experienced 'a great purgation' to rid herself of her disease and was 'restored to perfect health'. However, when Master returned and informed Barton that her 'speeches...came of God', she decided that it might be entertaining to play a trick on 'the people giving audience unto her, who were ready to make so much of her idle and trifling words'.[71] Right from the beginning of the sermon, then, it is clear that Barton was a liar who never really received divine revelations. However, it is also implied that her lies were at first less malicious than playful, intended not to have great consequences but simply to poke fun at her ignorant neighbours.

Why, then, did Barton's revelations take on such sinister proportions? The answer, according to the sermon, was the pernicious influence of Edward Bocking. When Bocking transported the young woman from Aldington to her priory after the miracle at Court at Street, we are told, 'she came with the

---

[69] *CSP Spanish*, IV, part 2, no. 1153.
[70] *Statutes*, III, p. 451; 'Sermon Against the Holy Maid of Kent', p. 464; for a suggestion that this sermon was preached elsewhere besides London and Canterbury, see *CSP Spanish*, iv, part 2, no. 1154.
[71] Whatmore (ed.), 'Sermon Against the Holy Maid of Kent', pp. 464–5.

said Dr. Bocking's servants to Canterbury in the evening; and Dr. Bocking brought her to the said priory of St. Sepulchre's in the morning'.[72] The insinuation is clear: Bocking sexually 'corrupted' the young virgin Barton on the very eve of her entry into the convent. Soon thereafter, we are told, she heard 'the said Dr. Bocking rail and jest like a frantic person against the King's Grace, his purposed marriage, against his acts of parliament, and against the maintenance of heresies within this realm, declaiming and blustering out his cankered malice to the said Elizabeth in the said matters, with all the persuasions that he could make to the detraction and derogation of those same'. Thus, although Barton had previously 'meddled not with the king's Grace's marriage', she began to feign revelations that if Wolsey or Warham allowed the king's divorce to go forward they would be 'utterly destroyed'. These revelations emanated neither from God nor from her own beliefs, but rather from a desire to please her lover, the monk Edward Bocking.[73]

We can see developing here a classic narrative of sexual danger in which Barton's own weakness caused her to tell lies, which led quickly to her sexual fall and corruption, which, in turn, left her open to manipulation by the evil Dr Bocking. From the government's point of view, this construction served two important purposes. First, it soiled the reputation for purity and innocence that was prerequisite to belief in Barton's holiness. Second, it made it clear that it was Bocking, a doctor of divinity and male member of the social elite, rather than the young female Elizabeth, who was responsible for her political revelations. In a sixteenth-century context, this latter purpose was crucial. It was inconceivable to most people that a poor maidservant could, on her own, devise elaborate treasons that would ensnare England's highest lords. The only choices available were thus that Barton was either the pawn of powerful men or else was truly inspired by God. It was therefore essential to the government that Barton appear not as the centre of the conspiracy herself but as a fallen woman susceptible to male corruption.

This tale of sexual corruption leading to political treachery continued throughout the sermon. We hear, for instance, that Barton was in the habit of sneaking out of her cell late at night: 'She used twice or thrice a week to go out of her cell secretly, and to be absent for an hour and sometimes more, when she perceived her sisters in their deep sleep. And it is to be supposed that then she went not about the saying of her Pater Noster!'[74] As a result of this illicit contact, it was always Bocking who was responsible for Barton's sedition. We are told, for instance, that he read her stories from the

---

[72] Ibid., p. 466.   [73] Ibid., pp. 466–7.   [74] Ibid., pp. 469–70.

none the less bitter disagreement over the practical problems facing England threatened to rip the rebellion apart. While the Pilgrimage of Grace was first and foremost a protest against government-sponsored attacks on Church and commonwealth, it was by no means agreed which attacks were being protested, for what reasons, and what new policies should be demanded. On the pressing issue of the monasteries, for example, a wide variety of opinions were canvassed, not only on the ostensible question of the king's prerogative to dissolve monastic houses, but also on the more subtle question of whether the government's actions were merely corrupt or were part and parcel of the new German heresy. This was far from an academic point. As defenders of Holy Church against heresy, the pilgrims could refuse to accept any settlement in which the monasteries were not restored. If the dissolution were corrupt but not heretical, however, significant space became available for negotiation with the regime.

For some, of course, the maintenance of monasteries was an absolute moral imperative. Thus a group of Yorkshire rebels described their mission '[to] put the religious persons in their houses again and live and die in the right of God's faith and the Church'.[36] In Lancashire, one rebel manifesto listed the ways 'certain heretics' had 'abominably confounded' the faith, including 'working most cruelly by spoiling and suppression of holy places, as abbeys, churches, and ministers of the same'.[37] Near Easby Abbey in Richmondshire, a visitor was told in December: 'Rather than our house of St. Agatha should go down, we shall all die.'[38] Far from rebel territory these sentiments could also be found. During the northern rebellions, for instance, the parson of Radwell, Hertfordshire told his parishioners, 'They that pull down abbeys and churches . . . without the great mercy of God they shall be damned.'[39] Such unequivocal support for the monasteries, not surprisingly, was encouraged by the monks themselves. It was with the survival of their own house in mind that monks of Furness told the commons: 'Now must they stick to it or else never, for if they sit down both you and Holy Church is undone; and if they lack company we will go with them and live and die with them to defend their most godly pilgrimage.'[40]

Something close to this level of devotion to the monasteries can be seen in the anger vented against persons and property connected to the Court of Augmentations, the administrative agency responsible for the dissolutions. It is no coincidence, for instance, that Richard Rich, chancellor of the Court of Augmentations, was habitually included in lists of highly placed

---

[36] PRO E 36/118, fol. 118r [*LP* XII, i, 29].

[37] Edward Derby, *Correspondence of Edward, Third Earl of Derby*, ed. T. N. Toller, Chetham Society, new series, 19 (Manchester, 1890), p. 48.

[38] PRO E 36/120, fol. 114v [*LP* XII, i, 491].   [39] SP 1/116, fol. 192r [*LP* XII, i, 572].

[40] *LP* XII, i, 841.

heretics whose heads were demanded by the rebels. Rich was certainly no evangelical, but enough rebels imagined the dissolutions as an outgrowth of heresy that the coordinator of those dissolutions could easily be perceived as a heretic himself. On a more concrete level, rebels sacked the houses of Leonard Beckwith, receiver for Yorkshire in the Court of Augmentations, and William Blitheman, receiver for Richmond.[41]

Yet belief that the dissolutions were not open to compromise or negotiation was always a minority opinion. Even Robert Aske, a staunch defender of the monasteries, listed practical reasons why they should be preserved, including their importance for alms-giving, prayers for the dead, hospitality and education. He never came close to claiming that the dissolutions partook directly of continental heresy, and (as will be discussed below) he signalled his equivocation by allowing some abbeys restored by the commons to be re-occupied by royal farmers pending the final settlement of the north.[42] This stance, while opposing the government's actions, tacitly admitted that the dissolution of monasteries had to be analysed on a case-by-case basis. This, indeed, was the argument that the king himself urged on the north in his printed declarations: many of his predecessors had dissolved individual abbeys without arousing spiritual concern, so his own actions had to be considered as different in degree rather than in kind.[43]

Other rebels had very different views of the monasteries. The first list of Lincolnshire grievances, for instance, demanded in highly equivocal fashion 'all the houses of religion that are suppressed to be restored again except such houses as the king hath suppressed for his pleasure only'.[44] Here the reversal of the dissolutions was imagined as an object of negotiation rather than a sine qua non for the resumption of ordinary order, and it was presumed that at least some abbeys would remain dissolved. Elsewhere the restoration of particular monasteries was demanded using language which implied that other monasteries could be dissolved with impunity; inhabitants of Craven, for instance, claimed that Sawley Abbey was worth defending because it provided for 'the charitable relief of those parts…standing in a mountain country and amongst three forests'.[45] In a very different sort of claim, Francis Bigod, the only known evangelical pilgrim, opposed the government's assaults on the monasteries but still suggested that clerical wealth could be appropriated so long as it was transferred to the poor. In his declaration to the commons

---

[41] Bush, *The Pilgrimage of Grace*, pp. 106–7.

[42] For Aske's views, see Bateson (ed.), 'The Pilgrimage of Grace and Aske's Examination', which has been usefully glossed with regard to the monasteries in Haigh, *The Last Days of the Lancashire Monasteries*, pp. 53–8.

[43] See Henry VIII, *Answere Made by the Kynges Hyghnes to Petitions of the Rebelles in Yorkeshire* (London, 1536).

[44] PRO E 36/121, fol. 116v [*LP* XI, 585].

[45] Bateson (ed.), 'The Pilgrimage of Grace and Aske's Examination', p. 338.

raising support for rebellion, he suggested that 'the fat priests' benefices of the south that were not resident upon the same, and the money of the suppressed abbeys, should feed the poor soldiers that were not able to bear their own charges'. This rhetoric may not have been mainstream, but it did not prevent Bigod from gathering his host.[46] And, of course, while many monasteries were restored by the rebels, many others were not restored, and we know that at least in some areas the issue was sufficiently peripheral that the monks had to send petitions to the rebels asking to be put back in their houses.[47]

The most divisive religious issue among the rebels was not the dissolution of the monasteries but the royal supremacy. As we have seen, the king's novel claim to be supreme head of the Church presented religious conservatives with an ecclesiological dilemma, and many defined the supremacy in narrow enough terms that they could at least nominally accept it. Thus, ironically, many participants in the 1536 rebellions accepted the king's authority over the Church even as they questioned his uses of that authority. On 14 November, for instance, Somerset Herald asked Lord Darcy: 'How say you to the excluding of [the] bishop of Rome and his authority, do you think that that is against our faith?' Despite having already subjected himself to treason charges during the interview, Darcy responded in the negative: 'By my truth I think that it is not against our faith, and what I spoke therein to Cromwell, he knoweth himself well enough.'[48] Archbishop Lee reported that 'at the beginning of the rebellion' he was required by 'the rebels . . . to deliver his opinion in some points of religion', resulting in a miniature colloquy over the Act of Ten Articles. His interlocutors 'took ill that mention was made but of three sacraments, and no purgatory', but they did not challenge the authority under which those articles had been issued or deny the legitimacy of the act itself.[49] George Huddyswyll, a captain of the commons in Lincolnshire, reported that early in the insurrection Sir William Ascue and other loyalist gentlemen asked him and his fellow captains 'what caused them to make this insurrection'. To this John Porman, another gentleman captain of the revolt, answered: 'They [the commons] will take the king to be the supreme head of the Church, and he shall have the first fruits and the tenth of every benefice, and shall have also the subsidy granted to him, but he shall

---

[46] PRO SP 1/115, fol. 215r [*LP* XII, i, 369].

[47] For these petitions, see Hoyle, 'Thomas Master's Narrative of the Pilgrimage of Grace', p. 65. I have not been specific here about how many monasteries were restored because this is unclear and has become an issue of some debate. For differing interpretations of the evidence, see Bush, *Pilgrimage of Grace*, pp. 180–1; Anthony Shaw, 'The Involvement of the Religious Orders in the Northern Risings of 1536/7: Compulsion or Desire?', *Downside Review*, 117 (1999), 89–114, at p. 92.

[48] Dodds and Dodds, *The Pilgrimage of Grace*, I, p. 304.

[49] Hoyle, 'Thomas Master's Narrative of the Pilgrimage of Grace', p. 76.

have no more money of the commons during his life nor he shall suppress no more abbeys.'[50] Elsewhere in Lincolnshire, when Sir William Sandon told William Leach and a force of one hundred rebels that they would likely be hung for their efforts, the commons were overcome with 'such a fury and rage that they called him traitor to the commonweal and to the Church of England [*sic*!]'.[51]

It is also remarkable that, although many rebels 'murmured' against the royal supremacy, the issue was left out of all their early manifestos and lists of grievances.[52] The Lincolnshire rebels' petition to the king, as may be assumed from the king's point-by-point response to it, discussed the dissolution of the monasteries and the Crown's claims to the first fruits of ecclesiastical benefices but made no mention of the royal supremacy.[53] Articles probably devised in Lincolnshire on 9 October demanded the restoration of monasteries and expressed grief at the promotion of bishops who had subverted the faith of Christ but made no mention of the royal supremacy.[54] Articles promulgated in Aske's name at the end of October demanded the 'maintenance of the Church', the 'reformation of the Church militant', and the removal of Cromwell, Cranmer and others 'of the same sect', but again made no explicit mention of the royal supremacy.[55] This prolonged silence was no accident; rebel leaders were aware that the issue of the royal supremacy was too hot to handle, and they crafted vague and ambiguous articles to encompass it. The demand that the king 'maintain the Church' in its traditional form, for instance, could be interpreted as an attack on the royal supremacy but could also be seen as a response to the Ten Articles. The exception that proves this rule was a bill in which the Lancashire commons claimed to defend the faith of Christ and support 'King Henry VIII, whose honour is entitled to be defender of the said faith'.[56] In so pointedly including the king's title of 'defender of the faith' but excluding his title of 'supreme head of the Church', the rebels made it clear that there was opposition to the royal supremacy in their ranks. But by refusing to denounce the royal supremacy in so many words or to utter the name of the pope, they also made it clear that – whether

---

[50] PRO E 36/118, fol. 56r–v [*LP* XI, 853].

[51] PRO SP 1/110, fol. 124r–v, cited in Hoyle, *The Pilgrimage of Grace*, p. 128.

[52] For 'murmuring', see Bateson (ed.), 'The Pilgrimage of Grace and Aske's Examination', p. 565.

[53] Henry VIII, *Answere to the Petitions of the Traytors and Rebelles in Lyncolnshyre* (London, 1536).

[54] PRO SP 1/108, fol. 50r [*LP* XI, 705(1)]. Hoyle, *The Pilgrimage of Grace*, pp. 455–6, prints this MS and glosses it as Lincolnshire articles from 9 October 1536, even though Fletcher and MacCulloch had described it as 'The York Articles'.

[55] PRO SP 1/109, fols. 255v–256r [*LP* XI, 902(2)].

[56] Toller (ed.), *Correspondence of the Third Earl of Derby*, p. 48.

because of theological disagreements or differing interpretations of the rule of law – they did not dare breathe that opposition openly.

These divisions came to the fore at Pontefract, where rebels debated articles of grievance to be submitted to the Duke of Norfolk. The final articles did indeed contain the rebels' first explicit rejection of the royal supremacy, but the precise language of that rejection is informative. The article in question, number two in the rebels' list of twenty-four, stated that they would 'have the supreme head of the Church touching *cure animarum* to be restored unto the see of Rome as before it was accustomed to be, and to have the consecrations of the bishops from him without any first fruits or pension to him to be paid out of this realm or else a pension reasonable for the outward defence of our faith'.[57] The second part of this demand, with its remarkable attack on Rome's fiscal policies, indicates that 'conservatism' alone is insufficient to describe the rebels' ideology. Anger at papal exactions had reached even the pilgrims of grace, and they demanded not a return to the *status quo ante* but a new arrangement in which the pope could not siphon wealth from English sees. The first part of the demand, moreover, was far more ambiguous than it sounds. The rebels rejected royal supremacy over the 'cure of souls', a power to which the king had first staked his claim during the 1530 praemunire manoeuvres.[58] Yet the idea that the king had cure of his subjects' souls was part of an extremely liberal reading of the royal supremacy that had never been accepted by such notable 'Henricians' as John Longland and Stephen Gardiner. Thus, while the rebels' support of papal authority was certainly critical of the regime, even the Pontefract articles stopped well short of condemning the royal supremacy as defined by Henrician conservatives.

Even more fascinating was the process by which the issue was debated and this compromise language was adopted. Robert Aske reported that the commons would have 'annulled the whole statute', that is condemned the royal supremacy outright, and that 'all men much murmured at the same, and said it could not stand with God's law' since it would cause 'a division from the unity of the Catholic Church'. Several of the Pilgrimage's leaders, however, most notably Lord Darcy and Sir Robert Constable, were not so convinced. As we have seen already, Darcy was willing to support the royal supremacy, and Constable, despite thinking ecclesiastical authority 'doubtful by the law of God to belong to a king', was not willing to condemn the royal supremacy outright. According to his own testimony, then, Aske himself

---

[57] Anthony Fletcher and Diarmaid MacCulloch, *Tudor Rebellions*, 4th edn (London, 1997), p. 135.
[58] Cited in Dodds and Dodds, *The Pilgrimage of Grace*, I, p. 6.

forged the ecclesiastical compromise, convincing the commons not to reject the king's supremacy altogether and instead putting in the saving clause that the king should not be supreme head 'touching *curam animarum*, which should belong to the bishop of Rome'.[59]

Aske's account is not entirely trustworthy, however, since it was written for the king's eyes, and other accounts suggest that the debate over the royal supremacy was considerably more complex. According to the testimony of Christopher Aske, for instance, Robert Aske first learned to appreciate the subtleties of the royal supremacy in conversations with Archbishop Lee. Aske requested Lee's opinion on the matter while the rebel convocation was in session, and Lee told him that 'touching cure of souls ... it belonged not to the king as king; but punishment of offences of sin and such other as the head of his people, at that therein he was the supreme head'. Aske was apparently enlightened by this precise theological reasoning, since that was 'the first time that ever the said Aske heard that division made touching the said supremacy'.[60]

Similar subtleties were employed in an anonymous ecclesiastical position-paper presented to the conference at Pontefract. The author suggested that:

Where his highness is recognised to be the supreme head of the Church of England, yet for because that he is a temporal man, and that the cure of souls and minis-tration of the sacraments of Christ's Church are spiritual where of necessity [there] must be one head only, and that the bishop of Rome is the most ancient bishop in Christendom ... that it would please our said sovereign lord to admit him to be head of the spiritual matters, so that he should give authority spiritual to the archbishop of Canterbury and the archbishop of York, and they to distribute the same within their provinces, and that the said bishop of Rome have no further meddling.[61]

Here, then, the title of 'supreme head' was retained for the king but utilised only in the temporal realm. The pope was to retain nominal cure of souls and responsibility for the sacraments, but in practice papal authority would ex-tend only far enough to appoint metropolitans for the two English provinces, who would then have absolute jurisdiction. The logical conclusion of this reasoning, although not spelled out explicitly, was that Archbishop Cranmer, having been given his authority by the pope, was within his rights when he annulled the king's marriage to Anne Boleyn. Hence, while this author in some sense opposed the royal supremacy, in practice his politics ran counter to those of more radical anti-Henrician activists.

Another, similarly complex position was laid out in an anonymous peti-tion, ostensibly directed to the king but probably presented to the Pontefract

---

[59] Bateson (ed.), 'The Pilgrimage of Grace and Aske's Examination', quotations at pp. 559, 565, 570.
[60] PRO SP 1/117, fol. 84v [*LP* XII, i, 698(3)].   [61] PRO SP 1/112, fol. 27r [*LP* XI, 1182(2)].

convocation. This petition begrudged not the royal supremacy but rather the fact that the famous saving clause of 1530, that the king was only supreme head of the Church of England 'in[sofar] that it may stand with the law of Christ', had been omitted from the king's more recent pronouncements. It thus argued that certain heretic bishops had corrupted the meaning of the supreme headship by 'naughtily understanding that term', in other words by interpreting the royal supremacy in unreasonably liberal fashion. For this writer, then, the verdict in the king's divorce case was flawed not because the pope had supreme authority but because it was poor legal practice for a man 'to be both judge in his own cause, and party'.[62]

The full extent of disagreement on the matter can be seen in the debate at the rebel convocation, recorded by John Dakyn, rector of Kirkby Ravensworth. He reported that on the article concerning the supremacy there was considerable controversy, with Dr Marshall speaking most vehemently for the pope's cause and Dr Sherwood most adamantly defending the king's authority. Several clerics were present who had been at the convocation where 'superiority' was granted to the king, and many of these registered protests that they had not dared present at the time; most of these, however, seem to have concerned the loss of the saving clause '*in quantum per legem Christi licet*' rather than the royal supremacy per se. Dakyn himself, along with Dr Cliff and Dr Rokeby, argued that the matter was by no means clear and should be referred to a general council. Finally they agreed that the king might be called '*Caput Ecclesiae*' but that he might exercise no clerical jurisdiction such as performing ecclesiastical visitations. This language was written down and 'read openly' in the convocation 'to the intent that every man's consent might be known'. The next day, however, when Aske discovered what the convocation had decided, this compromise language was suddenly reversed. Despite his apparent moderation when dealing with the secular arm of the pilgrimage, Aske was reportedly furious that the clergy had not taken a stronger position, and he threatened that 'the pope's law should have place or else he would fight'. Even at this point there was still controversy, however, as Archbishop Lee objected to the convocation's new, more strongly worded statement that the pope was head of the Church 'by the laws of the Church, general councils, interpretations of approved doctors, and consent of Christian people'. Lee rejected all of these rationales except the final one, then grudgingly allowed the article to be promulgated only on the grounds that it represented 'the consent of Christian people'.[63] Given all of these conflicting views and interests, all formed in dialogue with the rebel rank and file, it seems clear that any settlement of the north that

---

[62] PRO SP 1/112, fols. 31r–32r [*LP* XI, 1182(3)].
[63] PRO SP 1/117, fols. 201v–203v [*LP* XII, i, 786(ii)].

attempted to finesse questions of church government would necessarily create as many problems as it solved.

III

Differences over economic issues and the proper ordering of the commonwealth were also of tremendous significance. There were not only vertical divisions between gentlemen and commons over agrarian and tax policies but also horizontal fissures within the different social classes. Even when grievances received widespread support, moreover, different rebels often had vastly different and contradictory ideas about how best to see those grievances redressed.

There were some basic issues around which different classes could coalesce, and first and foremost among these was taxation. Lay taxes in the 1530s were both heavy and unorthodox, raising fears that ordinary constitutional restraints were being ignored. The fifteenth and tenth granted in 1534, for instance, did not include the ordinary rebate for poverty, nor was it justified on the grounds of military necessity which usually underlay extraordinary revenues. The subsidy granted at the same time was likewise controversial because it was granted in time of peace when the king should not have needed extraordinary revenues. The 1536 Statute of Uses, which closed a loophole through which nobles and gentlemen had long escaped feudal payments to the Crown, may not have concerned the commons directly, but in so far as it represented the Crown's goal of increasing revenues from feudal overlordship, all social classes shared a common financial incentive to stop the government in its tracks.[64] Clerical taxation was also extremely heavy and struck many observers as part and parcel of the king's larger attack on the wealth and independence of the clerical estate. In 1534, Henry VIII replaced traditional clerical annates (moderate fees due to the papacy on the appointment of priests to wealthy benefices) with the so-called 'first fruits', taxing all priests one whole year's income when they took up any new benefice. Soon afterwards, the *Valor Ecclesiasticus* assessed the value of clerical benefices, leading to a tax which annually claimed 10 per cent of all livings. These taxes were clearly oppressive, aimed not merely at raising revenue but at cowing the clergy.[65]

---

[64] Bush, 'Up for the Commonweal'; Bush, 'Enhancements and Importunate Charges'; Bush, 'Tax Reform and Rebellion in Early Tudor England'. It should be noted that tax grievances could be region-specific; the 1534 subsidy, for instance, exempted Westmorland, Cumberland, Northumberland and Durham: see Bush, 'Enhancements and Importunate Charges', p. 410.

[65] Richard Hoyle, 'War and Public Finance', in Diarmaid MacCulloch (ed.), *The Reign of Henry VIII: Politics, Policy and Piety* (New York, 1995), pp. 79–80.

Just as important as real taxes, moreover, were rumours of taxes. It was widely believed that the Crown would collect a tax on livestock, sometimes thought to be rated by the plough, sometimes by the head, and sometimes by the acreage of land under tillage. It was imagined that the nation's supply of gold would be called in to the Tower of London. Rumours held that 'no man shall eat in his house white bread, pig, goose, nor capon but that he should pay a certain [sum] to the king's grace'. It was thought that the Crown would impose a tax of one noble for the performance of priestly functions such as burials, christenings and weddings. It was even rumoured that a new tax would claim one-third of all men's goods. These rumours, if true, would have completely dismantled the exemptions which the poor peasantry traditionally enjoyed from direct royal taxation.[66]

Naturally complaints against royal taxation were crowd-pleasers; there was no party of high taxation in Tudor England. Differences between the rebels therefore centred on what sorts of compromises might be reached with the regime. The articles of the Lincolnshire rebels, for instance, which were later used by Robert Aske in Yorkshire, suggested that the fifteenth and tenth was unfairly burdensome because it involved a fixed payment, irrespective of economic conditions and changes in the real value of the goods being assessed. In particular, since livestock herds had recently suffered heavy losses, the tax effectively assessed the commons at the unreasonable rate of 4d for each cow and 12d for every twenty sheep. In spelling out grievances in such detail, these articles effectively offered a solution: a ratable or sliding scale.[67] The Pontefract articles of December 1536 were more blunt, not worrying about sliding scales but simply demanding that the nation be 'discharged of the quindene and taxes now granted by act of parliament'.[68]

Yet these 'official' demands fell well short of others being canvassed simultaneously among the rebels. John Porman, for instance, a gentleman captain in Lincolnshire, was willing to accept the subsidy already granted but announced that the king 'shall have no more money of the commons during his life'.[69] This idea that Henry VIII had exhausted his tax quota may also have been on the minds of the Louth crowd who bluntly told royal commissioners 'that they would pay no more silver', or on the minds of the rebels who wrote to the mayor of Lincoln demanding 'that his grace shall ask no more money of them'.[70] A slightly different but equally uncompromising position was pronounced by other Lincolnshire rebels, who told a Justice of the Peace

---

[66] *St.P.*, I, p. 482; *LP* XI, 567; see also Bush, 'Up for the Commonweal'; Bush, 'Enhancements and Importunate Charges'.
[67] PRO SP 1/108, fol. 50r [*LP* XI, 705(1)].
[68] Fletcher and MacCulloch, *Tudor Rebellions*, p. 136.
[69] PRO E 36/118, fol. 56v [*LP* XI, 853].
[70] PRO SP 1/106, fol. 248r [*LP* XI, 533] and PRO SP 1/106, fol. 271r [*LP* XI, 553].

that 'the king shall not now nor at any other time hereafter take nor demand no money of his subjects but only for the defence of the realm in time of war'.[71] This argument was also advanced in Yorkshire, where, according to the Imperial ambassador, the rebels believed that 'the king should not take money from his people except to make war on France and Scotland'.[72]

Similar disagreement existed regarding clerical taxes, with the fundamental division, not surprisingly, separating clerics from laymen. At the Pontefract convocation, rebel priests elaborated constitutional and ideological objections to the Act of First Fruits and Tenths, arguing both that 'the clergy of the north parts hath not granted nor consented to the payment of the tenths or first fruits of benefices in the convocation', and that 'no temporal man hath authority by the laws of God to claim any such'. The demands put to the king by the lay rebels, however, never demanded the complete elimination of clerical taxes, nor did they suggest that such taxes were not, within reason, the prerogative of the Crown. The Lincolnshire articles seem to have demanded not the abolition of first fruits and tenths but immunity for benefices with an income less than £20, protecting the more vulnerable parish clergy. The Pontefract articles demanded the abolition of first fruits and tenths for the religious houses only; it was suggested that secular priests would, by their own consent in convocation, agree to 'a rent charge in generality to the augmentation of the Crown'. Robert Aske himself distinguished between first fruits, which he called 'a decay to all religion', and clerical tenths, which he said could 'be borne well enough'.[73]

Even more potentially destabilising than issues of taxation were agrarian grievances. In Yorkshire, for instance, rebels objected to the increase of rents on demesne lands, the enclosure of common lands, and the corruption of landlords who had become entangled with royal office-holding.[74] These grievances were aimed to some degree at the king, both as dispenser of patronage and as landlord, but they were also aimed at local gentlemen. Similarly, in localities from the West Riding to Northumberland rebels objected to the unfair collection of 'gressums', fines paid by customary tenants to their landlords at the changing of either lordship or tenantship. This grievance was partially directed against the Crown, both because gressums had fallen due upon the recent death of Henry VIII's illegitimate son the Duke of Richmond and because of the potential changes in lordship created by the dissolution of the monasteries. But gressums had also been raised contrary to custom by other landlords, and the complaint carried a significant degree of local antagonism. In none of these cases was it automatic that agrarian grievances would pit peasants and smallholders against gentlemen; in the

---

[71] PRO E 36/121, fol. 116r [*LP* XI, 585].   [72] *LP* XI, 1143.
[73] Bush, 'Enhancements and Importunate Charges', quotations at pp. 413–14.
[74] Bush, *The Pilgrimage of Grace*, p. 55.

West Riding, for instance, the commons seem to have been willing to subjugate their private grievances to larger concerns for the commonwealth, while many gentlemen like William Stapulton seem to have been willing to accept agrarian reform.[75] While not *necessarily* leading to class tensions, however, in practice agrarian issues often did so. At Penrith, for example, a gentleman called Anthony Hutton was briefly made a rebel captain, but he was replaced by Robert Mownsey because, as Hutton himself put it, 'the commons would have no gentlemen to be their captains'.[76] In Kendal, the rebels had great difficulty recruiting the local elite to join the rebellion, and when they admitted this to rebels from Dent, the Dent men responded: 'If ye cannot rule them, we shall rule them.'[77] Such divisions were not limited to the far north. In Lincolnshire, gentlemen (and in one extraordinary case the gentlewoman Lady Willoughby) had their property sacked and were incarcerated when they refused to join the rebellion.[78]

Even among supporters of agrarian reform there was significant disagreement over what should be demanded of the government. In early 1537 the North Riding commons presented to Sir John Bulmer a bill which demanded that 'men should pay no gressums'. This proposal to eliminate gressums altogether would have significantly altered the relationship between tenants and landlords, and Bulmer responded: 'This will make the gentlemen and the commons fall forth!' This is not to say, however, that Bulmer and other gentlemen necessarily opposed the *reform* of gressums, nor that there were not intermediate positions available. One suggestion, for instance, was to generalise the payment of 'God's penny', a token payment that had become customary in lieu of gressums in some areas. Another solution demanded 'penny gressum, penny rent', in other words that gressums become fixed payments equal to the rent.[79] Yet another solution, which became normative when it was incorporated into the rebels' Pontefract articles, was that gressums become fixed payments of no more than double the rent.[80] Clearly it would be difficult for the rebels to construct a compromise around which all these different voices could rally.

Similar controversy emerged on the issue of tithes. The Cumberland rebels, for instance, demanded that 'all the tithes . . . remain to every man his own doing therefore according to their duty', in other words calling for tithes to become voluntary.[81] Remarkably, this radical solution was actually adopted in Westmorland, where the Appleby council declared that tithes would become

[75] Ibid., p. 55.   [76] Ibid., p. 332, citing PRO SP 1/117, fol. 55r.
[77] Ibid., p. 253, citing PRO SP 1/118, fols. 139v–140r.
[78] See S. J. Gunn, 'Peers, Commons, and Gentry in the Lincolnshire Revolt of 1536'.
[79] Bush and Bownes, *The Defeat of the Pilgrimage of Grace*, p. 267.
[80] Fletcher and MacCulloch, *Tudor Rebellions*, p. 136; see also Bush, *The Pilgrimage of Grace*, pp. 171–2.
[81] Dodds and Dodds, *The Pilgrimage of Grace*, I, p. 370; Hoyle, *The Pilgrimage of Grace*, pp. 252–3.

an optional payment rather than a requirement. To Barnard Townley, a Cumberland priest who was himself active in the rising, this shocking attack on the clerical estate would bring 'all to common' and result in radical social levelling. Other rebels, however, tried to construct compromises with which priests might make common cause, notably the proposal that tithes be payable in kind rather than in coin so that payments would always correspond to harvests rather than becoming fixed by precedent.[82]

With all these highly flammable social issues on the table, it should be no surprise that some rebels acted in ways that savoured of 'disorder'. In Lancashire on 28 November, for instance, a band of rebels expanded their recruitment efforts into a terror campaign, extorting money and harness from their neighbours. Unlike elsewhere in the north, these men came with their faces blackened to hide their identities, a tactic wholly alien to the 'society of orders' which the rebels had tried symbolically to recreate; in hiding their identities, these men could never petition the king, but only break the law.[83] There was also a 'common bruit' among the rebels that they would march on London and punish the king's evil counsellors in the manner of 1381.[84] As the gentry well understood, this would mean crossing the Rubicon: either they would force the utter capitulation of the regime, or else they would quickly be killed. Regardless of their support for the rebellion, it was only a small number of elite rebels who were so convinced that compromise and negotiation were impossible that they were willing to take this risk.[85]

A strain of radicalism can even be found within the pilgrimage which blamed the king himself rather than evil counsellors for the nation's ills. When the pilgrim host around Beverley received a letter praising their army as 'able to give battle to any king christened', some rebels misinterpreted this statement as an invitation to battle Henry VIII and became extremely excited about the prospect; as a horrified William Stapulton put it: 'the hearts of our wild people was set aflutter'.[86] Another controversy over the issue of royal culpability arose in Dent when William Breyar, a servant of the king, found himself in a crowd of rebels. One man, identified as a smith, heard that Breyar wore the king's livery and told him: 'Thy master is a thief, for he pulleth down all our churches in the country.' Others in the crowd, however, argued angrily against the smith's opinion: 'It is not the king's deed but the d[eed] of Crumwell, and if we had him here we would crum him [and crum]

---

[82] Bush, *The Pilgrimage of Grace*, pp. 303 and 336–42.
[83] *LP* XI, 1230.   [84] Bush, *The Pilgrimage of Grace*, pp. 119–20.
[85] As should be clear, I fundamentally disagree with Hoyle's assertion that elite captains of the revolt were unwilling participants. I think this argument enormously underestimates the complexity of the multi-sided game played by all the 1536–7 rebels, both elite and common, and reads intrinsically ambiguous evidence in highly selective ways.
[86] PRO E 36/118, fol. 77r [*LP* XII, i, 392].

him that he was never so crummed, and if thy master were [here] we would new crown him.'[87] With such disagreements over the most basic issues of loyalty, culpability and good order, it is not hard to imagine why a workable settlement proved elusive to the rebellion's ostensible leaders.

IV

With the rebellion's frenetic push and pull between cohesion and fragmentation now described, it becomes possible to place the collapse of the movement within the wider context of popular politics. The key to this process was the settlement reached at Doncaster between rebel captains and the Duke of Norfolk in December 1536. At this fateful meeting, Norfolk agreed on the king's behalf that a parliament would meet in northern England to consider the country's grievances, and he promised the rebels a full and unconditional pardon. In return, the pilgrims swore to put down their weapons and return home; Robert Aske, never lacking a flair for ceremony, publicly ripped off his pilgrim badge and declared his mission accomplished.

It has recently been argued that the Doncaster agreement represented a stunning victory for the rebels. If the north had remained unified after receiving the royal pardon, it is claimed, Henry VIII would have had no choice but to dismantle the Reformation:

> The Anglican church would have returned to Roman Catholicism; the dissolution of the monasteries would not have occurred; the subjection of the church to the state, and the clergy to the laity, would have been less extreme; most of what Thomas Cromwell stood for would have been rejected; the Reformation would have had to evolve as a social movement rather than as something imposed upon society by the state; and the massive redistribution of landed wealth that followed the Dissolution, with its well-recognized social and political consequences, would not have happened.[88]

Against this view, a contradictory argument has emerged suggesting that Doncaster was no victory for the rebels at all, since it won no concrete concessions besides a pardon. This view presumes that the gentlemen captains who struck the Doncaster bargain had been coerced into involvement with the rebellion and spent much of the autumn looking for ways to mitigate its ferocity and extricate themselves from its clutches. Doncaster thus represented the successful culmination of a gentry strategy to end the revolt peacefully, with or without any substantive changes in government policy; it was literally a 'gentlemen's agreement' in which the rebellious commons were betrayed by the very leaders in whom they had put their trust.[89]

---

[87] *LP* XI, 841.

[88] Bush and Bownes, *The Defeat of the Pilgrimage of Grace*, preface, p. i.

[89] Hoyle, *The Pilgrimage of Grace*, ch. 10, ch. 12 and *passim*; quotation on p. 359.

From these two very different interpretations of the Doncaster agreement, divergent understandings have emerged concerning the nature of the post-pardon revolts which shattered the Doncaster framework and gave the king an excuse to crush the north. In the former view, the post-pardon rebels were 'dedicated pilgrims' who fully subscribed to the 'basic aims of the pilgrimage of grace' but did not realise the magnitude of their victory and thus foolishly squandered it.[90] The post-pardon rebels, in other words, differed from the original pilgrims only in their lack of political acumen. In the latter view, on the other hand, the post-pardon rebels were rank-and-file pilgrims who were finally freed from dependence on their disingenuous gentry captains. The post-pardon revolts, in other words, represented the authentic, highly radical face of the Pilgrimage of Grace, an intrinsically popular movement now no longer muddied by manipulation from above.[91]

A third model for understanding the political fallout of the Doncaster agreement quickly becomes apparent, however, if we take as our starting point the arguments presented so far in this chapter: the Pilgrimage of Grace was not a unified revolt with 'basic aims' or an authentic core but rather was an intrinsically unstable and politically contested movement. This contestation, moreover, did not break down in any simple way along class lines; some issues separated commons from gentry, other issues separated clergy from laity, and still others grew out of the very real differences in ideology and religio-political temperament at the heart of popular politics. These observations suggest that the fragmentation of the Pilgrimage of Grace was part and parcel of a more general splintering of Catholic opinion in which the staunchest resistors to the Reformation were politically marginalised and defeated by their Catholic coreligionists.

To see this process at work, we need to consider the Doncaster agreement itself and the many wedges which it thrust into the rebels' ostensible unity. The agreement that the Duke of Norfolk negotiated in the king's name involved no concrete changes in government policy but merely promised a parliament to consider rebel grievances, effectively deferring the question of concessions to a later date. The rebels did win a pardon, which the Crown had strenuously resisted, but the Doncaster agreement demilitarised the Pilgrimage with Cromwell still in power, the Ten Articles still in force, the fifteenth and tenth and clerical subsidy still due, and so on. This arrangement, while certainly not ideal from the Crown's point of view, was no unmitigated success for the rebels, and many of the government's most vociferous opponents resented it from the start. Thus when Aske presented his tentative agreement with Norfolk to the commons assembled at Pontefract, according

---

[90] Bush and Bownes, *The Defeat of the Pilgrimage of Grace*, p. 289.
[91] Hoyle, *The Pilgrimage of Grace*, chs. 13–15.

to Marmaduke Neville 'diverse evil disposed persons bore such word unto the commons . . . that it was as much as gentlemen and of the most substantial of the commons could stay the rest, in so much that we thought we should be fain to divide, calling all them that were disposed to take the king's most gracious pardon to come to a side'.[92]

At the crux of disagreement about Doncaster was the issue of what exactly had been decided. The written pardon issued to the rebels, for instance, was supposedly a legally binding document; once it was issued, all questions concerning the rebels' legal jeopardy should have been put to rest. In practice, however, things were considerably more complex. The pardon was, in theory, a contract, and while it was offered to the rebels unconditionally, its *wording* bound recipients to a series of propositions that they were required to ratify by making 'humble submission' to the Crown.[93] Most noxious among these propositions was the statement that the person pardoned had 'attempted and committed manifest and open rebellion against his most royal majesty'. Many pilgrims utterly denied that this was the case, since they had merely 'petitioned' the Crown, and some northerners stated bluntly in the weeks following Doncaster that they would rather have had 'some of their petitions granted of the king than to have a pardon, for they never offended the king wherefore they should have any pardon'.[94] Of equal importance was the statement in the text of the pardon that the king had 'chief charge of you under God both of your souls and bodies'. This claim not only reaffirmed the royal supremacy, but seemed to echo a particularly radical interpretation of the king's powers that gave him cure of souls within his kingdom. These subtleties were not lost on the commons, and at least one post-pardon list of rebel articles described 'the great error which is in our pardon, that is that no man is pardoned but those which taketh the king for supreme head of the Church and to have cure and charge of every man's body and soul, and those that take him as king of his realm without cure of men's body and soul be

---

[92] PRO E 36/118, fol. 116r [*LP* XII, i, 29]. Hoyle mocks what he calls the Dodds' 'charming' notion that this 'division' referred to a vote, arguing instead that it indicated 'that the gentry thought that they might have to call on those who supported the treaty to fight those who opposed it' (Hoyle, *Pilgrimage of Grace*, p. 362). This mocking tone is unfortunate, since given what we know of votes and councils among the rebels, the Dodds' interpretation seems reasonable enough. More importantly, Hoyle underestimates how closely related elections and fights were in the sixteenth century. Any contested election could result in violence, and 'divisions' were very much physical representations of authority intended to convince minorities to accept the will of the majority rather than risk a fight. See Mark Kishlansky, *Parliamentary Selection: Social and Political Choice in Early Modern England* (Cambridge, 1986).

[93] Bush and Bownes, *The Defeat of the Pilgrimage of Grace*, appx. 4. Matters were further muddled by the fact that a differently worded pardon issued by Suffolk six days before was speedily withdrawn: Bush and Bownes, *The Defeat of the Pilgrimage of Grace*, p. 10.

[94] PRO E 36/119, fol. 29r [*LP* XII, i, 201]; see also PRO SP 1/115, fol. 215r [*LP* XII, i, 369].

all unpardoned every one'.[95] The pardon claimed, moreover, that leniency was being shown to the rebels because their 'offences proceeded of ignorance and by cause of sundry false tales... spitefully set abroad amongst you by certain malicious and seditious persons'. This not only trivialised the very real sense of grievance felt by many rebels, but also implied that those who had spread rumours the previous October, as opposed to those who had merely responded to them, remained 'seditious' and thus in some sense outlaws.[96]

As if this were not enough, there were numerous oddities in the form of the pardon which fuelled the fires of conspiracy theorists among the commons. The pardon, for instance, repeatedly referred to the king as 'he' rather than 'we', implying that it had been issued by Cromwell rather than the king.[97] This was a matter of grave concern, since only a royal pardon could guarantee the pilgrims' safety. Similarly, the pardon announced, on the one hand, that by its very promulgation all rebels were pardoned, but, on the other hand, it stated that 'his highness is pleased and contented that you and every of you from time to time shall and may have, upon your suit to be made hereafter in the king's chancery, his said most gracious and free pardon under his great seal thereof, and that you may sue without any further bill or warrant to be obtained for the same'. In other words, it was left extremely ambiguous whether the proclamation *was* a pardon or was merely a *promise* of pardon. Lastly, the pardon itself was issued on 9 December, while a pardon which was supposed to be final had been announced to the commons on 7 December and then read to them a day later. It appeared to the commons that the pardon issued was not the same pardon that had been agreed to, with the possibility that emendations had been made in the intervening period; there was no way this suggestion of tampering could be either proved or disproved.[98]

If the status of the pardon was open to interpretation despite being written down, other aspects of the agreement, relying entirely upon rumour and unverifiable accounts, were as fluid as public opinion. It was generally assumed, for instance, that a parliament was supposed to be convened at York to debate rebel grievances. But when would that parliament meet, and at what point in time would a failure to call that parliament constitute a violation of the agreement? Some rebels believed that the parliament was to meet immediately. For instance, an undated bill listing reasons why the Doncaster agreement was 'but feigned policy to subdue the commoners' suggested that 'we should have had a parliament at York at the twentieth day and had none'; this presumably was based on a rumour that the king had agreed to

[95] PRO SP 1/114, fol. 191r [*LP* XII, i, 138].
[96] For the text of the pardon, see Bush and Bownes, *The Defeat of the Pilgrimage of Grace*, appx. 4.
[97] See, e.g., PRO E 36/119, fol. 29v [*LP* XII, i, 201].
[98] Bush and Bownes, *The Defeat of the Pilgrimage of Grace*, pp. 39–40 and appx. 4.

convene the York parliament within twenty days and therefore had broken his word.[99] Robert Aske, on the contrary, told Bigod's rebels in January 1537 that the king had not broken his word at all because 'the parliament and the convocation is appointed to be at York at Whitsuntide', in other words in late May.[100] This in itself was something of a retreat from the ambiguous position enshrined in the Pontefract demand that a northern parliament must be 'shortly summoned'.[101]

All of these expectations, however, were a far cry from what the king envisioned. In a letter dated 4 December, for instance, the king instructed Norfolk to 'condescend to a parliament, to be holden at such place as we shall appoint, at Michaelmas next ensuing', in other words the following September.[102] An undated memorandum of the Privy Council from sometime after 1 January, moreover, referred to the possibility of 'his grace's repair this summer to York, for the parliament, coronation, and the perfect establishment of the country in quiet'.[103] Thus, while the rebels may have won a significant victory in principle by forcing the king to convene a parliament, in practice, without a set date for that parliament to meet, there was little they could do if he chose to stall and equivocate. They had either to renew their military option, as some chose to do, or else simply trust the king, as others chose to do. But, as long as the king held out the promise of a future parliament without actually convening one, he effectively regained the upper hand. This was not lost on the commons, some of whom believed that their strength lay in arms rather than in the institutional power of a potential parliament. Hence it was said to be 'a whole common voice' throughout Yorkshire in January that 'if their harness was taken from them before the parliament were holden, they thought and said that they would rise again, for they thought then that the parliament men should not obtain those things that they rose for'.[104]

The question of the dissolved monasteries was also problematic. According to the reconstruction of negotiations at Doncaster proposed by Michael Bush and David Bownes, it was at first agreed by Aske and Norfolk on 6 December that, in those places where the rebels had restored monks to their houses, those monks would be allowed to stay, alongside the new royal farmers of the houses, until the status of monasteries was reconsidered by the forthcoming York parliament. However, on 7 December some of the commons took issue with Aske's negotiating tactics and demanded that he accept no settlement in which royal farmers remained in the abbeys. Aske seems to have agreed to this condition in principle when addressing the rebels, but

[99] PRO SP 1/114, fol. 191r [*LP* XII, i, 138].   [100] PRO E 36/122, fol. 67r [*LP* XII, i, 103(4)].
[101] Fletcher and MacCulloch, *Tudor Rebellions*, p. 136.
[102] *St.P.*, I, p. 521. See Dodds and Dodds, *The Pilgrimage of Grace*, II, pp. 15 and 23.
[103] *St.P.*, I, p. 536.   [104] PRO E 36/119, fol. 25r [*LP* XII, i, 201].

then on 8 December he reverted to his original deal with Norfolk, accepting the presence of royal farmers in the final agreement. The northern commons were thus baffled in the weeks that followed over whether royal attempts to put farmers back on abbey lands were violations of the Doncaster agreement or not.[105] Perhaps the most extraordinary result of this confusion was a ceremony held at Easby Abbey in Yorkshire (and elsewhere in the weeks that followed) in which the canons were 'put forth of their house by the king's authority and ... taken in again by the same, and so remain until the determination of the next parliament'. In other words, the canons who had illegally re-entered their houses symbolically exited then re-entered again, believing that such re-entry, now supposedly occurring under the Doncaster dispensation, was legally valid and had the king's blessing. This was, in fact, very far from the case, and in late February the king ordered Norfolk to suppress Easby on the grounds of its 'resistance ... since the Doncaster appointment'.[106]

Taxation was also an issue of deep confusion. Many among the commons interpreted the Doncaster agreement to institute a moratorium on payments of all disputed taxes until the York parliament could settle those disputes once and for all. The discord created by this issue can best be seen from a meeting on 9 January in which Aske attempted to persuade the people of Beverley that the king 'hath granted us all our designs and petitions'. John Hallom responded by asking him: 'How happens it then if this be true that the tenths be gathered?' in other words implying that taxes (in this case clerical tenths) were being collected contrary to the agreement. Aske responded by muddying the issue, saying that he had not heard such reports, but that if they were true then they must refer to the clerical subsidy that was 'freely granted to the king's highness by the clergy'. This fudging may have helped Aske avoid a panic among his constituents, but it did not bring him much closer to the government's view, which was that the Doncaster agreement had not materially affected taxes in any way: since the law of the land gave the king taxes, those taxes remained due.[107]

On religious issues, the king did throw the rebels a bone during the truce in the weeks before the Doncaster settlement, but the concessions he offered were of the sort to exacerbate tensions between the rebels rather than soothe them. In a circular letter to the bishops dated 19 November, the king railed against religious radicals who preached against the 'honest, laudable, and tolerable ceremonies, usages and customs of the Church'. He also pronounced an absolute ban on clerical marriage and effectively suspended all preaching

---

[105] Bush and Bownes, *The Defeat of the Pilgrimage of Grace*, p. 16. See also *St.P.*, I, p. 534.
[106] Bush and Bownes, *The Defeat of the Pilgrimage of Grace*, pp. 93–4 and 118–20.
[107] PRO E 36/119, fols. 21v–22r [*LP* XII, i, 201]; see also Bush and Bownes, *The Defeat of the Pilgrimage of Grace*, p. 37.

licences, presumably in preparation for a block grant of new licences to more conservative clerics. These changes met with hearty approval among some rebels, and Lord Darcy remarked to Archbishop Lee that of the king's letter 'all true Catholics may joy'.[108] Yet, at the same time, the new circular was notable both for its omissions and for its reaffirmations of government policy. There was no reference to the royal supremacy, except the tacit assumption that by issuing such a letter to the clergy the king still claimed authority over the Church. There was no mention of monasteries, nor any hint of change on the issue of ecclesiastical wealth that had so incensed some rebels in October. The letter also ordered bishops to read 'our said articles' – in other words the Ten Articles – 'every holy day . . . openly in your cathedral church, or the parish church of the place where ye shall fortune to be . . . and in no wise, in the rest of your words which ye shall then speak of yourself, if you speak anything, utter any word that shall make the same or any word in the same doubtful to the people'. This order was, on the one hand, directed against evangelicals who had elaborately over-interpreted the omission of four sacraments from the Ten Articles to imply the abrogation of those sacraments. But, on the other hand, it clearly re-enshrined the Ten Articles as the law of the land, and its statement that the articles were to be read aloud on holy days pointedly reminded the commons that there were far fewer holy days than there used to be. Thus, while the king's circular would have been palliative to those who feared *further* innovation in the Church, to those who considered the royal supremacy and other *current* aspects of the Church of England heretical, it was utterly unacceptable.[109]

This line in the sand was reaffirmed by the Duke of Norfolk when he returned to the north in February 1537. In an undated letter, the king thanked Norfolk for his support for the royal supremacy, since Norfolk had throughout his travels declared 'the great usurpation of the bishops of Rome in this realm'. The king told Norfolk that he was gratified by 'how discreetly, plainly, and truly you paint and set forth those persons that call themselves religious in the colours of their hypocrisy, [so] that the ignorant people may perceive how they have been abused in them, and the [*sic*] rather leave the superstitions into which they have of long time trained them'.[110] This was hardly the sort of rhetoric which the northern commons wanted to hear, and it must have fuelled the perception of many of the more radical pilgrims that the York parliament, even if it occurred, would produce equivocal results at best.

[108] *LP* XI, 1336.

[109] The circular letter was issued in two versions, with slightly more forceful wording for the more radical bishops. See Gilbert Burnet, *The History of the Reformation of the Church of England*, ed. Nicholas Pocock., 7 vols. (Oxford, 1865), IV, pp. 396–9.

[110] *St.P.* , I, p. 538.

V

Thus a whole series of issues at the heart of the 1536 rebellions – the royal supremacy, the fate of the monasteries, economic abuses – was very much up for grabs in early 1537. The king had promised to listen to the north's grievances at a York parliament, had issued a pardon and had announced that he would symbolically renew his bonds with the north by having his new queen, Jane Seymour, crowned there. Yet, despite the promise of future redress, the king's public statements and actions suggested that the central policies of the Henrician Reformation, especially the royal supremacy, were not negotiable, while other policies might be finessed and compromised rather than yielded altogether.

It should be no surprise, then, that the north divided over whether to uphold the Doncaster settlement or push for more. For those who had expressed willingness to accept a partial or narrowly defined royal supremacy over the Church and whose livelihoods did not directly depend on monasteries, Doncaster seemed an acceptable compromise. No doubt they hoped that the king would sacrifice a royal counsellor or two, but, as long as he made some concessions, the king could be allowed to save face by remaining nominally head of the Church and perhaps keeping the monasteries he had already spoiled. Yet, for those who considered the royal supremacy, the Ten Articles and the dissolution of the monasteries grossly heretical, such a settlement was not acceptable. To these pilgrims, Aske had clearly sold the commons down the river when he agreed to a deferred settlement. When they read the king's repeated reaffirmations of his lordship over the Church, they must have had no doubt that renewed rebellion was necessary. To those whose lives were directly affected by the downfall of the lesser monasteries, moreover, especially the monks themselves, it must have seemed like they were being set up as sacrificial lambs, to be used by the York parliament as bargaining chips in negotiations to prevent *further* spoliation of the Church. The same logic applied to the pilgrims who had suggested the most radical social reforms, to whom it must have seemed folly to lay down their arms in anticipation of parliamentary negotiations which would inevitably result in compromise.

In villages and towns, then, vocal minorities among the ex-rebels began to agitate for renewed rebellion. From the beginning, their rhetoric was far more radical than it had been the previous October, because in an important sense these new outbreaks of violence were without recent precedent in their political implications. 'Risings of the commons' were assimilable within a traditional, hierarchical worldview because they were, at some level, elaborate public rituals in which grievances were put before the king for redress. In 1537, however, the nation's grievances had *already* been declared to the king and a pardon had *already* been granted. The post-pardon rebels thus appeared to have far more frightening goals: not to negotiate but to enact their will through violence and usurpation. In the West Riding, for instance, there was talk of raising a new army of 40,000 to march on London, execute Cromwell and 'put [the king] in such a fear that he would be glad to take the broad water'.[111] When the monks of Sawley wrote to Sir Thomas Percy at Christmas 1536 encouraging him to renew the rebellion, they sent him a 'bent royal', that is a coin bearing an image of the king bent in half; a bent coin was a traditional symbol for a pilgrimage vow, but in this context it also had unmistakable anti-government overtones.[112] One new rebel oath ordered 'if any lord or gentleman do deny to take this oath, then to put them to death, and put the next of his blood in his place, and if he do deny put him to death in like case, so one after another [until] one of the blood will take the oath'.[113] At Lenton Abbey in Nottinghamshire, an opponent of the Doncaster settlement remarked that it was 'alms to hang' the pilgrims who had negotiated at Doncaster, since 'he that will keep no promise with God Himself but pulls down His churches, he will keep no promise with them. But if they had gone forth onward up and stricken off his head, then they had done well'.[114]

The uprisings that followed the pardon invariably began with groups of pilgrims refusing to compromise on issues that had been finessed at Doncaster. The issue of the royal supremacy was often crucial; indeed, the ubiquity of ecclesiological arguments among the post-pardon rebels stands in stark contrast to their almost complete absence before the Doncaster agreement. Soon after Christmas in Richmond, for instance, John Dakyn (a former parson of the parish) exhorted the people 'that their belief in the Bishop of Rome's authority was *nihil ad salute*'. For his trouble, several 'lewd fellows of the town' tried to pull him out of the church at mass time, but they were prevented by 'Rauf Gower and other honest men' who persuaded them to desist. Even this action proved insufficient, however, and soon thereafter Gower found himself 'in jeopardy'.[115] A similar incident involved Robert Thompson, the priest who had led the 'captains' mass' at Penrith the previous autumn. At the end of January 1537, several parishioners told Thompson 'that it was the parish's commandment' that he should 'pray for the pope, for they said [in] all places thereabouts that they did so'. According to his own, obviously self-serving testimony, Thompson agreed out of fear and prayed for the pope just once (*after* he prayed for the king as supreme head

[111] Bush and Bownes, *The Defeat of the Pilgrimage of Grace*, p. 175.
[112] PRO E 36/120, fol. 114r [*LP* XII, i, 491]. On bent coins as pilgrim vows, see Eamon Duffy, *The Stripping of the Altars: Traditional Religion in England 1400–1580* (New Haven, 1992), p. 183.
[113] PRO SP 1/114, fol. 227r [*LP* XII, i, 163(1)].
[114] *LP* XII, i, 892.   [115] PRO SP 1/117, fol. 206r [*LP* XII, i, 788].

of the Church), after which he fled from his benefice.[116] In January 1537, likewise, a bill claiming to represent 'the whole assent of all the whole parishioners and tenants of my lords of Northumberland' ordered a priest named 'Master Deyn' to 'pray for the pope of Rome the head of our holy mother Church'; it included the thinly veiled threat, 'if ye will not, send us word to the contrary'.[117]

Perhaps the most remarkable parish conflict over the royal supremacy occurred at Kendal in Westmorland. On the Sunday after Christmas, 'certain of the lewd persons of Kendal town that were most busy in the first insurrection stirred up suddenly [at the] time of the beads' bidding and would have had the priest to bid the beads after the old manner and pray for the pope'. These agitators, estimated by one observer to be three-hundred-strong, found themselves opposing both a parish priest named Robert Appylgarthe and the 'twenty-four which is appointed for the weal of the church', a group of parish householders who, while called 'the twenty-four', in fact numbered closer to sixty. The bailiff of the town 'fetched the king's pardon' and read it to the commons, charging them in the king's name that 'as many as would enjoy the benefit of that the king's pardon' should 'be still and make no business'. Many of the parishioners, however, would not be mollified, crying: 'Come down, churl, thou art false to the commons.' One man bluntly announced that 'he cared for no pardon', and the agitators threatened to dunk Appylgarthe and the twenty-four 'in the water'. The bailiff eventually convinced the churchgoers to accept the status quo until Norfolk's return to the north, but, by the end of January, the same parishioners were agitating again for the papal primacy. On 4 February one Walter Brown, described as 'second curate there' and in fact one of the agitators from the previous month, announced: 'Commons, I will bid the beads as ye will have me', and he 'prayed for the pope and his cardinals'.[118]

Rejection of the royal supremacy also contributed directly to the large risings led by John Hallom and Francis Bigod. In early January, Bigod explained to Hallom his opinion that 'the king's office was to have no cure of souls' and that, while the head of the Church might be a spiritual man such as an archbishop, it could not be the king, since 'he should with the sword defend all spiritual men in their right'. From his uniquely evangelical perspective, Bigod also suggested that 'for heresy both the king and the bishop of Rome

[116] PRO E 36/119, fol. 79r [*LP* XII, i, 687(4)]; *LP* XII, i, 687(2), quoted in Bush, *The Pilgrimage of Grace*, p. 307.
[117] PRO *SP* 1/107, fol. 144r [*LP* XI, 655]. For the dating of this MS and the suggestion that it circulated widely, see Bush, *The Pilgrimage of Grace*, p. 233.
[118] PRO E 36/119, fol. 128v [*LP* XII, i, 914]; PRO SP 1/115, fol. 249r [*LP* XII, i, 384]; *LP* XII, i, 671(3).

might be deprived lawfully'.[119] Some days later, when the two conspirators met again, Bigod showed Hallom his treatise against the royal supremacy and discussed with him the deficiencies of the pardon, complaining that by it the king would claim cure of his soul. It was at this meeting that the two men plotted their assaults on Hull and Scarborough. Significantly, this meeting occurred at Watton priory, where at least two monks and the sub-prior seem to have been co-conspirators. Watton priory was already known as a hotbed of dissent against the royal supremacy; as one witness put it: 'The sub-prior, the confessor of the nuns, the vicar of Watton, and one Anthony, canon of Watton, be great founders and setters forth of this matter of sedition, for he heard them and every [one] of them since Christmas last at sundry times say that it would never be well as long as the king's grace should be the supreme head of the Church. And that the same would not be reformed without [that] the people did set forward again with a new insurrection.'[120] Also resident in the priory were William Swinburne, a friar of Beverley, and Thomas Asheton, another canon of Watton, both of whom had written manuscript tracts against the royal supremacy in 1536 which John Hallom is known to have read.[121]

Other outbreaks of disorder arose from the confusion over whether, according to the Doncaster agreement, monks were entitled to stay in the religious houses they had reoccupied. The monks of Sawley Abbey, for instance, had been informed by Robert Aske in the days immediately following the pardon that they were to remain in their house, which had been restored by the commons, until the expected York parliament decided their fate. Then, around 19 December, Aske gave a seemingly contradictory order, telling them to yield to anyone who commanded them in the king's name to vacate their house. This contradiction was probably part of a legalistic attempt by Aske to square the circle, letting monks remain technically in control of their houses while allowing royal farmers to receive the proceeds of the lands. To the monks and their supporters, however, Aske's actions must have seemed like a fundamental betrayal of the cause for which they had rebelled. As one bill put it in conscious repudiation of Aske, the restored monks were 'in their houses by the commons, and not by the agreement at Doncaster'.[122] Thus, at Christmas, the monks of Sawley wrote to Sir Thomas Percy, bluntly asking him to renew the Pilgrimage, and it was widely rumoured that any attempt to suppress the abbey would be met with violence.[123]

[119] A. G. Dickens, *Lollards and Protestants in the Diocese of York* (London, 1982), pp. 92–3.
[120] PRO E 36/119, fol. 23r [*LP* XII, i, 201].
[121] Bush and Bownes, *The Defeat of the Pilgrimage of Grace*, p. 44.
[122] PRO SP 1/114, fol. 191r [*LP* XII, i, 138].
[123] Bush and Bownes, *The Defeat of the Pilgrimage of Grace*, pp. 145–58.

At Cartmel Priory in Lancashire, disagreement over the fate of the monasteries had violent and tragic consequences. The monks were informed by John Dakyn and William Collyns that by the king's consent they should stay in their house until 'a further direction be taken in parliament' by which 'your monasteries [will] stand forever'. Not only did these monks stay in their house, however, but they also allied themselves with local peasants to resist attempts by the royal farmer, Thomas Holcroft, to reoccupy the priory's lands. Little is known of this altercation, although Bush and Bownes have cleverly argued that Holcroft may have been an object of particular violence because of his involvement in a scheme to tear down the priory church, which was also the parish church. What is clear, however, is that the government had a very different interpretation of the Doncaster agreement and considered events at Cartmel very serious indeed. As William Collyns later noted: 'Four of the brethren of the said house of Cartmel and eight yeomen were put to execution for withstanding the king's farmer, Mr. Holcroft, and stirring a new commotion.'[124]

On economic issues, as on issues of religious policy, post-pardon disturbances erupted when groups of pilgrims determined that the Doncaster agreement and its promised parliament would not provide sufficient redress. Of crucial concern in some areas, for instance, were tithes, particularly the demand that tithes be made optional or that they be payable in kind rather than in cash. Despite the importance of this issue in the Pilgrimage, the Pontefract articles submitted to the king had omitted tithes entirely, meaning that the issue would not be on the agenda at the hypothetical York parliament. This was presumably because clerics played a leading role in drafting the articles, as well as because the erosion of tithes ran contrary to the main thrust of the rebellion to preserve 'the privileges and rights of the Church'.[125] Thus, for pilgrims particularly agitated over the tithe issue, Doncaster provided no redress at all, and many among the post-pardon rebels made it a priority to call a new rebel council, to be convened at Richmond on 5 February, 'to meet the duke of Norfolk about their tithes'.[126]

In Westmorland an issue of particular concern to the rebels was enclosure, and here, as Michael Bush and David Bownes have shown, there is no question that the pilgrim high command really did betray their northern allies. In a letter to Lord Darcy dated 19 November, the Westmorland rebels had demanded the removal of enclosures that were 'noisome for poor men', which in local context meant recent attempts by the Clifford family to enclose areas of forest waste to create new pastures and farmsteads.

---

[124] PRO E 36/119, fols. 127r–129r [*LP* XII, i, 914]; Bush and Bownes, *The Defeat of the Pilgrimage of Grace*, pp. 231–7.

[125] Fletcher and MacCulloch, *Tudor Rebellions*, pp. 135–7.

[126] Bush and Bownes, *The Defeat of the Pilgrimage of Grace*, pp. 246–8.

When this demand was translated into the Pontefract articles, however, its language changed significantly, demanding that the existing 'statute for enclosures and intakes' be enforced and 'all intakes [and] enclosures since anno 4 Henry VII to be pulled down *except mountains, forest, and parks*'.[127] In other words, the grievances at the heart of the Westmorland revolt, which concerned enclosures of forest waste, were exempted from the articles submitted to the king. The result, not surprisingly, was renewed rioting in January 1537, most importantly attacks on fences erected by the Cliffords, beginning in Kirkby Stephen and spreading quickly through the neighbouring parishes.

We must not conclude from all these seemingly sensible arguments for renewed rebellion, however, that a majority of rank-and-file pilgrims were unhappy with the Doncaster accord. In practice most ex-rebels chose not to violate the Doncaster agreement but rather trusted that the king, now aware of the nation's grievances, would put Church and commonwealth right. Besides the work of pilgrim leaders like Aske and Constable to stop the post-pardon revolts, there is copious evidence of commoners opposing the new uprisings. When the abbot of Holm Cultram ordered his tenants to join an army outside Carlisle, those tenants unanimously refused.[128] When Francis Bigod wrote to the leaders of the town of Durham asking them to renew their rebellion, they refused on the grounds that they had accepted the king's pardon and were now sworn to rise for no man but the king or the Earl of Westmorland in the king's name.[129] When the rebels tried to raise a new host in Richmond, one of the leading centres of revolt the previous October, they found that 'the inhabitants of the said town would in no wise condescend in their opinion'.[130] The inhabitants of Hull largely refused to join with John Hallom when he tried to take that town, and even among Hallom's own company no fewer then four men separately betrayed him to town authorities. Such examples could be repeated endlessly.

The decision not to rebel again, of course, was motivated to a large degree by loyalism and the belief that it was the prerogative of the king to rule rather than be ruled. But, in the context of 1536–7, this loyalism had momentous consequences that were not lost on the pilgrims of grace. To accept the king's pardon and trust him to restore the Church and commonwealth *before* Cromwell was removed from power, the papal supremacy was restored, or the Ten Articles were revoked, was to accept that those issues were negotiable rather than absolute. The pilgrims who did not rekindle their revolt after the Doncaster agreement, in other words, believed that making a deal with

---

[127] My emphasis. Bush and Bownes, *The Defeat of the Pilgrimage of Grace*, pp. 292–3; Bush, *The Pilgrimage of Grace*, pp. 311–12.

[128] Bush and Bownes, *The Defeat of the Pilgrimage of Grace*, p. 276.

[129] *LP* XII, i, 148.   [130] PRO *SP* 1/115, fol. 208r [*LP* XII, i, 362].

Henry VIII, for all his faults, was *not* tantamount to making a pact with the Devil.

The effects of this choice for the fortunes of English Catholicism can be seen in the many former rebels who found themselves working as agents of the Cromwellian government in the years after 1536. Most strikingly, when the king constituted his Council of the North a year after the outbreak of rebellion, it included, under the leadership of Bishop Cuthbert Tunstall of Durham, no fewer than five former leaders of the Pilgrimage of Grace: Sir Ralph Ellerkar, Sir Thomas Tempest, Robert Bowes, William Babthorpe and Robert Chaloner. The appointment of Bowes was particularly problematic, since he had been responsible for plundering Bishop Tunstall's palace the previous October; Tunstall was evidently ordered to bury the hatchet. This council would, over the following years, interrogate, try and execute dozens of dissenters against the Henrician Reformation.[131] At a more humble level, the king also stocked dozens of grand juries and petty juries in 1537 with ex-rebels in order to encourage tangible acts of collaboration. This sort of participation did not imply love or even approval for the Henrician regime, but the participants did enact compromises on the very issues which Hallom, Bigod and others had declared incapable of compromise. They implied that the Henrician regime, while corrupt, was not out of the faith of Christ; while avaricious, it was not incompatible with the health of the commonwealth. These men chose to work from within the system, and indeed to work in concert with Cromwell, Rich, Audley, Cranmer and the other 'heretics' of 1536. In doing so, they separated themselves from their more radical neighbours in ways which significantly abetted the success of those 'heretics' in England.

VI

There is no greater testimony to the lasting divisions engendered by the post-pardon revolts than the remarkable number of rebels who, in the face of defeat and a return to the *status quo ante*, fled into exile in Scotland. In one sense, of course, this was a sensible precaution, especially for rebels on the government's list of exceptions to the final pardon granted in July 1537. But, in another sense, it represented an absolute repudiation of the Henrician regime, a conscious decision by some English subjects not to live under a heretical government.

[131] Dodds and Dodds, *The Pilgrimage of Grace*, vol. 2, pp. 268–71. On the Council of the North, see R. R. Reid, *The King's Council in the North* (London, 1921); G. R. Elton, *Policy and Police: The Enforcement of the Reformation in the Age of Thomas Cromwell* (Cambridge, 1972).

In all, at least twenty-seven rebels are known to have left England, although this is certainly an underestimate. Two of them, Thomas Danyell and Henry Bukbery, were banished by the government; both were Friars Observant, whose order had already been expelled from the realm. The other twenty-five, many of them priests or monks, fled of their own accord. Their ecclesio-political ideologies and their rationales for flight, when these can be ascertained, are informative.

Roger Hartlepool, for instance, was a monk of Jervaulx who fled into Scotland to escape the fate of his brother and co-conspirator John Staynton, who was executed. From December to February, Hartlepool had attempted to raise a company of men 'to destroy the Duke of Norfolk, affirming that if he were destroyed, their abbey should stand as it did and so should Holy Church in such state as it was in King Henry VII's days'.[132] This was an eminently sensible rationale for renewed rebellion; Hartlepool's desire for a Church 'as it was in King Henry VII's days' would not be achieved through the Doncaster framework, since Henry VIII had made it clear that the royal supremacy would stand. By abandoning England for Scotland, however, Hartlepool found for himself a solidly Roman Church where he could live unimpeded. The vicar of Watton, James Horsekey, also went into exile. He was one of a group of conspirators around Watton Priory who after Christmas 1536 agreed 'that it would never be well as long as the king's grace should be the supreme head of the church and that the same would not be formed without that the people did set forward again with a new insurrection'.[133] Among this group was Thomas Marshall, parish clerk of Beswick, who also escaped into Scotland.[134] Nicholas Musgrave, another exile, was leader of the revolts in Westmorland; his commitment to the papal supremacy is attested by the fact that, when the churchwardens of Brough commanded the vicar, Robert Thompson, to pray for the pope in early 1537, they threatened to set Musgrave on him if he refused.[135]

The decision to go into Scotland, furthermore, was fraught with political connotations and the threat of further rebellion. In May 1537, James V of Scotland, on his way home from France, anchored twice off the northern English coast, and on both occasions local fishermen and peasants urged him to invade England, insisting that if he had come five months earlier the rebels would have carried him in triumph to London.[136] Scotland, it seems, remained home to the hopes of disaffected Englishmen, despite the

---

[132] PRO SP 1/118, fol. 258r [*LP* XII, i, 1012].   [133] PRO E 36/119, fol. 23r [*LP* XII, i, 201].
[134] See *LP* XII, i, 202 (p. 105).
[135] Bush and Bownes, *The Defeat of the Pilgrimage of Grace*, p. 265.
[136] Ibid., pp. 224–5.

fears of some rebels that the Scots 'would rob or invade us'.[137] A man called John Petenson, moreover, reported rumours in October 1537 that 'many of them that were fled into Scotland be come forth and lieth about Hull Park and about Alnwick'. Petenson claimed that he had been asked by radical ex-rebels in Beverley, led by one William Spurryer, to serve as messenger between themselves and a group of exiles in Scotland which included Richard Wilson of Beverley and Robert Esch, friar of Knaresborough. The radicals in Beverley allegedly told Petenson to ask 'the said banished men to repair into England again with as convenient speed as they might, and to bring with them as great a company of Scots as they might get, and that the said William Spurryer and others aforesaid should cause the country about Beverley to assemble themselves in such like manner as the said country heretofore hath done, and that it would never be well with England till that were done'. The government investigated this story, decided that it was fiction, and executed Patenson for his troubles; regardless, there was at least significant fear that England had not heard the last of the banished radicals.[138]

Such fears smouldered long after the Pilgrimage of Grace. In 1538, an Englishman called Robert Dalyvell, who had lived in Scotland, reported to the English government a series of Scottish prophecies concerning the imminent downfall of Henry VIII. If the English king did not amend his ways, it was said, he would not live past the feast of the nativity of St John the Baptist in 1538, and before that time a horse worth 10s would 'be able to bear all the noble blood of England'. This story had grown, it seems, from prophecies current in Edinburgh the previous year that King James would make war on England with no less than 15,000 English exiles at the vanguard of his invasion force.[139] On at least one occasion, furthermore, ex-pilgrims led anti-English violence in Scotland. In 1541, the Lincolnshire exile William Leache and the Yorkshire exile John Priestman murdered Somerset Herald near Dunbar as he was returning from a mission to James V. This was the same Somerset Herald who, in 1536, had negotiated with Lord Darcy on behalf of the Crown.[140] It is no surprise, then, that the English government continued to look north with trepidation, fearing that the Scots would join with northern English Catholics to overthrow the Tudor regime.[141]

---

[137] Bush, *The Pilgrimage of Grace*, p. 335.

[138] PRO E 36/120, fols. 92r–95r [*LP* XII, ii, 918].

[139] Dodds and Dodds, *The Pilgrimage of Grace*, II, pp. 244–5.

[140] W. H. D. Longstaffe, 'The Connection of Scotland with the Pilgrimage of Grace', *Archaeological Journal*, 14 (1857), 331–44.

[141] When such an alliance was attempted in the 1569 rising, there were several rebel leaders who had been active pilgrims, for instance John Norton and his sons Richard and Thomas, who had helped besiege Skipton Castle in 1536. See Dodds and Dodds, *Pilgrimage of Grace*, I, p. 209.

The point of this analysis is not to suggest that the exiles and post-pardon rebels were somehow better Catholics than their more conformable neighbours, but rather to show how contested and volatile this very question was among contemporaries. Indeed, simply framing the question in this way draws attention to a crucial fact whose significance has long been overlooked: even though, in principle, the overwhelming majority of English subjects would have preferred if the religious alterations of the 1530s had never occurred, in the end some rebels accepted the government's terms while others did not. This division among Catholics, as important as the nascent division between Catholics and evangelicals, was based in deepening fault lines running through the polity, separating those willing to live in Henry VIII's vision of England from those who considered that vision incompatible with their own. Thus, while it is indisputable that the Pilgrimage of Grace was a revolt against the Reformation, this observation is insufficient to comprehend the rebellion's dynamics: the motives and actions of the pilgrims cannot be understood along a single axis running from right to left, from Catholic to Protestant, from conservative to radical. Rather, the rebellion must be conceptualised within a considerably more complex and multivariate system, where reactions to the government-sponsored Reformation were determined not only by theology but by interpretations of the royal supremacy, political temperament and economic circumstances.[142]

As the following chapters will show, these cracks within the Catholic population would increasingly allow new religious ideas to seep into English culture, spreading the cracks wider and wider until eventually there seemed more cracks than solid ground. For now, however, it is sufficient to notice that the Pilgrimage of Grace showcased a new mode of casuistic calculation, balancing civil and religious obligations, that would increasingly dominate the political landscape. The relationship between outward obedience and inward beliefs, built around notions of sovereignty, legitimacy and moral authorisation, was exactly the issue upon which the English Reformation primarily acted. The royal supremacy imposed upon people's religious sensibilities a paradigm of *political* loyalty in which obedience was due to the king so long as his policies did not violate God's law or undermine the fabric of the commonwealth. The fundamental divisions that emerged among English subjects thus concerned not whether individual policies were laudable but

---

[142] Here I take issue with Richard Hoyle's statement that 'a threefold division may profitably be made between the conservatives, some of whom supported the divorce and acquiesced in the royal supremacy and dissolution, the reform party or evangelicals, and the extremely small number of Lutherans': Hoyle, *Pilgrimage of Grace*, pp. 63–4. This equating of pro-Henrician and anti-Henrician 'conservatives' based solely upon their theology is in many ways an apt summary of the larger historiographical position against which the first three chapters of this book have argued.

whether those policies met the basic criteria of legality and legitimacy. Over the following century, English people would over and over again find themselves asking whether royal policies widely considered odious were or were not compatible with divine law and civil harmony; in the Pilgrimage of Grace they asked these questions for the first time and found, to their dismay, that they disagreed.

PART II

Points of contact: the Henrician Reformation and the English people

4

Anticlericalism, popular politics and the Henrician Reformation

On the first Sunday of Lent in 1540, John Gallampton and 'other misruled and wild persons' gathered outside their parish church in the town of Pawlett, Somerset. They entered the church 'with strength and violence', dragged out their vicar, Thomas Sprent, and 'cast him over the churchyard wall', nearly breaking his neck. On Easter Sunday the following month, with Sprent recovered from his injuries, John Gallampton 'stood at the chancel door' and 'kept the parishioners back' so that they could not receive communion from the vicar's hand. Then in July, Gallampton allegedly ambushed Sprent and beat him with a club. These violent actions, according to the vicar's opponents, were not without provocation. In the autumn of 1539, Sprent had abandoned his benefice for two weeks without providing a replacement, leaving two parishioners to die without last rites. Sprent was also accused of beating two of his parishioners, demanding 'more tithings of the parishioners than they were wont to pay', and meeting in his house with 'women of evil name and fame'. The conflict between the vicar and his parishioners became so heated that local modes of dispute resolution proved futile, and Gallampton and Sprent sued one another in rival actions in the King's Court of Star Chamber.[1]

This anecdote colourfully illustrates a mode of clerical–lay relations in the Reformation era, traditionally labelled 'anticlericalism', that scholars have often linked with the rise of English Protestantism.[2] Yet Protestantism is

---

[1] PRO STAC 2/31/120, fols. 25r, 24r, 12r, and 19r. The pages in this manuscript are confusingly and inaccurately numbered, so I have counted folios beginning at the front of the larger of the two bundles.

[2] For important assertions of the relationship between anticlericalism and English Protestantism, see A. G. Dickens, *The English Reformation*, 2nd edn (London, 1989); A. G. Dickens, 'The Shape of Anti-clericalism and the English Reformation', in E. I. Kouri and T. Scott (eds.), *Politics and Society in Reformation Europe* (Basingstoke, 1987); G. R. Elton, *Reform and Reformation: England 1509–1558* (London, 1977). Among earlier works, see J. A. Froude, *History of England: From the Fall of Wolsey to the Death of Elizabeth*, 12 vols. (New York, 1873); C. G. Coulton, 'Priests and People before the Reformation', in his *Ten Medieval Studies*, 3rd edn (Cambridge, 1930).

never mentioned in the voluminous depositions surrounding this case, and, while the affair at Pawlett involved violence against a priest, calling such violence 'anticlerical' is problematic. People in Pawlett objected to the conduct of their vicar, but it is not immediately clear how they regarded the status and privileges of the clergy as a whole; calling the affair 'anticlerical' might be no more analytically useful than calling attacks on corrupt merchants 'anti-capitalist'. Observations such as these have led many historians to challenge the notion that anticlericalism was a major contributing factor in the Protestant Reformation. As early as 1929, Lucien Febvre argued convincingly that many of the staunchest critics of the late medieval clergy were also some of the staunchest defenders of the Roman Church. In other words, there was a fine line between 'anticlericalism' and its opposite, and many who criticised priestly abuses did so in order to build up rather than tear down the reputation of the clergy as a whole.[3] These ideas were echoed by English historians who argued that the late-medieval clergy enjoyed strong popular support; disputes like the one between Sprent and Gallampton certainly occurred, but they were neither unusually common in the early years of the Reformation nor symptomatic of larger divisions within the Church.[4]

This revisionism was given it most aggressive form by Christopher Haigh in his 1983 article 'Anticlericalism and the English Reformation'. Haigh mocked the concept of anticlericalism as one of the 'convenience foods of historical study, which give us our past pre-packaged and frozen, in ready-mixed meals needing only to be warmed in the moderate oven of a mediocre essay or lecture'. He argued that historians had invented anticlericalism because without it the Reformation was 'inexplicable'; it was only his own view that the Reformation was far less successful than we had previously been led to believe which finally allowed such an ahistorical construct to be overthrown. Haigh suggested, moreover, that the interpretive weight of anticlericalism had been accepted for so long because 'thinking is a difficult business, and most of us prefer to do as little of it as possible'; historians had used anticlericalism as an 'historical cliché' in order to 'avoid the anguish and responsibility of independent thought'. Haigh won few friends with this blistering attack on his colleagues, but he enjoyed considerable success in shifting the debate on the English Reformation into the *second* half of the

[3] Lucien Febvre, 'Une Question Mal Posée: Les Origines de la Réforme Française et le Problème Général des Causes de la Réforme', *Revue historique*, 161 (1929), 1–73.
[4] J. J. Scarisbrick, *The Reformation and the English People* (Oxford, 1984); J. J. Scarisbrick, *Henry VIII* (Berkeley, 1968); P. I. Kaufman, 'John Colet's Opus de sacramentis and Clerical Anticlericalism: The Limitations of "Ordinary Wayes"', *JBS*, 22 (1982), 1–22; R. N. Swanson, 'Problems of the Priesthood in Pre-Reformation England', *EHR*, 105 (1990), 845–69.

sixteenth century, and discussions of anticlericalism and its relationship to the Reformation largely vanished from English historiography.[5]

This chapter reopens the question from a new perspective, suggesting that by analysing popular anticlericalism within the wider context of popular politics we can re-establish substantial links between religious innovation, royal policy and outbreaks of physical and verbal attacks against priests. It should be stressed that this is *not* to say that resentment against priests caused the Reformation. Whatever resentment existed between clergy and laity in the later Middle Ages was neither necessary nor sufficient to produce widespread spiritual upheaval, and, if not for the importation of an extrinsic Reformation, a high level of anticlericalism could have been contained indefinitely within the elastic boundaries of the Catholic Church. That being said, however, it is still the case that the Reformation radicalised existing anticlericalism, giving new and complex meanings to a previously well-understood genre of popular politics. The high-political events of the 1530s led to a widespread popular belief that the king and his government had turned against the clergy. Thus, parties in the country who felt aggrieved by priests began to appeal to the centre for support, with the language of anti-popery and the royal supremacy providing new and powerful weapons through which laymen could co-opt the power of the state in their local conflicts. Moreover, given the convergence of their interests in these cases, evangelicals and 'orthodox' anticlerical activists increasingly found themselves allied together in their attacks on local priests, allowing ever more ideological interpretations of clerical abuses to seep into popular political discourse. In short, anticlericalism became, to borrow Geoffrey Elton's term, a 'point of contact' between evangelicals, the government and the people, a point where new ideas insinuated themselves into the mainstream of English culture.

I

Before we can understand the relationship between popular anticlericalism and the English Reformation, we must first look more closely at the dynamics

---

[5] Christopher Haigh, 'Anticlericalism and the English Reformation', in Christopher Haigh (ed.), *The English Reformation Revised* (Cambridge, 1987), p. 56. This article was first published in *History*, 68 (1983), 391–407. Haigh reiterated and refined his views in his *English Reformations: Religion, Politics, and Society under the Tudors* (Oxford, 1993), part I. In continental Reformation historiography, the question of anticlericalism and its relationship to the Reformation is still very much open. For some key studies, see Henry Cohn, 'Anticlericalism in the German Peasants' War 1525', *P&P*, 83 (1979), 3–31; Robert Scribner, 'Anticlericalism and the German Reformation', in his *Popular Culture and Popular Movements in Reformation Germany* (London, 1987); and the many essays in Peter Dykema and Heiko Oberman (eds.), *Anticlericalism in Late Medieval and Early Modern Europe* (Leiden, 1993).

of physical and verbal attacks on priests. In this context, we must consider whether there was any underlying ideology that informed attacks on priests and might legitimate the use of the term 'anticlericalism', or whether these attacks were merely isolated instances of violence not unlike other brawls and slanders in late medieval society.

English historians assessing the usefulness of the term 'anticlericalism' have constructed various taxonomies of anti-priest sentiment in order to help answer this question. Most influentially, J. J. Scarisbrick has identified four varieties of the 'many-headed hydra of anticlericalism' which were 'often opposites or, at any rate, incompatibles'. First, there was the 'negative, destructive anticlericalism' practised by the common people in response to individual priests, an 'appetitive and basically selfish creed' that was 'often innocent of much philosophical or theological implication'. Second, there was the 'positive and idealistic, though secular, anticlericalism' of social reformers like Thomas Cromwell. Third, there was a 'positive, idealistic, and religious anticlericalism' practised by Erasmians who wished to reform the Church for its own sake. And fourth, there was the strongly anti-sacramental 'anticlericalism of heresy'.[6] Christopher Haigh has offered a comparable if slightly less refined tripartite taxonomy: 'the ideology of Erasmian reformers, the theology of the priesthood of all believers, [and] the gut reaction of neglected parishioners'.[7] These divisions are clearly crucial to any larger understanding of clerical–lay relations. We must not assume, for instance, that government schemes to confiscate clerical wealth were closely associated with Erasmian criticisms of clerical wealth, even though their programmes may have been similar. Likewise, contempt for rich, simoniac prelates was clearly a different animal entirely than contempt for the poor and under-educated clerical proletariat.

This atomising impulse has recently been questioned, however, by Peter Marshall, who carefully distinguished between different forms of anticlericalism yet located various practical and linguistic links between them that had the power, upon occasion, to render them compatible and resonant. The famous 'clerical' anticlericalism of John Colet, for instance, had little in common with Lollard heresy, yet Buckinghamshire Lollards are known to have attended Colet's sermons at St Paul's. Evangelical preachers who described the Catholic clergy as 'Baal's priests' did not shock their listeners nearly as much as they probably meant to, because the term was adopted from traditional, orthodox anticlerical sermons; the linguistic overlap allowed for a smoother transition as the laity wrestled with the new meanings their pastors applied to these words. The Londoner who was in trouble in 1491 for

---

[6] J. J. Scarisbrick, *Henry VIII* (Berkeley, 1968), pp. 243–4.
[7] Haigh, 'Anticlericalism and the English Reformation', p. 57.

wishing 'there was never a priest in England' was probably not influenced by Lollardy, and probably would not really have wanted to see his words translated into action; none the less he might have interpreted evangelical sermons in the 1530s very differently from those who reported him to the authorities.[8]

Building upon this more nuanced approach to the definitional problems attached to anticlericalism, it is worth reconsidering the nature of the popular form of lay–clerical tensions which Scarisbrick described as 'negative', 'destructive' and 'selfish', and which Haigh dismissed as the 'gut reaction of neglected parishioners'. These terms are the detritus of an outdated mode of scholarship, direct descendants of A. L. Rowse's condemnation of Cornwall's 'stupid and backward-looking peasantry'.[9] When we examine cases of popular anticlericalism more closely, we find that none of these prejudicial terms is appropriate. Rather than merely the unconsidered reactions of frustrated parishioners, attacks on priests, like grain riots or charivaris, had their own rules, meanings and underlying logic.[10] A great deal of popular politics in late medieval communities revolved around disputes over the suitability of local priests, especially in cases where those priests, like stipendiaries and others who lacked freehold of their benefices, were in some sense servants of the community. In many cases, parishioners claimed the right to discipline or even discharge errant priests, and they often attacked those priests in ways which symbolically mocked and undermined their spiritual status. As such, these attacks explicitly represented a reordering of the structural relationship between clergy and laity.

In the parish of St Clement's, Ipswich, for instance, the Augustinian canons of St Peter's had ceded to the parish their responsibility for finding a priest for the cure, so that an Elizabethan parishioner could claim that 'the inhabitants of the said parish . . . as well in the time of the late Cardinal Wolsey as since, have had the appointing, placing, and displacing of the ministers'.

---

[8] Peter Marshall, *The Catholic Priesthood and the English Reformation* (Oxford, 1994), ch. 8.

[9] A. L. Rowse, *Tudor Cornwall: Portrait of a Society* (New York, 1969), p. 318.

[10] On the political complexity of early modern violence, see Natalie Z. Davis, 'The Rites of Violence: Religious Riot in Sixteenth-Century France', *P&P*, 59 (1973), 51–91; E. P. Thompson, 'The Moral Economy of the English Crowd in the Eighteenth Century', *P&P*, 50 (1971), 76–136. See also John Walter, 'Grain Riots and Popular Attitudes Towards the Law: Maldon and the Crisis of 1629', in John Brewer and John Styles (eds.), *An Ungovernable People: The English and Their Law in the Seventeenth and Eighteenth Centuries* (New Brunswick, N.J., 1980); Louise Tilly, 'The Food Riot as a Form of Political Conflict in France', *Journal of Interdisciplinary History*, 2 (1971), 23–58. The *locus classicus* for all these studies is George Rudé, *The Crowd in History: A Study of Popular Disturbances in France and England 1730–1848* (New York, 1964). The importance of this body of scholarship and some criticisms of it have been usefully discussed in Suzanne Desan, 'Crowds, Community, and Ritual in the Work of E. P. Thompson and Natalie Davis', in Lynn Hunt (ed.), *The New Cultural History* (Berkeley, 1989).

This 'displacing' of ministers by the community, however legal it may have been in theory, in practice often carried an implicit sense of lay superiority in which priests' elevated spiritual status was eroded by their structurally weak position as salaried employees of the parish. One witness in the 1580s reported, for instance, that in Henry VIII's reign 'one Little Sir John, with whom this deponent went to school, was likewise placed there [in the cure] by the said inhabitants, and after by the said inhabitants displaced for his incontinent life with a young woman of the said parish'. Unfortunately we know nothing of the local politics behind this assertion of lay prerogative, but the mocking nickname 'Little Sir John', still remembered and used in an official deposition three decades after the fact, implies that, even in a case where the community had the right to remove errant priests, that action could carry significant critiques of clerical status.[11]

In the case of Shirland, Derbyshire, described in chapter 1 above, we can see how local politics interacted with and energised anticlerical activity. According to a variety of witnesses, a faction in the town led by Robert Revell ejected a phenomenal number of priests from the community; several people deposed that more than ten priests had been discharged from their livings, while one parishioner put the number at '17 or 18 priests changed out of the parish' within twenty years. Revell's attempts to eject priests, moreover, were tainted by blunt acts of degradation in which the sanctity of priests and their offices was publicly mocked. As noted above, one curate had a pudding stuffed in his mouth just as he was about to say mass, while a parson named Thomas was told, 'The devil's turd in Tom Tinker's teeth!' when he refused to ring bells according to his parishioners' bidding.[12]

We can see the same phenomenon in the case of William Lusher of Puttenham, Surrey, who was accused of violence against his parson, George Maychell, sometime before 1529. Lusher's excuse was that he had given fair warning: '[He] hath afore this said unto the said George Maychell, forso-much as he was of evil rule and did not say and minister divine service as he ought to do, that if he did not say and minister divine service in his cure there, that he would by the order of the law move him out of the said parsonage.'[13] Certainly the 'order of the law' allowed no such thing, but Lusher evidently believed that communities had an extraordinary prerogative to discipline their priests. Another statement of this prerogative comes from the Cornish

11 PRO E 134/28 ELIZ/Easter 29, fols. 2r–3r. I would like to thank Diarmaid MacCulloch for this reference.

12 PRO STAC 2/26/194. This abuse of the beneficed parson of Shirland, rather than simply the curate employed to sing divine service, implies that at least in some cases the legal status of priests' claims to their livings was irrelevant to parishioners who claimed a generalised right to unseat them.

13 PRO STAC 2/17/86. This MS refers to 'Bishop Richard of Winchester', which dates it to the episcopate of Richard Fox (1501–28).

parish of St Stephen's, Launceston, where in 1538 a chaplain called Thomas Frenche accused three husbandmen, two cordiners, a yeoman and twenty other 'riotous and misruled persons' of having 'menaced and threatened to murder' him. The defendants claimed in response that they had merely attempted to discharge an unsuitable priest:

[We] with diverse of the said parish of St Stephen's came unto the said Sir Thomas Frenche, saying unto him that for such inconvenient living that he the said Thomas Frenche did use within the said town of Launcheston and of long time before had done, and for other ill misdemeanors by him often times before that time committed and done, that he the said Thomas Frenche should no longer serve nay sing within the said church.[14]

The riots and disturbances through which priests were discharged from their duties, moreover, often displayed a generic, ritual form in which parishioners confiscated the priest's chalice, surplice, missal or other accoutrements necessary for saying mass.[15] A priest called Leonard Constable from Marston, Yorkshire, for instance, claimed in an undated deposition that '8 persons and above, by the procurement of one Sir Oswald Wyllestrolp, knight, and Sir Robert Wayd, clerk...violently came and took the chalice from the orator...and said: "Thou whoreson, poleshorn priest, thou shalt not say mass here, and therefore get thee out of the church, or we shall make thee repent it."'[16] On Palm Sunday, probably in 1531, John Vasye, parson of Lytchett Maltravers in Dorset, was listening to confessions when a number of parishioners burst in, threw Vesye out of the church, and took from him both his chalice and his keys. Afterwards the parishioners, 'without authority or colour of right, deputed and assigned one priest born in the parts of France, and also one other priest such as they pleased, to sing in the same church, without license and against the will of your said orator, parson of the same'.[17]

At Lawhitton, Cornwall, the parish priest went to his church on 1 October 1535 and found a small crowd waiting for him who took away his 'chalice, mass book, and other ornaments to that intent the said parish priest should not serve the cure there'.[18] On Easter 1541 a group of Londoners attempted to take a chalice away from Sir William Barton, a chantry priest in the parish of St Olave, 'whereby diverse parishioners there that were then ready to have received their maker at the said mass was by them and their means kept back from the same'.[19] At Alfreton, Derbyshire, the widow Anne Maryng told a chantry priest in June 1534 that he 'should say no mass' and afterwards

[14] PRO STAC 2/15, fol. 316r.
[15] Much of this paragraph duplicates work in Peter Marshall, *Catholic Priesthood*, pp. 67–8.
[16] PRO STAC 2/10, fol. 153r.   [17] PRO REQ 2/7/38, fol. 3r.
[18] PRO STAC 2/7, fol. 93r.   [19] PRO STAC 2/3, fol. 199r.

'took the chalice which belongeth to the said chantry...and with violence unreverently put the same chalice into the case and took it with her and went forth her way out of the church'. As a result of this action, as well as threats by Marying and her associates, the priest claimed that he 'dare not abide at his said chantry...but is compelled of necessity for the safeguard of his life to absent himself'.[20]

The symbolism of lay people discharging priests from their duties by confiscating liturgical paraphernalia was extremely significant. The idea that the goods of the church belonged to the commons was an old one in England and had played a role in many riots and rebellions, most significantly the 1381 peasants' revolt.[21] In temporarily reclaiming their goods from a corrupted clerical estate, then, the commons were asserting their prerogatives under the principle of the society of orders much as they had in the rebellions of 1536, when they temporarily reclaimed political powers usually vested in the Crown and nobility.[22] The chalice itself, moreover, was perhaps the most potent symbol in late medieval society for the superiority that priests claimed over the laity. The chalice was the vessel from which God's blood was drunk at mass, but only by the priest; medieval Catholic practice forbade the laity from drinking the wine, allowing them only the wafer. Indeed, for a layman even to touch the chalice rendered it ritually unclean, and as late as 1550 a Kentish priest announced that 'the chalice handled by a temporal man's hand was profaned, and that he would sing with none such'.[23] Thus when laymen confiscated chalices from priests in the course of their disputes, they were enacting claims to authority over their clergy in complex and powerful ways.

Moreover, attacks against priests often represented not the spontaneous combustion of a frustrated populace but rather the carefully enacted strategies of parishioners trying to achieve recognisable goals. In Boston, Lincolnshire, in 1535, a group of parishioners assembled their neighbours by ringing the church bells and then tried to beat down the door of a local priest's house with a 'great timber'. This riot, however, was part of a wider legal action for slander, and local justices of the peace had ordered the priest's arrest; the rioters claimed merely to have been following these instructions, although

[20] PRO STAC 2/27/41.

[21] Steven Justice, *Writing and Rebellion: England in 1381* (Berkeley, 1994), pp. 93–100; Marshall, *The Catholic Priesthood*, p. 189.

[22] See Michael Bush, *The Pilgrimage of Grace: A Study of the Rebel Armies of 1536* (Manchester, 1996). For similar ideology in the 1549 rebellions, see Diarmaid MacCulloch, 'Kett's Rebellion in Context', *P&P*, 84 (1979), 36–59; Ethan Shagan, 'Protector Somerset and the 1549 Rebellions: New Sources and New Perspectives', *EHR*, 114 (1999), 34–63.

[23] 'Extracts from Original Documents Illustrating the Progress of the Reformation in Kent', ed. C. E. Woodruff, *Archaeologia Cantiana*, 31 (1915), 92–120, at p. 97.

clearly they over-interpreted their brief.[24] In 1545, the parson of Chipping, Lancashire, encountered even more organised resistance, claiming that two gentlemen and two yeomen 'secretly doth counsel with all the residue of the parishioners...and willeth them also to stay their tithe corn and stop all their dues to the church, intending thereby to drive your said suppliant (being a stranger) out of his parish'.[25] In 1538 at Doveridge, Derbyshire, rioters broke into the house of a chantry priest and stole 'diverse evidences, escripts, muniments, and writings within the same house concerning the said chantry of Doveridge'. With the papers justifying the priest's title gone, the rioters then beat up his servants and occupied his house for several weeks; when the priest complained, one of the ringleaders mocked his impotence and 'bade [him] sue, for the birds were flown'.[26] In Swalcliffe, Oxfordshire, in 1543, when Richard Westburie became involved in a dispute with the parish priest over the sheep tithe, the village took up a collection to pay his legal fees, agreeing 'between them to pay for every yard [of] land that they have in the field 4d toward the cost and charge made and to be made in the suit hereof'.[27]

These cases, when taken as a whole, serve both to justify the use of the term 'anticlericalism' and to illustrate the complex world of popular politics into which the Henrician Reformation was thrust. Many laymen clearly believed that they had the right to force priests to conform to local power structures and norms of behaviour. Priests' exalted status as anointed servants of God was taken seriously, but so, too, was the necessity that priests act as the servants rather than the masters of their constituents. While rioters may not have explicitly denounced the priesthood as a caste, their actions implied a significant discrepancy between popular and official ecclesiology, underlining popular suspicions that priests did not deserve, or at least could easily forfeit, many of the legal, economic and spiritual prerogatives afforded to them by the Church.[28] Assertions of lay control over the celebration of mass thus amounted in practice to a significant incursion into the mysteries of the Church. It was only a small step, for instance, from parishioners stealing chalices to the actions of Thomas Dale of Canterbury, who at Easter

---

[24] PRO STAC 2/32/38, fols. 7r, 2r, 6r, and 16r.
[25] PRO DL 1/16, fol. 107r.   [26] PRO REQ 2/11/87.
[27] Oxfordshire Archives, MS Oxf. Dioc. Papers d.14, fols. 20r–27r. I owe this reference to Peter Marshall.
[28] In the fourteenth and fifteenth centuries, parishioners sometimes claimed the right to withdraw tithes from unsuitable clergy. While this position was generally associated with Lollardy, there is at least some evidence that orthodox parishioners flirted with it as well, for instance during anticlerical agitation at Saltash in 1404. This may suggest that, even before the Reformation, anticlericalism was a *locus* for cross-fertilisation between orthodox and heterodox attitudes towards ecclesiastical reform. See Swanson, 'Problems of the Priesthood in Pre-Reformation England', p. 850.

1540 'willingly and presumptuously did take the chalice in his bare hand, comparing that the priest's hand is no better than his'.[29] Similarly, it is no coincidence that the prerogative claimed by English parishioners to charge and discharge their own priests was also included by the German peasantry in the Twelve Memmingen Articles of 1525.[30] Thus, while far from Protestant in and of themselves, traditional forms of anticlericalism could, in certain circumstances, find a great deal of common ground with evangelical views of the priesthood as a class of public servants.

II

Over and above questions of theology, then, popular anticlericalism had a practical affinity for the first stage of English Reformation *politics*: Henry VIII's attacks on the independence of the priesthood.

When parliament met in 1529, the House of Commons was quickly engulfed in a sea of bills and proposals against the perceived abuses of the clergy. This flurry of legislative activity was unprecedented; according to Edward Hall, an evangelical member from Shropshire, no one had previously dared to oppose the clergy for fear of being accused of heresy.[31] The king's single-minded destruction of Cardinal Wolsey earlier in the year, however, and the government's increasingly vocal attacks on ecclesiastical prerogatives, led many subjects to expect that the Crown would respond positively to anticlerical agitation. Early debates addressed a variety of alleged abuses: probate and mortuary fees, the presence of priests in worldly professions, excesses in pluralism and non-residency, corruption in the ecclesiastical courts, and nepotism and simony in appointments to livings. There were even constitutional complaints about convocation's prerogative to pass ecclesiastical laws without the king's approval. Three bills passed in December 1529 began to address these concerns, curtailing probate fees, mortuary fees and clerical pluralism.[32]

It should be stressed that, while these proposals and bills were popular in the House of Commons, and while they were mostly Erasmian rather than evangelical in their rhetoric, they none the less engendered massive hostility from the spiritual peers. Bishop Fisher, for instance, got himself into considerable trouble for comparing the new proposals to the innovations of

[29] CCCC MS 128, p. 59. For a general discussion of the significance of laymen confiscating chalices, see Marshall, *The Catholic Priesthood*, pp. 66–7.
[30] Cohn, 'Anticlericalism in the German Peasants' War 1525'; Nicholas Tyacke, 'Introduction: Re-Thinking the "English Reformation"', in Nicholas Tyacke (ed.), *England's Long Reformation* (London, 1998), p. 14.
[31] Stanford Lehmberg, *The Reformation Parliament 1529–1536* (Cambridge, 1970), p. 83.
[32] Lehmberg, *Reformation Parliament*, pp. 76–86; Scarisbrick, *Henry VIII*; Haigh, *English Reformations*, ch. 5.

Martin Luther and John Huss. When the commons finally pushed through a bill eliminating most clerical pluralism, moreover, the spiritual peers refused to let it pass until the king intervened, forcing them to accept a compromise bill which allowed loopholes for many elite clerics like themselves. It was not the case, then, that the anticlerical legislation of 1529 was uncontroversial; on the contrary, it pitted clergy against laity on a grand scale.[33]

Between 1530 and 1532 these parliamentary manoeuvres against the clergy were augmented by Henry VIII himself. The king first threatened the entire clerical estate with praemunire for unlawful allegiance to a foreign monarch, in other words for performing their duties under obedience to the pope. In February 1531, the English clergy jointly purchased their pardon for £118,000, a sum comparable to the annual income of the English Crown. That same month, Henry demanded that the convocation of Canterbury recognise him as 'supreme head' of the Church within his kingdom; they agreed to do so 'so far as the law of God allows', a clause which protected their consciences but did little to protect the independence of the priesthood. Then, in May 1532, a browbeaten convocation agreed to give the king veto over ecclesiastical law and allowed the existing canons of the Church to be surveyed by a royal commission.[34] These early assaults on the prerogatives of the English clergy reached their apex with Henry VIII's assumption of quasi-papal powers in November 1534 and his confiscation of the vast wealth and lands of the monasteries beginning in 1536.

While this growing antagonism between the government and the priesthood is familiar terrain to historians of high politics, it has never fully been appreciated that contemporaries in the countryside also understood and even exaggerated this antagonism. As early as 1532, for example, the elderly Devonshire priest John Bentley was ambushed by a Somerset yeoman called Harry Evesham and two of his associates, who fraudulently claimed to be acting on orders from Thomas Cromwell. In explaining to the priest why he should fear Cromwell's wrath, Evesham revealed some startling assumptions about the regime: 'If he [Bentley] did know how sore that Master Cromwell was against priests and how grievously he had handled them, he would lever spend all the goods he hath than to come before him, for he is a man without any conscience against priests, I warrant you.'[35] Equally clear

---

[33] Lehmberg, *Reformation Parliament*, pp. 86–94. Not all anticlerical bills were Erasmian, and it is significant that a Lollard petition against clerical wealth from 1410 was resubmitted to parliament in 1529 even though Lollards had been prosecuted in the diocese of London only a year before. See Richard Hoyle, 'The Origins of the Dissolution of the Monasteries', *HJ*, 38 (1995), 275–305.

[34] On the events of 1530–2, see Lehmberg, *Reformation Parliament*; Elton, *Reform and Reformation*; Diarmaid MacCulloch, *Thomas Cranmer: A Life* (New Haven, 1996), ch. 3; Scarisbrick, *Henry VIII*, chs. 7–10.

[35] PRO E 36/120, fol. 121r–v [*LP* VI, 87]; see also *LP* VI, 104.

was the testimony of Alexander Clavell, who in 1535 reported a prophecy circulating among Sir Thomas Arundell's tenants that 'the priests would rise against the king' and believed that this rising 'was never more likely than now because they should pay so much money to the king's grace'. When Arundell tracked down different versions of the prophecy, he heard it said that 'the priests shall rule the realm three days and three nights, and then the white falcon should come out of the northwest and kill almost all the priests, and they that should escape should be fain to hide their Crowns with the filth of beasts because they would not be taken for priests'.[36] Some Catholic priests were particularly explicit in describing the government's enmity against them. For instance, the Lancashire priest James Harrison lamented in 1533 that the king would 'put down the order of priests and destroy the sacrament'.[37] Edmond Large, parish priest of Bishop's Hampton, was alluding to the Reformation parliament when he said in a 1535 sermon: 'Who put Christ to death but the peers of the realm in those days that were high learned men, both temporal and spiritual? And if Christ were now alive again he should die a cruel death, as ye see how their heads goeth off now daily.'[38]

These perceptions continued to grow throughout the 1530s, especially after the first dissolutions of monasteries in 1536 seemed to indicate that the king would use his ecclesiastical authority to raid clerical property. For example, Nicholas Staunton, parson of Woodborough, Wiltshire, told 'diverse poor men' in 1537 'that he had no money to give them, for the king had robbed him'.[39] In Wales, a parson called Robert ap Roger Heuster said in December 1536 that 'it was better for the men of the Church to die in the faith of holy Church than to let the king's grace to rob them'.[40] In January 1539, a Cornish priest spread rumours that 'the king's highness and his Council had decreed that there should no parson nor vicar within this realm of England have henceforth any more for their ... service [than] £6 13s 4d yearly to be paid for all manner of duties'.[41] And of course, the most famous rumours of the 1530s, those that precipitated the Pilgrimage of Grace, also implied royal enmity towards the clergy by alleging that the king would tear down churches and confiscate chalices and other ornaments. Indeed, those rumours might be reinterpreted given the ubiquity with which, as we have seen, anticlerical rioters confiscated those same chalices and ornaments: the king had become the greatest anticlerical rioter of them all.[42]

In the hands of evangelicals, this new public perception of government antipathy towards priests could result in remarkably blunt displays of political

---

[36] PRO SP 1/92, fol. 194r–v [*LP* VIII, 736].   [37] PRO SP 1/78, fol. 115v [*LP* VI, 964].
[38] PRO E 36/120, fols. 165r–166r.   [39] PRO SP 1/128, fol. 108v [*LP* XIII, i, 94].
[40] PRO SP 1/120, fol. 89r [*LP* XII, i, 1202].   [41] PRO SP 1/142, fol. 92r [*LP* XIV, i, 87].
[42] On the rumours, see Ethan Shagan, 'Rumours and Popular Politics in the Reign of Henry VIII', in Tim Harris, (ed.), *The Politics of the Excluded, c.1500–1850* (Basingstoke, 2001).

self-confidence. John Parkins, for instance, reported several priests and monks to royal authorities for alleged seditious words in early 1537. There turned out to be nothing substantial in his allegations, and Parkins was made to appear in the marketplace at Oxford with a sign around his neck bearing the words 'for false accusation'. Parkins was not dissuaded, however, and in a letter to the abbot of Osney, one of his enemies, he wrote: 'I see well both religious priests and secular priests be linked together like a chain of iron against our most dread and benign sovereign lord the king's grace.'[43] Parkins's link between royalism and anticlericalism was evidently untroubled by the fact that he rather than the priests he had accused stood condemned by royal justice. For another example, a series of public letters written by Bristol evangelicals in 1538 lambasted the town's leadership for their repression of radical preachers, warning them that they would 'all repent it shortly when my lord privy seal do hear of it'. One of these letters, addressed to the vicar of St Leonard's, Bristol, began by addressing him as 'thou shitting and stinking knave' and threatened him with the bishop's justice.[44] Such confidence on the part of anticlerical activists shows something of the radicalisation made possible by the Crown's activities in the 1530s.

The quintessential example of this growing perception of government anticlericalism occurred in the West Country, where in August 1545 'bailiffs, constables, tithingmen, and all other the king's majesty's officers' conducted a series of unauthorised raids on priests' houses. Local justices never determined who, if anyone, had ordered the raids; they learned only that a rumour had spread among local officials that the Crown had ordered priests to be severely handled. Thus officers throughout Dorset, Gloucestershire and Somerset searched priests' houses and confiscated 'all kinds of weapons, books, letters, and spits wherewith they roast their meat'. Despite attempts by Justices of the Peace to assure priests that these confiscations were illegal, in at least some areas there was a second round of raids in which the same officials made 'an inventory of all the priests' goods and chattels', clearly in preparation for an impending confiscation of clerical wealth.[45] What is remarkable about these raids is not only that people believed that such extraordinary orders had come from the Crown, but also that so many officials were willing to carry them out without so much as a glance at a letter of commission.[46] Clearly it was a commonplace belief

---

[43] PRO STAC 2/34/11, fols. 2r and 6r.   [44] BL Cotton MS Cleopatra E.V, fols. 390r–391r.
[45] The raids on priests' homes are documented in PRO SP 1/206, fols. 90r–94r [*LP* XX, ii, 186]; PRO SP 1/206, fol. 20r [*LP* XX, ii, 159]; and *APC*, I, pp. 234–6.
[46] An interesting continental analogy comes from the St Bartholomew's Day massacre, when rumours that the king himself had ordered the killings in Paris led to the spread of violence to provincial towns. In that case, too, people's perceptions of royal predilections unleashed a series of unprecedented, extra-legal acts. See Philip Benedict, 'The St. Bartholomew's Day Massacre in the Provinces', *HJ*, 21 (1978), 205–25.

that the king and the priesthood were enemies, and many subjects were eager to prove that, when push came to shove, they would always back the Crown.

III

These changing perceptions had enormous effects on the dynamics of anti-clericalism at the local level, inflecting even the most traditional disputes with the increasingly charged and ideological language of national politics. Parishioners who found themselves embroiled in conflicts with their priests often came to believe that the Henrician government was their ally, and thus, whatever their theological inclinations, they had strong incentive to collaborate with certain facets of the government's religious programme. By using the language of the royal supremacy and accusing priests of disobeying the king's religious policies, lay men and women gained a powerful new weapon in their struggles to discipline or displace offensive clerics.

One example of this new dynamic was a series of disputes between John Mydell, a weaver from Croscombe, Somerset, and his parson, William Bowreman. In a bill of complaint to the King's Court of Star Chamber in 1539, Mydell wrote that he had long been in conflict with the parson over a tree which was felled in the churchyard while Mydell was serving his term as churchwarden. Parson Bowreman had allegedly demanded the wood of the tree for his own use, and when Mydell refused to give it to him without the approval of the parish, Bowreman had him jailed. This relatively commonplace scenario was radicalised, however, by Mydell's accusation that Parson Bowreman was 'not the king's friend' and that he 'upholdeth and maintaineth a priest called Sir William Raynold, for speaking of high ill words at the insurrection of the north parts'. The parson also allegedly refused to give thanks at the birth of Prince Edward, commanded 'Peter's Pence' to be paid to Rome four years after its abolition, and demanded a mortuary fee from a parishioner after the act curtailing such payments, saying, 'I will have it, act or no act.' These accusations combined traditional anticlerical rhetoric with the brand-new language of the royal supremacy, imbuing a local dispute with broad political significance. By internalising the rhetoric of the Henrician Reformation, recasting what was essentially a financial dispute as a crisis of loyalty and a profound threat to law and order, the churchwarden acquired enormous leverage against his priest. Of course we cannot know whether Mydell's accusations were invented or genuine, but for our purposes it makes little difference; what matters is the profound interconnectedness of anticlericalism and the Henrician Reformation. If the Reformation had not occurred, Mydell's hatred for his priest might not have found an outlet;

conversely, if Mydell had not hated his priest, he might not have had occasion to embrace the Reformation.[47]

A case from Halifax, Yorkshire, in 1534 shows a similar radicalisation of a largely traditional dispute. Here a number of parishioners, including one identified as a gentleman, filed suit in Chancery against their priest, Dr Robert Holdesworthe. The suit alleged that Holdesworthe, an absentee priest with a number of benefices, had been negligent in his duty by not arranging for divine services to be held in his absence, had not provided 'bread, ale, and wine' to parishioners washing the altar, had refused to light candles because of the expense, and had even extorted money from his congregation. Most interestingly, however, Holdesworthe was accused of making his parishioners pay 'Peter Pence . . . contrary to the statute in that behalf provided and made, saying unto them if they would receive their maker they should pay the same'. In other words, unless the parishioners paid the traditional but now illegal tax to Rome, they would not be permitted to take Easter communion. At the end of the bill of complaint, furthermore, the plaintiffs added an absurdly superfluous reminder that the vicar should be made to answer the charges against him because 'the king our sovereign lord is the *supremum caput anglicanae ecclesiae*'. Here we are faced with unquestionably 'conservative' parishioners, people who objected to the lack of candles in church and volunteered to clean the high altar, none the less suing their priest in royal court for his attachment to the papacy and enlisting the supreme head of the Church of England as their ally in a local dispute.[48]

In 1538, the vicar of Chelington, Bedfordshire, was likewise accused of a combination of traditional clerical abuses and offences against the Reformation. In the former category, the vicar allegedly 'kept in his house a light woman with whom he hath carnal cognition'. Furthermore, he publicly announced the details of a confession made to him by the constable's wife, and, when she objected, he 'openly in the church did beat the said wife and make her black and blue'. The vicar, in other words, had upset his parishioners and by the conventions of popular politics they considered it within their rights to chastise or remove him. Yet the parishioners also accused the vicar of a very different style of misconduct. They claimed that when he heard a rumour that Henry VIII would begin collecting royal taxes called 'tenths' from the clergy, he answered: 'I trust that the king shall never live so long as to perceive any tenth.' Similarly, he commanded his parishioners that they should not eat eggs or cheese in Lent 'contrary to the license which your said highness did grant'. Here again, then, we have villagers with what seem to be traditionalist views (at least they valued the seal of confession) none

[47] PRO STAC 2/18/301.   [48] PRO C 1/827, fol. 1r–v.

the less using the language of religious reform, performing a sort of ostentatious conformity before the royal courts in order to score points in a local dispute.[49]

In the Essex town of Harwich, tensions between priest and parishioners reached boiling point in 1536 when the curate, Sir Thomas Curthope, objected to the licentiousness of traditional Christmas revels. When rowdy parishioners selected a Lord of Misrule, Curthope 'began a fury with the said young men and took the pipe out of the minstrel's hand and did strike the said minstrel on the head with the said pipe and after threw it against the ground and like a man full of malice did stamp upon the said pipe with his feet and so did break it in pieces and thus did bring the whole parish in a great disturbance'. The following day, far from apologetic, Curthope 'came into the pulpit within the church of Harwich and for his purpose brought in a text of the old law how the children of Israel did come dancing and piping in the honour of their idols, and applied the same unto his parishioners'.[50] These sound like the ravings of a stereotypical puritan preacher, and Curthope seems typecast for a Ben Jonson play, but, in fact, this could not be further from the truth. Following his Christmas antics, Curthope was reported to the government for a variety of Romanist offences: leaving the name of the pope in his books, refusing to admit into his church preachers licensed by Archbishop Cranmer, and defacing printed copies of royal circular letters that were placed on his pulpit. Some of his accusers, moreover, used bluntly evangelical language in their accusation that 'by reason of [Curthope's] slanderous preaching, the true preachers of the Word of God and setters forth of the king's title, style, and lawful jurisdiction are had and brought into great slander and infamy, and...are called the new-learned fellows and teachers of new doctrine, even as the Pharisees called our saviour Christ and his apostles'. Here, then, a dispute between an overzealous priest and his parishioners was transformed by its Reformation context into something much more. Because the Romanist priest's activities were so obviously contrary to the norms of community behaviour, traditional and newfangled attitudes towards clerical misconduct converged, and Curthope's evangelical opponents found themselves in the unusual position of representing wider community sentiment.

These cases, and many of others like them, show something of the resonance between traditional anticlericalism, the 'new learning', and the perceived priorities of the Crown. Evangelicals co-opted the genre of popular

---

[49] PRO STAC 2/26/15. The date of 1538 seems likely for this case, as it was in that year that Henry VIII issued a controversial dispensation from Lenten fasting.

[50] PRO SP 1/99, fols. 200r–204v [*LP* IX, 1059]. It is obvious from the case that it involved events from June 1535 to February 1536, though it is dated to 1535 by *LP*.

only the husks of buildings standing. Sometimes even these husks were attacked: one man carried away 'a great bar of iron holding up the wall going up the stair to the dorter', while another removed 'the ceiling over the window in the prior's great chamber'.[3] Trees were removed from abbey lands. Three hives of bees were taken for their honey. Paving stones were plundered, while within the church itself the stones of the floor were stripped away. And, beyond all this, the commissioners noted that still 'there be many diverse spoils daily done within the said late monastery, to a great substance over and above these above written, but by whom as yet it is not known'.[4]

It has long been known that the legal dissolution of the English monasteries was followed by the physical destruction of the houses themselves. Yet this destructive process, for all its intrinsic interest, has been more of a minefield than a gold mine for scholars seeking to understand popular involvement with and attitudes towards the English Reformation. It would seem that such a massive and outrageously sacrilegious project as the destruction of abbeys could not have been undertaken without some degree of popular support. But, within a historiographical framework focused on religious conversion, the downfall of the monasteries has proven singularly disappointing as a subject for research, since it is clear that greed often trumped spiritual conviction in the minds of the men and women who participated. One Elizabethan clergyman, for instance, recalled his Catholic father's guilt-ridden explanation for monastic plunder, an explanation more reminiscent of opportunistic looting than principled iconoclasm: 'Might I not as well as others have some profit of the spoil of the abbey? For I did see all would away; and therefore I did as others did.'[5] Within the 'revisionist' interpretation of Henry VIII's reign, then, the dissolution of the monasteries has been almost wholly divorced from the Reformation as a spiritual process, since it was apparently so easily assimilable by traditionalist Catholics. Hence, we have the odd spectacle that the two great histories of the English Reformation written in the 1990s, Eamon Duffy's *Stripping of the Altars* and Christopher Haigh's *English Reformations*, both almost entirely omit one of the English Reformation's central themes.[6]

---

[3] PRO SP 5/5, fol. 10v.   [4] PRO SP 5/5, fol. 10r.

[5] J. J. Scarisbrick, *The Reformation and the English People* (Oxford, 1984), p. 70, citing the Elizabethan Yorkshire clergyman Michael Sherbrook. Sherbrook's whole treatise is printed in A. G. Dickens (ed.), *Tudor Treatises*, Yorkshire Archeological Society Record Series, 125 (Wakefield, 1959).

[6] Haigh limited his discussion of the dissolution to a few examples of resistance: Christopher Haigh, *English Reformations: Religion, Politics, and Society under the Tudors* (Oxford, 1993), pp. 130–1, 143–50 and a few other scattered references. Duffy declined to discuss monasteries almost entirely, limiting his analysis to 'the parish setting' in order to save space: Eamon Duffy, *The Stripping of the Altars: Traditional Religion in England 1400–1580* (New Haven, 1992), p. 6.

Yet, when we move beyond the question of religious conversion and examine the cultural and political impact of the English Reformation, popular participation in the dissolution of the monasteries looms large indeed. After all, once we accept the fact that conscientious Catholics *could* support the dissolution, that leaves us with the central question: what did it *mean* for ostensible followers of Eamon Duffy's 'traditional religion' to participate in the wholesale destruction of a central pillar of Catholic religiosity? Since the sources have never before been available to reconstruct these meanings, historians have assumed that the spoil of monasteries was a wholly profane and expedient response to an intrinsically 'unpopular' Reformation-from-above. The records of the spoliation of Hailes Abbey, however, provide a unique opportunity to examine the active and productive engagement of English subjects with their new spiritual environment.[7] In these manuscripts, we have the most complete record known of a community's involvement in dismantling a religious institution, and, by tracing the prehistory of religious disputes at Hailes that formed the background to their destructive behaviour, we can glimpse how people's actions fit into the larger structures of Reformation. What we will find is a remarkable and unexpected series of interactions between Protestantising forces and the more nakedly political and economic aspects of the dissolution of the monasteries. This is not to argue that a significant percentage of the Gloucestershire population were evangelicals, nor that the destruction of Hailes was somehow a 'Protestant' event. What it does suggest, however, is that evangelicals were active in every step of the destructive process, that they were extremely successful in facilitating more radical interpretations of the dissolution than the government officially recognised, and that they were able to convince many of their 'conservative' neighbours to collaborate in activities that would have been unthinkable only a few years before. The spoliation of Hailes Abbey, then, was another 'point of contact' between religious reformers, the Crown and the people, a site where we can view directly the effects on a community of nearly a decade of sustained revolution.

I

The parish of Hailes is located near the town of Winchcombe in the Gloucestershire hundred of Kiftsgate, thirteen miles northeast of Gloucester. To understand the process of Reformation in this obscure parish, we must begin

---

[7] These manuscripts are in PRO SP 5/5, fols. 10r–18r. Despite various discussions of Hailes in recent years, these manuscripts have not previously been closely examined by scholars. See Peter Marshall, 'The Rood of Boxley, the Blood of Hailes and the Defence of the Henrician Church', *JEH*, 46 (1995), 689–96; Caroline Litzenberger, *The English Reformation and the Laity: Gloucestershire, 1540–1580* (Cambridge, 1997), ch. 2.

three centuries before Henry VIII's reign, when an unexpected storm threatened to sink the ship in which Richard, Earl of Cornwall, brother to Henry III, was travelling home from Gascony. In the fury of the storm, Richard swore to found a monastery if he survived, and when he reached port he made good his promise, choosing the village of Hailes where he owned a manor. The Cistercian abbey of Hailes thus became home to twenty monks and ten lay brothers when its church was solemnly hallowed in November 1251.[8]

The fame of Hailes, however, was owed not to its illustrious founder but to his son Edmund, who while travelling in Germany procured for the abbey one of England's most impressive relics: a vial filled with the holy blood of Jesus Christ. The blood had entered Europe in the 1250s, accompanied by a certificate of authenticity under the seal of Jacques Pantaleon, Patriarch of Jerusalem and later Pope Urban IV. Edmund purchased the blood in 1267, and a portion of it was presented to the abbey of Hailes on the festival of the Exaltation of the Cross in September 1270; not having a suitable place to display so holy a relic, a new apse with five chapels was added to the east end of the monastery with a shrine for the blood at its centre.[9] Immediately, Hailes became one of western England's major pilgrimage destinations, and the precious relic was put under the care of a special custodian, or '*altararius*', who welcomed pilgrims into its shrine, displayed it to them at appointed times, and accepted their payments to the monastery.[10]

Throughout the Middle Ages indulgences for venerators of the relic were regularly granted from Rome, and these perks helped bring enough money-carrying pilgrims to keep the abbey safe and solvent even during the turbulent years of the Wars of the Roses.[11] Hailes also became a major beneficiary of the late fifteenth-century renaissance in lay patronage and church-building, with extensive renovations underwritten by such prominent donors as Sir John Huddleston, Sir William Compton and the Earl of Northumberland.[12] The steady stream of pilgrims who came to see the blood was attested by Hugh Latimer, who wrote in the early 1530s that 'they come by flocks out of the West Country to many images, but chiefly to the blood of Hailes'.[13] Popular folk belief held that the holy blood was only visible to those free from sin, so many chose Hailes as a pilgrimage destination to guarantee that their transgressions had been forgiven. This myth may have been on the

---

[8] *VCH Gloucester*, II, p. 96. The chronicle of the abbey is in BL Harleian MS 3725.
[9] St Clair Baddeley, 'The Holy Blood of Hayles', *TBGAS*, 23 (1900), 276–84, at pp. 277–8.
[10] Ibid., p. 278.
[11] Bodleian MS Hearne's Diaries 42, pp. 95–6; Baddeley, 'The Holy Blood of Hayles', pp. 279–80; *VCH Gloucester*, II, p. 98.
[12] Baddeley, 'The Holy Blood of Hayles', p. 281; William Hazeley, 'The Abbey of St Mary, Hayles', *TBGAS*, 22 (1899), 257–71; see also anonymous reports in *TBGAS*, 52 (1930), 4–9 and *TBGAS*, 23 (1900), 10–12.
[13] Cited in John Foxe, *Actes and Monuments* (London, 1563), p. 1316.

minds of more elite pilgrims as well, such as the Duke of Buckingham, who visited the abbey shortly before his execution in 1521.[14] Hailes thus seems to provide a fine example of the 'popularity' of the Catholic Church in the later Middle Ages; certainly local inhabitants must have felt both pride in their abbey and gratitude for the wealth that pilgrims brought into local shops, inns and alehouses.

Yet for all its popularity, there were cracks in the abbey's ideological foundation that would be available for exploitation when the Crown turned against the religious houses. Individual relics like the bones of saints or pieces of the True Cross were always open to speculation that they were fakes, but as classes of relics they were ordinarily beyond doubt; bones of saints obviously had survived and could be discovered, while the True Cross was such a powerful symbol in Christianity that few would have denied its capacity to endure. The existence of a vial containing the blood of Christ, however, presented very real Christological dilemmas for theologians and laymen alike. When Christ had ascended to heaven, could he have left bits of himself behind? If so, in what sense were those bits still God? Was the physical, carnal blood shed by Christ the very blood that washed away the sins of the world, or was the world saved by spiritual or metaphoric blood?

Among the first to raise specific doubts was no less a figure than Thomas Aquinas, who in his *Summa Theologiae* denied that relics such as the blood of Hailes could possibly be portions of the blood spilt by Christ in his Passion. Aquinas argued that Christ, in both His incarnation and His resurrection, was and will be an integrated whole, so that 'all of the blood which poured forth from Christ's body also rose with it'. Thus 'blood which is preserved as relics in certain churches . . . did not flow from Christ's side but . . . poured forth from an image of Christ when it was struck'.[15] This was not, of course, tantamount to calling the relics fakes; miracles of bleeding images were thought to be common in the Middle Ages. Yet there was at least a touch of irony and perhaps serious criticism in the Angelic Doctor's prose: relics like the blood of Hailes were intimately bound up with the story of the Passion and the legend of Longinus,[16] and any suggestion that they arose from a

---

[14] Baddeley, 'The Holy Blood of Hayles', p. 282.

[15] Thomas Aquinas, *Summa Theologiae*, gen. ed. Thomas Gilby, 61 vols. (Cambridge, 1964–1981), part 3, question 54, article 3: 'Totus sanguis, qui de corpore Christi fluxit, cum ad veritatem humanae naturae pertineat, in corpore Christi resurrexit. Et eadem ratio est de omnibus particulis ad veritatem et integritatem humanae naturae pertinentibus. Sanguis autem ille qui in quibusdam ecclesiis pro reliquiis observatur [*sic* for 'conservatur'?] non fluxit de latere Christi, sed miraculose dicitur effluxisse de quadam imagine Christi percussa.'

[16] See the anonymous early Tudor work *A Little Treatise of Divers Miracles Shown for the Portion of Christ's Blood in Hayles* (n.p., n.d.), in Bodleian Dep. d. 324, on loan from the Gloucester Library, where pilgrims are invited to come to Hailes 'to see and visit the precious portion of his blood / which dropped from the wound that was full wide / made with the spear of Longinus in his side': sig. B2v.

more recent source implied that the Church's myth-making machinery was open to doubt.

The potentially inflammatory nature of Aquinas's statements was revealed in the bitter partisan controversy which followed between Franciscans, who had a number of relics of Christ's blood in their possession, and Dominicans, who followed Aquinas in doubting their veracity. In 1351 there was a controversy over blood-of-Christ relics at Barcelona, and Pope Clement VI was appealed to at Avignon for a judgment; he declined to intervene on such a divisive issue. Nearly a century later, three Franciscans debated the issue against three Dominicans in front of Pope Pius II; once again the pope ended the debate without passing judgment. While these were, in principle, strictly academic debates, vast sums of money and the reputation of the Church's relic-procuring business potentially hung in the balance. Thus, even though two separate popes declined to decide the matter, it seems likely that we can read at least some of the indulgences granted for worshipping the blood of Hailes as defensive manoeuvres by the papacy against attempts by Dominicans to undermine the relic's legitimacy.[17]

Besides this orthodox theological debate, there was also a much more heated rhetoric of opposition among Lollards. Of all the thousands of relics worshipped in English churches in the fifteenth century, the blood of Hailes was among a handful singled out by Wyclif's followers as particularly odious and absurd. In 1485, a Lollard in Coventry called Roger Brown was brought before diocesan authorities for, among other things, saying that he would 'not adore an image, the blessed Mary of Walsingham, nor the blood of Christ at Hailes'.[18] In 1464, a heretic as far away as Lincolnshire knew the myth that the blood of Hailes was invisible to unrepentant sinners, and he lambasted the relic as a fraud: 'The blood of Hailes is but the blood of a dog or a drake, and goeth by a vice, and all thou that liveth upon it shall go to the devil, and as well a sinner shall see it as a good man whom the monks will [allow] for silver.'[19] In 1518, Sir John Drury, vicar of Windrush, Oxfordshire, announced after paying 18d in veneration of Our Lady of Worcester and the blood of Hailes that 'he had done as an ill husband that had plowed his land and sown it, but nothing to no purpose; for he had worshipped man's handiwork, and cast away his money'.[20]

It could reasonably be objected that Latinate debates and the ramblings of heretics did not add up to real public scepticism about the blood of Hailes. Yet

---

[17] Baddeley, 'The Holy Blood of Hayles', p. 278–9.
[18] Lichfield Record Office B/A/1/12, fol. 166v: 'non adoravet ymaginem, beatam Mariam de Walsingham, nec sanguinem Christi apud Heylys'.
[19] Lincolnshire Archive Office Episcopal Register XX, fol. 61r.
[20] Cited in E. P. Loftus Brock, 'On the Cistercian Abbey of Hailes', *Journal of the British Archaeological Association*, 32 (1876), 355–62, quotation at p. 358.

a very different kind of source implies that this scepticism was far-reaching indeed. In the years around 1500 at least two short books were written to advertise the shrine at Hailes. Surprisingly, both books spoke in highly defensive terms to a notional audience who had heard scepticism about the blood of Hailes and had doubts about its legitimacy. One of the books asked, for instance, 'Why is it more against man's wit / to believe that Christ's Blood is in Hailes' than to believe in other, similar relics at Rome? It then recommended to its readers: 'But for mettle of the hearer oft in doubt / of the precious Blood that in Hailes is / to know how it was brought about / take heed and read over this.'[21] The other book described a series of disasters that befell those who doubted the power of the blood of Christ as a relic. One priest near Derby, for instance, 'heard of this holy pilgrimage / how pilgrims sought Hailes the monastery / which to his mind he thought full contrary'. He thus tried to impede the passage of the pilgrims, and in punishment for his sacrilege his missal began to bleed when he said mass; the priest quickly concluded that Christ's blood truly was at Hailes. A Shropshire priest had a similar experience after denying the veracity of the blood, this time with the wine of the holy sacrament boiling in his chalice.[22]

The blood of Hailes, then, was never a univocal symbol and must always have been a mixed blessing to the monks who kept it. On the one hand, the abbey owed its tremendous popularity to the reputation of the blood, and the monks could both rejoice in its holiness and profit from its rarity. On the other hand, Hailes found itself at the centre of a very unpleasant debate, waged simultaneously in popular culture and among theologians, over the legitimacy of an intrinsically suspect relic. While most English relics enjoyed nearly unanimous popular support if not great fame, the blood of Hailes enjoyed great fame but was always vulnerable to a minority of English subjects who doubted its holiness and resented its existence. For the monks of Hailes, regardless of whatever personal doubts about the relic they may have had, it must have seemed a good trade-off for most of the Middle Ages. It was only in the 1530s that the precariousness of their position became clear.

II

Debates over the authenticity of Hailes' great relic were serious but far from fatal; there is no reason to believe that scepticism was more prevalent in 1530 than it had been a century before. That scepticism, however, provided an unusually pregnant context for the polemic against monastic abuses which

---

[21] BL Royal MS 17.C.XVII, fol. 147r.
[22] *A Little Treatise of Divers Miracles Shown for the Portion of Christ's Blood in Hayles*, sigs. A2v, A4v and A3r.

began to flow from England's pens and printing presses in the early 1530s. Most people presumably still believed in the blood's holiness, but many would also have been aware of the debate surrounding it and knew that not only Lollards but also Aquinas and the luminaries of the Dominican order had cast doubts on the relic. It was this context that led reformers within the English ecclesiastical hierarchy to choose Hailes as a test case for their attack on the 'merchants' and 'jugglers' of Rome. Hence the full weight of the Church of England, along with a healthy dose of only semi-official evangelical theology, was thrown against a small vial of liquid in an obscure Gloucestershire village.

As early as 1535, before either the dissolution of the monasteries or the government's attack on images began in earnest, there is evidence that Hailes had been noticed by leading reformers. The evangelical Anthony Saunders was appointed by Cromwell in 1535 'to read the pure and sincere word of God' to monks at the neighbouring abbey of Winchcombe, an assignment which evidently included preaching at Hailes, since Saunders complained that 'among all others the abbot of Hailes, a valiant knight and soldier under antichrist's banner, doth much resist, fighting with all his power to keep Christ in his sepulchre'. Saunders had preached in favour of salvation by faith alone, but the monks had been very reluctant to attend since they 'set so much by their popish service'. Moreover, he complained that the abbot of Hailes had 'hired a great Goliath, a subtle Duns man, yea a great clerk (as he saith), a bachelor of divinity of Oxford' to preach against him.[23] Despite these complaints, however, Saunders's preaching seems to have had some success: the abbot of Winchcombe complained in December 1535 that two of his monks had eaten meat during Advent 'contrary to the good and wholesome custom of our said monastery' and then had refused to perform the penance required of them.[24]

Another evangelical who chose Hailes as a subject for particular venom was the radical preacher and future bishop Hugh Latimer, who discussed the blood at length in a written defence of his controversial 1533 sermons at Bristol. In particular, he challenged on a number of grounds the belief that sight of the relic assured people 'that they be in clean life and in state of salvation without spot of sin'. Some of his rationales were comparable to orthodox medieval scepticism, but others were more-or-less explicitly 'new-learned'.

---

[23] BL Cotton MS Cleopatra E.IV, fol. 60r. Due to a change in foliation, this MS is listed in the catalogue of Cotton MSS at fol. 47.

[24] PRO SP 1/99, fol. 129r [*LP* IX, 934]. It seems likely that Saunders was sent to Gloucestershire at the request of Anne Boleyn, who was on progress at Winchcombe with her husband and the rest of the court in the summer of 1535. See William Latymer, 'William Latymer's Cronickille of Anne Boleyn', ed. Maria Dowling, *Camden Miscellany* 30, Camden Society 4th series, vol. 39 (London, 1990), pp. 60–1. I owe this reference to Peter Marshall. See also E. W. Ives, *Anne Boleyn* (Oxford, 1986), pp. 308–9.

First, he noted that he could not find it in Scripture that 'I am translated from death to life because I see with my bodily eye the blood of Hailes'. This attack not only presupposed the primacy of Scripture, but also utilised an increasingly (though by no means exclusively) evangelical emphasis on the Pauline distinction between letter and spirit, stressing that seeing Christ's blood with bodily eyes was not equivalent to seeing it with 'the eye of my soul, which is true faith'. Second, he wrote that 'it is very probable that all the blood that was in the body of Christ was united and knit with his divinity, and then no part thereof shall return to his corruption'. This was essentially equivalent to the scholastic critique, although with typical humour Latimer added his surprise that 'Christ shall have two resurrections'. Third, he noted that the men who 'scourged Him and nailed Him to the cross' had certainly not been of 'clean life' yet indisputably saw Christ's blood. Fourth, and most potentially subversive, he mocked the relationship between the blood of Hailes and the consecrated wine at mass, asking why a pilgrimage should be made to Hailes if the wine in the chalice was really Christ's blood as well.[25]

William Tyndale (a Gloucestershire man himself) also noticed the relic, and, while Tyndale attacked many aspects of what he considered popish superstition, it is significant that he discussed Hailes in the context of the most blatantly heretical of his opinions, his denial of the Real Presence. In his *Treatise of Christ and His Office*, published in 1536 but written several years earlier, Tyndale argued that by Roman doctrine the blood consecrated in the chalice at mass was the very blood of Christ, yet also by Roman doctrine the blood at Hailes was a portion of that blood; was it therefore true that the blood of Hailes was present in every chalice in the world at the time of consecration? Tyndale also expounded the more subtle argument that the Christ to whom we should pray is the entire Christ, both human and divine, containing blood, flesh and soul. Thus prayers should be directed to the Christ who 'sitteth on the right hand of the father' rather than to the blood of Hailes, which was not 'animate with the soul of Christ'.[26]

The full frontal assault on the blood of Hailes began, however, in February 1538 when John Hilsey, Bishop of Rochester, preached a sermon at St Paul's Cross against idolatrous images. According to Wriothesley's Chronicle, Hilsey included the following story:

[25] Cited in Foxe, *Actes and Monuments*, p. 1316.
[26] William Tyndale, *Doctrinal Treatises and Introductions to Different Portions of the Holy Scriptures, by William Tyndale, Martyr 1536*, ed. Henry Walter (Cambridge, 1848), pp. 383–5.

He [Hilsey] said how he confessed a woman twenty years ago in Oxford, which woman was the miller's wife, by the abbey of Hailes, and how she showed him how the abbot of the same place had given her many jewels that had been offered there at the holy blood, and how he would have given her one jewel which she knew very well hanged about the said holy blood, and she said to the abbot that she would not have that blood [*sic*, presumably for 'jewel'] because she was afraid because it hanged by the holy blood. And the Abbot said, 'Tosh! Thou art a fool, it is but a duck's blood.'[27]

This sermon may have raised controversy on a number of fronts; many in Hilsey's audience must have been as shocked by his violation of the seal of confession as by the content of his tale. None the less, Hilsey's sermons against 'superstitious' relics were already a well-understood part of English political culture, and when preached from the nation's leading pulpit they produced action.

Eight months later, the king's commission was issued to Hugh Latimer (by now Bishop of Worcester), the prior of Worcester, the evangelical Gloucestershire gentleman Richard Tracy, and, for form's sake, the abbot of Hailes, to investigate the blood. In a letter to Cromwell written on 28 October, Latimer described their efforts:

Sir, we have been bolting and sifting the blood of Hailes all this forenoon. It was wonderfully closely and craftily enclosed and stopped-up for taking of care, and it cleaves fast to [the] bottom of the little glass it [was] in. And verily it seemeth to be an unctuous gum and compound of many things. It hath a certain unctuous moistness and though it seem somewhat like blood while it is in the glass yet when any parcel of the same is taken out it turneth to a yellowness and is cleaving like glue.[28]

Having thus assured themselves that the blood would be appropriately unimpressive when publicly displayed, the commissioners opened the blood 'in the presence of a great multitude of people'. We can only assume that Bishop Latimer, the foremost preacher of his era, took the opportunity to explain to the assembled multitude his views on idolatry, but all that survives is his brief description of the anti-ceremony in which the blood was displayed:

The said supposed relic we caused to be taken out of the said beryl, and [we] have viewed the same being within a little glass, and also tried the same according to our powers, wits, and discretions by all means. And by force of the view and other trials thereof we think, deem, and judge the substance and matter of the said supposed relic to be an unctuous gum ... which being in the glass appeared to be a glistening red resembling partly the colour of blood, and after we did take out part of the said

---

[27] *Wriothesley*, I, p. 75.
[28] W. H. St John Hope, 'Notes on the Holy Blood of Hayles', *Archaeological Journal*, 68 (1911), 166–72, quotation at pp. 170–1.

substance and matter out of the glass, then it was apparent glistening yellow colour like amber or base gold.[29]

The blood was then transferred to London, where Hilsey again preached against it and paraded it through the city. According to Wriothesley:

The 24th day of November, being Sunday, the Bishop of Rochester preached at Paul's Cross, and there showed the blood of Hailes, and recanted certain words that he had spoken of the said blood that it was a duck's blood, and now showed plainly that it was no blood, but honey clarified and coloured with saffron, and lying like a gum, as it evidently had been proved and tasted before the king and his counsel. And [he] did let every man behold it there at Paul's Cross, and all the way as he went to dinner to the mayor's, to look on it, so that every person might well perceive the abuse of the said thing.[30]

Radical set pieces like these were becoming standard fare in the metropolis, but in a small Gloucestershire village it was remarkable for such powerful men and their retinues even to visit much less for them to take such extraordinary actions under colour of the king's commission. It was of incalculable significance for the men and women of Hailes, then, that they experienced the Henrician government's authority most deeply at the exact moment when that government was at its most radical; few communities could have had as little doubt that political and Protestant 'Reformations' were inseparable. More important than the government's precise theological complexion, moreover, was the fact that Latimer's performance at Hailes, like Hilsey's performance in London, was the sort of relentlessly *public* event at which the reformers were so adept. Its significance was not merely in exposing a fraud or even altering beliefs but in implicating ordinary people in the very process of Reformation. The men and women who gathered to watch the bishop and his colleagues open the vial and desecrate its contents were not only observers but participants. They were asked to certify the government's claims with their own eyes and act as the unconscious vanguard of government propaganda as they told their friends and neighbours that they had seen for themselves that the blood of Hailes was a fraud. In other words, they were not only exposed to new ideas but actually took part, almost without realising it, in an enormously volatile act of iconoclasm.

III

Against such sustained attack, the abbey of Hailes bore little chance of survival. The abbot, Stephen Sagar, made some early attempts at self-defence, hiring the theologian George Cotes, Bachelor of Divinity at Magdalen College, Oxford, and later Marian Bishop of Chester, to preach against

---

[29] Brock, 'On the Cistercian Abbey of Hailes', p. 359.   [30] *Wriothesley*, I, p. 90.

the sermons of Cromwell's local agent Anthony Saunders. Sagar's rebellion, however, was short-lived. Sometime before July 1536, Cromwell sent for Cotes to be examined for his views, and Hugh Latimer's joke that Cotes was 'Dunsly learned [and] Morely affected' less than a year after Thomas More's execution suggests the severity of the charges against him.[31] Sagar thus subtly but promptly withdrew his patronage from the unfortunate theologian, informing Cromwell that while he 'liked the man very well', he had recently discovered that Cotes was not yet 'sworn to the king's succession, nor yet hath subscribed against the bishop of Rome, and therefore I am not minded that he shall read any longer with me'.[32]

This kind of quick retreat was to become standard operating procedure for the abbot. In his earlier days Sagar had been patronised by Thomas Cromwell himself, and as late as 1537 Cromwell recommended him as a royal chaplain (a recommendation more than a little irksome to his diocesan, Hugh Latimer).[33] None the less, Sagar's ability to stay in good grace with the vicegerent in spirituals was heavily dependent upon his willingness to embrace the revolution. In a remarkable letter to Cromwell written in the months between Hilsey's first sermon and the arrival of the commissioners to investigate the blood, Sagar reported having experienced something close to a conversion experience and actually asked Cromwell to send his investigators to the monastery. He wrote that God's truth was only now for the first time 'perched in my very heart... which I had never come to if I had not had liberty to read Scripture in English'. As a result of his new knowledge, he claimed that he had 'conceived a conscience' against all forms of 'superstition or idolatry':

It is not unknown unto your honour how that there is in the monastery of Hailes a blood which hath been reputed as a miracle a great season, and now I come to tell your lordship plainly that I have a conscience putting me in dread lest idolatry be committed therein, giving the very honour of the blood of Christ to that thing, which I cannot tell what it is... And for discharge of my conscience in voiding of idolatry, and to save my honesty towards the world, I do most humbly beseech your honour to send thither a commission by whom shall please you to examine my truth and honesty in this matter.[34]

Not everyone was convinced by Sagar's change of heart. In 1539 Richard Tracy, one of the commissioners sent to investigate the blood and a prominent evangelical, said that he was 'right sorry to see and perceive the king and

[31] Hugh Latimer, *The Works of Hugh Latimer, Sometime Bishop of Worcester, Martyr, 1555*, ed. G. E. Corrie, 2 vols. (Cambridge, 1844–45), II, pp. 373–4.

[32] PRO SP 1/88, fol. 178r [*LP* VII, appx. 35].

[33] For Cromwell's memorandum mentioning the promotion, see *LP* XII, i, 1323. For Latimer's response, see Corrie (ed.), *The Works of Hugh Latimer*, II, p. 380.

[34] PRO SP 1/129, fol. 120r–v [*LP* XIII, i, 347].

his counsel to favour (but rather to punish) such an enemy as he hath of the abbot of Hailes'.[35] Similarly, Latimer referred to Sagar with typical humour as 'the bloody abbot' and suggested that he would steal the jewels of the monastery from under the king's nose.[36] None the less, the proof was in the pudding, and with the abbot bound over for £500 to insure his good behaviour, Cromwell's trust in his man proved well placed.[37] Sagar may have used his office to enrich himself in the months before the monastery was dissolved by issuing illegal leases under the abbey seal, including one to his brother which may have been part of a scheme to funnel money back into his own pocket.[38] But this was small beer as far as the government was concerned so long as Sagar acquiesced in the removal of the blood and the dissolution of his house.

And acquiesce he certainly did. Sagar was called down to London, perhaps as early as 1537, and told in advance of the expected dissolution of his house; from Richard Layton's mention of his 'privy surrender' it seems that he agreed not to challenge the government's decision.[39] Indeed, Sagar wrote to Cromwell in September 1538 asking for permission to tear down the shrine where the blood had stood, and it is clear from his tone that he was more concerned with his own reputation than the fate of his abbey. He wrote that his reason for destroying the shrine was to prevent it from memorialising the false relic 'during that time it shall please God, our sovereign lord the king's majesty, and your good lordship, that this poor house may stand'.[40] Sagar clearly knew the score. For his willingness to play ball, when the monastery was dissolved on 24 December 1539 he was given an annual pension of £100, roughly the same sum as the combined total given to the other twenty-one monks of the house. In addition he was given a 'mansion house', a stable, several plots of land, and 'forty loads of fire-wood' so that he would not be cold in winter.[41]

When Hailes was dissolved, the commissioners responsible for its demise carefully noted the value of the monastery and its contents and began the

[35] PRO SP 1/150, fol. 178v [*LP* XIV, i, 828].
[36] PRO SP 1/135, fol. 228r–v [*LP* XIII, ii, 186].
[37] PRO SP 1/137, fol. 58r [*LP* XII, ii, 481].
[38] These charges were levelled against Sagar in a later Star Chamber case: PRO STAC 2/1, fols. 15–21. Sagar may indeed have been hiding something, since at least two large chunks have been ripped from the abbey's cartulary, including all entries after 1 September 1539, exactly the period when Sagar would have been making illegal grants: Shakespeare Birthplace Trust Record Office MS DR 18/31/5. I would like to thank Clair Walton, archives conservator of the Shakespeare Birthplace Trust Record Office, for examining this manuscript and discussing its provenance with me.
[39] PRO SP 1/137, fol. 58r [*LP* XII, ii, 481]. This manuscript is undated but was placed by the editors of LP in 1537. The reason for this dating is unclear.
[40] PRO SP 1/136, fol. 221r [*LP* XIII, ii, 409].   [41] PRO E 315/245, fol. 73r–v.

process of turning that value into profit for the Crown. Over £330 in annual rents due to the abbey came into the Crown's possession, along with over £400 in 'ornaments, goods, and chattels' which were immediately 'sold by the said commissioners'. While we have no details of this fire-sale, it was ordinary practice for suppression commissioners to sell monastic ornaments locally, both to raise money quickly and to encourage tangible acts of collaboration.[42] The Crown also received advowson of nine clerical livings and claimed precious metals amounting to twenty-eight ounces of gold and nearly eight hundred ounces of silver. The buildings and livestock of the monastery were put in the custody of Robert Acton, a Worcestershire gentleman with court connections, and then leased to him *in toto* on 7 March 1540.[43] Thus the Crown followed what by the end of 1539 were standard procedures, skimming a certain amount of cash off the top of Hailes and then leasing the rest to a loyal servant. Henry VIII still maintained a firm interest in the land – a twenty-one-year lease was very different from outright alienation – but for the moment the Crown withdrew from its dealings in Hailes, confident that its potential value would remain available when royal coffers were running low.

By the beginning of 1540, then, the juggernaut of the Henrician Reformation had overtaken this small corner of Gloucestershire. The abbey that had provided the community of Hailes with much of its identity had been dissolved, its riches absorbed into the Crown's coffers and its properties distributed amongst the laity. The people who lived near the monastery had listened to debates between reformist and traditionalist preachers. They had watched while the abbot of Hailes, undoubtedly known as a religious conservative, had seemingly of his own initiative pulled down the shrine in which the blood had stood so that it would not encourage remembrance

---

[42] For examples, see *Three Chapter of Letters Relating to the Suppression of the Monasteries*, ed. Thomas Wright, Camden Society 1st series, 26 (London, 1843), pp. 266–78.

[43] The commissioners' accounts of the dissolution of Hailes are in PRO E 315/494, pp. 67–72. The grant of the monastery to Robert Acton is in PRO E 315/212, fol. 102r–v. The buildings and livestock were at first divided by the commissioners into two groups. Some were 'assigned to remain undefaced': 'the late abbot's lodging extending from the church to the frater southward, with pantry, buttery, kitchen, larders, cellars, and the lodgings over the same; the baking [and] brewing houses and garner; the gatehouse; the great barn, two stables, the oxhouse and sheephouse'. Other properties, however, were 'deemed to be superfluous': 'the church with aisles, chapels, and steeple; the cloister chapter house, dormitory, and frater; the infirmary with chapels and lodgings to them adjoining; the prior's chamber and all other chambers lately belonging to the officers there'. As we shall see, this distinction proved of little consequence to those who ransacked the abbey in the months that followed, and certainly local inhabitants who broke into the abbey acted against the law even if they raided 'superfluous' properties. It is possible, however, that in the instances where *Acton's servants* raided the 'superfluous' properties, *if* they did so with Acton's permission, they may have acted within the law. The government obviously did not think this was the case.

of the defrocked relic. They had watched a public sale of monastic goods. And they had witnessed the gold and silver of the abbey being systematically counted, loaded onto carts and hauled away by men endowed with the unimpeachable legitimacy of royal letters of commission. It should be clear, then, that, while officially the government's attack on relics was unrelated to the legal suppression of religious houses, in their practical application the two programmes were perceived as intimately linked. It could have escaped no one's attention, for instance, that, at the same time that the blood of Hailes was being removed from its shrine in 1538, other monasteries throughout England were being suppressed. After the removal of the holy blood and sudden cessation of the massive pilgrimage to Hailes, moreover, the downfall of the abbey itself must have seemed inevitable.

Much of this activity took place after 16 November 1538, the date on which, we have recently been told, 'Henry VIII stopped the Reformation dead'.[44] Yet, even though there was no inherent theological agenda in the dissolution of Hailes, it would be absurd to deny that this process was a crucial component of the English Reformation. The effects of such a revolution being enacted on a local level are immeasurable. The people in and around Hailes experienced their first taste of iconoclasm in an impeccably legitimate form, perpetrated by a wide variety of ecclesiastical and secular authorities. With such good teachers, they would learn their lesson well.

IV

Given how actively involved the people of Hailes were in the profoundly ideological events leading up to the dissolution of the abbey, it should not surprise us that those people were not content to stand meekly by during the theoretically non-ideological divvying-up of the spoils. Thus, in the months following the dissolution, local people began breaking into the ex-monastery and systematically tearing it apart.

Before we can begin analysing what the spoliation of Hailes meant to the people involved, we must begin by examining the activity itself, since, clearly, people's perceptions were shaped not only by questions of conscience but by the much more mundane difficulties of actually dismantling the very imposing structures of the monastery. This work was made more difficult by its illegality; wrecking crews had to work at night. Richard Griffin of Hailes, for instance, was a young man of twenty-three who, as a servant to the local worthy Ralph Passy, was often required to do this dirty work. 'By night to nights' he carried lead from the abbey's kitchen out the back door of the monastery, then 'through the park and lakehouse close to the house of

[44] Haigh, *English Reformations*, p. 152.

the said Ralph Passy . . . at the least 10 times, every time loaded with pieces of lead rolled together'. Two of these burdens 'were so heavy to carry that the said Ralph did help him to carry them', but it seems that Griffin was well compensated; he was pleasantly surprised to be given 2d for his labour.[45] Similarly, one Christopher Wevar of Stow told one of his neighbours that 'he brought from Hailes on three several nights 6 horse loads of glass' and at the same time saw 'a servant of the parson of Battishere bring to his master's cart at Hailes certain glass nailed between 2 boards in hay, as much as 2 men might bare it safe'.[46] John Burges, a forty-year-old servant from Didbrook, 'carried in a morning by three of the clock a load of stuff, as boards, a stair of timber, and other like gear of one Richard Reve, servant to Richard Andros, gentleman, out of the convent garden to the house of the said Richard at Didbrook, and had for his carriage 4d'.[47]

The commissioners investigating the spoliation attempted to compile a complete catalogue of what was removed by whom, resulting in a manuscript more than 8,000 words long; we can do no more than summarise here. The variety of items mentioned individually was staggering: locks, tables, doors, pipes, drains, pots, windows, hooks, iron bars, hinges, ceiling beams, floorboards, stairs, beehives, trees, paving stones, grinding stones, wooden frames, and so on. A sample deposition will serve to give the flavour of the whole:

John Richards of Winchcombe of the age of 33 years, sworn and examined, saith that he bought of the said John Harres, servant to the said Robert Acton, a floor of boards in the little chamber within the prior's chamber and paid him therefore 5s. Item he bought of the same John 2 or 3 lights of a glass window, the foots [i.e. their length] uncertain, and paid therefore 12d. Item he bought of the said William Bough and William Brode the ceiling over the window in the prior's great chamber and paid them therefore 16d. Item he bought of the said Bough and Brode the boards of the floor in the little chamber next unto the jakes where one Townley did lie, and as much lead as came like to weight of 100 [i.e. a hundred-weight] and paid them for all 8s. Item he bought of the same Bough a hook of iron that had borne a door and paid for it 1d. Item the said John Harres did give him a door in recompense for a door lacking of a cell which afore he had bought of [the] said Harres.[48]

It is worth noting that the monetary values involved here were comparatively small because the spoils were divided so many ways. There were exceptions, of course; a smith called Robert Ray from Todington paid £4 13s 4d for a load of iron, as well as buying 12s in other goods.[49] But the average price for a given purchase was less than two shillings, and many items, like John Richards's iron hook, were no more than a penny or two.

---

[45] PRO SP 5/5, fol. 10v–r. These folios are out of order, with 10v preceding 10r.
[46] PRO SP 5/5, fol. 13r.   [47] PRO SP 5/5, fol. 13r.   [48] PRO SP 5/5, fol. 12v.
[49] PRO SP 5/5, fol. 14r.

These were transactions conducted at the level of ordinary local life, albeit often the lives of the local elite. Even Robert Ray's payment of nearly £5 for iron is part of a very different economic world than the picture usually drawn of the dissolution of the monasteries, with its large-scale accumulation and speculation by powerful gentlemen.

If transactions were small-scale, however, it was because of the small size of individual bundles and the low value of the items being sold, not because of any lack of volume. On the contrary, overall quantities were massive. Lead, for instance, was sometimes described in the depositions by weight, sometimes by price, and sometimes in unquantifiable terms like 'sheets'. Of those bundles whose weight is given, the total amounts to about one hundred 'hundredweight'. If we estimate this as a third of the lead mentioned in the depositions, that gives us a total of more than fifteen tons of lead stolen from the monastery, removed cartload by cartload in the black of night. An equally staggering amount of wood was removed in the form of timbers, planks, beams and doors, with somewhat less (although still impressive) quantities of the more expensive building materials, iron and stone.

The pillaging of Hailes was clearly a massive operation, and it presents us with a contradiction between the plunderers' very real need for secrecy and the intrinsically public nature of their activities. On the one hand, it is clear that much of the spoliation was illegal. The thoroughness of the government's investigation is proof of how seriously the plunder was taken, and, while we have no evidence of punishments meted out at Hailes, there is evidence that in other parts of the country similar thefts were brutally repressed. In Pipewell, Northamptonshire, for instance, a tinker who 'stole out of the said monastery iron and lead' was hanged for his trouble.[50] On the other hand, there can be no doubt that, when taken as a whole, the nightly activities at Hailes were known to everyone in the community. These activities must have been extremely loud and disruptive: besides the sounds of breaking glass and scraping metal, one ambitious plunderer solved the problem of removing timbers from upper-floors by hurling them out of the steeple.[51] Furthermore, nearby communities must suddenly have been up to their necks in iron, lead and suspiciously coloured glass at the very same time that the monastery's outward appearance was quickly deteriorating. We must draw the conclusion, then, that, while not announced publicly, the spoil of Hailes was an open secret.

When we begin to examine how different individuals became involved in the process of spoliation, furthermore, we see just what a communal activity it became. The depositions taken by the royal commissioners, which themselves admit to being a woefully incomplete version of events, list more

[50] PRO E 315/109, fol. 23r.   [51] PRO SP 5/5, fols. 12r and 14v.

than seventy-five people who either bought fragments of the abbey, sold fragments, or were paid to extract fragments from the abbey itself. In significant ways, moreover, this number heavily underestimates the number of people involved. All but two of the people mentioned in the depositions were men, no doubt because it was assumed that men were responsible for financial transactions; none the less we can safely assume that many of the named culprits had wives and families who were in various ways also implicated. Moreover, in the depositions we hear only of the first tier of spoilers, those who received property directly from the abbey in more-or-less original form. But the surrounding communities must have been unable to believe their luck as prices for many commodities dropped, specie flooded into the locality, and formerly dilapidated houses were suddenly restored.

Of the seventy-five-odd people mentioned in the depositions, many were, of course, prominent members of the community, the local gentry and yeomanry who already held a disproportionate amount of the community's wealth. For instance, John Richards of Winchcombe, who 'had the ceiling over the window in the prior's great chamber', was assessed in the 1544 subsidy at £18 in goods, making him one of the more prosperous men in the locality.[52] William Couper, who bought ten loads 'of stone out of the church', was assessed for the same subsidy at £12 in goods.[53] When the Crown convened a manor court at Hailes under its temporary new ownership in January 1540, the jury contained several future-plunderers of the abbey: John Issode, Ralph Passy, Anthony Griffith, Richard Reve and William Goodall.[54] These men were all respected local worthies, although not all so rich as John Richards: Richard Reve was assessed in 1542 at £4 in goods, while Anthony Griffith was only assessed at 40s.[55]

Further down the social spectrum it is more difficult to identify people's status, since they are unlikely to appear in financial records, but it is sometimes possible. A man called Ralph Stile, for instance, was implicated in the spoliation only in the purchase of 'one broken locket and one bar of iron' for which he paid 3d; in 1542 he was assessed at 20s in goods.[56] Thomas Fouche and his two sons, all of them smiths, were involved in the spoil; Thomas was respected enough to appear on the Crown's manor court jury for Longborough in January 1540, but his sons, being younger artisans, were unlikely to have been so secure.[57] Similarly, a man identified in the depositions simply as 'the plumber of Winchcombe' was probably no higher than the middling sort.[58] John Burges of Didbrook bought from John Fouche a door with iron hinges, for which he paid 6d; he was able to afford this

[52] PRO SP 5/5, fol. 10v; PRO E 179/114/268, fol. 7v.
[53] PRO SP 5/5, fol. 13v; PRO E 179/114/268, fol. 7v.   [54] PRO SC 2/175/1, fol. 51v.
[55] PRO E 179/114/247, fol. 13r.   [56] PRO SP 5/5, fol. 13r; PRO E 179/114/247, fol. 12v.
[57] PRO SC 2/175/1, fol. 44r.   [58] PRO SP 5/5, fol. 13r.

purchase, it seems, because he had earned 8d for hauling loads out of the monastery at 3 o'clock in the morning and carrying other loads 'from Hailes to Tewksbury in pipes and barrels'.[59] One man called John Owen is described as a servant to a smith, while servants of other local men such as Roland Morton and Richard Andros are ubiquitous in the depositions; it is unclear whether these men were enriching themselves or their masters, but in either case they were actively employed in the spoliation of the abbey.[60]

The plunder was thus not limited to the wealthy or powerful, but pervaded all levels of the local community. That does not mean, however, that everyone involved had an equal role, or that the event was entirely unorganised. Rather, when we start to distinguish more carefully between the purveyors of monastic property and their customers, we find that many of the people selling bits of Hailes were in fact associated with one another: they were servants of Sir Robert Acton, the Worcestershire gentleman who had acquired the Crown lease of the abbey. In all, twelve of Acton's servants took part in the spoliation, including several (most notably William Bough, William Brode and John Harres) who were among the most active pillagers. Also, Sir Thomas Hopkins, chaplain to Sir Robert Acton, comes across in the depositions as something of a ringleader. It was Hopkins who orchestrated some of the most astonishing acts of destruction, including selling 'five loads of stone digged within the ground under the paving stone in the body of the church' – presumably a reference to grave stones.[61] One man was even advised by a servant of Acton's that if he kept his knowledge of the spoliation secret he would receive 'a good reward of his master'.[62]

This begins to look like an inside job: Acton might have wanted to squeeze more money out of his holdings by orchestrating the thefts. This inference is strengthened by the fact that the abbey was re-leased in March 1542 to the local gentleman Richard Andros, indicating that the property had somehow reverted back to the Crown by that point.[63] The significance of Acton's involvement, however, should not be exaggerated. Acton did not live in or around Hailes and had a wide variety of properties in Worcestershire, Gloucestershire and Southwark; he was, in fact, returned as an MP from Southwark in 1542, shortly after the commissioners at Hailes finished their work. There is no evidence that Acton ever micromanaged his Hailes properties, or even that he ever visited them. He was not called to appear before the commissioners, does not seem to have fallen out of favour with the regime in any significant sense, and certainly would not long have

---

[59] PRO SP 5/5, fol. 13r.   [60] PRO SP 5/5, fols. 13v and 10r.   [61] PRO SP 5/5, fol. 13r.
[62] PRO SP 5/5, fol. 14v.
[63] PRO E 315/214, fol. 98r–v. Richard Andros was also implicated in the Hailes spoliation (see SP 5/5, fols. 10v and 13r) which may explain why his new lease was quickly cancelled (the cancellation is included on the MS of the lease itself).

endorsed a spoliation in which dozens of people unconnected with him made off with possessions that had been leased to him. Acton also had less than cordial relations with some of the people named in the depositions, becoming embroiled in a land dispute in October 1541 in which he complained of riotous behaviour on the part of Thomas Fouche, John Fouche and other men involved in the plunder of the abbey.[64] It seems likely that, while Acton may have known about the spoliation, winked at it, and occasionally profited from it, he certainly did not orchestrate it.

Even to whatever extent the raids were an inside job by Acton's servants, the geographic range of the black market in monastic goods belies any suspicion that collaboration was thin on the ground. People who profited from the plunder of the abbey came from all of the local towns and villages, including Hailes itself, Didbrook, Stanway, Toddington, Pinnock and Winchcombe. They also came from farther afield, including Stanton three miles away, Condicote seven miles away, Longborrow eight miles away, and Stow-on-the-Wold nine miles away. There are even references to significant purchases of monastic spoils in Tewkesbury and Bristol, fifteen and forty miles away respectively. Given this geographical range, the depositions must surely show only a fraction of the people who collaborated by carting goods, spreading news of the plunder, organising financial deals, and so forth.

Thus, like the famous examples of Cornish communities supporting themselves through the plunder of wrecked ships, the people of Hailes and the surrounding communities integrated the wealth of the dissolved abbey into their economy.[65] There had always been thieves willing to rob churches, and there had always been unscrupulous fences willing to resell stolen goods; even the 'age of faith' had its share of frankly sacrilegious individuals. But this was an example of an entire community taking part in such robbery or profiting from its proceeds, of whole villages willingly expending their energies plundering great Gothic monuments and even a hallowed monastic church. In the later Middle Ages, we have recently been told, communal or corporate solidarity was at the centre of Christian worship; at Hailes such solidarity seems to have been neatly turned on its head.

V

With the physical and social details of the spoliation now established, we can return to the central matter at hand: the interconnections between religious change and the dismantling of the abbey. The standard scholarship

---

[64] PRO STAC 2/1, fols. 15r–21v; PRO KB 9/978, fol. 70r.

[65] John Rule, 'Wrecking and Coastal Plunder', in Douglas Hay, Peter Linebaugh, John G. Rule, E. P. Thompson and Cal Wirslow (eds.), *Albion's Fatal Tree: Crime and Society in Eighteenth-Century England* (New York, 1975).

would suggest that there were few such interconnections. Not only was the fall of English monasticism a story of greed rather than iconoclasm, we are told, but Gloucestershire was one of the more conservative counties in England. According to Caroline Litzenberger, the most recent authority on Tudor Gloucestershire, only a tiny minority of surviving Gloucestershire wills from Henry VIII's reign show evangelical tendencies, while in the Gloucestershire Cotswolds (Hailes' region) not a single will showed clear signs of Protestantism in the years 1541–7. In the 1540s, Litzenberger writes, 'the Gloucestershire laity appear to have settled quietly into a modified version of the old religion', and by 1553 'most would have welcomed the return of the public practices and private devotions of the old religion'. Litzenberger cites the trauma of the Reformation itself as evidence that the population favoured a conservative reaction: 'Exposed to the opposing beliefs of the last two bishops of Worcester, Hugh Latimer and John Bell, witnessing the removal of shrines such as the blood of Hailes, and presented with the dissolution of the monasteries, the laity generally seem to have welcomed the more conservative policies of the early 1540s.'[66]

Yet, in fact, among the individuals implicated in the destruction of the abbey were a considerable number of people who can be linked to new religious ideas either in the early 1540s or later. Such numbers do not add up to anything like a majority of the people who plundered the abbey, and the point is not to suggest that the plunder was somehow a 'Protestant' event. Yet, given the ideologically charged nature of the assault on Hailes in the 1530s, it would be surprising if whatever evangelicals there were in Gloucestershire had *not* rushed to participate in the abbey's destruction, spreading their own interpretation of its meanings among their more conservative neighbours. The point, then, is that the participation of evangelicals in the plunder of Hailes provided significant opportunities for cooperation and productive engagement among people of very different theological views.

The evidence for evangelical tendencies among the spoilers of Hailes begins with the gentleman John Stratford the younger from Sudeley, a significant landowner in both Winchcombe and Hailes. Stratford made a total of 9s from abbey goods, selling to one Ralph Hornby 'a little house called a scripture' and 'a ceiling of boards containing 30 yards'.[67] When he made his will in July 1549, he left none of his substantial wealth to the Church or to the care of his soul, but rather stated in the preamble: 'I give and commend my soul to almighty God my creator, trusting assuredly that only by the death

[66] Litzenberger, *The English Reformation and the Laity*, pp. 43, 58, 82, 161 and 183.
[67] PRO SP 5/5, fol. 13v. This John Stratford the younger was almost certainly the son of the John Stratford the elder who was one of the royal commissioners investigating the spoliation (see PRO SP 5/5, fol. 17r).

of his dearly beloved son Jesus my sins be washed clean and forgiven.'[68] Another wealthy man, Thomas Harres from the nearby town of Condicote, was summoned to testify before the royal commissioners but failed to appear, rather unconvincingly alleging 'inability to labour'; his son John Harres, who had no such excuse, was heavily implicated in the plunder.[69] When Thomas Harres died in March 1548, he bequeathed his soul 'unto almighty God only, the which is the maker and redeemer of the world'.[70] These men's use of the unequivocal formula that they were saved 'only' by God certainly points towards the new religion, as does their complete lack of traditional bequests, although Litzenberger considers them to lie on the reformed end of the 'ambiguous' spectrum.[71]

Among men of more moderate financial means, tendencies towards the 'new learning' can also be glimpsed. Anthony Griffith of Didbrook, probably the same man whom John Harres paid to break into Hailes, died in April 1569, leaving his soul 'to almighty God my saviour and redeemer by whose death and blood shedding I trust to be saved and by none other means'.[72] The inclusion of the term 'and by none other means' is sufficient to mark Griffith as unambiguously evangelical even by Litzenberger's demanding standards.[73] Griffith was not a poor man, having been assessed at 40s in goods at the 1542 subsidy and having been included on a local manor court jury in 1540.[74] As his 'tools' were divided among his sons at his death, however, he was clearly no gentleman. Roger Croswell, who was extremely active in the spoliation, occupies a similar place in our records. He was assessed at £3 in goods in 1542, making him a significant local figure but almost certainly not a gentleman.[75] At his death in 1572, Croswell bequeathed his soul 'to almighty God my savior and redeemer by whose death and blood shedding I trust only to be saved and by none other means', and left nothing of any sort to the Church.[76] Richard Roberts, a 'joiner' from

---

[68] GRO Will 1550/17. This will was written in July 1549, but proved in January 1550.
[69] SP 5/5, fol. 10r–v.   [70] GRO Will 1548/100.
[71] Litzenberger, *The English Reformation and the Laity*, p. 172.   [72] GRO Will 1569/5.
[73] Litzenberger, *The English Reformation and the Laity*, p. 172.
[74] PRO E 179/114/247, fol. 13r; PRO SC 2/175/1, fol. 51v.
[75] PRO E 179/114/247, fol. 13r.
[76] GRO Will 1572/132. This soul bequest is very similar to Anthony Griffith's and came from the same parish, raising the possibility that this formula was provided to them by their scribes. Often, however, scribes offered testators a choice of formulae, while sometimes scribes were chosen exactly because they shared the religious beliefs of the testator. Thus, as in all uses of evidence from wills, these conclusions must remain tentative in lieu of independent corroboration. See Margaret Spufford, 'The Scribes of Villagers' Wills in the Sixteenth and Seventeenth Centuries and their Influence', *Local Population Studies*, 7 (1971), 28–43; M. L. Zell, 'The Use of Religious Preambles as a Measure of Religious Belief in the Sixteenth Century', *BIHR*, 50 (1977), 246–9; J. D. Alsop, 'Religious Preambles in Early Modern English Wills as Formulae', *JEH*, 40 (1989), 19–27; C. Marsh, 'In the Name of God? Will-Making and Faith in early Modern England', in G. H. Martin and Peter Spufford

Toddington who died in 1570, may or may not be the same Richard Roberts of Wodstanway who bought 4s 6d worth of stolen wooden boards from Hailes Abbey. If so, he is yet another middling-sort evangelical involved in the destruction of the abbey, since he, too, bequeathed his soul to 'Almighty God my saviour and redeemer by whose death and blood shedding I trust to be saved and by none other means' and left no bequests for the Church.[77] While it could be objected that none of these men betrayed any signs of Protestantism until Elizabeth's reign, when such sentiments were legal and encouraged, it should be pointed out that, according to Litzenberger, only 4.3 per cent of testators in the Gloucestershire Cotswolds used Protestant will formulae between 1559 and 1569, and only 11.3 per cent used such formulae between 1570 and 1580.[78] Thus, while there is no proof that either Griffith, Croswell or Roberts had evangelical sympathies when they broke into the abbey of Hailes, it is clear that they later became quite abnormally vociferous in their support for the new religion.

Another evangelical involved in the assault on the abbey was John Pynnock of Longborough, whose will has been singled out by Litzenberger as one of the most quintessentially Reformed documents to emerge from Gloucestershire during Queen Mary's reign. Addressing God directly in his 1555 will, Pynnock prayed, 'let all the merits of thy passion be my salvation for in them I trust and not in any works that I have done', and he asked that 'the sweet sacrifice of [Christ's] body and blood may now make atonement betwixt the wrath of God which I have deserved and me'.[79] Pynnock's role in the 1540–1 spoliation was undeniable but, at least according to his own testimony, small scale; he bought 12d worth of coloured and white glass, 16d worth of iron, and 'took himself one board, without authority, which was worth 4d'.[80] Despite this apparent moderation, the fact that Pynnock was involved at all is extraordinary, since before the dissolution he had been farmer of the abbey's manor of Longborough and as recently as July 1537 he and his wife had been granted leases by the abbot for lands, a sheep house, liberty of pasture, and tithes of wool and lambs.[81]

Among laymen whom we might suspect of evangelical leanings, however, the most important is Robert Acton, the gentleman to whom the abbey was leased and whose servants were so instrumental in its destruction. Acton's will, written during Mary's reign in September 1558, is slightly ambiguous

---

(eds.), *The Records of the Nation* (Woodbridge, 1990); Duffy, *Stripping of the Altars*, pp. 504–23; Litzenberger, *The English Reformation and the Laity*, Appendix A and *passim*.

[77] PRO SP 5/5, fol. 13v; GRO Will 1571/161. Although listed as being from 1571, this will is dated 27 June 12 Eliz.I, i.e. 1570.

[78] Litzenberger, *The English Reformation and the Laity*, p. 183.

[79] Ibid., pp. 93–4.   [80] PRO SP 5/5, fol. 13v.

[81] Shakespeare Birthplace Trust Record Office, MS DR 18/31/5, fols. 101v–107r.

in its religiosity since he left money for the poor to be distributed on the day of his burial (a reflection of traditional practices) and included among his executors both Cardinal Pole and the Catholic bishop of Worcester. Neither of these items is strong evidence for his Catholicism, however, since many elite evangelicals left charitable bequests and included their diocesan and metropolitan in their wills. On the other hand, Acton left no money for the Church, candles or masses, practices that were both legal and encouraged in Mary's reign, and he did not mention saints or the virgin. He also used a quintessentially evangelical soul bequest: 'I, most miserable and wretched sinner, do commend my soul to almighty God and to his blessed son Jesus Christ and to the Holy Ghost, three persons and one God, most humbly beseeching that most holy and blessed trinity to have mercy upon my soul and to forgive me my sins that I may arise again at the latter day with such as be his elect and chosen people ordained to salvation, and have the fruition of his godhead according to my true belief.'[82] Other evidence for Acton's evangelical leanings confirm this picture, most importantly the verdict of Hugh Latimer that Acton was 'faithful and hearty in all good causes, no man more ready to serve God and the king'.[83]

Besides these laymen, there were also many priests involved in the destruction of the abbey, several of whom show clear evangelical sympathies. Most importantly there was Thomas Hopkins, the man responsible for both hurling timbers from the steeple and pulling up gravestones in the church. Hopkins is identified in the records of the royal commissioners as 'chaplain to the said Robert Acton', and, given Acton's religious predilections, this at least marks him as suspicious.[84] Moreover, one Thomas Hopkins was a monk of Hailes when it was dissolved late in 1539 and was given an annual pension of 16s 8d by the Crown.[85] If this was the same man, then the plot thickens: we have a monk taking a job as chaplain to the reform-minded gentleman who had been granted his former abbey. Most importantly, however, in June 1545 the chancellor to the Bishop of Gloucester brought suit in ecclesiastical court against '*Thomas Hopkins et Elizabeth Hopkins eius uxorem in causa mutue cohabitacionis*'.[86] If this Thomas Hopkins is also the same man, then his credentials as a married priest in Henry VIII's reign mark him as an evangelical indeed.

There were also two priests involved in the plunder of the abbey named Nicholas Wyks, one of whom was parson of Condicote and the other of whom was rector of Bachesore; a variety of sources show that these really

---

[82] PRO PROB 11/42A, fols. 154v–156r.
[83] S. T. Bindoff (ed.), *The House of Commons, 1509–1558*, 3 vols. (London, 1982), I, pp. 291–2.
[84] PRO SP 5/5, fol. 12r.   [85] PRO E 315/245, fol. 73r.   [86] GRO GDR 2, p. 46.

were two different men rather than a single pluralist cleric.[87] Later evidence shows that one or both of these men had evangelical leanings. When Nicholas Wyks of Condicote was examined on the fundamentals of the faith by the zealous Protestant bishop John Hooper in a 1551–2 visitation, he was '*potens respondere ad omnes articulos supra memoratos*'; while this does not necessarily make Wyks a reformer, Hooper was not promiscuous with his praise.[88] More importantly, a Nicholas Wyks described as parson of Colne Rogers in Gloucestershire, who could have been either of the two men who were at Hailes in 1541, left a will in 1570 in which he left a variety of bequests to his 'daughter Margaret'. For Margaret Wyks to have been of legal majority in 1570, she must have been born no later than 1552; in other words, this priest had sired a daughter whom he considered legitimate by the middle of Edward VI's reign at the latest.[89]

There is also the case of a man called William Fisher, named only briefly in the Hailes depositions and described as a servant of Robert Acton.[90] The title 'servant' is a general one, as we know from other parts of the Hailes depositions, so it is unclear whether this man either was or became a priest. If so, then he could well be the William Fisher who purchased lands formerly belonging to the abbey in the early 1540s, and who was presented by the king to the vicarage of Longborough in August 1546. This William Fisher was subsequently deprived of his living by Queen Mary in 1554, making it very likely that he, too, had non-traditional religious views.[91]

Even if some of this evidence is open to doubt, the cumulative effect of all these coincidences is enough to force us to reconsider the conventional notion that the dissolution of the monasteries was unconnected to theology. Of the roughly seventy-five people named as involved in the spoil of Hailes, wills and church court records allow us to make a guess at the religious views of seventeen.[92] Of these, ten can be either tentatively or strongly identified

---

[87] For instance, in a 1540 visitation book from the diocese of Worcester, the Nicholas Wyks of Condicote was referred to as '*dominus*' while the Nicholas Wyks of Bachesore was referred to as 'Mr': WRO MS 802 BA 2764, p. 313. In a 1551–2 visitation book from the diocese of Gloucester, the Nicholas Wyks of Condicote answered all Bishop Hooper's questions satisfactorily, while the Nicholas Wyks of Batsford (*sic*) was described as '*mediocrites*': Dr Williams Library, Morice MS 31L/3, pp. 39 and 44. And in the manuscript describing the spoliation at Hailes, the Nicholas Wyks of Battashere is described as being thirty years old, while on the same page the Nicholas Wyks of Condicote is described as being thirty-three years old: PRO SP 5/5, fol. 18r.

[88] Dr Williams Library, Morice MS 31L/3, p. 44.   [89] GRO Will 1570/128.

[90] PRO SP 5/5, fol. 11r.   [91] GRO GDR D1/177; PRO E 323/2A, fol. 15r–v.

[92] Three people can be described as traditionalist Catholics: John Butler (GRO Will 1546/88) and William Coopar (GRO Will 1557/451) left wills in which their souls were bequeathed to 'all the blessed company of heaven', while the rector of Staunton, Kenelme Deane, was threatened with deprivation in 1551 for his attachment to 'superstitions' (GRO GDR 6, p. 48). Four other wills of ambiguous religiosity are also extant. Thomas Fouche: GRO Will 1555/102; Thomas Harres: GRO Will 1548/100; Richard Andros: GRO Will 1559/250

as evangelicals by the time of their deaths. Clearly the most heterodox members of the community, those either already enamoured with the new learning or most open to such views, internalised the rhetoric of Hailes' detractors in the 1530s and took the lead in plundering the abbey's wealth in the 1540s.

VI

On the other side, it is important to note that the spoliation was not a univocal process, and we can locate several cases where people who participated in the spoil of the abbey may have had pious motives and attempted to protect objects of devotion until the Old Religion was ascendant again. As will be shown below, the depositions from Hailes make it clear that this was only the case for a minority of participants. None the less, it is important to recognise that the dissolution of Hailes, far from creating any sort of consensus, divided the community. Thus, just as the minority of evangelicals who took part in the plunder deserve special attention as a crucially influential interest group, so, too, those who put a conservative gloss on the spoliation must be given their innings.

Some of the most interesting evidence of liturgical reuse of the fabric of Hailes comes not from manuscripts or printed books but from the stones themselves. In 1899–1900, excavations at Hailes revealed for the first time the details of the abbey's structure. Thirty years later, this information was put to good use by W. H. Knowles, who, in his investigation of the parish church of Teddington, Worcestershire, discovered that structural elements from Hailes Abbey, such as arch mouldings and capitals, had been incorporated into the west tower of that church when it was built in 1567.[93] While it cannot be proven that these stones were taken from Hailes in 1540–1 rather than over the subsequent quarter century, it seems reasonable to suspect that at least one of our plunderers successfully reused the abbey's constituent materials for spiritual purposes.

More evidence of possible devotional uses of Hailes's remains can be found in the depositions taken after the spoil. For instance, John Harres gave Richard Reve, servant to the local gentleman Richard Andros, '2 painted boards from the altar where the blood stood'; this is the only reference to the blood of Hailes in the entire manuscript, and the fact that these boards were given as a gift rather than sold may imply that they retained special

(NB: This Richard Andros is described as a shoemaker, so he is probably not the same man as the Richard Andros in the Hailes depositions); Robert Hogges: GRO Will 1558/389.

[93] W. H. Knowles, 'Teddington Church, Worcestershire, in Which Are Structural Fragments from Hayles Abbey', *TBGAS*, 52 (1930), 93–101.

significance. This conclusion must remain tentative, however, since many other, non-devotional objects were also given as gifts in the depositions (especially by John Harres) and since Richard Reve also stole a variety of objects (such as wooden stairs) with no apparent spiritual significance.[94] Another possible example of a devotionally motivated consumer was the wealthy Winchcombe man William Couper, who bought from Thomas Hopkins '2 chapels of stone out of the church there containing 10 loads' and 'paid him therefore 6s 8d'.[95] This certainly sounds like a devotional purchase, and there is corroborating evidence that Couper remained a religious conservative; when he died in 1557 he bequeathed his soul to 'almighty God and to the prayers of our blessed lady St. Mary and to all the blessed company of heaven'.[96] Once again, however, Couper's interest in chapels did not prevent him from buying a variety of other objects such as lead sold by weight. Another possible traditional purchase was that of Nicholas Wyks, parson of Condicote, who bought from John Harres 'the decks in the cloister and 4 forms and a door of a chapel out of the church, and paid him therefore all 2s 8d'. Again, this evidence is ambiguous, since this same Wyks also bought lead pipes from the abbey, and since at least one of the two men called Nicholas Wyks was later a religious reformer.[97]

Other evidence of public reaction to events at Hailes suggests that some people vigorously opposed the spoliation. The government first heard of the thefts, for instance, from two former suppression commissioners, Richard Poulet and William Berners. These men not only intervened to stop the nightly raids but also told of another man, a servant of one of the abbey's most important patrons, Lady Huddleston, who risked his life to prevent further thefts: 'More spoil would have been made there, as we have been credibly informed, if this man had not been vigilant and attendant for the saving thereof.'[98] Another man, called Robert Hoggez of Longborough, obstinately refused to take part in the spoil; he refused to carry 'a horse load of lead to Longborough' on behalf of Thomas Fouche and then with uncommon zeal reported to the authorities a variety of stolen objects he had seen hidden about Fouche's house.[99] Most interestingly, Thomas Norres of Longborough told the royal commissioners a complex tale of disagreement over the spoil, implying both his own opposition and the opposition of some of his neighbours: 'One Joan Tham, woman servant at one Thomas Harres

[94] PRO SP 5/5, fol. 12r.   [95] PRO SP 5/5, fol. 13v.   [96] GRO Will 1557/451.
[97] PRO SP 5/5, fol. 18r. The word I have rendered as 'decks' is actually 'dex' in the manuscript. According to the *OED*, the word 'deck' in the early modern period could mean any covering. Another possible interpretation would be 'dexe', which the *OED* gives as an attested form of 'desk'.
[98] PRO E 315/165, fol. 9r.   [99] PRO SP 5/5, fol. 10v.

of Condicote...did say to the wife of this deponent that she did see one come by night to the house of the said Thomas Harres with certain locks from Hailes in bags, and part of them were great and substantial. And then the said Joan said to her master, "Fie, alas, why do you receive thus this stuff?" And then the said Thomas said to her, "Hold thy peace, for it is there now. Catch that may catch."[100]

There is thus evidence that some people chose to gloss the spoliation at Hailes as unacceptably sacrilegious and sought either to stop that spoliation or make the best of it within a traditionalist framework. This position is certainly not a surprise, and it reflects the views of people elsewhere in the country who are known to have actively resisted the dissolution of the monasteries. At Norton Abbey in Cheshire, for instance, the abbot 'gathered a great company together to the number of two or three hundred persons' to prevent royal commissioners from seizing monastic jewels.[101] At Exeter, a mob of women with pikes and shovels broke open a monastic church and attacked the men pulling down the rood loft.[102] The parson of Radwell, Hertfordshire, told his parishioners in 1536 that 'they that pull down abbeys and churches...without the great mercy of God they shall be damned'.[103] The existence of such attitudes at Hailes, however, only serves to underline the radicalism of what was happening there in 1540–1. The plunder of the abbey was not a simple act of theft, devoid of religious significance and easily assimilable within a late-medieval devotional framework. Rather, the spoliation almost instantly became a 'wedge issue' for Catholics, dividing them into those who saw monasteries as essential elements of Christ's Church and those willing to reimagine those monasteries as mere lead and stone. The conservatives who objected to the assault on the abbey thus found themselves opposing not only a 'predatory Crown' but also their own friends and neighbours.

VII

If there was a minority of plunderers at Hailes who were reformers, and another minority who were traditionalists, there was still a majority who were neither. These were the people who participated in the spoil without any clear ideological objective, who collaborated in an unprecedented act of sacrilege without any obvious motive other than the desire for material profit. It was for this great mass of souls that Catholics and evangelicals battled in the sixteenth century, and it is for these same reluctant participants in the drama of Reformation that historians battle in the twenty-first. What was the

---

[100] PRO SP 5/5, fol. 18r.   [101] Bodleian MS Tanner 105, fols. 60r–61v.
[102] Joyce Youings, *The Dissolution of the Monasteries* (London, 1971), p. 164.
[103] SP 1/116, fol. 192r [*LP* XII, i, 572].

relationship between their beliefs and their actions, and to what extent can meaning be read into their desecration of the abbey? The answer suggested by the Hailes depositions is that, regardless of their theological views, the plunderers internalised the reordering of the relationship between Church and state promulgated by the government and accepted that the dissolution of the abbey had profound spiritual consequences, effectively desacralising monastic space. They thus enacted a new set of assumptions – assumptions that were themselves a significant point of contact between the official view of the dissolution of the monasteries and the evangelicals' more radical views – about the irrelevance of physical objects and places in the spiritual life of the Church.

A variety of devotional items, for instance, are described in the depositions as having been handled in unambiguously sacrilegious ways by people whom we cannot otherwise label religious reformers. For instance, George Fouche, son of the plumber Thomas Fouche, admitted that he bought from William Bough 'the lead in the holy water vat without the church door, and certain pipes of lead, and paid him for all 12d'.[104] We have no evidence to link George Fouche with religious reform, and no reason to doubt that he considered himself a conventionally pious Catholic. Yet this particular purchase clearly amounted to iconoclasm of a much higher order than pulling lead gutters out of buildings; holy water was of enormous significance to medieval worship, and the containers for that water were items of significant devotion. A second person was also implicated in Fouche's sacrilege, namely William Bough, who both ripped the vat out of its accustomed place and sold it to a smith who he must surely have known would melt it down. George Fouche's father, Thomas Fouche, was also not above stealing expressly devotional objects. Robert Hoggez, for instance, reported seeing in the elder Fouche's house 'a bell rope pertaining to the late monastery'. Given that church bells were consecrated objects, the theft of the bell rope must have had significant implications.[105]

Thomas Hopkins, who was certainly a religious reformer himself, committed many of the gravest acts of desecration in the abbey. Interestingly, however, he sold the products of his labours to people whom we cannot identify as sharing his spiritual views. The forty-year-old Nicholas Wainwright of Winchcombe, for instance, 'bought of the same Sir Thomas 5 loads of stone digged within the ground under the paving stone in the body of the

---

[104] PRO SP 5/5, fol. 10r.
[105] PRO SP 5/5, fol. 10v. The bells of Hailes were not apparently stolen, and in Mary's reign they were sold to the parish of Stratford-upon-Avon (PRO E 117/14/98). For an example of church bells in this period being sanctified by the diocesan, see c. 14 of the deposition of Edmund Canworthy of Halberton, Devon in PRO STAC 4/8/47.

church there and paid him 3s 4d'.[106] Since we learn about this incident from his own deposition, Wainwright clearly knew that the church floor had been destroyed to procure his goods, an act of particular significance because it would have required the desecration of graves. Similarly, John Dobins of Stanley bought from Thomas Hopkins '7 frames of timber whereupon the copes were wont to hang'. It is clear from the deposition that Dobins was not saving these frames for devotional use; in fact he bought a significant quantity of wood, including 'one door and 9 yards of ceiling boards', so it seems likely that he needed the materials for house repairs.[107] Here we have financial transactions between Catholics and evangelicals in which the Catholics accepted and profited from the sacrilegious activities of a man whose religious proclivities they must surely have known.

It is also striking how many smiths and plumbers were implicated in the spoil of Hailes. The three Fouches of Longborough, Thomas and his two sons John and George, were all smiths, and appeared to their interrogators to be 'privy great meddlers' in the destruction of the abbey.[108] Robert Ray, a smith from Todington, bought large quantities of iron and lead.[109] John Harres delivered several horse-loads of lead to 'a smith of Stow'.[110] Roger Croswell sold 7s worth of lead to 'the plumber of Winchcombe'.[111] These men were clearly in the business of melting down the metal and recasting it; Robert Ray's servant, John Owen, even described his master's haul by explaining how the metal would be refashioned, saying he had received 'as much iron as made a pair of hand-irons and 3 pairs of cross gimmals which weighed about 80 pounds'.[112] This was clearly not a reuse of monastic fabric but its destruction.

It could be argued that, besides these rather clear-cut cases, the other people involved in the plunder of the abbey were unintentional participants, conscientious Catholics dragged into unwitting collaboration by the vast quantity of monastic goods on the market. Yet people did not simply buy anonymous metal, wood or glass; in nearly every deposition it is clear that the buyers of flotsam and jetsam from Hailes knew not only that it came from the abbey but even from what room their particular purchases had been removed. William Goodall, for instance, knew that wooden boards he bought from William Brode had come from 'the bachelor of Hailes's chamber'.[113] Anthony Griffith knew that the boards he bought came from the 'second dorter and the boards of the partitions betwixt each of them'.[114] Ralph Passy knew that the 'small stair of timber' that he bought came from

[106] PRO SP 5/5, fol. 13r.   [107] PRO SP 5/5, fol. 13v.   [108] PRO SP 5/5, fol. 10r.
[109] PRO SP 5/5, fols. 13r–14r.   [110] PRO SP 5/5, fol. 14r.   [111] PRO SP 5/5, fol. 13r.
[112] PRO SP 5/5, fol. 13v.   [113] PRO SP 5/5, fol. 10r.   [114] PRO SP 5/5, fol. 10v.

the 'kitchener's chamber'.[115] Richard Cheshere knew that the wooden boards that Robert Garfote gave him were 'boards out of the steeple which stood in [the] window there'.[116] Dozens more examples could be cited.

To summarise, then, the majority of thefts and purchases from Hailes were conducted by people who, despite having no positive evangelical ideology, none the less knowingly laid claim to monastic property for thoroughly irreligious purposes. These people consciously and systematically committed acts that only a few years before would have been considered sacrilege and which, even more importantly, some of their neighbours *still* insisted were sacrilege. Our inevitable conclusion, then, is that for vast numbers of people in and around Hailes the abbey had within a few short years been successfully desacralised. This was not merely a function of the *legal* dissolution of the abbey; for the rebels who tried to resuscitate monasteries in 1536, after all, such legalisms evidently had little spiritual impact. More important was the *gloss* placed on the dissolution in this local context, an interpretation thoroughly alien to traditional religion and its obsession with physical manifestations of holiness: objects were merely stone, wood and metal, and reverence for those objects was a form of superstition and idolatry, just as Anthony Saunders, Hugh Latimer and even the abbot of Hailes had said.

Yet even this conclusion is insufficient, since the people of Hailes did not merely accept the desacralisation of holy objects but actually broke the law in order to participate in that desacralisation themselves. Here, then, we must conclude that the plunderers' understandings of their own actions were not centred on the king's prerogative to dissolve abbeys, nor were they at all bound by issues of legal jurisdiction, spiritual adiaphora, or other interpretations of the dissolutions peddled by Henrician conservatives. Their understandings rather centred on their own prerogative to confiscate ecclesiastical wealth, and as such they were closer to John Wyclif's interpretation of the medieval maxim *bona ecclesiae sunt bona pauperum*: 'The goods of the Church belong to the poor', and when a churchman 'unjustly consumes the goods of the Church' he is an 'apostate, a seducer, and a heretic'.[117] Certainly not everyone at Hailes felt this way, but what is most important in this context is that, at Hailes, evangelicals and Catholics plundered the abbey *together*, creating a broad coalition of local residents who cooperated in opposition to their more conservative neighbours. Those who had internalised aspects of the new religious ideology were able to discuss that ideology with their neighbours not as proselytisers but in the context of a common project.

---

[115] PRO SP 5/5, fol. 11r.   [116] PRO SP 5/5, fol. 12r.

[117] Steven Justice, *Writing and Rebellion: England in 1381* (Berkeley, 1994), pp. 93 and 84.

In practical terms, then, if not in the purest theological sense, the impact of religious change on the English people was already beyond dispute. Hailes Abbey, the focus of both national pilgrimage and community devotion for centuries, had been dismantled without hesitation by the same people to whom Queen Mary would soon appeal for help in the revival of monasticism. The abbey church, with its side chapels for private masses, holy-water fonts, devotional statuary, stained glass and stone altars had been converted in people's minds back into the constituent elements from which it had been made. With their collaboration in the spoil of Hailes, the inhabitants of the surrounding communities gave their assent to this process, an assent which a decade before would have been unthinkable. This was the progress of the English Reformation.

VIII

In his 1984 trumpet blast for revisionism, *The Reformation and the English People*, J. J. Scarisbrick argued that 'there are no examples in England of the dissolution unleashing pent-up violence against monks and nuns or of mobs ransacking religious houses as they were vacated, as was to happen elsewhere'.[118] While it may or may not be true that there was no violence against monks and nuns, the statement that mobs did not ransack religious houses is severely misleading. Admittedly, such 'ransacking' was comparatively orderly, and the people of Hailes did not display unambiguous hatred for the institution they plundered. Yet their actions were remarkably far removed from our received model of late medieval religiosity. It is simply impossible to imagine the practitioners of Eamon Duffy's traditional religion engaging in such breathtakingly sacrilegious activities; either Duffy is wrong, or something very significant had occurred in the first decade of the Henrician Reformation.

And, while Hailes, with its great relic, cannot be taken as typical, the elements present there were also present, in varying degrees and configurations, throughout the country. In an undated letter from Philip Hoby to John Scudamore, for instance, there is evidence for a comparable plunder at the monastery of Evesham in Worcestershire: 'As concerning the spoil or waste that ye wrote to me of that hath been done there, I assure you both I and mine be guiltless thereof, besides that it did cost me money to persons for a long time nightly to touch and to take heed lest anything should . . . be misordered there.'[119] At Pipewell monastery in Northamptonshire, royal commissioners found destruction comparable to the plunder at Hailes, although they

---

[118] Scarisbrick, *The Reformation and the English People*, p. 72.
[119] Wright (ed.), *Three Chapters of Letters Relating to the Suppression of the Monasteries*, pp. 283–4.

documented it less fully: panes of glass from the church, iron from the cloister, lead, wood, plaster and much else was removed.[120] Near Reading, a chapel owned by Notley Abbey was dissolved in 1538 by the royal commissioner John London, who reported that as soon as he had taken its surrender, 'the multitude of the poverty of the town resorted thither, and all things that might be had they stole away, insomuch that they had conveyed the very clappers of the bells'.[121] In Derby, a labourer called Richard Camerdaye was arrested for having illegally entered 'the church and houses of the late black friars in Derby' and stolen 'two grave stones of marble with certain glass, iron, lead, and timber...to the value of £4'. While Camerdaye may have acted alone, the spectre of conspiracy was raised when two local bailiffs, Humphry Sutton and Edward Lenton, were accused of having 'suffered the said Camerdaye wilfully to escape'.[122] And, most remarkably, at Warwick John London reported that he and the 'honest inhabitants' had tried everything in their power to prevent spoliation:

but the poor people thoroughly in every place be so greedy upon these houses when they be suppressed that by night and day, not only of the towns but also of the country, they do continually resort as long as any door, window, iron, or glass, or loose lead remaineth in any of them. And if it were so done only where I go, the more blame might be laid to me, but it is universally that the people be thus greedy for iron, windows, doors, and lead. In every place I keep watch as long as I tarry, and imprison those that do thus abuse themselves, and yet others will not refrain.[123]

Throughout England, then, there were large numbers of people willing to follow on the heels of the suppression commissioners, claiming for themselves a piece of monastic spoils even at the risk of the law's fury. Why was this revolutionary activity possible? One explanation is simply greed: desire for riches outweighed moral scruples. This is certainly true, but it fails to explain why such greed was suddenly unleashed against an ancient and venerated institution. Should we really believe that at any other time in English history the commons would have ripped apart the monasteries and stolen their wealth if only they had believed they would not be caught? This notion defies common sense. Rather, something had changed in the years before the plunder: not only had the monasteries themselves been vacated, but their meaning had been eroded, their powerful symbolism and aura of holiness turned on its head.

The coercive power of the early Tudor state was meagre, but with its panoply of royal and religious imagery, its sophisticated propaganda machine and its core of ideologically committed evangelicals, its persuasive power

[120] PRO E 315/109, fols. 23r–26r; PRO E 315/109, part 2.
[121] Wright (ed.), *Three Chapters of Letters Relating to the Suppression of the Monasteries*, p. 222.
[122] PRO STAC 2/29/1, fol. 7r.   [123] *Original Letters*, III, part 3, p. 139.

could be immense. At Hailes, the relic that had supported the reputation of the abbey for centuries was exposed as a fraud and the monks who guarded it were exposed as charlatans. Evangelical preachers and even an evangelical bishop explained to local inhabitants how they had been duped by both the monks and the bishop of Rome. Even the conservative abbot came down on the government's side, and at least one ex-monk was quickly drawn into the evangelical fold. At the same time, the government directly challenged the holiness of the abbey itself. The physical stripping of the monastery by agents armed with royal commissions represented a direct contest between Church and Crown, the two powers which, to most English subjects, seemed to rule the world. When only one was left standing at the end of the day, can we be surprised that it altered English people's conceptions of the sacred?

This desacralisation of Catholic space was not, of course, tantamount to nascent Protestantism; here the views of A. G. Dickens, who saw a decrease in outwardly Catholic religiosity as synonymous with the 'progress of Protestantism', have rightfully been overthrown. Yet we also cannot attempt to disassociate de-Catholicisation and Protestantisation altogether.[124] As the evidence from Hailes shows, the two were intimately related processes. Catholics who collaborated with the destruction of Hailes could not have been ignorant of the fact that their actions had spiritual connotations; they were constantly being told as much by their more intransigent co-religionists. Besides following directly in the footsteps of Hugh Latimer (denounced as a 'heretic' by the pilgrims of grace), the plunderers certainly knew from their more worldly neighbours that similar destruction of monasteries had occurred wherever the heresies of Luther, Zwingli and Bucer had put down roots. Of course this does not mean that Catholics could not collaborate with the dissolution of the monasteries without abandoning their faith; many did just that. But on the ground at Hailes, as opposed to looking down at the dissolutions from the bird's-eye perspective of great magnates and Henrician courtiers, collaboration required much more than scrawling numbers in ledgers and collecting rents. It required ripping gravestones out of churches and patching roofs with lead melted from abbey walls, enacting with one's own hands the physical destruction of all that was holy. Whatever its motivations, then, it required sloughing off beliefs in the ability of the Church to sanctify spaces and objects– and hence to bridge the gap between the sacred and the profane – that were at the heart of medieval religion.

---

[124] Cf. Jeremy Gregory, 'The Making of a Protestant Nation: "Success" and "Failure" in England's Long Reformation', in Nicholas Tyacke (ed.), *England's Long Reformation 1500–1800* (London, 1998); Robert Whiting, *The Blind Devotion of the People: Popular Religion and the English Reformation* (Cambridge, 1989), ch. 8 and passim.

While the people of Hailes may have remained ostensibly followers of the old faith, then, they none the less found themselves behaving in ways which their parents would have found appalling and which committed resistors could barely comprehend. This promiscuous seepage of ideas and motivations between people of rival faiths may not help to explain the conversion of England to Protestantism, but it does explain how a regime so weak that it twice capitulated to tax revolts managed to achieve almost universal compliance with an unprecedented and radically destructive policy against one of the great pillars of the Catholic Church.

6

'Open disputation was in alehouses': religious debate in the diocese of Canterbury, c. 1543

As important as it is to recognise how much of the Reformation English people experienced through the mediation of political debates and property disputes, it would be absurd to deny that they were also exposed to great swathes of systematic theology. Thus, when people adapted aspects of the evangelical programme to suit their needs, they were not unaware that they were sailing into potentially dangerous waters. In this chapter, then, I want to shift my analytical focus and consider the sorts of theological positions that were canvassed among ordinary English subjects. Yet, because the goal remains to trace a political process rather than one of national conversion, the argument of this chapter will necessarily appear somewhat perverse. While I discuss technical questions of theology, I make no claims about the relative popularity of different theological positions or the growth of Protestantism, the standard fare of most Reformation history. Rather, I want to demonstrate the crucial importance of a new phenomenon – rampant and public theological *division* – for the ways people received and responded to the state-sponsored Reformation. In other words, instead of privileging the experiences of actively partisan minorities, this chapter examines those minorities in order to show how their debates – conducted publicly and appealing for support at all social levels – affected English political culture more generally.

To bring order to such a potentially wide-ranging subject, this analysis focuses on the evidence created by a unique and fascinating event: the Prebendaries' Plot of 1543.[1] During that year in the diocese of Canterbury, prominent Catholics hatched an ecclesiastical *coup d'état* intended to oust Archbishop Cranmer and his evangelical clients and ultimately have them

---

[1] On the Prebendaries' Plot, see Diarmaid MacCulloch, *Thomas Cranmer: A Life* (New Haven, 1996), ch. 8; Glyn Redworth, *In Defence of the Church Catholic: The Life of Stephen Gardiner* (Cambridge, Mass., 1990), ch. 8; M. L. Zell, 'The Prebendaries' Plot of 1543: A Reconsideration', *JEH*, 27 (1976), 241–53; Peter Clark, *English Provincial Society from the Reformation to the Revolution: Religion, Politics, and Society in Kent 1500–1640* (Hassocks, 1977), ch. 2.

burned at the stake. The conspirators collected extensive evidence that Cranmer and his allies were using their authority to promote heresy and protect evangelicals who ran afoul of the law. When those conspirators presented their evidence to Henry VIII, they expected the king to arrest Cranmer and begin a new round of attacks against the evangelical establishment – a reasonable assumption given the king's brutal destruction of Thomas Cromwell and his allies in London only three years before. Yet Henry VIII, ever skilful at confounding his subjects' expectations, dithered instead of acting forcefully against the evangelicals. He encouraged a swing towards conservative policy, but he also decided that the traditionalist faction should not be allowed to grow too strong, and he thus used the Canterbury conspiracy as an excuse to move against potentially disloyal Catholics. In a tragicomic scene in the Privy Council, the king made clear to the plotters the depth of their folly by appointing Cranmer himself to investigate the charges they had laid against him. Using his new investigative authority, the archbishop uncovered evidence of Romanist activities in Kent which precisely mirrored the conspirators' discoveries of rampant heresy, and on the basis of this evidence Cranmer purged Catholics from positions of power in the diocese.

The story of this failed *coup d'état* is well known, but there is much that we have still to learn from the *evidence* collected by both sides during the crisis, evidence which provides a treasure-trove of information about religious conflict at the local level.[2] While the Prebendaries' Plot itself was an event in the elite politics of the cathedral and the court, it was generated by fears of popular heresy and was intimately linked to the dynamics of popular politics. As John Mills, one of the plotters, later testified, the conspiracy began when 'justices of this shire ... did greatly fear ... seditious preaching and occupying of corrupt books, by the which two things schism did engender among the people, open disputation was in alehouses, and in households reasoning among servants, of the which did also arise much debate and strife, [so that] a commotion would or might be among the people'.[3] It is this potential for 'commotion' among the people that is our subject. As early as 1542, the Kentish evangelical Thomas Becon asked: 'To whom is it unknown what dissension reigns among the spirituality and temporality?'[4] Taking his question as rhetorical, we might ask what effects the evident schism among the Kentish clergy and gentry had upon ordinary subjects who looked to them for spiritual and political guidance. To what extent did religious conflict

[2] This evidence is preserved in Corpus Christi College, Cambridge, MS 128, which has been extremely fully and accurately calendared in *LP* XVIII, ii, 546.
[3] CCCC MS 128, p. 297.   [4] Clark, *English Provincial Society*, p. 64.

colour social relations, local politics and the responses of Kentish men and women to royal religious policy?[5]

In this chapter, then, evidence gathered during the Prebendaries' Plot is used to explore religious controversy in the early 1540s, usually seen as a period of 'conservative reaction' when Catholics regained the reins of government and religious life returned more or less to normal. It argues instead that, far from returning to the *status quo ante*, the early 1540s were in fact the years when confessional conflict began to settle into predictable patterns and shape the politics of local communities. Previously, popular reactions to the Reformation had been largely (if never entirely) shaped by interpretations of its unique English corollary, the royal supremacy over the Church. From the Act of Six Articles in 1539 onwards, however, the realities of religious plurality and doctrinal difference were publicly acknowledged with increasing bluntness. As so many of the priests and gentlemen to whom the commons appealed for patronage and intervention chose sides in confessional disputes, the minority of commoners who adopted the rhetoric of religious conflict (whether out of belief or expediency) acquired disproportionate influence in their localities. Thus, while most English subjects did not imagine the Reformation as a straightforward battle between incompatible worldviews, popular politics none the less became increasingly confessionalised as people sought to make their way in a political world whose rhetoric was shaped by assumptions of binary opposition. The principal effect of public Reformation polemic, in other words, was not to convert the people of England to a new religion but rather to build a culture in which division rather than unity was acknowledged as the fundamental wellspring of politics.

I

As various historians have observed, the so-called Prebendaries' Plot was not merely a conspiracy by the canons of Canterbury Cathedral, as the name would imply, but a much wider movement by religious conservatives against the rising tide of heresy in southeastern England.[6] Active plotters included not only five prebendaries, but also two 'six preachers' (a new cathedral office created in 1541), a variety of priests not associated with the cathedral, and a wide range of local gentlemen including Thomas Moyle, Edward

---

[5] Two recent attempts to use the Prebendaries' Plot materials to inform our views of local religion are Brian M. Hogben, 'Preaching and the Reformation in Henrician Kent', *Archæologia Cantiana*, 101 (1984), 169–85; and Eamon Duffy, *The Stripping of the Altars: Traditional Religion in England 1400–1580* (New Haven, 1992), ch. 12.

[6] MacCulloch, *Thomas Cranmer*, ch. 8; Redworth, *In Defence of the Church Catholic*, ch. 8; M. L. Zell, 'The Prebendaries' Plot'; Clark, *English Provincial Society*, ch. 2. The two paragraphs which follow are based on these analyses.

Thwaites and Cyriac Pettit. Pulling the strings behind much of the conspiracy, and coordinating agitation in Canterbury with agitation in Windsor, was Bishop Stephen Gardiner of Winchester, using as an intermediary his secretary and nephew, Germain Gardiner. Also involved was Sir John Baker, a Privy Councillor who was instrumental in bringing Cranmer's heresies to the attention of the Crown, and Dr John London, a former commissioner for the dissolution of the monasteries who, like many of his erstwhile colleagues, turned out to be a religious conservative.

Long-term interconnections and loyalties among the elite of the diocese were also instrumental in hatching the conspiracy. Among the prebendaries involved in the plot, for instance, was William Hadleigh, formerly a monk of Christ Church who in 1526 had been a colleague of Edward Bocking on the archiepiscopal commission that pronounced Elizabeth Barton's divine revelations genuine.[7] It was as a Barton supporter, no doubt, that Hadleigh became friends with Edward Thwaites, one of Barton's propagandists, and with another conspirator and prebendary of the cathedral, Richard Parkhurst, who at the time had been Archbishop Warham's secretary. Another complex web of relationships surrounded John London, who had known the six preacher and conspirator Robert Serles at Oxford, where John London had been warden of New College while Serles held the living in the neighbouring church of St Peter's. As a persecutor of Oxford evangelicals in the 1520s, moreover, London would have known three prominent conservatives who had been wardens of Canterbury College, Oxford, and would later be prebendaries of Canterbury Cathedral: William Hadleigh, Richard Thornden and William Gardiner. To top off the list of interconnections, the *ex officio* visitor of John London's New College was none other than Bishop Stephen Gardiner. All of these personal ties, many of which flowed from the patronage network Archbishop Warham had created in the 1520s, served as a bulwark against the encroachment of Archbishop Cranmer's evangelical clients, who themselves had an equally complex basis in family ties, Cambridge University connections and the patronage network left behind by Thomas Cromwell.

These Byzantine webs of interpersonal relationships would seem to be far removed from popular politics, but in practice the boundaries between popular and elite politics could be remarkably porous. Indeed, the range of the conspiracy and its potential for impacting ordinary people's lives may be gleaned from the fact that no less than 240 priests and 60 lay men and women were accused of wrongdoing in the Prebendaries' Plot, with many hundreds more acting as accusers or witnesses.[8] Many of the people accused,

---

[7] See chapter 2 above.   [8] Hogben, 'Preaching and the Reformation in Kent', p. 170.

moreover, were Kent county officeholders or functionaries of Canterbury Cathedral, the same priests and politicians through whom ordinary people experienced governance. These petty officials had close relationships with local community leaders like parsons, churchwardens and landlords who themselves acted as social intermediaries and had close relationships with their poorer neighbours. Thus local religious disputes could quickly become intertwined with national politics when – often at the behest of these social intermediaries – members of the county, city or diocesan establishment intervened in the spiritual affairs of a community.

In the Canterbury parish of St Alphege, for instance, the parson, Sir Humphrey Cherdayn, was accused by several of his parishioners of denying the necessity of auricular confession; it later became apparent that these accusers had been encouraged by two powerful conservative clerics, the prebendary William Gardiner *alias* Sandwich and Edmund Shether, a six preacher of Canterbury Cathedral. In response to this accusation, two members of the parish, Thomas Batters (described as 'the king's servant') and William Salter (described as 'the king's bead man'), wrote a petition testifying to the 'honesty' of the parson and convinced their friends to sign it. Much to the anger of conservatives, however, many of the people whose signatures were procured were not members of Cherdayn's parish at all but rather were evangelical sympathisers from elsewhere in the city. In other words, outside weight was being brought to bear on what was, at least in the minds of Catholics, a legitimate grievance pursued through proper channels. In counterattack, then, four Catholic parishioners of St Alphege reported the activities of Batters and Salter to William Gardiner, including in their report the probably apocryphal but very potent story that Batters had claimed that Gardiner would 'quail' at the first sign of opposition. With his hackles thus raised, Gardiner wrote the whole story to the Privy Councillor Sir John Baker, asking him to intervene against the reformers. That same John Baker was, furthermore, one of the Kentish gentlemen working closely with Gardiner to gather evidence against Archbishop Cranmer and other heretics. We can see, then, that the boundaries between local and national politics were extremely fluid in Canterbury, with parish disputes feeding off and, in turn, contributing to the plot against the archbishop.[9]

The fraught issue of idolatry could also interweave local and national politics. In the Kentish parish of Chilham, for instance, the vicar, Dr John Willoughby, also happened to be a royal chaplain, a client of the ex-maid of Kent supporter Edward Thwaites, and a plotter with the prebendaries of Canterbury Cathedral. Thus, when Archbishop Cranmer and his commissary

[9] CCCC MS 128, pp. 201 and 267.

ordered the removal of 'abused' images in Chilham, those orders received an icy response. One image, a shrine which Thwaites had brought to Willoughby's parish from the dissolved monastery of St Augustine, the vicar simply ignored, later claiming that he had never been asked to pull it down. When he was commanded to pull down the parish rood, however, more complex machinations were necessary. Willoughby claimed that the rood was too big for him to pull down alone, so he went to some of his parishioners for aid. When he showed them the order to pull it down, however, they objected on the grounds that the order contradicted the King's Book, the recently published doctrinal statement of the Church of England. According to Willoughby's account, several parishioners claimed that only images to which 'oblations' were commonly made were required to be pulled down, and, since the rood of Chilham had not been the object of such dubious devotions, it might lawfully stand. Those same parishioners thus 'caused that same article [i.e. the passage from the King's Book] to be read, and then all said there should none be pulled down there, and by and by caused a lock [to] be set of the door'. This was clearly a staged protest; not only does Willoughby's story sound strained, but one of his concerned parishioners was identified as 'Master Pettet', almost certainly Cyriac Pettit, founder of a Catholic recusant dynasty, client of Sir John Baker, and Clerk of the Peace for Kent.[10] Willoughby's activities did not go unchallenged, however. A week after a lock was set on the church door, Edward Thwaites was allegedly 'marred'; this probably meant not that he received a physical injury, but rather that he was bothered by parishioners objecting to the continued presence of the rood. The matter was then appealed to Sir Thomas Moyle, Speaker of the House of Commons and yet another conspirator, who reportedly said that if no oblation were made to the rood 'then I warrant you let him stand'. Here, once again, a small parish outside Canterbury was the site of a complex religious dispute; the fact that elite players on the national political stage participated in the conflict did not mean that the parishioners of Chilham were not equally involved, agitating both for and against their village crucifix.[11]

Similar events occurred at Milton beside Canterbury, where there was an image of St Margaret 'to which was a common pilgrimage' before the Reformation. The parson of the parish, Sir Thomas Bynge, took down the image according to his duty, since there could be no argument that it had not been 'abused'. However, on St Margaret's Day in 1543, 'Mr. John Cross, sometime cellarer of Christ Church, came to the same church and did set the same image again with a garland of flowers on the head of it, and did strew the church and said mass there'. There can be no doubt that Cross's

---

[10] On Pettit, see MacCulloch, *Thomas Cranmer*, p. 312.   [11] CCCC MS 128, p. 99.

timely intervention came at the request of the parson; not only had the image itself presumably been in his safe-keeping, but another part of the deposition referred to the parson as the agent 'by whose means' the image was re-erected. Given that John Cross had been one of the leading monks of the cathedral priory of Canterbury, we have here an elite intervention in what must have been a contentious local dispute over an honoured icon. However, a note scribbled in Cranmer's hand also called for an inquiry into 'how many of Chartham were of counsel' in the re-erection of the image; evidently elite participation did not preclude popular activity.[12]

Sometimes interactions between local *engagés* and ecclesiastical authorities could be unpredictable and attempts to achieve interventions from Canterbury could go dangerously awry. In one case, a priest from the Isle of Thanet came to Canterbury 'to labour to have preachers to come to preach with them, for they said that they lacked their quarter sermons and could get no preachers'. While it does not say so in the depositions, this priest from Thanet was almost certainly an evangelical reformer. Much to the horror of the politically naïve priest, however, he seems to have accidentally walked into the wrong room at Canterbury Cathedral, making his request not to the Protestant archdeacon or commissary but to a small meeting of Catholic plotters against the archbishop: Robert Serles, William Gardiner, Edmund Shether and John Mills. They asked the priest how many churches there were in Thanet, and when he responded that there were eight, the four Catholic clerics 'agreed to go thither all upon one ... every one of us to preach at two parish churches, and so to do all their sermons in one day'. This was clearly not the outcome that the priest had ridden to Canterbury to achieve, and from the tone of questions which were later put to Serles and his associates about the incident, it seems that the sermons they preached in Thanet were more than usually divisive in tone.[13]

Another crucial mode of elite intervention in popular politics was manipulation of the judicial process. One of the central charges levelled in the Prebendaries' Plot, for instance, was that Christopher Nevinson, commissary of the diocese of Canterbury and a devoted evangelical, had routinely subverted the church courts to protect heretics. Complaint was made to Nevinson, for instance, that 'the Holy Sacrament of the altar was not renewed in the church of Buckland near Faversham by the space of two years', but Nevinson allegedly 'passed over the cause without reformation'.[14] Similarly, James Newman, a priest in Chartham, refused to use the name of Our Lady and would not cense the crucifix, 'which things, presented by the churchwardens to Mr. Commissary, was never punished'.[15] Nevinson also worked to procure

---

[12] CCCC MS 128, pp. 16 and 38.   [13] CCCC MS 128, pp. 175 and 256.
[14] CCCC MS 128, p. 13.   [15] CCCC MS 128, p. 76.

the release of Joan Boucher, a notorious sacramentary, and he suppressed evidence that the accused heretic Margaret Toftes had previously abjured her heresies in the diocese of London in an effort to save her from the fire.[16]

Archbishop Cranmer was equally notorious for his biased handling of accusations. For instance, a flurry of rumours that he was 'remiss in punishment' of evangelicals like Lancelot Ridley was accelerated by his public humiliation of the Catholic Robert Serles, who was made to preach a recantation of his opinions upon a stool.[17] The accusations against Serles, moreover, were hotly contested, and Cranmer made every effort not to let them be undermined. After Serles was accused of preaching popish sermons in the town of Hothfield, for instance, three men of the parish came to Canterbury to testify that he had been falsely accused; they were told, however, that their evidence would not be admitted because 'a negative in the law could never be proved'.[18] Such manipulations were well known and affected the tenor of popular politics. As William Gardiner put it: 'As Christ was accused by two or three false knaves, so a man may be accused by two or three false knaves, and the judge as false a knave as the best, and so be condemned.'[19]

Catholics, too, could use the justice system to protect their friends and punish their enemies. John Barrow, for instance, Clerk of the Peace for Kent and former client of the late attorney general Sir Christopher Hales, was accused in 1543 in a slew of judicial corruption charges. In several cases he was thought to have packed juries, refusing to impanel known religious reformers for the Kent sessions enforcing the Act of Six Articles. He was also accused of arranging the heresy conviction of a young woman from Benenden by testifying against her himself, based entirely on hearsay, without putting forward a single witness to her alleged words.[20]

Thus, just as it has been meticulously shown that the Prebendaries' Plot was a creature as much of the gentry as of the clergy,[21] so it seems that the plot resonated far lower down into Kentish society. Many of the incidents used as evidence by the conspirators or their opponents took place in ordinary communities, and the majority of these incidents were in fact local religious disputes that were merely enlarged by elite intervention. The same men who oversaw the religious life of the diocese, moreover, had cure of souls in a wide range of parishes throughout Kent, and these parishes were to be the front lines in the religious disputes of the 1540s. It is to the nature of those disputes that we now turn.

---

[16] CCCC MS 128, pp. 78–80.   [17] CCCC MS 128, pp. 297–8.
[18] CCCC MS 128, p. 171.   [19] CCCC MS 128, p. 10.
[20] CCCC MS 128, pp. 105–9.   [21] Zell, 'The Prebendaries' Plot'.

II

Given the outpouring of recent scholarship on 'popular piety' in the sixteenth century, remarkably little attention has been paid to the actual theological debates raging in English parishes during Henry VIII's reign. The reasons for this omission are threefold. First, revisionist emphasis on the unyielding conservatism of the English people has increasingly made theological controversy seem like a quaint footnote rather than a central component of the early Reformation. Second, pulpit disputes have been imagined largely as a continental rather than an English phenomenon, leading scholars of popular religion to rely instead on less dynamic and confrontational sources like wills and churchwardens' accounts.[22] Third, some historians have stressed the unreflective nature of parish religion, imagining theological debates performed in front of uninformed parishioners as pearls cast before swine rather than invitations to participate in the great debates of the age.[23] Evidence from Kent renders the first two of these arguments hollow; the third is more complex and requires greater consideration. We will return below to a more nuanced discussion of how ideas canvassed in the parishes were received; for now we will explore the complex and polemical nature of those ideas themselves.

Salvation and the sacrifice of Christ

Nothing was more central to sixteenth-century theological disputes than the issue of salvation, not only in the solifidean rejection of merit-through-works or the Reformed emphasis on predestination, but in the fundamentally different ways that people interpreted the significance of Christ's sacrifice on the cross. For Catholics, Christ's death and resurrection wiped clean the slate of human sin, allowing people living after the Incarnation to be saved, irrespective of the sins of Adam, according to their own faith and works. For proponents of the 'new learning', on the other hand, Christ's death not only wiped clean the slate of human sin but effectively threw that

---

[22] The standard work on English Reformation preaching, J. W. Blench, *Preaching in England in the Late Fifteenth and Sixteenth Centuries: A Study of English Sermons, 1450–c.1600* (Oxford, 1964), relies almost exclusively on printed editions of sermons and contains little discussion of either pulpit debates or local controversies except for Hugh Latimer's famous disputes in Bristol. This gap should soon be filled by the forthcoming work of Susan Wabuda, and I would like to thank her for discussing Tudor preaching with me. There is now a lively historiography on Elizabethan and early Stuart preaching, for which a useful introduction is Lori Anne Ferrell and Peter McCullough (eds.), *The English Sermon Revised: Religion, Literature and History 1600–1750* (Manchester, 2000).

[23] The classic statement of this viewpoint in the European context is Jean Delumeau, *Catholicism Between Luther and Voltaire: A New View of the Counter-Reformation* (London, 1977).

slate away, forgiving not only original sin but all the sins that ever would be forgiven. Protestants made the crucifixion the uniquely potent moment in human history, when God's elect were not merely offered the chance of salvation but were in fact saved. Thus, any ceremonies, sacraments or prayers that purported to contribute to human salvation were for evangelicals the grossest form of sacrilege, usurping from God the victory He had won on the cross.

Such complex ideas were the commonplace stuff of sermons in Kent in the early 1540s, with both sides argued before large, heterogeneous audiences. Thomas Dawby, parson of Wichling, for instance, preached at Christmas 1542 that 'Christ's passion is alone sufficient for all our sins', arguing against the necessity of good works and penance in salvation.[24] While this sermon was probably preached at Wichling, it is significant that Dawby had until not long before been curate of Lenham, the parish where Robert Serles was vicar. The parishioners of Lenham must have heard a great deal of Dawby's heterodoxy, which was undoubtedly why Serles took up the challenge there in August 1543, preaching in a mocking and highly polemical tone, 'They say...that only faith justifieth, and that it maketh no matter how we do live. Christ died for us and by his blood hath washed all our sins away. Therefore what needeth us to fast or pray?'[25] Preachers in other parts of the diocese also addressed this issue. One Swan, vicar of Sheldwich, allegedly preached to his flock an extreme version of the Catholic position that 'Christ did not die neither for you nor for me, nor your fathers nor my fathers, but for the fathers of the old law, and left us to be saved by our works'.[26] On the opposite side, Richard Turner preached in eloquent language, probably at the cathedral, that 'God was the sole priest and sung the last mass of requiem, and other masses profiteth not them that be departed'.[27] This was remarkably close to the language employed by a layman called Archibald of Faversham. When a priest told him, 'If I were your ghostly father I would neither absolve you nor give you penance', Archibald responded: 'Hast thou authority to absolve me or give me penance? Nay, thou mayest keep sheep. Christ said mass upon the Mount of Calvary and that is sufficient for my soul.'[28]

A closely related issue was the stain of original sin and its status in the post-Incarnation world. The Catholic six preacher Edmund Shether, for instance, sounded much like the vicar of Sheldwich when he preached 'that Christ and baptism did nothing but wash away our original sin, and if that any man after

---

[24] CCCC MS 128, p. 82.   [25] CCCC MS 128, p. 34.   [26] CCCC MS 128, p. 55.
[27] CCCC MS 128, p. 62. It is not clear whether Turner meant 'soul priest' or 'sole priest'; perhaps it was an intentional play on words.
[28] CCCC MS 128, p. 64.

baptism did fall, he must purchase remission of his sins by penance as Mary Magdalene did'.[29] Robert Serles took this argument a step further in a funeral sermon, preaching that even though 'by the receiving of the sacraments and penance all a man's deadly sins were forgiven', none the less 'the venial sins remained', and the dead would be punished for those sins unless 'they were relieved by masses and *Diriges* after their death'.[30] These arguments skilfully wove together several key strands of Catholic theology, suggesting that Christ's sacrifice purged the sins with which human beings were born, but that for their own sins Christians required the sacraments of the Church, including a new miracle, the sacrifice of the mass. For evangelicals, on the other hand, the mass was neither a sacrifice nor a miracle; as John Bland preached at Boughton under the Blean in April 1541: 'the mass did not profit for sins, for then Christ had died in vain'.[31] Original sin, furthermore, was still (at least in mainstream Reformed theology) resident in human beings even after the crucifixion. To believe otherwise was a form of perfectionism, the belief that human beings could achieve a state of grace while still on earth, which ran contrary to the whole thrust of Protestant anthropology: its profound pessimism and emphasis on the degradation of fallen humanity. Thus John Scory, six preacher of Canterbury and future Bishop of Rochester, preached in 1542 at the parish church of St Elphin's: 'Ye have a saying, "the child which is born between man and wife, it is born in original sin", and so it is. And ye say that the sin is taken away by the water of baptism, but it is not so. But look how that the wife that occupieth the fire all the day and at night covereth it with ashes to preserve the fire; so doth the sin remain under the sacrament.'[32]

   Another crucial area of disagreement with profound effects on the experience of religious worship was the theology of confession and penance. The Catholic position was that confessing to a priest and performing the prescribed penance purged the soul of sin. For most late-medieval Christians, therefore, confession was a crucial act of purgation performed once a year in preparation for receiving the body of God, while the receipt of 'shrift and housel' before death was almost a sine qua non of salvation. For evangelicals, however, confession to God required no human intermediary, and no priest could absolve intrinsically sinful human beings. In 1539 in the parish church of Lenham, for instance, a priest called Sir Ralph told the congregation, 'There be some priests do use to give penance in confession for sin; but I tell you . . . whosoever giveth penance for sin robbeth God of his honour. I

---

[29] CCCC MS 128, p. 91.   [30] CCCC MS 128, p. 41.   [31] CCCC MS 128, p. 70.
[32] CCCC MS 128, pp. 80–1.

myself have done so, but I cry God mercy. I did it of ignorance.'[33] Similarly, in February 1543 John Bland allegedly preached that 'auricular confession was the most abomination that could be'.[34] Nicholas Ridley, prebendary of Canterbury and future Bishop of London, gave a more subtle but equally heterodox interpretation in a sermon at St Stephen's, Hackington, during Rogation week 1540: 'Auricular confession was but a mere positive law, and ordained as a godly mean for the sinner to come to the priest for counsel; but he could not find it in Scripture.'[35] Among lay people listening sympathetically to these new teachings, new forms of confession arose that challenged the beliefs of the Catholic priests attempting to give them absolution. We have already seen how Archibolde of Faversham told his priest: 'Hast thou authority to absolve me or give me penance? Nay, thou mayest keep sheep.' Similarly, the notorious heretic Bartholomew Joye confessed to his curate merely in general terms: 'I am a sinner'; and when asked for particulars he responded 'that he had confessed himself to the Lord already and that he would make none other confession'.[36] John Fishecock of Headcorn would not confess in the normal fashion but rather said, without asking the priest to bless him: 'I knowledge to God that I am a grievous sinner, and none so grievous as I, for I am not able to keep the commandments; for who so offendeth in one offendeth in all. And therefore I cry God mercy.'[37] These new interpretations, while angering many priests, received at least some direct support from the ecclesiastical establishment. When Bartholomew Joye's priest, Sir John Write, objected to Joye's improvisation in confession, he received a stern rebuke from the archbishop's commissary.[38]

What took the place of worldly deeds in the evangelical view of purgation was absolute faith in Christ's sacrifice as the sole mediation between humanity and oblivion. That message of salvation through faith alone was on a great many Kentish lips in the 1540s. When 'James Wourley's wife' of Wichling said that her prayers and deeds would save her from the devil, for instance, her evangelical parson Thomas Dawby told her: 'Not so, thou shalt not be saved by thy deeds but only by faith.'[39] Another priest, Hugh Cooper, argued that neither alms, fasting nor prayer helped the soul 'but faith only', and anyone who trusted to be helped by prayer committed idolatry.[40] John Scory preached from Canterbury Cathedral's pulpit in Lent 1542 'that only faith justifieth, and he that doth deny that only faith doth justify would deny, if he durst be so bold, that Christ doth justify'.[41] This message strongly affected some lay people, and not merely the sympathetic audience of pre-existing Lollards. A man called Hammond Bett, for instance, announced that

[33] CCCC MS 128, p. 84.   [34] CCCC MS 128, p. 70.   [35] CCCC MS 128, p. 47.
[36] CCCC MS 128, p. 31.   [37] CCCC MS 128, p. 64.   [38] CCCC MS 128, p. 61.
[39] CCCC MS 128, p. 84.   [40] CCCC MS 128, p. 91.   [41] CCCC MS 128, p. 42.

when he died he would 'neither have ringing nor singing nay any manner of alms deed to be done for his soul', and he 'repented himself that ever he did so much alms and good deeds for his father's soul'.[42]

All of this brings us to the most radical and contested aspect of Reformed theology: the denial of the Real Presence of Christ in the Eucharist. Even at the most Protestantising moments of the Henrician Reformation, sacramentaries were still burned for heresy, and in the 1530s even Thomas Cranmer presided over such executions, as his enemies gleefully reminded him in the weeks before his own pyre was lit. Yet denying the sacrificial nature of the mass carried an explicit corollary for many evangelicals that the body and blood of Christ were not physically present in the consecrated elements. This belief had long been a centrepiece of Lollard theology, and many Kentish lay people, perhaps some with Lollard backgrounds, expressed similar ideas in the early 1540s. A woman called Joan Frenche, for instance, was accused of saying that the sacrament of the altar was 'but a figure or memory of Christ's passion'.[43] The Canterbury shoemaker Anthony Ager and his neighbour Simon Castelyn said that 'God is in no place made by man's hands'.[44] At Easter 1541, a courier in Sandwich shouted to the people that the sacrament of the altar was 'but a signification and a sign, as the sign of a Bull or the sign of the Rose set up and standing at taverns'.[45] Catholic investigators in 1543 also dug up a story more than a decade old that they considered too outrageously heretical to let stand. In 1531, Raynold Bucker of Boxley was left unpunished despite allegedly telling his neighbours 'that the sacrament of the altar was bread as other bread was, and that the knave priests did receive Him before noon and did piss and shit Him out at whores' arses at afternoon'.[46] Priests occasionally expressed sacramental heterodoxy themselves. The cleric Thomas Carden, for instance, allegedly said at Selling church in 1541 that it was wrong for people to say that they received 'their maker' at Easter, but rather they should say, 'we shall receive our housel'.[47] John Bland allegedly said in Faversham church that the mass was 'no satisfaction for sin' but only a 'remembrance or memory of the passion of Christ'.[48] These priests advocated a remarkable break from the past, drawing their parishioners onto a path which led straight to the fire.

The Bible and 'unwritten verities'

Besides the issue of justification, another heated controversy concerned the role of the Bible in the militant Church. This issue was partially defined by

---

[42] CCCC MS 128, p. 53.   [43] CCCC MS 128, p. 47.   [44] CCCC MS 128, p. 65.
[45] Clark, *English Provincial Society*, pp. 60–1.   [46] CCCC MS 128, p. 87.
[47] CCCC MS 128, p. 46.   [48] CCCC MS 128, p. 67.

the evangelical doctrine of *sola scriptura* and its rejection of 'unwritten verities', those doctrines that had accrued to the Church since the completion of the Gospel. Equally important in the English context, however, was the debate over vernacular Bibles. In much of continental Europe, vernacular Bibles had long been legal and available, albeit in small numbers, for devotional use. These Bibles could not substitute for the Vulgate in technical matters, but even so prominent a Catholic as Erasmus looked forward to the day when farmers and weavers would sing biblical verses while they worked.[49] In England, however, Lollard biblicism led to an absolute ban on the reading or publication of English Bibles.[50] In 1538 that ban was officially lifted, but by 1543 the king and anxious conservatives grew fearful that Bible-reading had led to a resurgence in heresy, and the King's Book once again prohibited poor men and all but the richest women from reading Scripture.[51]

Kentish subjects in the 1540s heard and participated in debates over biblicism to a remarkable degree. On the Catholic side, the king's legalisation of vernacular Bibles did little to mitigate the opposition of some stalwarts to any unmediated contact between lay people and the Scriptures. The chantry priest Humphrey Cotton, for instance, allegedly 'said that there be heresies in the Bible', a position which likely referred not to all Bibles but specifically to the contested translations of William Tyndale and his successors.[52] On Candlemas in 1542, the layman John Thatcher supposedly told 'one Starkey, a barber of Canterbury, that the Bible was made by the devil'.[53] Just after Easter 1542 Vincent Engham, jurat of Sandwich, commanded that no man should read or hear the Bible upon pain of imprisonment, and he actually arrested two people for disputing his order despite the king's legalisation of vernacular Bibles.[54] In August 1543, Robert Serles preached in the parish Church of Ashford: 'You fellows of the new trickery that go up and down with your Testaments in your hands, I pray you, what profit

---

[49] Desiderius Erasmus, 'The Paraclesis', in *Desiderius Erasmus: Christian Humanism and the Reformation*, ed. John C. Olin (New York, 1965). See also Werner Schwartz, *Principles and Problems of Biblical Translation: Some Reformation Controversies and the Background* (Cambridge, 1955); Alister McGrath, *The Intellectual Origins of the European Reformation* (Oxford, 1987), chs. 4–5.

[50] As Lucy Wooding has pointed out, some English Catholics influenced by Erasmian humanism favoured the translation of the Bible, at least in principle: Lucy Wooding, *Rethinking Catholicism in Reformation England* (Oxford, 2000). In practice, however, agitation for direct lay access to Scripture was a sure sign of evangelical sensibilities.

[51] See Susan Wabuda, 'The Woman with the Rock: The Controversy on Women and Bible Reading', in Susan Wabuda and Caroline Litzenberger (eds.), *Belief and Practice in Reformation England: A Tribute to Patrick Collinson from His Students* (Aldershot, 1998).

[52] CCCC MS 128, p. 54.   [53] CCCC MS 128, p. 55.

[54] CCCC MS 128, p. 29; Zell, 'The Prebendaries' Plot', pp. 249–50. Engham's wife was a kinswoman of the Catholic conspirator Robert Serles.

take you by them?...As Adam was expelled from paradise for meddling with a tree of knowledge, even so be we for meddling with the Scripture of Christ.'[55]

Equally vociferous were Catholic defences of the traditions of the Church from charges that they were non-scriptural. In a May 1543 sermon, for instance, the prebendary William Gardiner defended the patristic tradition, mocking what he perceived as Protestant disavowals of post-biblical learning: 'They will have none of the holy doctors. They will not have St Augustine, St Ambrose, St Jerome, St Gregory, Basil, [or] Gregory Nazianzene.'[56] Similarly, Edmund Shether told an audience in the chapter house at Canterbury: 'All the constitutions, decrees, and ordinances of our holy mother the Church are most godly, most holy, and therefore are to be observed of all her children, Christian people, without disputing or reasoning of any of them.'[57] Robert Serles promoted non-biblical tradition less explicitly, not defending it in so many words but using it liberally in his sermons; he told one audience, for instance, that 'Moses sent letters from hell to teach the state thereof, and how men should live, and another likewise out of heaven'.[58]

On the evangelical side, support for Bible-reading was, at its most basic level, an issue of devotion and edification; hence Margaret Toftes, in angry reaction to the new restrictions promulgated in 1543, said that it was a 'pity that God's Word shall so little be set by that it may not be read openly'.[59] As the phrase 'read openly' indicated, many evangelicals wanted the Bible read aloud in public places and believed that Bible-reading should take the place of large portions of the liturgy that were mere popish survivals. For instance, the Canterbury barber Thomas Makeblythe neglected to bear a palm in procession on Palm Sunday, but instead read the Bible.[60] One 'Sir Bing' likewise was denounced to ecclesiastical authorities in 1543 as 'a reader of the Bible in corners'.[61] In July 1542, John Toftes of Canterbury 'openly and with loud voice read the Bible in English in the church to his wife, Starkey's wife, George Toftes's wife, to the midwife of the same parish, and to as many other as then were present'.[62] Thomas Dawby, when he was curate of Lenham, procured lay people 'to read the Bible, even at the quire door where divine service was sung or said, from the beginning of the service to the ending, with as low a voice [as] they could'.[63]

The disruptive potential of Bible-reading was exemplified by the words of Roger Strawghwyn to the parishioners of Davington church: 'You be not bound...to believe anything which is not written or contained in the Holy Scripture, nor ought to believe any other thing than God's Word found in

---

[55] CCCC MS 128, p. 40. [56] CCCC MS 128, p. 35. [57] CCCC MS 128, p. 11.
[58] CCCC MS 128, p. 34. [59] CCCC MS 128, p. 53. [60] CCCC MS 128, p. 51.
[61] CCCC MS 128, p. 270. [62] CCCC MS 128, p. 31. [63] CCCC MS 128, p. 82.

Holy Scripture.'[64] Yet this radicalism could easily be linked to the royally sanctioned anti-Romanism of the day; the evangelical six preacher Michael Drum, for instance, argued in a sermon at Canterbury that 'they which went about to take away the reading of the Bible did even go about to pluck Christ's Word and the Holy Ghost from the people, as the Bishop of Rome hath done in time past, which by restraining the people from reading the Bible took first an occasion by that mean of his usurped power'.[65] In other words, evangelicals argued that opposition to vernacular Bibles implied support for Rome.

This anti-Romanist subtext extended to a more general argument for English-language prayers, insisting that people understand the words they spoke not only for their edification but as protection against future usurpations of Christ's authority. This argument was helped significantly by the fact that prayers in English had never actually been illegal but merely suspect because of their connection with Lollardy. English primers had circulated before the Reformation, although much less commonly after about 1450, while English versions of basic prayers, the Ten Commandments and the Creed circulated in a variety of printed editions in the early sixteenth century.[66] The 1536 and 1538 royal injunctions, moreover, had called for the clergy to educate their flocks in basic vernacular prayers. In the Protestant imagination, it was but a small step from legality to ubiquity, and from ubiquity to exclusivity. John Scory, for instance, argued that 'no man may pray in anywise in Latin or other tongue, except he understand what he prayeth'.[67] Michael Drum preached in the cathedral that 'we may not pray in an unknown tongue, for if we do we do but mock with God . . . and for that before God thou art but a fool'.[68] At Herne, where Nicholas Ridley was vicar, the *Te Deum* was commonly sung in English.[69] Nicholas Fitzwilliams likewise was accused of explaining the *De Profundis* in English at the hospital of St James.[70] Richard Turner was accused of teaching some children of Northgate, Canterbury (not his parish) to say the Ave Maria in English.[71] Christopher Nevinson even used his authority as commissary to instruct the clergy to refuse absolution to any who came to confess unable to say their Paternoster and Creed in English; Nevinson in fact did not believe in priestly absolution at all, but he knew how to use the carrot and the stick on the English laity.[72]

On the Catholic side, opposition to English prayers was fierce, doubtless because, as Eamon Duffy has shown, Latinate prayers carried talismanic properties with meanings in popular religion far more complex than

---

[64] CCCC MS 128, p. 57.   [65] CCCC MS 128, p. 56.
[66] Duffy, *Stripping of the Altars*, pp. 213 and 80–2
[67] CCCC MS 128, p. 42.   [68] CCCC MS 128, p. 48.
[69] CCCC MS 128, p. 47.   [70] CCCC MS 128, p. 74.
[71] CCCC MS 128, p. 75.   [72] Duffy, *Stripping of the Altars*, p. 438.

any translation would allow.[73] Edward Dyngleden of Rolvenden, for instance, was reported by his evangelical curate for obstinately refusing to learn his Paternoster, Ave, Creed and Ten Commandments in English.[74] His refusal, and that of many of his contemporaries, was supported by numerous Catholic priests. The parson of Ripple, for instance, told his parishioners: 'I am commanded to show you the Paternoster in English. You may do as you will in learning of it, but it is against mine opinion. For I liken the Paternoster in English to the hard shell of a nut and the Paternoster in Latin to the sweet kernel.'[75] The vicar of Faversham likewise was accused of having 'moved in confession John Tacknal to use his Paternoster in English no more, for he knew not how soon the world would change'.[76] Edmund Shether, in a sermon at St Stephen's, Canterbury, in May 1543, gave his audience a subtle and beautiful defence of Latin prayer: 'He did discourage men from praying in the mother tongue, saying, "Some of you say that men cannot pray in an unknown tongue because they understand not what they say. But I say that no man understandeth what he prayeth, as St Paul sayeth, *nescit homo quomodo orandum sit, sed spiritus hominis docet quomodo orandum sit.* And therefore, though you do not understand what you pray, yet pray so still."'[77]

Closely linked to the debate over English prayers was the potentially more disruptive debate over the liturgy of the Church. Not only did evangelicals want church services performed in English, but they believed that many of the ceremonies and practices of the Church of England were popish accretions with no place in the worship of God. Emblematic of this conflict was an extraordinary pulpit dispute in the town of Lenham. On 1 November 1541, Robert à Stotte, curate of Davington, came into the pulpit at Lenham and preached that 'there was heresy sung in the church that present day', in other words denouncing the traditional liturgy. Afterwards, the prebendary Robert Serles, vicar of the parish, came into the same pulpit and (according to conservative deponents) 'made a good sermon there' defending Catholic practices. This enraged Stotte, who:

hearing thereof, came from Davington to Lenham the Sunday following. And after evensong the same day there was an anthem sung of Our Lady, and he said openly in the church that it was heresy. And incontinent he went unto the Bible and turned to the same Gospel that Mr. Serles had preached the Sunday next before and expounded the contrary to Master Serles in every word, with threatening words towards him, saying, 'All pickpurses' ears are not set on the pillory as yet.' Whereupon diverse were offended with him and many words were multiplied and great variance [was]

---

[73] Ibid., chs. 6, 7 and 8.   [74] CCCC MS 128, p. 30.
[75] CCCC MS 128, p. 15.   [76] CCCC MS 128, p. 12.
[77] CCCC MS 128, p. 11. 'Man does not know how he should pray, but the spirit of man teaches how he should pray.' This appears to be a rather loose rendition of 1 Corinthians 2:11–12.

among the people, insomuch that diverse persons thought there should have been a fray. And thus he came six or seven times within half a year and preached half an hour at the least, always moving the people to give no credence to Mr. Serles or Mr. Shether.[78]

This idea that there was heresy in the traditional liturgy was commonplace among Kentish evangelicals in the 1540s. John Bland, for instance, preached in the parish of Northgate, Canterbury, in 1542 'that if women did understand what was read and sung in the matins, mass, and evensong, they would be ashamed one of another, for there was in it both heresy and treason'. Bland allegedly even went so far as to say that 'in christening of children, priests be murderers'.[79] The notorious heretic Joan Boucher expressed similar disapproval for ceremonies, saying that 'matins and evensong was no better than rumbling of tubs'.[80] John Scory gave one audience an extremely cogent argument against the ceremonies of the medieval Church: 'Think you ... that the devil will be afraid or flee away cross-making, hurling of holy water, ringing of bells, and such other ceremonies when he was not afraid to take Christ himself and cast him on his back and set him on a pinnacle?'[81]

Foremost among the post-biblical traditions of concern to evangelicals was fasting, especially the complex traditions surrounding the Lenten fast. In 1538, Henry VIII had struck a blow against Lent, using the royal supremacy to dispense the nation from the six-week fast on the dubious grounds that there was a scarcity of fish and that the Lenten fast, as 'a mere positive law of the Church', existed at the discretion of the Crown.[82] Yet despite this appeal to adiaphora, the 1538 dispensation was not established as precedent and the fast was not officially eliminated. In the 1540s, therefore, fasting was still required but breaking the fast was unlikely ever to be prosecuted, creating a situation bordering on chaos. An evangelical called Broke, for instance, preached on Palm Sunday 1542 'that masters and mistresses were bound to eat eggs, butter, and cheese in Lent to give example to their household'.[83] This was to become a typical Protestant gloss on adiaphora, arguing that, while ceremonies were themselves indifferent, the abuse of such ceremonies led the masses into error, and community leaders therefore had a positive obligation to provide a godly example against them. Another evangelical strategy was to agree that fasting was an acceptable form of self-denial, but to argue that it did not matter *when* people fasted, as there was no scriptural prohibition against eating on any particular day. John Bland, for instance,

---

[78] CCCC MS 128, pp. 84–5.   [79] CCCC MS 128, p. 71.
[80] CCCC MS 128, p. 71.   [81] CCCC MS 128, p. 34.
[82] Duffy, *Stripping of the Altars*, p. 405; MacCulloch, *Thomas Cranmer*, p. 198.
[83] CCCC MS 128, p. 45. It is unclear who this 'Broke' might be, although it could be Thomas Brooke of the Cobham family, who was one of Archbishop Cranmer's servants: MacCulloch, *Thomas Cranmer*, p. 249.

preached that 'fasting profiteth nothing one time more than other'.[84] John Rich denied that God made fasting days and added that the 'embering days' (a Wednesday, Friday and Saturday fast kept in each of the four seasons of the year) were popish, having been 'made by the intercession of one Emme, the bishop of Rome's concubine'.[85] Hugh Cooper of Tenterden stated succinctly in February 1543 that God was 'neither pleased with fasting nor discontent with eating', and he added in a sermon two weeks later that fasting did not help the soul, but faith only.[86]

On the Catholic side, however, the king's brief flirtation with heterodoxy in 1538 did not keep priests from demanding traditional observance. In response to questions about the king's previous dispensations, for instance, Clement Norton, the vicar of Faversham, said 'that if the king were examined he would confess that he gave no leave to eat white meat in Lent but unto sick persons'. On another occasion, the same vicar commanded one of his parishioners, a tanner's wife, not to have sexual relations with her husband during Lent.[87] At the church of St Paul's in Canterbury, the vicar 'did dissuade one Cruse, of his parish, from eating of white meat in Lent...and rebuked him therefore'.[88] To many Catholics, invitations by radical preachers to ignore the traditions of the Church in favour of salvation by faith alone seemed like a licence to all forms of disorder. It was with this idea in mind that the curate of Stroodmarsh not only rebuked men who ate white meat in Lent but also preached an extraordinary attack on those who sought salvation outside the parameters of the established Church, allegedly arguing that 'men should love and fear God, but not to trust Him too much'.[89] Some embattled priests, it seems, were too shocked by the sacrilege around them even to remember where their trust belonged.

Images and idolatry

The third great subject of debate was idolatry. The legal status of images was highly ambiguous in the 1540s and, as Margaret Aston has observed, no place 'displayed to the full the open-endedness' of this issue so well as Archbishop Cranmer's diocese.[90] The king had waged a full-scale war against idolatry in the 1530s, culminating in the 1538 destruction of St Thomas Becket's bones, the rood of Boxley and other famous relics. By 1539, however, the pendulum had begun to swing, and, while government attacks on images continued in the early 1540s, they were limited to 'abused' images, those to which pilgrimages or offerings were commonly made. In 1543, this

---

[84] CCCC MS 128, p. 14.   [85] CCCC MS 128, p. 54.   [86] CCCC MS 128, p. 63.
[87] CCCC MS 128, p. 12.   [88] CCCC MS 128, p. 16.   [89] CCCC MS 128, p. 33.
[90] Margaret Aston, *England's Iconoclasts: Volume I, Laws Against Images* (Oxford, 1988), pp. 237–8.

conservative shift was ratified in the King's Book. The 1537 Bishops' Book had interpreted the second commandment to mean that people were 'utterly forbidden to make or to have any similitude or image, to the intent to bow down to it or worship it'. In the King's Book, this was rewritten to say that 'we be not forbidden to make or to have similitudes or images, but only we be forbidden to make or to have them to the intent to do godly honour unto them...And therefore, although images of Christ and his saints be the works of men's hands only, yet they be not so prohibited but that they may be had and set up both in churches and other places'.[91] This was not a significant change in substance, but it marked a profound change in emphasis, leading to endless debate over the exact meaning of the revised text.

This question of whether images could ever lawfully be used in Christian worship, in other words whether the danger of idolatry lay in the erection of images or in their abuse, was at the heart of conflict in Kent. In Canterbury Cathedral, itself the scene five years earlier of England's most radical act of iconoclasm, the potential for conflict was manifest when Robert Serles preached 'that no idolatry might be to an image of Our Lady' because images were merely representations of saints rather than idols. In other words, he suggested that since everyone understood that images were not literally divinities, no images in England were ever technically 'abused', and thus by the King's Book all images should stand. Thomas Cranmer was present at this sermon and confronted Serles afterwards, arguing that all images were idols, since '*idolum* and *imago* in Greek was one'. This was a humanist interpretation of the King's Book, suggesting that, since the Vulgate's '*imago*' was simply a translation of the Greek word for 'idol', it was absurd to draw a distinction in spiritual matters between images that were treated as idols and those that were not. At this point, Prebendary Gardiner stepped into the conversation with a more moderate argument, telling Cranmer: 'Pleaseth your grace, I think nay, for an idol is a thing which hath given unto him such honour as is due unto God or unto some saint.' This was closer to the spirit of the King's Book but still maintained a view of saints that sounded unhealthy to evangelical ears. Cranmer responded disdainfully to the less learned prebendary: 'You know not the Greek; for in the Greek *idolum* and *imago* are all one.' Gardiner retorted, 'My lord...although I know not the Greek, yet I trust I know the truth, and that by St Paul.'[92]

For many traditionalist Catholics, of course, the question of 'abuse' of images was moot, since images were indeed taken to have special powers, allowing worshippers direct access to the saints they represented. For

[91] Ibid., pp. 240–1.   [92] CCCC MS 128, pp. 228–9.

instance, the vicar of Chilham, John Willoughby, had a dangerous conversation about the shrine of Our Lady of Court at Street with a local miller called Dawson, telling the miller that 'images had power of God to help sick people vowing unto them'.[93] The subtext of this conversation was undoubtedly the 'cure' which Elizabeth Barton had received at that same shrine almost two decades before, a 'cure' which the government had later pronounced a fraud. Willoughby's words, then, were not only of questionable orthodoxy, but were also of questionable loyalty to the Henrician regime.

Given the prevalence of these attitudes, it is not surprising that there were often conflicts over images. Indeed, since the images that were to be removed according to the King's Book were exactly those that received the most popular devotion, royal policy was a recipe for conflict. In Canterbury, for instance, disorder was engendered when one 'Bartholomew the surgeon' confronted Cranmer's general apparitor and allegedly told him: 'Thou art he that would have pulled down our St George, but your master lieth by the heel, and we have showed the taking down thereof to the king's Council and were bid set it up again.'[94] At North Mongeham, Thomas Bleane ordered the priest and churchwardens not to deface images, 'saying that such ways should continue but a while'.[95] On the opposite side, a variety of arguments against images were presented to Kentish parishioners. John Scory, for instance, preached at Faversham church in 1542 that 'this sumptuous adorning of churches is against the old fashion of the primitive Church. They had no such copes or chalices nor other jewels, nor gildings, nor paintings of images as we now have, and therefore if I were curate I would sell all such things, or lay them to pledge to help the poor'.[96] A more advanced position was taken by Michael Drum, who preached in Canterbury Cathedral on Whitsunday 1543 that 'images were dangerously permitted in the church', using as his text Deuteronomy 4, where Moses told the Hebrews that God had not spoken to them in any form or similitude, so they should make no form or similitude in speaking to God.[97] Drum, then, opposed all religious images, but even he might not have gone so far as John Bland, who preached at Faversham church that 'to kneel or bow unto a cross, yea, though it were the very cross that Christ died on, it was idolatry'.[98]

With these arguments in mind, evangelical priests and parishioners pulled down images faster than conservatives could erect them. In Sandwich, the laymen Thomas Holly and William Morris pulled down sundry images in St Clement's church, while in the nearby parish of St Mary's the vicar pulled down images 'of St George and others' estimated to be worth £30.

---

[93] CCCC MS 128, p. 37. [94] CCCC MS 128, p. 14. [95] CCCC MS 128, p. 29.
[96] CCCC MS 128, p. 43. [97] CCCC MS 128, p. 56. [98] CCCC MS 128, p. 68.

In Newington-next-Sittingbourne, the vicar Robert Howe also pulled down images in his church; in Howe's case we might suspect financial motives, since he was reported to have 'scraped off the gilding of diverse other images' in the church, and two of the images he tore down later re-emerged in London parishes.[99] John Bland, who by his own admission would have pulled down the very cross on which Christ died, was more than happy to pull down mere modern replicas; he was accused of having 'defaced a chapel at Ospringe, pulled down the images, and sold all the stuff'.[100]

All of these incidents must have engendered hostility and recriminations, but even more electrifying than the mere removal of images was the *violence* towards images that sometimes occurred. For instance, the curate of Lenham, Sir John Abbey, took the advice of the former curate, Thomas Dawby, 'to take the key of the church door secretly from the sexton's house and to go privily into the church, and take down one image more of Our Lady Pity, and break her in pieces'.[101] In Canterbury, Christopher Levenysh burned the bones of St Blaise, formerly a relic of St Peter's parish, in his own home.[102] In Walmer, it was alleged, 'the priest and clerk have taken down images, not abused, and burnt them'.[103] George Wyborne, of an undisclosed parish, 'did head and quarter St Stephen, and also burned him'. The symbolism here is important, since not only was the image burned for heresy, but it was also given the traditional punishment for treason, equating religious traditionalism with political opposition.[104] The Canterbury radical John Toftes pulled down a picture of Our Lady in December 1542 'and had her and the tabernacle home to his house, and there did hew her all in pieces'.[105] It was alleged that the archbishop's brother, Archdeacon Edmund Cranmer, 'did violently break the arms and legs of the rood' in the church of St Andrew's, Canterbury.[106] Commissary Nevinson was likewise accused of commanding that images in various churches be not only pulled down but also 'hewed with axes'.[107]

Words against saints and images could be as violent as deeds. Thomas Carden, for instance, was accused of preaching in Selling church that 'he supposed St Katherine was rather a devil in hell than a saint in heaven'.[108] Margaret Toftes the younger of Canterbury said in July 1543 that 'images in the church were devils and idols, and wished that the church and they were on a fire'.[109] Thomas Hasylden of Elmsted 'asked why he should do more reverence to the crucifix than to the gallows'.[110] These statements, made openly before hostile audiences, underline the very public nature of the attack on idolatry. While evangelicals had to be cautious about expressing many of their opinions, attacks on images could be glossed as consistent with royal

[99] CCCC MS 128, p. 65.   [100] CCCC MS 128, p. 14.   [101] CCCC MS 128, p. 82.
[102] CCCC MS 128, p. 74.   [103] CCCC MS 128, p. 59.   [104] CCCC MS 128, p. 55.
[105] CCCC MS 128, p. 31.   [106] CCCC MS 128, p. 30.   [107] CCCC MS 128, p. 7.
[108] CCCC MS 128, p. 46.   [109] CCCC MS 128, p. 52.   [110] CCCC MS 128, p. 53.

policy. In November 1539, for instance, Canterbury radicals pulled down all the images in the church of Northgate except for the rood, Mary and John, the twelve apostles, Our Lady and John the Baptist. These particular omissions were no coincidence; they were all scriptural saints, the ones whose feast days had been spared the axe in 1536. By leaving them intact, then, evangelicals were working to remain within the law, interpreting royal policies broadly but still in their own minds obeying them.[111] John Toftes made explicit this rationale some years later when asked by his conservative neighbour Andrew Kempe why he had spoiled so many images; he said that he had done 'nothing but his prince's commandment'.[112] This appeal to legality was precisely why the issue of images proved so explosive. Conservatives hoping to reconcile Catholic orthodoxy with loyalty to the regime were desperately trying to imagine the Reformation as a jurisdictional rather than a theological event. The king's abysmal record of destroying the Church's most holy treasures was thus precisely what they were trying to forget, and these constant reminders were salt in their wounds, pushing them ever closer to the boundary where religious 'conservatism' intersected with political dissent.

III

The purpose of this overview of religious conflict in Kent has not been to show the strength of the evangelical party, as attempted with the same evidence by A. F. Pollard, nor to show 'the strength and character of traditionalist beliefs under pressure', as attempted with the same evidence by Eamon Duffy, but rather to show the depth of *division* that had already washed over English communities by the early 1540s.[113] It seems clear that complex theological issues were being regularly canvassed in Kentish parishes, sometimes in difficult and technical terms, sometimes in terms designed for lay people to understand, and sometimes by those lay people themselves. At every turn, moreover, polemic was matched by polemic, argument matched by argument. Parishioners in doubt about some aspect of traditional religion would not have had to base their opinions upon a single conversation or sermon but would have had easy access to a variety of points of view, not only from preachers in the pulpit but from neighbours in the alehouse. The question to which we must now turn, then, concerns the impact of this endemic debate on the lives, and particularly the politics, of Kentish subjects.

---

[111] CCCC MS 128, p. 31.   [112] CCCC MS 128, p. 73.
[113] A. F. Pollard, *Thomas Cranmer and the English Reformation, 1489–1556* (New York, 1904); Duffy, *Stripping of the Altars*, p. 434.

Given the limits of sixteenth-century education, the isolation of many communities, and the severe limitations of our sources, it would be rash not to accept that a significant proportion of the Kentish population neither understood nor cared about the theological maelstrom swirling around them. That being said, however, anecdotal evidence suggests that Reformation issues found an engaged audience in Kent not merely among the literate elite but throughout a cross-section of the population. Richard Turner's evangelical sermons, for instance, are known to have attracted large audiences, especially at Chartham, strategically located just off a main road out of Canterbury; while Eamon Duffy is certainly correct that many were horrified by what they heard, people still came to see what all the fuss was about.[114] Catholic sermons could be equally popular; as early as 1535 an evangelical complained of the 'great audience' of lay people who flocked to Herne to hear a friar from Canterbury 'blame these new books and these new preachers' for the nation's ills.[115] In the 1520s, Elizabeth Barton had attracted thousands to watch her miracles at Court at Street, and when she turned her efforts against both Protestant heresy and the royal divorce there is no doubt that her words energised a large population both in Kent and elsewhere.[116] In the late 1530s, when Henry Goderick, parson of Hothfield, preached that the consecrated host was only a remembrance of Christ's passion, a sympathetic observer wrote that his sermon 'turned a hundred hearts to his opinion and devotion'; whether exaggerated or not, such a statement surely implies a large, engaged audience.[117] Furthermore, in many cases we have oblique evidence of the constant flux of rumours about what was said and done in Kentish churches; an unadorned mention of 'much murmuring' caused by Thomas Holly's refusal to bear a candle in Sandwich church, for instance, undoubtedly obscures a wealth of debate about which we will never know.[118]

Isolated laypeople also found their way into the historical record by speaking seditious words against the king, suggesting concern with ecclesiastical events if not necessarily great theological sophistication. In December 1539, for instance, the Canterbury tailor Edward Woodhouse said that 'we should never have merry world as long as this king reigneth, for he know no good that he did but pull down abbeys'. His accusers, far from being Cromwell's agents, were a baker and a labourer.[119] In Dartford in May of the same year, a baker at an alehouse raised a pint to the king, saying, 'God save King Henry, here is good ale.' To his horror, a miller and a labourer took offence at his words, one of them replying, 'God save the cup of good ale, for King Henry

[114] MacCulloch, *Thomas Cranmer*, p. 303; Clark, *English Provincial Society*, p. 60; Duffy, *Stripping of the Altars*, pp. 435–6.
[115] PRO SP 1/91, fol. 176r [*LP* VIII, 480].   [116] See above, chapter 2.
[117] BL Cotton MS Cleopatra E.V, fol. 397r–v.   [118] CCCC MS 128, p. 67.
[119] PRO KB 9/544, fol. 119r.

shall be hanged when twenty other shall be saved.'[120] According to Geoffrey Elton, forty-one such accusations of treason in Kent reached government ears during Cromwell's years in power, more than in any other county where there was not a rebellion to artificially inflate the numbers.[121] Such accusations do not imply peculiar opposition to the government (there were very few accusations in the far north, for instance) but rather a heightened level of conflict, with local tempers hot enough to produce both dangerous words and angry accusations.

If significant numbers of people in and around Canterbury were thus cognisant of Reformation debate, how did that engagement affect their responses to government religious policy? The answer is not that the Kentish population turned en masse towards reform, but rather that they came to think of themselves as living in a divided nation where religious conflict, far from an aberration, was the fundamental wellspring of politics. Even though only a small percentage of the Kentish population became active religious partisans in the 1540s, the rhetoric of partisanship was ubiquitous, and to whatever extent ordinary subjects had political agendas they had to pursue those agendas within the new reality of religious division. The minority who were religious ideologues and those who were willing to appeal to religious divisions became increasingly influential, while those who tried to remain neutral or disengaged were increasingly marginalised from the creation of local religious culture. Thus even with only a minority of actively partisan subjects, Kentish life became remarkably 'confessionalised'.

To comprehend the importance of this shift, it must be recognised that Tudor political theory held that religious consensus was the basis of political stability. Since the earthly polity ideally reflected the City of God, any religious division represented a potentially devastating failure. It was thus far more shocking than we can easily understand when in June 1541 Thomas Cranmer informed the Catholic prebendary William Gardiner that of the six preachers to be named to Canterbury Cathedral, the king would appoint 'three of the old, three of the new'. This statement not only accepted the notion of a fundamental opposition between old and new but also implied that this bifurcation would be permanent, consciously imbedded by the king within the ecclesiastical establishment. Gardiner's anguished response, 'My lord, that is a mean to set us at variance!' neatly encapsulates the political changes taking place within the diocese of Canterbury.[122]

---

[120] PRO KB 9/541, fol. 2r.

[121] G. R. Elton, *Policy and Police: The Enforcement of the Reformation in the Age of Thomas Cromwell* (Cambridge, 1972), p. 397. Elton did not account for all of these cases, so his numbers cannot be corroborated.

[122] CCCC MS 128, p. 229. This choice of 'three of the old, three of the new' might be seen as a reiteration of Henry VIII's famous, simultaneous execution of three Catholics for

Whatever Gardiner's misgivings in 1541, however, by 1543 he and many other Kentish clerics found themselves contributing to this 'variance' through a series of explicitly partisan sermons. On Easter Day 1543, for instance, Gardiner delivered a fierce tirade against evangelical radicalism, ending with cries of 'Heretics! Faggots! Fire!'[123] This sermon was the culmination of months of *ad hominem* preaching. In late January he had preached from the same pulpit that 'of late days you have had here so many waterlaggers, which have turned your good wine into water, that you could have no good doctrine taught nay preached unto you but the fantasies of their own brains'.[124] This sermon evidently caused great consternation, since a week later Gardiner was back in the pulpit, stubbornly refusing to apologise: 'You are grieved with me because I called them waterlaggers which have changed our good wine into water. Truly I could invent no fitter name for them, but even as I said then, so I say again . . . they must be smoked and purged round about with fire, or else we shall never be rid of them.' In the same sermon he answered accusations of Romanist treason with equally virulent accusations of Protestant heresy, saying: 'Some of you thought that some should have been hanged. But if you had deserved no more to be burned than they have to be hanged, you should do well enough.'[125] And soon after his Easter 1543 sermon he stated explicitly the connection between Henrician novelties and Protestant heresies that was so often left implicit by Catholics attempting to accommodate the regime: 'Since the time that we have been given to newfangles, the spirit of newfangles hath brought in the spirit of error.'[126]

The six preacher Robert Serles, one of the 'three of the old' appointed by the king, was so incessant in his *ad hominem* attacks that it was included in the charges against him that 'he preacheth no sermon but one part of it is an invective against the other preachers of Christ Church'.[127] In several sermons Serles even told his audiences that if they had been seduced by evangelical preachers, God would forgive them, since it was the preachers' fault rather than theirs: 'Good people, you have been deceived with preachers, but if you have received any poison and learned any false doctrine, and believed by ignorance, you be not to blame, neither God is discontent with you.'[128] So much for freedom of the will in salvation. Edmund Shether was equally stark in his dichotomy between Christians and heretics. In one sermon he preached:

treason and three Protestants for heresy in 1540. Yet, since the point of selecting the six preachers was clearly to balance religious factions rather than demand their submission, we might question interpretations which see the king's actions as self-consciously promoting a *via media*. Promoting six moderates, after all, would have been far more 'Anglican' than promoting three evangelicals and three conservative activists.

[123] CCCC MS 128, p. 13.   [124] CCCC MS 128, p. 9.
[125] CCCC MS 128, p. 10.   [126] CCCC MS 128, p. 35.
[127] CCCC MS 128, p. 41.   [128] CCCC MS 128, pp. 9 and 34.

Beware of these false preachers, which preach to you newfangles. Will you know how to discern a true preacher from a false? You have a dog, which is your conscience. Whensoever you shall come to any sermon, ask your dog what he saith unto it. If he say it be good, then follow it. But if your dog bark against it and say that it is naught, then beware and follow it not... If you will ask your conscience what she thinketh of such newfangles as is brought into the Church of God, she will say that they be naught.[129]

All these sermons taught people to think of the world in terms of religious conflict.

Evangelicals were equally unyielding in their division of the world into rival camps. According to William Gardiner, for instance, Canterbury conservatives first began discussing a *coup d'état* after an evangelical preached in the cathedral on the subject of Haman and Mordecai from the Book of Esther, saying that 'as Haman made a scourge for Mordecai and yet suffered himself, so nowadays [some] men went about to displease other, and now the matter lieth in their own necks'. In other words, the preacher was suggesting that the Catholics who had ousted Cromwell in 1540 had overreached and were about to be hoist by their own petard.[130] This rhetoric terrified Catholics, who were justifiably fearful of another of Henry VIII's factional pirouettes. Other evangelicals were equally confident of their own strength. Thomas Dawby, parson of Wichling, told a priest called Thomas Huxley: 'That knave thy master, the parson of Boughton, is a false heretic and a popish knave, and thou also. And I shall make forty in the parish of Doddington to bark at thee, and I shall make 10,000 of my set against thee in Kent.'[131] The laywoman Margaret Toftes the elder told an antagonist, 'When my lord of Canterbury's grace cometh down to Canterbury, we trust to have a day against you.' Again, the use of the word 'we' and the confidence in archiepiscopal support are important indications of partisan assumptions.[132]

The result of all of this rhetoric was that 'confessional' antagonisms often spilled into everyday life. In the town of Pluckley, for instance, a layman named Stephen Giles told the parson, apparently in casual conversation, that every day and night he prayed 'in the honour of God and Our Lady and all the company of heaven'. Giles did not imagine this to be a controversial statement, but he quickly found himself socially alienated from the parson, who replied that 'if he knew it of truth that the said Stephen used the same form of prayer, he would not accompany him, nor once drink with him'.[133] Similarly, at Chartham a man named Browne promised a lease to one James Terry, but after the indenture was drafted Terry reneged on the deal because the king's title of supreme head of the Church of England had not been

[129] CCCC MS 128, pp. 44–5.   [130] CCCC MS 128, p. 340.
[131] CCCC MS 128, p. 84.   [132] CCCC MS 128, p. 53.   [133] CCCC MS 128, p. 29.

included in the preamble. This clearly was not a simple case of scribal laxity, or else the error would have been corrected and the case would never have come to our attention. Rather, Browne and Terry seem to have tested each other's predilections and discovered that they were on opposite sides of a growing social gulf.[134] The most disruptive incident of this kind occurred in Canterbury, where personal hatred along confessional lines engendered scandalous behaviour by a Catholic functionary of the cathedral, Ralph the bell-ringer. According to 'all the quire that were present', 'Ralph, the bell-ringer of Christ church, at the burial of Dr. Champion, after the priest had censed [the] grave, and a boy was bearing away the censers and the coals, called again the boy and took the censers and poured the hot coals upon him in the grave, to the great slander of the said Dr. Champion, as though he had been an heretic worthy [of] burning.'[135] The import of all these examples is that the use of doctrinal litmus tests penetrated community life and began to affect social relations in ways which allowed decreasing latitude for public neutrality, regardless of people's private hopes for moderation and consensus.

The level to which religious polarisation came to structure parish disputes can best be seen in a violent row over the use of an English-language liturgy in the parish of Milton-next-Sittingbourne in 1545. In June of that year, apparently acting on direct orders from Cranmer, a priest attempted to undermine the solemnity of the parish's traditional procession by using the archbishop's newly published English litany in place of the Latin processional service. News of this impending alteration leaked out, however, and when the priest began his English-language service, traditionalists in the parish were ready for him. Mr John Fynche, a local gentleman, enlisted John Lacey, a churchwarden, as a sort of parish conservative whip. Lacey ordered the sexton of the parish to take up the cross and march out the church door, telling him 'not to stay for any commandment of the priest'; this was evidently a carefully chosen tactic, since the priest had previously told the parish that due to pain in his eyes he could not read his service in direct sunlight. Lacey then ordered the other churchwardens and clerks to follow the cross out the door, pulling hesitant parishioners behind them; in at least one case they used force. While still within the building, they all 'sang with the priest the king's majesty's procession in English'. As soon as they crossed the threshold, however, 'they left that and sang the ordinal in Latin', maintaining their traditional service against the will of the priest.

From the version of the story told by traditionalists, it would seem that the priest was unique in his desire for liturgical reform. Indeed, according to one conservative deponent the priest was left 'in the church alone' when

---

[134] CCCC MS 128, p. 36.   [135] CCCC MS 128, p. 31.

the procession left the building. From other accounts, however, it is clear that the parish was deeply divided over the issue. The complaint against the conservatives John Fynche and John Lacey was undersigned by at least four men; it is mutilated in such a way that there may be names missing. Beneath their signatures, moreover, is the following addendum: 'These persons whose names are underwritten cannot write their own names: Thomas Trowtes, Robert Blyton, William Skelton, Richard Anderson, Thomas Heywarde, Dennis Bradley, William Hilles and William Inglond.' In other words, the priest's use of an English liturgy was supported not only by local worthies but by a variety of illiterate parishioners. It is also clear from the depositions that the priest did not decide to experiment with the liturgy of his own accord but rather had been pushed into it by a group of parishioners who had complained to the archbishop; this was not a situation where the clergy 'outstripped the laity in radicalism', as Eamon Duffy has stressed was often the case, but rather an example of lay initiative in religious reform.[136] In this small Kentish parish, then, we can see a new dynamic at work. The issue in dispute here did not revolve around questions of loyalty to the regime; neither St Paul's Cathedral nor any other official organ of the Crown adopted an English litany until more than four months after the Milton row.[137] Rather, large numbers of humble subjects, whatever their motives, explicitly chose doctrinal sides in a debate structured by religious partisanship.

It was the Prebendaries' Plot itself, however, that was most instrumental in allowing theological tensions to disrupt the social lives of communities. Over the course of 1543, both Catholic conspirators and Cranmer's deputies scoured the countryside for evidence of religious 'abuses' by their enemies. The number of witnesses who came forward with accusations against their neighbours was enormous. Indeed, the number of allegations of religious impropriety collected in this brief period from this one diocese approaches the total number collected by Thomas Cromwell in his eight years collecting such stories. This massive outpouring shows how the Kentish laity could take an active role in their communities, as well as acquiring new weapons in their feuds with local enemies, if they were willing to adopt the rhetoric of religious division.

The sheer scale of denunciations can often give us a sense of the local conflicts that underlay them. For instance, no fewer than fifteen men reported the evangelical six preacher John Scory for preaching against the 'sumptuous adorning of churches' at Faversham in 1542. This should be no surprise – Scory was an outsider preaching against the parish's sense of propriety at

---

[136] PRO SP 1/203, fols. 86r–89r [*LP* XX, i, 1118]. Duffy, *Stripping of the Altars*, p. 436. On the litany, see MacCulloch, *Thomas Cranmer*, pp. 328–32.
[137] Ibid., p. 332.

a moment chosen to be most controversial, the feast of the dedication of Faversham church.[138] Much less easy to explain is the fact that no fewer than twelve men denounced Scory's opponent, the Catholic six preacher Edmund Shether, for preaching that Christ's death only cleansed original sin and that other sins had to be cleansed through penance.[139] Perhaps the most extraordinary case of wholesale denunciation concerned Vincent Engham of Sandwich, who, as we have seen, upset many of his parishioners by flouting the king's injunctions concerning Bible-reading in 1541. When Engham extended this disregard for the law and 'repugned against the doing of the commissary for taking down the image of St John by the king's commandment', he was denounced by 'Mr John Master, Thomas Pynnocke, Peter Holam, Daniel Cranmer, and all Christmas men'. This last phrase seems to refer to players in a Christmas pageant, providing yet more evidence that, when disloyalty to the sovereign became entangled with religious conservatism, even seemingly 'traditionalist' laymen were willing to take action against conservative clerics.[140]

It should also be noted that while in many cases priests and gentlemen acted as denouncers, elsewhere even people very low on the social ladder could take an active role. When John and Joyce Benson made seemingly heretical statements against the Virgin Mary and the sacrament of extreme unction, for instance, they were reported by, among others, a smith and a servant to John Culpepper, both fellow parishioners of the Bensons at All Saints, Canterbury.[141] When Sir William Kempe, vicar of Northgate, Canterbury, refused to read the Bible in his church or announce the king's injunctions on ceremonies, the witnesses against him were listed as simply 'the parish'.[142] In these cases, even quite humble people helped to define the bounds of acceptable behaviour in their communities.

In a few cases, moreover, the depositions taken during the Prebendaries' Plot provide enough information for us to unravel some of the local disputes which underlay religious conflict. In 1543, for instance, a Canterbury barber named Thomas Makeblythe refused to participate in the Easter procession, and six months later on 26 September 1543 he was denounced for this and other heterodox behaviour by James Rolf, John Thatcher the elder, John Maske and Thomas Brameston. The inclusion of John Thatcher the elder in this list is interesting because his son, John Thatcher the younger, had been denounced only four days earlier by another Canterbury barber named John Starkey for saying that 'the Bible was made by the devil' and calling Archbishop Cranmer 'a maintainer of heretics'. This John Starkey,

---

[138] CCCC MS 128, p. 43.   [139] CCCC MS 128, p. 91.

[140] CCCC MS 128, p. 29. I have no evidence that Daniel Cranmer was a relative of the archbishop.

[141] CCCC MS 128, pp. 62 and 92.   [142] CCCC MS 128, p. 31.

who happened to be a churchwarden of Northgate as well as a barber, was himself denounced (by whom we do not know) on 26 September for refusing to light candles before the rood. We can only assume that the denunciation of the two barbers was a retaliation for the denunciation of John Thatcher's son. Most interestingly, John Thatcher the younger was the nephew (and hence John Thatcher the elder was presumably the brother-in-law) of William Gardiner, prebendary of Canterbury Cathedral and leading plotter against the Archbishop. Here, then, we seem to have two factions – the Thatcher family and their allies versus the barbers of Canterbury – intermingling their personal feuds with complex theological issues and the high politics of the realm.[143]

While usually we cannot know whether people's willingness to denounce their neighbours preceded or followed their doctrinal opinions, in some cases it is clear that religious denunciations were little more than a pretext for the pursuit of politics by other means. In one deposition, for instance, we learn that 'Johanna Meryweder of St Mildred's parish, for displeasure that she bore towards a young maid named Elizabeth Celsay and her mother, made a fire upon the dung of the said Elizabeth and took a holy candle and dropped upon the said dung 7 times. And she told unto her neighbours that the said enchantment would make the cule [i.e. the buttocks] of the said maid to divide into two parts'. Clearly the denunciation of Johanna Meryweder by Elizabeth Celsay and her allies was an example of personal animosity rather than Reformation debate, and, since one of the archbishop's investigators scribbled in the margin of the deposition, 'she did it not, but said she would do it', it is clear that the alleged act of sorcery was never even performed. The salient point for our purposes, however, is another word scribbled by investigators in the margin: 'superstition'. Elizabeth Celsay might not have had a theological axe to grind, but she knew that the use of 'holy candles' for magical purposes was unacceptable to the new ecclesiastical regime, and she knew how to use the harsh reality of religious division in her private affairs. Popular politics in early modern England always depended upon carefully structured appeals to pockets of elite power, and in the context of Kent in the 1540s, that meant learning the rhetoric of Reformation debate.[144]

IV

If religious agitation in the diocese of Canterbury affected how lay people perceived the polity and modulated their responses to government initiatives, the implications for our study of the English Reformation are significant. Kent was not representative of England as a whole, of course, but its

---

[143] CCCC MS 128, pp. 51, 55, 58 and 313.   [144] CCCC MS 128, p. 31.

large population and proximity to the capital made it extremely important as a staging area for ideological conflict. As Eamon Duffy said of Kent, 'The struggle between the old and the new ways was more intense and more existential than in most other parts of England, but the issues involved were not in essence different from those raised by the progress of reform, or the lack of it, in parishes up and down the country.'[145] The widespread acceptance of religious divisions in the 1540s, then, warns us not to underestimate the education which even quite humble people received in Reformation controversy.

On a more general level, the Kentish disputes of the 1540s can also teach us to think of the English Reformation as surprisingly similar to religious events across the Channel. Historians have imagined England as somehow unique, driven by its own internal dynamics and thus outside the mainstream European experience. This theme has recently been expounded by Christopher Haigh, who insisted that 'Reformations' in England 'were not *the* Reformation, exported across the Channel and installed in England by Luther, Calvin, and Co. Ltd.'. He suggested that in England acts of religious reform 'did not come in swift and orderly sequence, as consecutive steps of a pre-planned programme or a protest movement', but rather as 'the accidents of everyday politics and the consequences of power struggles'. This was, he claimed, in sharp contrast to the continent, where Reformation came 'with violence and enthusiasm', the rapid implementation of Protestant services, and the wholesale destruction by rampaging mobs of 'the symbols with which priests had kept them in awe'. In England, Haigh wrote, it was different: 'change was piecemeal, and it took twenty years to get from the first real attack on Church jurisdiction in 1532 to the first Protestant church service in 1552'.[146]

This view of the continental Reformation is rather idiosyncratic and would be largely unfamiliar to most European Reformation historians. The supposed firm of 'Luther, Calvin, and Co. Ltd.', for instance, was beset by constant battles between the Lutheran and Reformed Churches from 1529 onwards, even before Calvin arrived in Geneva. In France, twenty years elapsed between the posting of Antoine Marcourt's infamous *placards* in 1534 and the arrival of Genevan missionaries in the 1550s. Iconoclasm was always a hit-or-miss affair, for instance in the Low Countries where cities with strong local militias avoided the 'iconoclastic fury' of 1566 yet still unquestionably

---

[145] Duffy, *Stripping of the Altars*, p. 434.

[146] Christopher Haigh, *English Reformations: Religion, Politics, and Society under the Tudors* (Oxford, 1993), p. 13. Another version of this position has recently been canvassed by Lucy Wooding, who argues that similarities between moderate Catholic and moderate Protestant ideologies in England allowed for a level of flexibility and consensus not available on the Continent: Wooding, *Rethinking Catholicism*.

experienced Reformations.[147] 'The Reformation', as Haigh defined it, existed in no more than a few locations, and perhaps only in reformers' dreams and conservatives' nightmares; everywhere else the assault on traditional religion was a long process of advance and withdrawal, compromise and negotiation, as diverse factions laboured to create their own disparate visions of Christian society.

None the less, to whatever extent there was a general pattern of Reformation, events in Kent make England suddenly seem a great deal more 'European' than we have been taught to expect. Certainly the phenomenon of the pulpit dispute, long stressed by continental scholars but usually confined in England to Hugh Latimer's confrontations with conservatives in Bristol, here takes on a new importance. Similarly, it is clear that in Kent images were not 'carefully removed on government orders' but violently pulled down and destroyed. The iconoclasm which followed on the heels of John Bland's sermons in towns like Faversham and Ospringe, for instance, might reasonably be compared to the iconoclasm which proceeded from 'hedge-preaching' in the Low Countries in 1566.[148] Something approaching continental radicalism can also be glimpsed in the agitations of 'persons that have made themselves priests and were none', lay preachers who were allegedly abetted by the archbishop's commissary.[149] But the most important connections between English and continental Reformations were the most basic: profound theological continuities that mark them as subsets of a wider phenomenon. The issues canvassed in Kent were remarkably familiar ones to European ears: justification through faith, the idolatry of images, the sacrilege of post-biblical accretions on the visible Church, and the diminution of the sacraments and other ceremonies in Christian worship.

These similarities should not be surprising, since there were numerous links between continental reformers and Kentish religion. In Lenham, for instance, lived the Partrich family, whose favourite son Nicholas had become friends with the Protestant leaders Heinrich Bullinger and Rudolf Gualter when he travelled abroad in 1536; Gualter himself stayed with the Partrich family twice in 1537 during his perambulations of southern England.[150] John Butler, another Kentishman from Sandwich and a protégé of Cranmer, also travelled to Zürich in 1536 and was received warmly by Bullinger before returning home.[151] Nicholas Wotton, the prominent Kentish diplomatist and cleric, was ambassador to the Duke of Cleves in 1539–40 and had certainly absorbed evangelical views by the time he was made Dean of Canterbury

---

[147] Geoffrey Parker, *The Dutch Revolt* (Ithaca, N.Y., 1977), ch. 2.
[148] See Phyllis Mack Crew, *Calvinist Preaching and Iconoclasm in the Netherlands 1544–1569* (Cambridge, 1978).
[149] CCCC MS 128, pp. 72 and 7.   [150] Clark, *English Provincial Society*, p. 60.
[151] MacCulloch, *Thomas Cranmer*, pp. 176–7.

in 1541.[152] A more complicated case involves John Twyne, an evangelical who sat on the common council of the city of Canterbury in 1540. Twyne had translated Philip Melanchthon's *Philosophiae Moralis Epitome* into English and dedicated it to Thomas Cromwell in the 1530s; by 1543 he was acting as Cranmer's overseas liaison agent. Twyne is known to have had secret discussions in Easter 1543 with yet another Kentish radical, the archpriest of St Martin's in Dover, Robert Singleton, who afterwards ostentatiously spread 'news from Germany' around Canterbury and was thus accused by William Gardiner of being a spy.[153] And, of course, Thomas Cranmer himself, the font of so much Reformation in his own diocese, had cut his evangelical teeth while on embassy in Central Europe in the early 1530s.

The books of European reformers also came into Kent in significant numbers. As early as 1530, the Maidstone curate Thomas Hitton was burned for carrying Lutheran books into England. In 1536, John Twyne was in trouble with Canterbury authorities for maintaining a printer who 'does print and sell diverse and sundry books to diverse rude and unlearned people which books are deemed to be in many sentences clearly against the faith of a true Christian man'; we can only guess at the identity of these books, but given Twyne's strong interest in Melanchthon we might reasonably take them for European works. By 1538, the powerful landowner and two-time sheriff of Kent Sir Edward Wotton (elder brother of Nicholas Wotton) was known to be a voracious reader of Bullinger's works, showing a level of academic interest not at all common in Tudor magnates. And Commissary Nevinson collected an enormous library of continental theology while resident at Canterbury, including works by John Calvin, Martin Bucer, Peter Martyr and many others.[154]

Just as evangelical activities in Kent looked surprisingly like evangelical activities in Europe, so, too, did the reactions of English Catholics resemble the reactions of Catholics abroad. The Catholic clergy provided their flocks with well-reasoned and politically sensitive responses to heretical ideas. In Rouen, for instance, Catholic sermons denounced the city's heretics as sexually deviant and carnally gluttonous, reflecting conservative fears of the disorder that would arise from Protestant attacks on clerical chastity and Lenten fasting.[155] Those angry French Catholics might have appreciated Edmund Shether's sermons in Canterbury Cathedral denouncing

[152] *DNB*, under Nicholas Wotton.
[153] MacCulloch, *Thomas Cranmer*, p. 311; Clark, *English Provincial Society*, pp. 29–30, 38 and 40–3; CCCC MS 128, pp. 153 and 267.
[154] Clark, *English Provincial Society*, pp. 34–5, 40, 52 and 60.
[155] Philip Benedict, *Rouen During the Wars of Religion* (Cambridge, 1981).

his opponents who 'preach nothing but a carnal liberty'.[156] Similarly, the ebb
and flow of Catholic control over the diocese of Canterbury might usefully
be compared to the fortunes of Catholics in Amsterdam. There a powerful
Protestant minority in the 1520s overreached during the 1530s, carried away
by eschatological excitement associated with Anabaptism, and after a failed
Protestant *coup* in 1535 Catholics burned a large number of heretics and
reclaimed control over the city for forty years.[157] Such was the goal of the
1543 conspirators, and if not for the unlikely leniency of Henry VIII towards
'the greatest heretic in Kent' (as he facetiously called Archbishop Cranmer at
the height of the crisis) this Catholic reaction against evangelical enthusiasm
might well have succeeded.

In conclusion, then, the recent scholarly obsession with English peculiar-
ity in the Reformation has been based upon an unwillingness to distinguish
between a 'Reformed polity', on the one hand, and 'Reformation politics',
on the other. The former, exemplified by Genevan discipline or the promulgation of new liturgies by the oligarchies of Imperial free cities, of course
never existed in Henrician England; localities lacked the autonomy to es-
tablish their own forms of worship, and all ecclesiastical authorities were
beholden to the king's maddening weaves across the theological spectrum.
The latter, however, exemplified by pulpit disputes, battles for control of
local offices and courts, and the overflow of theological debates into the ordinary discourse of communities, was present in England by the early 1540s.
Just as in so many places where Protestantism was neither immediately triumphant nor immediately suppressed, places like Bavaria, northern France
and the Low Countries, these conflicts moulded political disputes within a
well-understood, 'confessional' dynamic. Disputes between evangelicals and
Catholics, rather than the clear triumph of either, would shape the politics of
these regions throughout the sixteenth century, firmly entrenching the idea
of religious conflict within their political cultures.

It was despair at this new fact of English life, so foreign to the worldviews
of plebeians and politicians alike, that led Henry VIII to make the last major
address of his reign at the concluding ceremony of parliament on Christmas
Eve 1545. In an impassioned plea to the nation, the old king lamented that
the 'perfect love' between himself and his kingdom could not long continue
unless English subjects took pains 'to amend one thing, which surely is amiss
and far out of order... which is that charity and concord is not amongst
you, but discord and dissension beareth rule in every place'. Citing St Paul's

---

[156] CCCC MS 128, p. 45.
[157] Alastair Duke, 'Building Heaven in Hell's Despite: The Early History of the Reformation
in the Towns of the Low Countries', in his *Reformation and Revolt in the Low Countries*
(London, 1990).

sermon on *caritas*, he told his subjects, 'Charity is gentle, charity is not envious, charity is not proud', and he therefore asked them, 'What love and charity is amongst you when the one calleth the other "heretic" and "Anabaptist", and he calleth him again "papist", "hypocrite", and "Pharisee?"' Henry singled-out priests for blame, telling them: 'I see and hear daily that you of the clergy preach one against another, teach one contrary to another, inveigh one against another without charity or discretion. Some be too stiff in their old mumpsimus, other [*sic*] be too busy and curious in their new sumpsimus. Thus all men almost be in variety and discord, and few or none preach truly and sincerely the word of God.' Yet the laity, too, he decried as divisive and unkind: 'You of the temporality be not clean and unspotted of malice and envy, for you rail on bishops, speak slanderously of priests, and rebuke and taunt preachers, both contrary to good order and Christian fraternity.' Most importantly, he told them that the Scriptures had been given to them only for their edification, not for their interpretation:

I am very sorry to know and hear how unreverently that most precious jewel, the Word of God, is disputed, rhymed, sung and jangled in every alehouse and tavern, contrary to the true meaning and doctrine of the same. And yet I am even as much sorry that the readers of the same follow it in doing so faintly and coldly. For of this I am sure, that charity was never so faint amongst you, and virtuous and godly living was never less used, nor God himself amongst Christians was never less honored or served.[158]

Such was the rationale of the Henrician *via media*: not a self-conscious programme of religious moderation but a Sisyphean task of reconciliation put to a rancorous and divided nation. Neither the old king's eloquence nor his wrath could put so self-righteous a jinnee back in its bottle again.

---

[158] Edward Hall, *The Triumphant Reigne of Kyng Henry the VIII*, ed. C. Whibley, 2 vols. (London, 1904), II, pp. 354–8. See also Peter Marshall, 'Mumpsimus and Sumpsimus: The Intellectual Origins of a Henrician *Bon Mot*', *JEH*, 52 (2001), 512–20.

PART III

Sites of Reformation: collaboration and popular politics under Edward VI

7

Resistance and collaboration in the dissolution of the chantries

In February 1539, Archbishop Cranmer's client John Marshall wrote to Thomas Cromwell describing the progress of the Reformation in the East Midlands. Marshall's report was at times unabashedly biased, but he also was not afraid to deliver bad news, for instance regarding people's fears of new taxes and unwillingness to work on abrogated feast days. In particular, he was concerned to describe the social repercussions of the dissolution of the monasteries, and in the process he left us a fascinating, if all too brief, analysis:

> Abbeys be now nothing esteemed or pitied, for the commons say they now perceive more commonwealth to grow to them by their suppressing than was afore. For they say many good farms and other benefits come thereby daily abroad, which they [the monks] heretofore kept and had accumulated in great number to their own singular profits and advantages, saying they [the monks] were but the bellymonds and gluttons of the world, and the most vicious persons of the world, saving they [the commons] think there is much and great losses of their prayers.[1]

The last clause in Marshall's analysis belies the easy confidence of his initial observations. The commons may have been pleased with the material benefits gained from the dissolution of the monasteries, but the great tragedy they perceived in the downfall of the religious orders was the elimination of so many prayers. These prayers, particularly prayers for the dead, were the *raison d'être* of medieval monasticism and one of the principal outlets for lay religiosity in the early sixteenth century. Vast numbers of lay people left provisions in their wills for prayers to speed their souls through purgatory. Fraternities provided masses for the souls of their members, while perpetual endowments ensured masses for the souls of their wealthy founders. If people were pleased with the dissolution of the monasteries but uncomfortable

---

[1] PRO SP 1/143, fol. 81r–v [*LP* XIV, i, 295]. On Marshall's correspondence, see Geoffrey Elton, *Policy and Police: The Enforcement of the Reformation in the Age of Thomas Cromwell* (Cambridge, 1972), pp. 329–31; on his possible kinship to Cranmer and attachment to Welbeck Abbey, see Diarmaid MacCulloch, *Thomas Cranmer: A Life* (New Haven, Conn., 1996), p. 12.

with the elimination of prayers, then, it was symptomatic of a larger contradiction within English society. Ordinary subjects, torn by conflicting loyalties and pressured by new ideas, accomplished deft feats of cognitive dissonance, accepting and profiting from the dissolution of the monasteries while simultaneously lamenting the decline of one of monasticism's central functions.

Less than a decade after Marshall's observations, however, the dissolution of the monasteries was eclipsed by the dissolution of the chantries, begun slowly in the later years of Henry VIII's reign and then systematically implemented in the reign of his young son Edward VI.[2] This dissolution struck at exactly that component of medieval Christianity whose diminution, according to Marshall, was most regretted. It not only dismantled all institutions specifically created for intercessory prayers but, in concert with the 1547 injunctions, effectively anathematised all prayers for the dead in England. Chantries, guilds, fraternities, colleges, free chapels, obits, lights, lamps, bede-rolls and all the other institutions that upheld the cult of the dead and the prominence of purgatory in the medieval Catholic worldview were banned. Chalices, pyxes, vestments and other paraphernalia of the Catholic mass were confiscated from thousands of chantry priests, foreshadowing the abolition of the mass itself two years later. The 1547 Chantries Act, moreover, left no doubt about the explicitly evangelical rationale behind these actions, describing purgatory as a 'superstition...brought into the minds and estimation of men by reason of the ignorance of their very true and perfect salvation through the death of Jesus Christ'.[3] Here, then, the regime's ideological colours were laid bare. Henry VIII had always relied upon a strategy of incrementalism, maintaining plausible deniability about the spiritual connotations of even his most radical policies. Now there was no question that the regime was promoting a revolution.

This chapter will explore how the Edwardian government was able to implement so remarkable and unprecedented a project. It will suggest that the regime's success depended, to a hitherto unacknowledged level, on the involvement, cooperation and collaboration of the populace, fuelled by an amplification of the same cognitive dissonance that John Marshall found so disquieting in the 1530s. Late in Henry VIII's reign, in the aftermath of more than a decade of attacks on the wealth of the Church, opponents of the Reformation increasingly shared with its adherents a view of chantry endowments that privileged their economic value to the living over their spiritual value to the dead. With so much money at stake, the defensive strategies of all but

---

[2] The word 'chantry' usually refers to institutions endowed for intercessory masses in which a priest is employed full time, but it can also be used as a general term for all intercessory institutions.

[3] *Statutes*, IV, pp. 24–33.

the most preternaturally pious of subjects came to centre on the protection of scarce resources from royal predations, siphoning wealth away from the Church before the government could seize it. In practice, these strategies, no less than the polemic of evangelicals, eroded confidence in purgatory and prayers for the dead, forcing people to imagine alternative avenues for both investment and salvation. By the time Edward VI came to power, then, only a small minority of English subjects were willing to resist the spiritual (as opposed to financial) impact of the dissolution of the chantries, while many were willing to contribute to the collapse of intercessory institutions if they themselves rather than the government reaped the rewards. With fiscal considerations so intertwined with spiritual ones, moreover, many communities divided over appropriate responses to the government's policies, and local factions often used the dissolutions as pretexts for financial manoeuvres and power plays. In other words, the dissolution of the chantries was such a financially and politically adulterated event that even its explicitly evangelical character did not prevent it from cutting across ostensible lines of ideology and belief, leading even many conservatives to implicate and invest themselves in a central pillar of the Protestant Reformation.

I

To understand the revolutionary nature of the Chantries Act of 1547 and the significance of collaboration with it, it is necessary briefly to review the centrality of intercessory prayer within Catholic voluntary religion. Late-medieval theology held that the sacrifice of Christ on the cross, as received by individual Christians through baptism, washed away the stain of original sin, making it possible for human beings to be redeemed through the mediation of the Church and its sacraments. The venial sins committed in the post-biblical era, however, were not washed away by Christ's sacrifice, nor was the human propensity for sin, so in practice the achievement of salvation depended upon Christians cleansing their souls through confession and absolution and then providing satisfaction for their sins through penance. Since virtually no degree of penance could satisfy the burden of human degradation, however, when human beings died all but the holiest of saints had payment still to make, a condition which did not warrant eternal hellfire but was sufficiently serious that they could not be permitted to come face to face with God. For these sinners, the overwhelming majority of human beings, there was purgatory, literally a place of purgation where penance could be completed, doubts could be alleviated and the immaculate faith necessary for entry into heaven could be achieved. In the late-medieval English imagination, purgatory was a place of terrible pain and hardship, no limbo but a taste of the inferno where souls were boiled in oil, suspended by meat hooks, or fed on excruciating poison.[4] Only through thousands of years of such tribulations was it believed that the sinfulness of human beings could be expunged; Catholics believed that works contributed to salvation, but they foresaw hard work indeed.

The amount of time people might expect to endure these torments depended upon the gravity of their sins and the extent of their penance. Every sinner naturally wanted to shorten their stay in purgatory, and it was thus upon the fertile ground of self-interest that the concept of intercessory prayer took root. Just as individual works could be performed by people seeking to speed their way into heaven, so those people could pay priests to contribute to their salvation by praying for them after their deaths. This idea had been present within Christianity since at least the third century, when St Cyprian referred to an offering of the Eucharist to help the soul of a recently deceased Christian. The idea of intercession gained credence with the further development of the doctrine of purgatory by Gregory the Great in the sixth century, and in the high Middle Ages when the doctrine was formalised intercessory prayers became common both in monasteries and in the form of 'anniversary masses' for illustrious benefactors. By the thirteenth century, the endowment of daily masses for the souls of wealthy laymen had become common, and corporate institutions providing intercessory prayer for more humble Christians were growing in popularity. Since canon law forbade priests from saying mass more than once per day, however, the proliferation of intercessory masses required that new livings be instituted especially for the purpose: chantries were born.[5]

The ubiquity of chantries by the first quarter of the sixteenth century is hard to overestimate. When intercessory institutions were surveyed between 1546 and 1548, the Crown's commissioners counted 2,189 separate institutions supporting at least one full-time priest. These 'greater' intercessory institutions, including chantries, guilds, free chapels, colleges, stipendiary services and hospitals, could be found in 23 per cent of all English parishes.[6] Many of these were full-fledged ecclesiastical benefices, and chantry priests

---

[4] On views of purgatory in late medieval England, see Eamon Duffy, *The Stripping of the Altars: Traditional Religion in England 1400–1580* (New Haven, 1992), ch. 10; Stephen Greenblatt, *Hamlet in Purgatory* (Princeton, 2001), ch. 2; Peter Marshall, *Beliefs and the Dead in Reformation England* (forthcoming), ch. 1. Occasionally in medieval European literature, purgatory was portrayed as a place of waiting rather than torment: see Greenblatt, *Hamlet in Purgatory*, pp. 61–4.

[5] On the history of intercessory prayers, see K. L. Wood-Legh, *Perpetual Chantries in Britain* (Cambridge, 1965), ch. 1; Jacques Le Goff, *The Birth of Purgatory*, trans. Arthur Goldhammer (Chicago, 1984); Jacques Le Goff, *Your Money or Your Life: Economy and Religion in the Middle Ages*, trans. P. Ranum (New York, 1990); Joel Rosenthal, *The Purchase of Paradise: The Social Function of Aristocratic Benevolence, 1307–1485* (London, 1972).

[6] Alan Kreider, *English Chantries: The Road to Dissolution* (Cambridge, Mass., 1979), pp. 16–17.

had to be presented to the bishop for institution like other priests. In these cases, the physical space occupied by the chantrist could be merely a chapel within a church, but it could also be a free-standing chapel erected for the purpose. At a slightly less exalted level were 'stipendiary services' with priests endowed to say masses like chantrists but paid by laymen and functioning entirely outside the ecclesiastical establishment.[7]

Among the intercessory institutions initiated by the laity, the most important were the fraternities, also known as guilds, confraternities and brotherhoods. A fraternity was, by J. J. Scarisbrick's useful definition, 'an association of layfolk who, under the patronage of a particular saint, the Trinity, Blessed Virgin Mary, Corpus Christi or similar, undertook to provide the individual member of the brotherhood with a good funeral – as solemn and well-attended a "send-off" as possible – together with regular prayer and mass-saying thereafter for the repose of the dead person's soul'. Living members paid regular dues to provide masses for the dead, trusting that future members would do the same for them; fraternities were thus institutions whose very existence, like a social security tax, was predicated on stability and permanence. While smaller fraternities could be modest, using chapels in pre-existing churches and asking only a few pennies each year from brothers, others could be very grand indeed. In Boston, St Mary's guild had an annual income of over £900, while in Coventry the fraternity of the Holy Trinity was the second largest landowner in the city and had 390 members in 1533. In Cambridge, two town fraternities even combined resources to found a university college, Corpus Christi. The number of fraternities in England was enormous. In the early sixteenth century, there were over 100 in Northamptonshire and 120 in Lincolnshire. Large cities could all boast several, while even some smaller towns and villages could have more than one; at Yaxley, Huntingdonshire, for instance, there were seven fraternities, with a guildhall. London itself had over forty separate fraternities. These were institutions, in other words, that enjoyed massive lay support, whether among wealthy urban elites or modest village artisans and small landholders.[8]

Several rungs down from fraternities were the obits, lights, lamps, tiny guilds and other institutions that were not wealthy enough to maintain a priest but none the less paid for prayers and good works to be done for the souls of their founders. Obits were endowments, far less expensive than full-time chantries but still founded in perpetuity, which paid priests to say an annual requiem mass as well as vespers, matins, lauds for the dead, and

---

[7] Wood-Legh, *Perpetual Chantries*, ch. 2.
[8] This paragraph is based on J. J. Scarisbrick, *The Reformation and the English People* (Oxford, 1984), ch. 2.

other prayers on every anniversary of the death of the founder. At a lower level, people of even very modest means could leave money in their wills for candles to be lit at saints' shrines or at an altar in the parish church so that priests could read their missals. Bequests could also pay for a finite number of masses to be sung for the dead parishioner's soul, often five for the five wounds of Christ or the thirty masses of the 'trental'. Christians on their deathbeds were often creative; one parishioner in Croscombe, Somerset, for instance, left money for 'the ringing of the curfew nightly within the parish church'. Sometimes these modest foundations derived their incomes from land, but often they were derived from agricultural products such as the milk of a single cow or the honey of a single beehive.[9] At the poorest levels of society, of course, they would simply be one-time cash payments as a deceased person's meagre possessions were divided between their heirs and the Church. At any given time, England's churches had thousands of these temporary grants at some intermediate stage of completion.[10]

The most universal form of intercessory prayer, however, was nearly as socially levelling as death itself: the parish bede-roll. In every church, a great list was kept of the deceased members of the parish, recited in full once a year with prayers for their souls. While technically parishioners had to contribute to the fabric of the church to be included on the bede-roll, in practice poorer people could simply provide a couple of pennies. In some parishes, then, these lists could grow to hundreds of pages, containing thousands of names, providing a 'social map' of the community that stretched back centuries. As Eamon Duffy has written, these documents became '*the* parochial documents *par excellence* in pre-Reformation England', unifying the living and the dead of the parish in a single, seamless community. With the living constantly praying for the souls of those who came before them in an unbroken chain, the bede-rolls acquired an eschatological significance, wedding together Christian history with the parish's own history. In Duffy's analysis: 'The presence of the parishioner's name on the bede-roll [was] more than an assurance of continuing intercession: to have one's own name or that of a parent, spouse, or child enrolled was to affirm one's unity in salvation with the parish community, and to seek to perpetuate that unity beyond the grave.'[11]

Taken together, all of these thriving institutions point to a society which poured its financial and creative resources into the health of its souls after death, a society which regarded purgatory rather than heaven or hell as the

---

[9] Kreider, *English Chantries*, p. 8.

[10] For an analysis of the full range of intercessory activities in a locality, see Clive Burgess, ' "For the Increase of Divine Service": Chantries in the Parish in Late Medieval Bristol', *JEH*, 36 (1985), 46–65.

[11] This paragraph is based on Duffy, *Stripping of the Altars*, pp. 153–4 and 327–37.

first destination of the departed and thus made the shortening of suffering after death one of the primary goals of life. The speeding of souls through purgatory was perhaps the single most dominant preoccupation in people's religious lives, shaping how they spent their time and money, structuring how they prayed, and shaping, in Duffy's words, 'the organization of the Church and the physical layout and appearance of the buildings in which men and women worshipped'.[12] The destruction of intercessory institutions and the banning of intercessory prayers in the 1540s thus struck not at a peripheral aspect of English Catholicism, as some people chose to interpret the dissolution of the monasteries, but at the still-beating heart of traditional religion.

II

Despite the popularity of intercessory prayers, in Henry VIII's reign the institutions that supported them were subjected to low-level but significant and sustained attacks. The idea of intercession for souls in purgatory depended, of course, upon the existence of purgatory, and this concept was relentlessly challenged by the reformist wing of the Henrician government. As early as Easter 1534, in a compromise designed to prevent popular religious division, Cranmer and the conservative bishops agreed to ban preaching on either side of contentious subjects, of which the first subject listed was purgatory.[13] While this hardly amounted to a condemnation of traditional beliefs, it certainly marked purgatory as controversial, and church-goers could not have failed to notice the absence of sermons on a subject so central to their salvation. Then in another compromise in 1536, an example of virtually nonsensical theology-by-committee, the Ten Articles explicitly called for intercessory prayers yet at the same time denounced papal pardons and stated that we cannot know where souls go after death since 'the name thereof, and kinds of pains there . . . be to us uncertain by Scripture'.[14] Seven years later the King's Book, despite its generally conservative tone, was overwhelmingly dismissive of purgatory, stating that prayers for the dead were laudable not because of their intercessory potential but because all members of the mystical body of Christ are bound by charity to pray for one another. Even more radically, it insisted that 'it is not in the power or knowledge of any man to limit and dispense how much, and in what space of time, or to what person particularly the said masses, exequies, and suffrages do profit and avail'. In other words, prayers and masses for the dead were not efficacious in salvation,

---

[12] Ibid., p. 301. [13] Ibid., p. 381.
[14] Gerald Bray (ed.), *Documents of the English Reformation* (Minneapolis, 1994), pp. 173–4.

since only God 'knoweth the measures and times of his own judgment and mercies'.[15]

Among English evangelicals there was also an incessant drumbeat against purgatory. In 1537, for instance, there were printed ballads circulating in Yorkshire that attacked purgatory, encouraging the Rotherham schoolmaster William Senes to argue that every soul after death went either to heaven or to hell, and that no prayers could avail for them.[16] Hugh Latimer preached against purgatory as early as 1531 in London, and then afterwards in countless sermons in West Country parishes; in 1536 he even took up the theme in front of the convocation of the province of Canterbury, mocking purgatory as a 'pleasant fiction' and a 'pick-purse' designed to garner profits for the Bishop of Rome.[17] In the same year, the preacher John Swynerton denied the existence of purgatory, while one Robert Wymond was denounced for saying that 'purgatory is pissed out'.[18] In 1538, Thomas Wylley, vicar of Yoxford, Suffolk, offered Cromwell a radical stage-play against purgatory entitled 'Woman on the Rock, in the Fire of Faith Affining and a Purging in the True Purgatory'.[19]

At the same time as these explicit attacks against the doctrine of purgatory, there was a decline in lay bequests for intercessory prayers. In a sample of West-Country wills studied by Robert Whiting, for instance, 58% included bequests to religious guilds in 1530–5, 45% included them in 1536–9 and only 28% included them in 1540–6. Intercessory prayers and masses were requested in 70% of wills in 1520–9, 51% of wills in 1530–9 and only 26% of wills in 1540–6.[20] Similarly, of the Gloucestershire wills from 1541–7 studied by Caroline Litzenberger, only 14% included provisions for prayers for the dead; Litzenberger does not have earlier data, but such a low percentage is far removed from our assumptions about late medieval devotional practices.[21] Fraternities also suffered decreasing enrolments in the 1530s and 1540s. The guild of Corpus Christi, Boston, averaged ten new members per year in the 1520s, but added only four in 1533, three in 1536, only a few scattered through the rest of the decade, and none in 1540–2. Subscriptions fell similarly at the guild of Holy Trinity, Coventry, and Holy Trinity, Sleaford.[22] This trend was by no means universal, and certainly it cannot tell us anything

---

[15] Kreider, *English Chantries*, pp. 151–3.

[16] A. G. Dickens, *Lollards and Protestants in the Diocese of York* (London, 1982), p. 40.

[17] Kreider, *English Chantries*, pp. 101–2 and 119–20.   [18] *LP* XI, 1424.

[19] Seymour Baker House, 'Literature, Drama and Politics', in Diarmaid MacCulloch (ed.), *The Reign of Henry VIII: Politics, Policy and Piety* (New York, 1995), p. 188.

[20] Robert Whiting, '"For the Health of my Soul": Prayers for the Dead in the Tudor South-West', *Southern History*, 5 (1983), 68–94, at p. 74.

[21] Caroline Litzenberger, *The English Reformation and the Laity: Gloucestershire, 1540–1580* (Cambridge, 1997), p. 187.

[22] Scarisbrick, *The Reformation and the English People*, pp. 34–5.

substantive about popular piety. What it can tell us, however, is something more mundane but no less important: as a whole, chantries and guilds were taking in far less money than they had before. This decline in demand for intercession was exacerbated by a marked trend among testators after about 1530 to provide for relatively short-term endowments of prayers rather than the more lavish and long-term endowments that had predominated before.[23] In all of these cases, the reasons for the shift probably had to do with well-founded fears of the regime's sticky fingers more than profound changes in religious attitudes. None the less, the recently thriving chantries were not faring well.

For a variety of reasons, then, lay confidence in intercessory institutions was shaken by the 1540s. The government had spent years demonstrating its ruthlessness towards Church property, and anyone with their finger in the wind would have been nervous about pouring money into religious institutions. At the same time, theological attacks on purgatory and prayers for the dead must have made people nervous about entrusting their wealth to such abstract concepts. Even many people who never showed significant interest in Protestant ideas would have instinctively backed away from controversial issues and perceived 'risk' when bequeathing their lives' savings. A vicious circle was thus created in which the controversy surrounding prayers for the dead made people nervous about paying for them, and people's nervousness about paying for them increased the perceived controversy surrounding the issue. Out of this vicious circle emerged a new phenomenon, a trickle that was to become a flood: the dissolution of chantries, both by private individuals and by the Crown, without statutory authority or ecclesiastical consent.

There had always been chantries that lapsed for lack of funds, either because of diminution of the principal for the endowment or because memories of the beneficiaries grew cold and their descendants needed ready cash. In the context of the dissolution of the monasteries, however, with predations seemingly so normal and natural, liquidations of intercessory endowments became commonplace. In Yorkshire, for instance, Thomas Boswell claimed chantry lands at Conisborough in 1537, Sir Edmund Ackroyd took possession of the lands of Frith chantry in 1539, and Thomas Markenfield seized the lands of St John's chantry at Wathe in 1542.[24] At Exeter around 1538, Richard Drew appropriated the property bequeathed to two parish churches for intercessory masses, while in the same year the prominent citizen John Blackaller confiscated obit lands at Shillingford.[25] At Nuneaton,

[23] Peter Marshall, *The Catholic Priesthood and the English Reformation* (Oxford, 1994), p. 54.
[24] Dickens, *Lollards and Protestants in the Diocese of York*, p. 207.
[25] Whiting, 'For the Health of my Soul', pp. 74–5.

Warwickshire, in 1542, parishioners conspired with the descendants of a chantry's founder to convert the priest's service into a grammar school; this was certainly laudable in worldly terms, but it did little for the soul of the founder, still presumably awaiting release from purgatory. Similarly, at Monmouth, parishioners converted chantry funds into an endowment for a church organist, while at Harwich in Essex chantry funds were used to repair the town's sea walls.[26] At Olney, Buckinghamshire, in 1542, one Edward Brymley detained the rents of 'a certain house called the Katherine Wheel' which was owed to the 'Earl of Warwick chantry'.[27] In London, the Goldsmiths' Company was sued in 1540 because masses were no longer sung for Robert Butler, founder of an intercessory endowment maintained by the Company. The Goldsmiths claimed that the income had been stolen and that therefore a priest could not be paid, rather a telling argument for such a rich London guild.[28]

The Crown's own dissolutions prior to the first Chantries Act in 1545 were particularly significant, not only because of their scale but because they underlined the hypocrisy of a government which justified the 1545 statute on the grounds that chantry property was being embezzled by unscrupulous subjects. Between 1540 and 1545, the government dissolved at least nineteen chantries and fraternities, six free chapels, ten hospitals and twenty-five colleges, all institutions whose endowments included provisions for intercession for the dead. While the number of chantries and chapels was modest, twenty-five colleges amounted to more than one-quarter of all the colleges in the realm, and ten hospitals amounted to one-eleventh of the total; even the universities of Oxford and Cambridge feared for their continued existence in the wake of these extraordinary dissolutions. Some predations were particularly eccentric; at Burton-upon-Trent, for instance, the king sent commissioners in 1545 to dissolve a college that he himself had founded only four years previously on the site of a recently suppressed monastery. According to Alan Kreider, the government's selection of intercessory institutions to dissolve was based not on the nature of the institutions themselves but on the attractiveness of their endowments: in many cases the king's hand was encouraged by influential courtiers or magnates who requested the grants from these properties.[29]

The motivations for private dissolutions, where they can be discerned, ran the gamut. On the one hand, there is no question that some confiscations represented pious attempts to pre-empt anticipated assaults by the government. In the extraordinary case of Richmond, for instance, the borough took

[26] Kreider, *English Chantries*, p. 157.   [27] PRO E 301/108.
[28] Susan Brigden, *London and the Reformation* (Oxford, 1989), p. 387.
[29] Kreider, *English Chantries*, pp. 160–4.

control of the endowments for six chantries, two chapels, and ten obits in December 1544, then provided pensions for the priests out of the town's regular income so that they could continue their intercessory activities. With the complicity of the community's leadership, Richmond successfully hid the existence of these institutions until late in Edward VI's reign.[30] This may seem extraordinary for 1544, before the Crown had made any official move against the chantries, but it was a natural reaction to Henry VIII's reputation for impiety concerning prayers for the dead. As early as 1536, the abbot of Woburn had noted that 'his grace as yet hath built no house of prayer, not so much as one chantry for himself that I know'.[31]

The continued maintenance of mass priests from dissolved chantries as occurred at Richmond, however, was extremely rare. Far more often, individuals or communities dissolved intercessory institutions for financial reasons, taking no action to continue their religious function; wealth was protected within the locality, but prayers came to an abrupt end. In 1536, for instance, the city of York, long suffering from recession, obtained a private bill in parliament allowing it to suppress three obits and nine chantries whose priests the corporation had been required to support; the bill granted the remaining property of their endowments to the 'mayor and commonalty' of the city. The only thing unusual about the York case was that the town got permission. Elsewhere, as in Walkeringham, Nottinghamshire, where the community created a fund for the 'Trent banks and a highway leading to the same', confiscations proceeded behind the king's back, with no provisions made for priests' livings. Whether these actions show any self-conscious change in beliefs about purgatory is questionable, but they certainly show a remarkable willingness to put the financial needs of the living above the spiritual needs of the dead.[32]

On the opposite end of the spectrum from events in Richmond, moreover, in some cases there clearly were reformist motives behind the dissolution of intercessory institutions. In the London parish of St Matthew Friday Street, for instance, the churchwardens tried illegally to remove a chantry priest in 1540; one of these churchwardens, William Etis, was indicted in the same year for harbouring evangelicals. Another London parish with a powerful early Protestant tradition, All Hallows Lombard Street, had an income of almost £6 per year for a chantry priest but provided for no such priest after 1540.[33] In the village of Holflete, Lincolnshire, an undated dispute over 'a chapel and alms house ... and eighteen acres of land belonging to the same'

[30] Ibid., p. 158.   [31] BL Cotton MS Cleopatra E. IV, fol. 111r.
[32] Kreider, *English Chantries*, pp. 159–60 and 157; A. G. Dickens, 'A Municipal Dissolution of Chantries at York, 1536', *Yorkshire Archaeological Journal*, 36 (1945), 164–74; *Statutes*, vol. 3, 27 Hen. VIII, c. 32, pp. 582–4.
[33] Brigden, *London and the Reformation*, p. 387.

was radicalised by an accusation that 'the inhabitants of the said hamlet of Holflete did continually use in the said chapel papistical ceremonies and the usurped power of the bishop of Rome'.[34] In some instances, the stripping of chantries and free chapels could even look uncannily like the plunder of monasteries, with subjects breaking in and removing anything of value. In June 1544, for example, remarkable spoliation occurred at a chapel of St John in South Willingham, Lincolnshire:

One Thomas Marbery, squire, William Twydale, Richard Thomson, Thomas Grene, John Redhed the elder, George Grene, Henry Johnson, Thomas Bard, Charles Bury, and John Redhed the younger, by the commandment and procurement of Francis Askew, squire, unlawfully assembled themselves ... and the doors and windows of the same chapel then and there did riotously break, and a chest of books there being to the value of 12d, and a bell with a clock and the seat and desks of the said chapel, did then and there riotously take away and converted the same to their own uses ... and pulled down and threw down all the leaf and covering of the same chapel and carried away the same ... to the value of £40 sterling, and also took down out of the windows of the same chapel all the glass and iron ... to the value of £5 sterling at the least ... and left nothing there but only the bare stone walls.[35]

We do not know how Francis Askew 'procured' his accomplices, but, given that he was the brother of Anne Askew, we may reasonably assume that events at South Willingham had evangelical implications.[36]

In other instances the raiding of chantry wealth could be glossed, whether disingenuously or not, as a form of obedience to royal policy. In Chester, for example, the chantry priest Thomas Warnyngham claimed that he was 'wrongfully expelled' from his intercessory post at the collegiate church of St John the Baptist by 'the dean of the said collegiate church with other the ministers of the same church' who allegedly colluded in their 'covetous and perverse minds' to withhold his £3 8d stipend. The dean's reply to these accusations, however, was that Warnyngham's office had been not merely to say prayers for the dead but also to read lessons to visitors who gave oblations 'unto the image of the rood in the said church of St John'. Recently, this image had been removed, so the dean and chapter had ceased payment to the superfluous priest. Here, then, the elimination of a chantry priest was a by-product of the Henrician attack on idolatry. The clergy of Chester may not have opposed intercessory prayer, but they knew better than to support a chantry priest whose activities were linked too closely with prayers to an outlawed image.[37]

---

[34] PRO STAC 2/2, fol. 152r.   [35] PRO STAC 2/10, fol. 140r.

[36] On Askew, see Steven Gunn, *Charles Brandon, Duke of Suffolk, c.1484–1545* (Oxford, 1988), pp. 210–11; *Narratives of the Days of the Reformation*, ed. J. G. Nichols, Camden Society, old series, 77 (London, 1859), p. 39. I would like to thank Diarmaid MacCulloch for these references.

[37] PRO REQ 2/1/96.

Similarly, in Lancashire a free-chapel priest called Thomas Barlowe sold off the ornaments in his possession as early as 1537. He was accused eight years later of having 'converted … to his own purpose' not only the chalice and other valuables but also 'certain jewels called relics', including 'one cross of silver with a piece of St Andrew's cross closed in the same' and 'one great piece of silver the which did stand upon some feet of silver and in the same was closed a piece of the garment of St Laurence'. Barlowe's sanguine response to these charges was that 'according to the injunctions and commandments of our said sovereign lord the king's majesty' he had indeed taken 'diverse things called relics and the same spoiled and did cast away as his duty was'.[38] We cannot be sure whether Barlowe was a conscientious reformer or merely a time-server reaping the benefits of royal policy, but once again the wealth of an intercessory chapel was substantially diminished for ostensibly reformist purposes.

Attacks on chantries and other intercessory institutions, then, were not necessarily motivated by disdain for prayers for the dead, but they were substantially legitimised and exacerbated by the Crown's multifaceted assault on the established Church. Regardless of the respect that prayers for the dead still enjoyed in principle, in practice the institutions that supported those prayers were increasingly seen as inessential, and any number of circumstances could lead English men and women to reclaim the wealth of the dead for the sake of the living.

III

Despite the profit-taking that occurred in Henry VIII's reign, of course, active plunderers were always a small minority, and, even within the growing population who were willing to imagine the wealth of chantries flowing into their own purses, few people approved of attempts to appropriate that wealth by the Crown. When we move to the more systematic, governmental dissolutions of Edward VI's reign, therefore, the crucial phenomenon with which we must begin is the resistance that those dissolutions generated. This resistance has served as the centrepiece of the revisionist narrative of the dissolutions, and rightly so; the magnitude of resistance across the length and breadth of England was remarkable. Yet, just as important as identifying resistance is differentiating one form from another and analysing their varying goals, methods and political dynamics.

The most spectacular resistance to the Edwardian dissolutions, and the kind most appealing to historians, was violent confrontation. Although very rare, these confrontations had an importance far outweighing their numbers.

---

[38] PRO DL 1/16, fols. 50r–51r.

Protector Somerset's government, already strained by wars in Scotland and France, could not expend serious military resources suppressing riots over chantries, and the Amicable Grant risings a quarter-century before had taught both government and people how effective popular protest could be in undermining offensive government programmes. These confrontations, then, always potentially carried within them the seeds of wider rebellion.

Generally the dissolution of a chantry did not produce violence on its own, but rather violence became possible when a dissolution was tied to threats of a more root-and-branch assault on local religion. One of the most spectacular examples was in Cornwall, where a despised ex-Cromwellian stooge, Archdeacon William Body, was responsible for the implementation of religious change. On 5 April 1548, Body's surveys of the chantries, combined with his removal of images from churches on the Lizard peninsula, produced an explosion. The timing of the incident was not coincidental, resulting from the elimination of candles on Palm Sunday and 'creeping to the cross' on Good Friday the week before. Regardless of their exact motivations, a mob led by a chantry priest and two yeomen attacked Body in his lodgings and lynched him. A small-scale, localised rebellion followed, but it was quickly suppressed, and the chantry priest was executed despite the reprieve of many of his accomplices; clearly the regime had a point to make about chantries and their priests.[39] An equally violent incident occurred at Seamer, Yorkshire, where a parish clerk and a yeoman lit a beacon to raise the country, and the assembled crowds lynched a chantry commissioner and his wife, the servant of another chantry commissioner, and a former mayor of York. Again, various grievances motivated this rising, but strong amongst them was the complaint that the dissolution of two local chantries had deprived the community of a chapel of ease, forcing people to walk to a church more than a mile distant.[40]

Sometimes violence could emerge from the complex economic arrangements that supported intercessory institutions. At Ashburton, Devon, for instance, the rents on the town's weekly market had been used to support a priest at the fraternity of St Lawrence. When the fraternity was dissolved and a servant of the local chantry commissioner arrived to collect the Crown's new revenues from the market in July 1548, he was confronted by a local Justice of the Peace and a crowd composed of mercers, pewterers, bakers, smiths and other artisans. Whether the incident which followed amounted to a riot is contested in the records, but there is no question that three

[39] A. L. Rowse, *Tudor Cornwall* (New York, 1969), pp. 257–9; Duffy, *Stripping of the Altars*, pp. 456–9.
[40] A. G. Dickens, 'Some Popular Reactions to the Edwardian Reformation in Yorkshire', *Yorkshire Archaeological Journal*, 34 (1939), pp. 151–69; Duffy, *Stripping of the Altars*, p. 459.

months later on Michaelmas Saturday stalls at the market were violently thrown down.[41] Similarly, at Keighly, Yorkshire, a husbandman called Henry Ambler who in 1548 had become Crown farmer of local chantry lands complained that three men had 'entered into the premises, breaking up the hedges, fences, and enclosures of the same'. It is unclear why the three men (all surnamed 'Hall') chose to confront Ambler, but since they reploughed the land and continued to occupy it afterwards, it seems likely that they were pursuing a legal claim in opposition to Ambler's rights under the Chantries Act.[42]

All of these incidents were potentially destabilising, but it is worth pointing out that there were only a handful of violent confrontations. Elsewhere, it seems, those who wished to resist the Crown's assault on intercessory institutions found more orderly ways of doing so. One more subtle mode of resistance was through the use of the royal courts, where the dissolution statutes could be parsed, definitional issues could be raised and diverse technicalities and exceptions could be invoked by those subjects with the resources to hire good counsel. This mode of resistance has gone almost completely unnoticed by historians, but, among subjects trying to remain outwardly loyal to a dangerously heterodox regime, legal action provided a respectable way of protecting local institutions without appealing to controversial doctrines. Most importantly, the 1547 statute mandated the dissolution of free chapels maintained for intercessory purposes, but it made exceptions for 'chapels of ease' in which sacraments and other ordinary parochial functions were regularly performed.[43] To lawyers, such loopholes were the stuff dreams are made of, and dozens of lawsuits suddenly appeared in which people argued, whether truthfully or not, that due to the distance or inaccessibility of parish churches they had always received the sacraments in their local chapel.

The chapel of Carleton, Yorkshire, for instance, was allegedly separated from the parish church by a river which 'oftentimes by abundance of water in rough weather as well by reason of great ruin as by sudden tempests . . . is so dangerous that no man can or dare pass over the same'.[44] Parishioners in Overland, Kent, claimed that their path to the parish church was 'in winter very foul . . . and in summer very dewy and wet'.[45] Inhabitants of Rossendale, Lancashire, claimed that without their chapel the inhabitants would have to go 'six or seven miles to churches over high hills and mountains in as perilous and dangerous ways as ever man rode or went', and that the forest of Rossendale was 'one of the coldest places within all your majesty's

---

[41] PRO STAC 3/2/14.   [42] PRO E 321/26/63.
[43] *Statutes*, vol. 4, 1 Edw. VI, c. 14, pp. 24–33. Chapels of ease were exempted from dissolution only so long as they did not possess significant properties.
[44] PRO E 321/19/61.   [45] PRO E 321/5/29. This location may be Overland or Oversland.

dominions'.[46] Perhaps the most unusual claim came from Northampton, where the mayor and burgesses argued that 'the inhabitants of such houses as were infected with the plague within the said parish' used a chapel of Saint Katherine as a chapel of ease so that they need not resort to the parish church and risk infecting their neighbours.[47]

Doubtless many of these claims were true, and others were reasonable interpretations of ambiguous situations; others sound rather far-fetched. What is important for our purposes, however, is that these claims were made by local communities as an alternative to riot or disorder, 'resisting' the dissolution of the chantries through legal rather than extra-legal means. And such methods sometimes worked: the Court of Augmentations on several occasions reversed the rulings of local chantry commissioners and allowed chapels to stand. At Cresswell, Staffordshire, for instance, the court ruled that commissioners had erred in declaring an institution to be a mere free chapel when in reality it served as a parish church. At Northampton, a house commonly called 'the chantry house' was given back to the incumbent on the grounds that the name 'chantry house' was merely a 'corruption of speech'. Sometimes these rulings can be tentatively traced to local politics. In Ulcombe, Kent, for instance, there was a long dispute over lands that had allegedly funded candles in the parish church. The Court of Augmentations ruled finally that 'the presentment made for the king's title in that behalf is imperfect and insufficient in the law', a ruling almost certainly explained by the fact that witnesses were examined by the notorious conservative and erstwhile plotter against Archbishop Cranmer, Sir Thomas Moyle.[48] What we can see in these cases, then, is a strictly legal method through which resistors could postpone local dissolutions for long enough to let the vagaries of the court system and local politics work; sometimes, whether through the honesty of their claims or the skill of their lawyers and lobbyists, they hit the jackpot.

In situations where, for whatever reason, no legal remedies presented themselves, individuals or communities could use another strategy which was outside the law but fell short of open violence: embezzling chantry goods before the government's agents could find them. In the Yorkshire town of Scotton, for instance, 'shortly after the making of the act or statute concerning the gift of chantries, fraternities, [and] guilds', a gentleman called Walter Pullyn 'minding to defraud his grace . . . embezzled out and from the chantry and chapel of Scotton aforesaid certain bells, vestments, goods, chattels, and other things belonging to the same, and that concealed and to his own use converted'. Pullyn got away with his theft for more than three years

---

[46] PRO DL 42/96, fols. 35v–36r.   [47] PRO E 321/27/4.
[48] PRO E 315/105, fols. 118r–v, 80v–81r and 140r.

until his vanity brought him down; he bragged to his neighbours about fooling the king's commissioners, saying that he would soon use the slate tiles of the chantry to repair his house, after which he was denounced to the authorities.[49] In Skipton, Yorkshire, three chalices and numerous vestments from the chantries of Our Lady, the Rood, and St Nicholas were embezzled by 'the churchwardens and parishioners', while in the nearby community of Newton all the ornaments of the dissolved chapel were spirited away by the local gentleman Thomas Banke.[50] At the fraternity of the tailors' guild in Bristol, the master, William Preston, admitted that 'he, by the advice of all the company of the said fraternity', sold the ornaments because otherwise they 'would have been destroyed'. This was not the only institution in Bristol where embezzlement occurred: a suspicious number of Bristol chantries claimed to have stored their valuables in wooden chests that flooded during heavy rains which coincidentally fell just before the 1547 Chantries Act, allegedly destroying the contents.[51]

Embezzlements often reflected well-organised and concerted efforts by local inhabitants to keep the government's hands out of their pockets. In Nesscliff, Shropshire, for instance, more than a dozen men and women were accused of dividing up a herd of livestock that supported the chantry: 'Anne Gistens, widow' took three cows, John Battie took one cow, David Vicham took one sheep, and so on.[52] In Berkshire, a gentleman called Edward Slegge claimed that he had lawfully purchased from the Crown £96 worth of cattle which had previously been given to 'superstitious' uses. When he went to collect his cattle, however, he found that the previous owners had colluded to avoid giving him his property:

Some hath answered that they would do as William Kele of Shippon, being a rich farmer there, would advise them to do. And some would do as Richard Bene of Didcot, Richard Arnold of Didcot, Thomas Mayne of North Moreton, the parson of Fifield, and the parson of Hagborne would advise them to do. And after much travelling and much riding unto them, their answers hath been, through the sinister labour and counsel of the parties above said, that some hath none such cattle, and some that they would pay no more then as they were certified to the surveyor.[53]

By far the most common form of resistance to the dissolutions, however, was the concealment of chantry lands. Failure to report the endowments of intercessory institutions often allowed lease-holders to reclaim proceeds that had previously gone for spiritual purposes without the Crown ever learning that those proceeds existed. In the Somerset village of Donyatt, for instance,

---

[49] PRO DL 1/27, fols. 70r–71r. Pullyn denied the charge of theft, claiming that he had paid for the items in dispute.
[50] PRO E 315/123, fols. 151r–154r.   [51] PRO E 314/40/118(ii).
[52] PRO E 321/24/8. Another copy of this whole case file is in E 321/24/16.
[53] PRO E 321/26/76.

one acre of pasture which had paid 4d per year to maintain lamps was concealed until 1572. In the village of Combe Florey in the same county, three acres of pasture that had paid 1s 4d per year to maintain obits in Mary Magdalene's chapel remained concealed until 1575.[54] In Stokesley, Yorkshire, land was concealed whose annual rent of 10s had gone to the chantry of Our Lady.[55] Sometimes concealments could step even farther afoul of the law. In Stratton, Cornwall, for instance, the churchwardens forged documents to conceal the fact that a parcel of land 'was given for the maintenance of masses'.[56] In Langar, Nottinghamshire, a man chosen by his village to report local intercessory endowments to the authorities was asked upon his return: 'What have you done concerning our chantry land?' He quickly responded, 'Hold your peace! You may not call it "chantry land".'[57]

The phenomenon of concealment has been studied in a deservedly famous essay by C. J. Kitching.[58] Kitching's emphasis on the late-Tudor land market and the Elizabethan efforts to unearth concealments, however, prevented him from fully exploring the main issue here: the magnitude of fraud in the immediate wake of the Edwardian Chantries Act. The records of the Court of Augmentations and the various commissions for concealments over the subsequent half-century reveal that scarcely a community in England could have been free from these extra-legal manoeuvres. Large-scale investigations invariably uncovered dozens or hundreds of separate concealments. Frances Boldero, for instance, informed the Edwardian Court of Augmentations of twenty-two separate properties concealed by dozens of people in Essex and Suffolk.[59] A 1553 survey of Staffordshire chantries and their property 'not afore surveyed' yielded an enormous manuscript with dozens of entries, many of them trivial to the government but obviously of immense significance to the people doing the concealing; a cottage in Weston, for instance, was 'in the holding of Walter Walker' despite the fact that its rent, a paltry 2s, had been used for 'St Katherine's masses'.[60] In Devon and Cornwall, there was a survey of collegiate, chantry, and obit lands taken late in Henry VIII's reign; when this survey was repeated late in Edward VI's reign witnesses presented lands amounting to £220 less in annual rents, representing what must have been several hundred separate concealments.[61] Literally thousands of concealments are documented, uncovered at various points from the reign of Edward VI to the reign of James I, and no doubt large numbers also

[54] *Calendar of Somerset Chantry Grants, 1548–1603*, ed. G. H. Woodward, Somerset Record Society, 77 (Taunton, 1982), pp. 105–9.
[55] PRO E 321/25/54.   [56] PRO E 321/26/50.
[57] C. J. Kitching, 'The Quest for Concealed Lands in the Reign of Elizabeth I', *TRHS*, 24 (1974), 63–78, at p. 65.
[58] Ibid.   [59] PRO E 321/26/90.   [60] PRO E 315/123, fols. 189r–192r.
[61] PRO SP 10/18, fol. 34r–v.

remained permanently hidden from the authorities. This resistance suggests that even if few people were prepared to risk violent confrontation with the regime, many were willing and able to defraud the government of vast sums of money that had been unjustly granted to it.

IV

All these strategies may be lumped together under the heading of 'resistance', but it is clear from the outset that different people were at times 'resisting' different things for different reasons with different results. Violent resistance, such as the murder of William Body in Cornwall, could undoubtedly be intended as one facet of a broader defence of traditional religion. Actions in the law courts could sometimes be intended to protect the contours of local religious observance, while thefts of chalices and vestments could sometimes preserve them for later Catholic revival. Other examples of resistance, however, held no such spiritual function, and in many cases the religious activities of chantries were eliminated just as efficiently as, or sometimes even more efficiently than, if there were no resistance at all.

There are a handful of extant cases where chantries were concealed, or chantry wealth embezzled, for the explicit purpose of preserving their religious function. In Lancaster, for instance, one almshouse chantry priest continued to pray for the founders until 1560.[62] In several cases, moreover, the pious motives of concealers can be inferred from the re-foundation of the concealed institutions in Mary's reign. In Arnold, Nottinghamshire, a man called Henry Gibson reported in 1574 that a piece of land there provided a lamp in church 'till lights went down in *primo Edwardi Sexti*, and after the lamps were put down [the land] did for a certain time pay for the same five shillings to the churchwardens, and in Queen Mary's time it found the said lamp again'.[63] In Liskeard, Cornwall, a 'lamp before the rood loft' was 'taken away in King Edward's days' but the rents maintaining it were hidden; in Queen Mary's reign 'the lamp was again revered... by order of the mayor'.[64] In Gainsborough, Lincolnshire, two guilds which had maintained lights and processions prior to Edward VI's reign were converted to more secular activities in 1548 but then renewed in their former state at Mary's accession.[65]

These examples, however, represent only a small minority of the extant cases of concealment or embezzlement; in the vast majority of cases intercessory activities permanently ceased and 'local resistance' merely funnelled

---

[62] PRO DL 44/29.   [63] PRO E 178/2927, fol. 8r.
[64] PRO E 134/9ELIZ/HIL4. More about this case is in E 134/9ELIZ/EAST4.
[65] PRO E 178/1315.

wealth into lay hands rather than the hands of the Crown. In Lincoln Cathedral, for instance, it had long been a tradition to display an image of the Virgin on the high altar on principal feast days and to illuminate the image with tapers. The practice ceased 'within one year after the death of King Henry VIII' and was never revived, but in Elizabeth's reign there was still an elaborate inquisition into the concealment of lands whose income had provided the tapers.[66] Similarly, in the town of Corsham, Wiltshire, rents from 'Our Lady lands' had been annually collected by 'Our Lady proctors' and then given to two priests who said masses for the dead in the parish church. Witnesses in 1577 confirmed that the priests had not said mass since 'about the beginning of King Edward VI his time' and that the altar itself was soon afterwards pulled down, but the revenue from 'Our Lady lands' never reached the Crown; not surprisingly, suspicion fell heavily on the 'proctors'.[67] At the chantry of Our Lady in Wick Rissington, Gloucestershire, the priest reported to royal commissioners late in Edward VI's reign that 'the clerk stole the paten and went away'; whatever the clerk's motives, religious functions at the chantry ended and the priest was forced to pay for the missing paten out of his own pocket.[68]

The ubiquity with which people 'resisted' chantry dissolutions for thoroughly secular motives can be seen most clearly from the difficulties Queen Mary had in recovering liturgical ornaments formerly belonging to chantries even though her regime was publicly committed to putting those ornaments back to traditional use. In May 1555, for instance, the queen issued a commission to investigate thefts in Lancashire after being 'credibly informed that there is diverse stocks of kine, chalices, jewels, plate, bells, ornaments, and such like which were given to the use and maintenance of the late chapel of Farnworth . . . remaining in diverse men's hands, which were never answered to us nor any our progenitors'. Remarkably, Mary experienced these difficulties even after the chapel was declared 'a chapel of ease for the administration of sacraments and sacramentals' and she ordered that the recovered goods be given 'to the churchwardens of the said chapel' for 'the maintenance of God's service'.[69] In the North Riding of Yorkshire, where Marian commissioners compiled a list of embezzled intercessory goods, parishioners gave a variety of creative but unhelpful responses to government demands. Sometimes there were flat denials, for instance in the parish of Eston, where in reply to queries about 6s 8d 'given to the finding of a light there' the wardens simply announced that 'there was no such stock'. Elsewhere in the neighbourhood, parishes issued refusals rather than denials. In Whitby, where a group of parishioners split the stock into shares and took 12d each, the queen's

[66] PRO E 178/1312.   [67] PRO E 134/19ELIZ/HIL9.
[68] PRO E 314/40/118(i).   [69] PRO DL 42/96, fol. 122r–v.

agents wrote: 'These be but poor fishermen, and nothing can be levied.' At Sneaton, likewise, 13s 4d was concealed but commissioners concluded that 'they be poor men and not able to pay it'.[70]

More Marian presentments survive from Kent. Thomas Bet of Elmstead, for instance, refused to yield eleven tapers that 'did burn in the rood loft beside the chantry of Our Lady'. William Sanders of Woodnesborough would not return a 'church cow, wherewith the paschal was always maintained'. Thomas Keys of Folkestone refused to yield 'a house of 12d a year out of a piece of land that should find a canopy light to burn before the sacrament'.[71] Another batch of presentments survives from the diocese of Ely, where in the town of Sutton a rash of concealments were discovered as late as the summer of 1557. Robert Frost 'withheld from the church 12d by year to keep an obit for his friends', for instance, while another man was ordered to 'keep the light before the crucifix in the rood loft' that he had formerly provided.[72]

Countless refusals to turn over chantry goods were also encountered by the queen's principal commissioners for church property, William Berners, Thomas Mildmay and John Wiseman. In a letter to James Starkey in February 1555, for instance, the commissioners wrote that £159 in cash and 113 ounces of plate due to the Crown, much of it from dissolved chantries, remained in private hands in Cheshire; accompanying this letter they sent a list of twenty-eight individuals who had failed to deliver their goods, and they procured twenty-eight privy seals to encourage compliance.[73] The same commissioners investigated Margaret, Countess of Lennox in 1557 for embezzling ten ounces of plate and 13s in goods from the chantry of Newsham in the parish of Wressle, Yorkshire. She at first sent a servant to deny the charges, but finding that the commissioners were 'not satisfied in my said servant's answer', she was forced to write another letter reaffirming that she 'never had the value of one farthing'. Whether she was telling the truth or not, *someone* had stolen the chantry's goods and refused to return them even under a Catholic regime.[74] In 1556, a privy seal was issued to Richard Jones of Thornbury, Gloucestershire, 'for the delivery . . . of one cross of silver belonging to the late chantry of Our Lady in Thornbury'. When the commissioners investigated Jones's claims of innocence, they were told by numerous witnesses that Jones never had the cross, but rather that it had been in the keeping of the churchwardens, 'which said cross among and with diverse other things . . . before the time of the late inventory made, was embezzled and stolen away out of the said church'.[75]

[70] PRO E 117/14/125.
[71] 'Extracts from Original Documents Illustrating the Progress of the Reformation in Kent', ed. C. E. Woodruff, *Archaeologia Cantiana*, 31 (1915), 92–120, at pp. 109–10.
[72] CUL EDR D2/4, fols. 6v–7r.   [73] PRO E 117/13/83.
[74] PRO E 117/14/119.   [75] PRO E 117/14/31.

It has been assumed that widespread embezzlement of chantry goods in Edward VI's reign represented attempts to save church fabric from the Crown's predations. These cases confirm, however, that at least in many places thefts were far from pious. If embezzlers had intended to save chantry property for 'better days', then surely those better days had arrived with Mary's accession and the revival of traditional Catholic observance. The fact that Mary's government was, in practice, little more successful than the governments of her brother and sister in reclaiming chantry property implies that, to say the least, many 'resistors' to the dissolution of the chantries did not have the health of departed souls in the front of their minds.

Sometimes the desire to avoid giving the Crown its due presupposed or even encouraged the end of religious functions in a chantry; in these cases ostensible 'resistance' shaded almost imperceptibly into collaboration. In 1548, for instance, a group of claimants led by Sir William Drury and Sir John Constable petitioned Protector Somerset regarding lands in Yorkshire that had for sixty years supported chantry priests to pray for the soul of one Henry Sotehill. Drury and Constable argued that their wives were Sotehill's heirs, and that, since the lands in question were held by Sotehill in fee tail rather than fee simple, he could not legally have alienated the lands outside his bloodline. The property thus legally belonged to them, the claimants argued, and they had been trying to reclaim it in the Court of Common Pleas at Westminster even at the time of Henry VIII's last illness. They therefore claimed that it was grossly unfair for the lands to be claimed by Edward VI under the Chantries Act, since if only their case had reached its conclusion before the late king's death the lands would not have been legally considered chantry lands at all. We do not know how the government responded to this claim, but Drury and Constable, far from trying to protect their ancestors' souls, were even more anxious to dissolve the Sotehill chantry than the government was.[76]

Sometimes what looks like resistance was merely corruption plain and simple. Land near Shrewsbury, for instance, had been used 'towards the finding of a priest to sing for the company or brotherhood of the shoemakers in the parish of St Chad's'. When that guild was dissolved, one Richard Mytton paid £12 to the shoemakers in return for the documents concerning the land and a promise to conceal the transaction, and he thereupon 'converted the profits thereof to his own use'.[77] For another example, when the college of Lothropp in Yorkshire was dissolved, one John Bradysbye dutifully delivered £80 due to the college 'unto the hands of John Bellow, esquire and Thomas Heynes'. But Bellow and Heynes apparently absconded with the money, and four years later Bradysbye's widow was surprised to receive

[76] PRO SP 10/5, fols. 57v–58r.   [77] PRO E 321/24/70.

a bill from the government; Bradysbye should have kept his receipts.[78] In yet another example, papers concerning concealed properties belonging to the Rood Guild in Ripon, Yorkshire, were hidden by Sir Richard Tyrrey, 'last priest of the said guild', because the guildsmen promised to 'recompense him'. Before we jump to the conclusion that this priest had conservative motives, it should be noted that we learn of these concealments in a 1577 deposition given by 'Jennet Tyrrey, widow', formerly 'wife unto Sir Richard Tyrrey'. No pious traditionalist he![79]

While 'resistance' to the dissolution of the chantries was ubiquitous, therefore, historians should be wary of assigning spiritual motives, or indeed any sort of ideological unity, to that resistance. While at times successfully undermining the regime's efforts to profit from the chantries, the sum total of resistance offered was less than helpful for the souls of so many English men and women still languishing in purgatory. Indeed, those who opposed the government's assault on intercessory institutions were often just as effective as the government in profiting from the demise of those institutions. The rioters who lynched William Body in Cornwall, then, were not the visible edge of an underground reservoir of 'ideological' resistance, but rather the small minority within the diffuse amalgam of 'resistors' who let their beliefs in purgatory and prayers for the dead outweigh their desire to profit from the Edwardian Reformation.

V

The existence of vigorous resistance to the dissolution of the chantries serves, on the one hand, to demonstrate dissatisfaction with the Edwardian regime. On the other hand, it also raises into stark relief the widespread collaboration that enabled Edward VI's government so successfully to annihilate the purgatorial system. The regime announced consistently that chantries were to be torn down because they contributed to superstition, and events like the lynching of William Body made it clear to all observers that at least some Catholic traditionalists considered chantries worth killing and dying for. Those who collaborated with the government's programme, then, could not have been ignorant of its spiritual significance, and they acted in conscious contradistinction to their more conservative neighbours.

The simplest form of cooperation (not yet collaboration) with the dissolutions, and the form requiring the least ideological engagement, was acquiescence. Many English subjects obeyed the commissioners who arrived in their localities, truthfully disclosed the wealth of their intercessory institutions,

[78] PRO E 321/25/86. It is unclear whether 'Lothropp' is *sic* for Longthorpe.
[79] PRO E 178/2609.

and accepted the dissolution of those institutions as lawful under the king's authority. Financial inducements undoubtedly lay behind the acquiescence of many priests, who were given lifetime pensions at rates comparable to their ordinary salaries, a level of financial security they could not have maintained either in illicit chantries or as conscientious objectors trying to make a living in a rapidly dwindling job market. In the East Riding of Yorkshire alone, for instance, ninety-seven chantry priests received government stipends, of whom three-quarters received annual sums exactly equal to their former livings.[80] In Devon, a comparable number of chantry priests received pensions, which were dutifully paid by every government until the last priest died in 1589.[81] Lay people, too, largely acquiesced in the changes required by Edward VI's government, for instance by reorganising their guilds and fraternities around licit social works and renouncing their former intercessory functions.[82] In one case, the town of Chipping Sodbury, Gloucestershire, even voluntarily gave half the landed income of their guild to the Crown, only to be told later by royal commissioners that they 'might have kept the whole lands'.[83] Eamon Duffy has correctly argued, in reference to the larger religious changes of Edward VI's reign, that such cooperation 'should not be read as approval'.[84] Yet, regardless of the motives that produced it, this sort of acquiescence had significant spiritual repercussions. Former chantry priests en masse entered the employment of the Crown, dependent upon the goodwill of the regime for their very lives, while lay people diverted their wealth from intercessory prayers into programmes like poor relief and primary education – programmes supported by the Edwardian government yet convergent with popular priorities.

Some priests, moreover, did more than merely accept government pensions in lieu of their former wages: they actively manoeuvred to be granted pensions by the government, sometimes in suspicious or fraudulent ways. When a chantry within Wells Cathedral was dissolved in 1548, for instance, an elaborate legal squabble resulted between two priests, Peter Jacket and Walter Shepherd, over which of them was the rightful incumbent of the chantry and should receive the pension pertaining to it.[85] In a similar case from Somerset, the gentleman Giles Kaylwaye claimed before the Court of

---

[80] C. J. Kitching, 'The Chantries of the East Riding of Yorkshire at the Dissolution', *Yorkshire Archaeological Journal*, 44 (1972), 178–94, at p. 183.

[81] Nicholas Orme, 'The Dissolution of the Chantries in Devon, 1546–8', *Report and Transactions of the Devonshire Association*, 3 (1979), 75–123, at p. 85.

[82] See Muriel McClendon, ' "Against God's Word": Government, Religion and the Crisis of Authority in Early Reformation Norwich', *SCJ*, 25 (1994), 353–69; Muriel McClendon, 'A Moveable Feast: St. George's Day Celebrations and Religious Change in Early Modern England', *JBS* 38 (1999), 1–27.

[83] PRO E 134/15ELIZ/TRIN3.   [84] Duffy, *Stripping of the Altars*, p. 462.

[85] PRO E 321/20/57.

Augmentations that one Richard Aylonde had pretended to be the incumbent of the chantry of East Horrington in Croscombe and had fraudulently obtained letters patent for an annual pension of £5.[86] In Lancashire, one deceptive priest allegedly went so far as to have an institution dissolved specifically so that he could receive a pension:

There was certain lands belonging to the churchwardens or inhabitants of Burnley parish which the parishioners intended to have been used to the maintenance of their school. And at such time as they were destitute of a school master, [they] did suffer Sir Steven Smith to have the rents of the same until such time as they could be provided of a school master. And in the mean time chantries were dissolved, and then the said Sir Steven, for his own gain, did certify the same as a chantry.[87]

In such cases, mere acquiescence to the Edwardian dissolutions gave way to active connivance.

A more explicitly collaborational strategy, though again a complex and multivalent one, was the purchase of ex-chantry lands from the Crown. As with the dissolution of the monasteries, most of the people who bought chantry property were not evangelicals and had no ideological motivation for purchasing particular lots. To be a person of substance in sixteenth-century England meant holding lands and collecting rents, and chantry land was priced to move. On the other hand, these transactions required a high level of cognitive dissonance in the minds of prospective purchasers. Chantry lands had been bequeathed by testators to ensure the passage of their souls through purgatory. For acquisitive landowners to participate in the interruption of that passage without guilt or dread for their own souls surely implied that those landowners had lost some of their belief in the power of intercessory prayer. Certainly they had grown deaf to the screams of pain and agonised pleas for aid with which, in Thomas More's *Supplycacyon of Soulys*, the dead constantly bombarded the living.[88]

The actual purchasers of chantry lands were as diverse as the English landed classes. In Somerset, for instance, ninety-two men appeared before the commissioners for chantry sales to receive a rating for chantry property. Of those, thirty-one resided within Somerset, while sixteen resided in the adjacent counties of Wiltshire, Devon and Dorset. Of the Somerset men, there were two knights, ten gentlemen, five merchants, three esquires, three yeomen, one clerk and seven men of unknown status. Thirty-nine other men who rated Somerset chantry property are known to have worked in London, showing the importance of proximity to the Court of Augmentations. In addition to the ratees of lands, fifty-two men were granted Somerset chantry lands by letters patent, of whom 90 per cent lived in London or the Home

---

[86] PRO E 321/27/54.   [87] PRO E 315/170, fol. 2r.
[88] Thomas More, *The Supplycacyon of Soulys* (London, 1529).

Counties.[89] In some cases it is clear that locals who invested in chantry land were simply buying back from the Crown the same lands they had previously held from religious institutions. Two laymen in Padiham, Lancashire, for instance, bought from royal commissioners 'eighteen acres of land which was then in their own occupation for the sum of twenty marks', land with an annual rent of 10s 8d which had previously gone to the Church. These men thus effectively became their own landlords.[90] Likewise, in the Northamptonshire town of Wellington guild lands confiscated by Edward VI were 'bought and purchased again by certain men of our town'.[91]

Yet, even if some purchases of chantry lands had only the most oblique spiritual connotations, in other cases purchases had wider implications and represented more active collaboration with the regime's spiritual project. C. J. Kitching noted that many Elizabethan gentlemen 'hunted' for concealed chantry lands in hope of being granted or sold those newly discovered lands by the Crown.[92] Kitching failed to note, however, that this practice was already common in Edward VI's reign practically from the moment the chantries were dissolved, and it represented a method of purchasing chantry lands that explicitly reinforced the legitimacy of the government's predations. William Wharton of Richmond, for instance, wrote to the Court of Augmentations:

that there is concealed in Richmond aforesaid from the king's majesty by Raff Goore, Charles Jonson, James Manne, John Ortone, Richard Bankes, Raff Lymewraie, and Richard Tompsone, inhabitants and burgesses of the said Richmond, these chantries (commonly called by that name) ensuing, viz. the chantry of the Blessed Virgin Mary, the chantry of St. John the Baptist, the chantry of St. Thomas the apostle, the chantry of St. Katherine, the chapel of the Trinity, and the chantry called St. James chantry, to the which did belong certain lands and tenements of the yearly value of £28.

Wharton asked that 'in recompense of his travail and costs' in making these discoveries he be granted 'preferment of the said chantries'.[93] In a similar case, a man called Robert Bures petitioned Protector Somerset that one William Mayre of Long Melford, Suffolk, had 'restrained and keepeth to his own use the lands of one priest's service... of the yearly value of ten marks'. Bures asked that his 'diligence' be rewarded with the 'preferment of the sale of the same lands, or a lease thereof for so many years as to your noble grace shall be thought mete'.[94] William Engledue informed the Court of Augmentations of concealed chantry lands in Stokesley and Kirkby in Yorkshire, and he asked for 'all the said lands and tenements by lease for term of

---

[89] Woodward (ed.), *Calendar of Somerset Chantry Grants*, pp. xiv–xix.
[90] PRO E 315/170, fol. 5r.   [91] PRO E 315/168, fol. 31r.
[92] Kitching, 'The Quest for Concealed Lands'.
[93] PRO E 321/5/35.   [94] PRO E 314/64, fol. 46r.

years, paying to the king's majesty the accustomed rent thereof'.[95] Anthony Rowlesey of Breadsall, Derbyshire, likewise informed the Court of Augmentations of concealed lands in Staffordshire and concealed cattle in Derbyshire; he asked to farm the lands 'by lease of the king's majesty in recompense towards his charges' and offered to pay 10s per cow for the livestock.[96]

Perhaps the most interesting examples of this sort of self-interested collaboration occurred in cases where communities split along pre-existing factional lines and the dissolution of the chantries became the occasion for local political conflict. In the town of Northampton, for instance, ornaments belonging to 'fraternities and guilds' were allegedly embezzled by local artisans. According to the investigating commissioners, these embezzlers claimed that they had been 'ready to deliver the things above mentioned' but were stopped from doing so by the mayor, a glover named John Brown, who 'countermanded' their efforts to obey the law. Here we can see the contours of local politics rising to the surface. We do not know if these Northampton men were telling the truth, and we do not know anything about their religious beliefs, but we do know that they used the dissolution of local guilds as an excuse to put their mayor on the government's enemies list.[97]

A more elaborate case of local dispute can be seen in Mestrange, Shropshire, where Vicar Thomas Botefeld 'menaced and threatened diverse of the inhabitants' to prevent them from disclosing concealed chantry property. In this case, the chantry priest himself testified on the king's behalf against his own chantry, apparently because he was kinsman to one of the local commissioners, Robert Clough. The vicar, seeing the chantry priest's collaboration, 'did call him knave and reviled him, and so rebuked diverse others that were there . . . and made such business with the poor men that the commissioners were fain to leave their business'. When the commissioners returned and called fourteen men as witnesses, Botefeld 'did all that he could to inveigle and persuade the said deponents not to depose', including allegedly procuring writs in London to have his enemies arrested if they testified. Yet the commissioners none the less found numerous informants in the community, nearly all of whom took the opportunity to denounce the vicar, accusing him not only of concealing chantry lands but also of stealing a chalice from the endangered chantry and bringing it to use in his own church. They made this accusation on the bluntly loyalist grounds that 'the parish would fain have their own chalice, and the king's grace to have the chalice that did serve the chapel'.[98] It thus appears that the dissolution of the chantries became entangled with pre-existing animosities, and many of the vicar's enemies seem

---

[95] PRO E 321/25/54.   [96] PRO E 314/64, fol. 10r.   [97] PRO E 321/28/80.
[98] PRO E 314/39/57. That Botefeld had a propensity to make local enemies is attested by a riot against him in 1529, when he was vicar of Ness, Shropshire: see Peter Marshall, *The Catholic Priesthood and the English Reformation* (Oxford, 1994), p. 84.

to have supported government policy as a strategy for undermining his local authority. The point, then, is not only that money and power could play a crucial role in people's reactions to the dissolution of the chantries, but also that in those reactions the fate of the chantries themselves often became peripheral.

VI

Nearly all the collaboration described so far involved people obeying, supporting or profiting from the 1547 Chantries Act in ways that could be glossed, whether disingenuously or not, as 'merely following orders' with varying degrees of enthusiasm. This would indeed be the common excuse for collaboration when the religious pendulum shifted again at Queen Mary's accession. Yet the most radical forms of collaboration with the Edwardian dissolutions were not excusable as mere obedience, since they were in fact illegal. Men and women, emboldened by the king's policies and happy to claim a share of the spoils of institutions in which they no longer believed, often made claims to chantry wealth which crossed the line into illegality and banditry. Wherever there was controversy over whether a particular chapel should legally be dissolved, there were factions eager to press the issue and claim the spoils. Often when a chapel was left standing by royal commissioners, there were radicals willing to interpret the law according to the spirit rather than the letter and tear the chapel down themselves. These were the shock troops of Edwardian collaboration: an uneasy alliance of evangelicals and thieves who elaborately over-interpreted the 1547 Chantries Act, taking it as licence to pillage ecclesiastical wealth.

At Catcott, Somerset, for instance, a man named William Coke argued before the king's commissioners that a chapel described by some of his neighbours as a 'chapel of ease' was really a chantry and should be dissolved. Coke succeeded temporarily and acquired the chapel for his own use, but soon afterwards his opponents appealed the case. A commission out of the Court of Augmentations quickly certified the chapel 'to be a chapel of ease and no chantry', and it thus reverted back to the community. Notwithstanding this ruling, however:

William Coke, accompanied with Richard Coke of Glaston in your said county of Somerset, husbandman, Robert Capron of Catcott aforesaid, husbandman, and diverse other riotous persons...to the number of eight persons...in most riotous manner broke and entered the said chapel of Catcott and from thence took and carried away two bells...and defaced the cage made and provided for the said bells, and on the next day following the said riotous persons in like forcible manner riotously assembled, came to the said chapel of Catcott, and with like force did pluck up the font there and broke the same, and also the seats made for the said inhabitants of

Catcott within the said chapel, and the pulpit within the said chapel, and broke down the glass windows of the said chapel, and the windows of the said chapel and the iron of the said windows [they] hath taken away and brought to the house of the said William Coke at Catcott.

Coke's initial defence against these charges was to argue that he had been granted the chapel legally by letters patent, ignoring the pleas of his opponents that the Court of Augmentations had changed its ruling. In a continuation of the suit in the very different political atmosphere of Mary's reign, however, Coke admitted that he had been wrong to raid the chapel and attempted to negotiate a settlement. Clearly, then, Coke and his colleagues had no legitimate claim to the chapel, but they none the less committed acts which, at least in the descriptions given by their accusers, looked like iconoclastic riots.[99]

At Cockthorpe, Oxfordshire, there was a chapel founded in Edward III's reign that was, according to some locals, almost two miles from the nearest parish church and provided sacraments for the community. This should have exempted it from dissolution, but according to the chapel's defenders two men, William Boxe from London and Leonard Yate from Witney, Oxfordshire, 'falsely surmised and presented to the surveyor of the shire that the said church . . . ought lawfully to come and be vested to the king's highness by virtue of the last act concerning the dissolution of chantries'. According to this same version of the story, the king's commissioners refused to believe Boxe and Yate and let the chapel stand. However, not to be foiled, the two men raided the chapel anyway:

One William Boxe of London, Grocer, Leonard Yate of Witney in the county of Oxford, clothier, and Thomas Taylor of Witney aforesaid, with other accompanied to the number of 23 or thereabouts, forcibly arrayed, some having forest bills, some swords, some staves and daggers, came to the said chapel the Friday next following the end of the last term and broke open the church door with an axe, uncovered the lead of the said chapel, and that day and the Saturday the next morrow following defaced and spoiled the same chapel and left the same in such plight as it now is.

The rioters' actions were allegedly so violent that they seemed 'rather like to move a tumult and cause rebellion than otherwise', and the thefts from the church, including chalices, ornaments, vestments, books and crosses, left the villagers 'in fear lest all their churches should in like manner be spoiled'. The attitude of the rioters also caused grave concern among local

---

[99] This case is in PRO STAC 2/8, fols. 190r–192r and STAC 4/6/2, along with a variety of other supporting documents. The case has been analysed in Geoffrey Woodward, 'The Destruction of the Catcott Chapel at the Reformation', *Somerset Archaeology and Natural History*, 125 (1981), 67–71.

conservatives. A villager named John Bullock, for instance, claimed that he saw the armed men coming to spoil the church and begged them 'to suffer the said chapel to stand until such time as they had commission or other sufficient warrant'. One of the armed men answered him that 'it was but folly, for down it must, and more in this country as that'. Similarly, John Smyth claimed that one of William Boxe's servants told him 'not to be grieved with pulling down of that little chapel, for he trusted to see 20 pulled down more than that in this country'. If these words were really spoken, their arrogance lends credence to the idea that the spoilers were comfortable with the havoc that they were wreaking and considered the destruction of the chapel a fringe benefit rather than an unfortunate byproduct of their thefts. In Cockthorpe, then, there was rampant collaboration with the spirit, if not the letter, of the Edwardian dissolutions.[100]

Equally extraordinary spoliation occurred at Farnley, Yorkshire, where royal commissioners had let a chapel stand because it lay 'between two rivers' and was the only church accessible when flood waters rose. Unfortunately, in the three years after this reprieve the chapel's priest was gravely ill, so no divine services were performed there. This raised the suspicions of local chantry commissioners, John Lambert and William Clapham, who went to Farnley to investigate. According to defenders of the chapel, these two commissioners and their servants 'without any lawful authority did deface the said chapel, and pull down all the lead lying upon the said chapel, and also the rood loft, pews, stalls, glass windows, bells, irons, priest chambers, and all the same hath taken and converted to their own uses at their pleasures'. Lambert and Clapham, however, told a very different story. According to their version, the chapel was not nearly so far from the parish church as some parishioners alleged, besides which 'a costly and goodly bridge of stone of 5 or 6 arches' had been built so that the church was now accessible regardless of the depth of the river. More interestingly, Lambert and Clapham claimed that they had come to the chapel not to spoil it but because they had received word that it had *already* been spoiled. When they arrived on the scene, they found that lead, iron, vestments and the chalice had been stolen and the windows of the chapel had all been broken. In addition, they found 'the quire defaced, the rood loft riven and taken down, the doors set open for all men to enter and spoil and steal at their pleasure, and the chapel made a sheepfold and a vile and profane place'. We cannot know in this case who was telling the truth, but one piece of evidence suggests that reality lay somewhere in between and that a partnership developed between official corruption and local spoliation: Lambert was forced sheepishly to admit that 'Richard Kendill, servant to Mr Clapham, gave to one John Cawdray

---

[100] This case is in PRO E 315/125, fols. 147r–154r and STAC 4/4/53.

of Newall a little piece of lead worth 2d or 3d to solder and stop a little hole in his brewing lead'.[101]

A less fully documented incident occurred in the last year of Edward VI's reign at Burnley, Lancashire, where 'by colour of commission . . . concerning the sale of copes, vestments, chalices, and other ornaments, and jewels belonging to free chapels and chantries', four men including the gentleman Sir Richard Towneley broke into a chapel on 6 May 1553. They allegedly 'without any just cause, title, or ground defaced and spoiled the said parish church [*sic*] of Burnley and [took] away the said bells, chalices, copes, vestments, and other premises with other the jewels and ornaments', supposedly amounting to the lordly sum of £120.[102] In the same year, a comparable incident occurred in the town of Billinge, Lancashire. There was allegedly a 'certain chapel commonly called Billinge chapel', four miles away from any church, where local inhabitants had always supported a priest to say divine service and administer the sacraments. It is unclear how this chapel was judged by the 1548 commissioners, but it was still standing on 6 August 1553 (during the chaos generated by the Jane Grey *coup*) when the gentleman James Winstanley and twenty of his associates broke in. The description of their activities is extraordinary:

Being assembled with force and arms, [they] in very riotous manner did enter into the said chapel and one bell (price £3), one chalice with a paten (price 10s), two vestments, two surplices, a cross and a cruet, and also one chest or coffer of the goods and chattels of your said orators then and there found, so being for the administration of God's service, with all and singular ornaments belonging to the same, [they conveyed away] . . . Also not being therewith contented but minding utterly to destroy the said chapel forever, of very malice and hate that he had and bore towards the service of God which he perceived the queen's majesty was minded to advance and set forwards, [they] did likewise, pulling down the glass which did stand in the windows of the said chapel, and casting out the forms, chairs, and other things ordained for the ease of your said orators within the same, converting the same to his own use. [They did] stop up the said windows and walls with bows and brooms, and hath thereof made a barn, wherein he hath set his corn and hay and hath ever since with like force and arms . . . so kept the said chapel so that there could not be any divine service said or sung or any sacraments ministered.[103]

Whether accurately or not, the inhabitants of Billinge who brought this suit described the incident as an act of evangelical iconoclasm performed specifically in response to Queen Mary's accession. This interpretation of events of course may have been slanted for the new monarch's ears, but regardless of the details it is remarkable that in both the Burnley and Billinge cases we see violent acts of local collaboration with Edward VI's Reformation

---

[101] This case is in PRO E 315/520, fols. 24r–26r; E 315/521, fols. 6r–7r; E 314/37, fol. 12r; E 315/123, fol. 239r.
[102] PRO DL 1/35, fol. 6r.   [103] PRO DL 1/37, fol. 11r.

even within the conservative stronghold of Lancashire. This suggests that collaboration and conflict may have been much more prominent, even in the realm's 'dark corners', than we have previously been led to believe.[104]

VII

Given the importance of prayers for the dead in traditional religion, the obvious question is: why did so many English subjects contribute to or collaborate with the dissolution of intercessory institutions? One obvious answer is greed. The conservative Elizabethan chronicler Michael Sherbrook summarised the acquisitiveness of the Edwardian commons with brutal honesty: 'Many other persons there were then of the like consciences and conditions to the commissioners, which persons took many things away without commissions, seeing all things were put to the spoil.'[105] Yet, as with the monasteries, greed alone cannot account for people's actions. English people still cared for the health of their souls, and widespread attacks on houses of prayer could not have proceeded so successfully without some changes in popular attitudes. We must admit, then, that notwithstanding how few English people had actually converted to Protestantism by 1548, some evangelical ideas had expanded into mainstream culture. These ideas may not have been in the front of most people's minds, but they were now thinkable in ways they had not been a decade before, and those who flirted with them enjoyed the greatly enhanced authority that went with government support and patronage.

We can see this changing dynamic through the negotiations that sometimes occurred between chantry commissioners and the defenders of local chapels. In the parish of Dent, Yorkshire, for instance, inhabitants claimed that their chapel should be allowed to stand as a chapel of ease because parishioners had to walk six miles to church and pass through 'dangerous mountains' along the way. In this case, however, backroom manoeuvring led to the chapel being preserved 'with condition that they shall buy a great Bible in English, and the *Paraphrases* of Erasmus also in English, and that their priest shall read and use the same in like manner as is used in parish churches to the king's subjects'. An almost identical deal was struck in the nearby village of Bentham, where commissioners allowed a chapel to stand so long as the community purchased 'a Bible of the great volume and the *Homilies* all in English, and to see they be read and used to the king's subjects'.[106] These

---

[104] See Christopher Haigh, *Reformation and Resistance in Tudor Lancashire* (London, 1975). The Burnley and Billinge cases each receive one sentence from Haigh (p. 32 and p. 149).
[105] A. G. Dickens (ed.), *Tudor Treatises*, Yorkshire Archaeological Society Record Series, 125 (Wakefield, 1959), p. 139.
[106] PRO E 315/115, fol. 4r–v.

were Faustian bargains in which parishes won the right to keep their chapels in return for active acceptance of some of the most important aspects of Edwardian Protestantism. From one perspective, of course, the parishioners who made these deals were 'merely following orders', complying with the government's programme just like priests and parishioners up and down the country. But we must also realise that they did have choices – elsewhere, after all, people chose very different defensive strategies – and that, by thinking the unthinkable and admitting the inadmissible, they performed their obedience in ways which gave them power over their more intransigent and actively resisting neighbours.

A story of more bluntly evangelical collaboration comes from Buxton, Derbyshire. According to complainants at Queen Mary's Court of Chancery, the chapel of St Anne at Buxton, site of the famous 'St Anne's well', had been allowed to stand after long litigation in the Court of Augmentations, but the evangelical layman who had wrongfully occupied the chapel, Roger Cottrell, locked the door rather than allowing it to be used by parishioners. This familiar scenario was radicalised by Cottrell's extraordinary strategy for undermining the chapel's sacredness, encouraging young people to make it the focus of adolescent rebellion: '[He] doth suffer such youthful persons as do resort to Buxton aforesaid to wash and bathe them in the well called St Anne's well not only to tipple and drink within the said chapel over the Sundays and holidays, but most irreverently also to pipe, dance, hop, and sing within the same, to the great disturbance of the said complainants.' The youth of the parish, moreover, seem to have taken Cottrell's desacralisation of the chapel to heart and did 'make affray upon the... honest, sage, and discrete persons of Buxton aforesaid because they required them to desist from their foolish youthful fashions aforesaid and hear God's service, or else to avoid and suffer the complainants and others to hear it'. Here, then, the experimentalism of evangelical religion was exploited to the fullest, giving licence to youthful iconoclasm and in the process implicating a whole generation in the Protestantising project.[107]

I certainly do not want to argue from this evidence that the dissolutions – much less Protestantism itself – were 'popular' in the sense of proceeding 'from the bottom up'. What I would suggest, however, is that the Edwardian regime could not have succeeded in so outrageously sacrilegious a project unless that project offered sites of convergence between government and popular interests that encouraged significant collaboration from below. Sometimes this collaboration included radical and ideologically motivated

---

[107] PRO C 1/1322, fol. 57r. On the subject of adolescent rebellion in the Reformation, see Susan Brigden, 'Youth and the Reformation', *P&P*, 95 (1982), 37–67.

actions against local institutions, sometimes it consisted of simple profit-taking, and sometimes it involved the pursuit of local politics through the new opportunities for patronage (or denunciation) that the dissolution of the chantries provided. We cannot know, and we should not try to guess, how many collaborators fell into each category, but the crucial point for a study of English Reformation politics is that all these people found themselves *on the same side*. All over England, then, the familiar hum of intercessory prayers, so crucial to traditional Catholicism, was efficiently and methodically silenced by the very same men and women who, only a short time before, had poured their resources into prayers for departed souls.

Historians will continue to debate the role of Protestantism in this process. The goal of this chapter has not been to settle this question, but rather to suggest that religious reform was itself a multivalent phenomenon that could involve complex transactions between government and people, a series of decisions to accept or profit from new programmes as much as a series of ostensibly spiritual conversions. In this way, then, religious, political, and economic considerations were woven together in re-enforcing and over-determined responses to a fundamentally unsustainable gap between the theoretical imperatives of religious traditionalism and the practical realities of religious change. The rejection of old ideas and institutions – what Stephen Greenblatt has called 'a huge enterprise of recycling and reorienting' – could emerge along the axes of political loyalty and economic self-interest as efficiently as along the more closely studied axis of confessional loyalty.[108] Similarly, the acceptance of new ideas and institutions did not require conversion to a new religious system but could emerge organically from the logic of one's own behaviour. If purgatory was deemed no longer important enough to warrant financial investment, it was but a small step to declaring purgatory itself a myth, and for people who started along this road there were plenty of self-consciously evangelical neighbours, preachers and politicians in Edwardian England who might help them to rationalise, systematise and contextualise their own beliefs in explicitly 'newfangled' fashion.

The result is that by 1553, for a variety of not-explicitly-Protestant reasons, large numbers of English people had added the dissolution of the chantries to a résumé that already included the dissolution of the monasteries, the elimination of relics and pilgrimages, the use of English Bibles, the adoption of an English liturgy, and the rejection of papal authority. These were the very projects that were being actively promoted by evangelicals within the government and given explicitly Protestant public glosses, while among Catholics even such noteworthy casuists as Stephen Gardiner denounced the

---

[108] Greenblatt, *Hamlet in Purgatory*, p. 40.

government that sponsored these programmes as heretical. Surely, then, we cannot dismiss as merely secular the actions of people who, in vast numbers, collaborated with this allegedly heretical government. Surely, in some important sense, if not in the most technical, theological sense, in the act of separating from their actively resisting neighbours, these collaborators stepped over the line and partook of heresy themselves.

8

The English people and the Edwardian Reformation

Elite observers in Edward VI's reign were well aware that regardless of whether most English people unequivocally accepted *sola fide* and *sola scriptura*, the 'new learning' was acquiring significant political weight in the countryside. With evangelicals increasingly monopolising the 'points of contact' through which Tudor subjects traditionally communicated with their government, Catholics leaders fretted, not without reason, that avarice and ambition would lead their coreligionists to 'take truce with the world'.[1] Perhaps more surprisingly, many influential Protestants were equally uneasy with their own growing ascendancy, worrying that political expediency would take the edge off of evangelical religion. If dedication to true religion resulted not in worldly suffering but in worldly advancement, after all, how could the sheep be reliably separated from the goats? Hence the great bugbear of Edwardian Protestantism was not the ability of crypto-Catholics to 'counterfeit the mass', but rather the incentive for ambitious pseudo-evangelicals to counterfeit an outward affectation of Protestantism.

The charge of lukewarm or expedient religion could be brought against all social classes, giving it a gratifying appearance of evenhandedness in an era of social strife.[2] The evangelical John Hales, for instance, castigated greedy landlords who 'in their talk be all gospellers, and would seem to be favourers of God's Word'.[3] Thomas Lever used similar rhetoric against corrupt ministers, excoriating 'carnal gospellers, which by their evil example of living, and worse doctrine, do far more harm than they do good by their fair reading and saying of service'.[4] But at heart the threat of the 'carnal gospeller' was a *popular* threat, rooted in the dangerous promiscuity of the

---

[1] John Redman, *A Compendious Treatise Called the Complaint of Grace* (London, 1556), sig. G3r. While not published until Mary's reign, this tract was written shortly before the author's death in 1551.
[2] Diarmaid MacCulloch, *The Boy King: Edward VI and the Protestant Reformation* (New York, 2001), p. 152.
[3] BL Lansdowne MS 238, fol. 320v
[4] Thomas Lever, *Sermons*, ed. Edward Arber (London, 1871), pp. 65–6.

reformers' message and their growing realisation that the people to whom they preached could respond actively and creatively to what they were told.[5] Hence John Hooper, rarely one to dilute his message of salvation through the gratuitous gift of grace, warned preachers not to 'flatter those hypocrites, epicures, and lascivious gospellers with the promise of faith, until such time as they amend'.[6] On Christmas 1552, likewise, Hugh Latimer mocked the idea that the populace had truly been converted, suggesting that just as the virgin birth 'begot a wondering and a gazing: everybody marvelled at it, and was desirous to talk of it, because it was a new matter', so now 'in this our time, a great number of people pretend the Gospel, and bear the name of gospellers, because it is a new thing'.[7] Perhaps most forcefully, Peter Martyr preached a stinging sermon against the rebellious commons in 1549, attacking Englishmen for 'pretending a zeal . . . in their lips, and not in their hearts, counterfeiting godliness in name but not in deed'. These counterfeiters, despite 'always having in their mouth "the Gospel, the Gospel", reasoning of it, bragging of it', none the less showed by 'their conversation' that they 'live after the world, the flesh, the devil'.[8]

This chapter will suggest that this phenomenon of direct, popular engagement with Protestantism, in many ways the logical conclusion to our story of popular politics in the English Reformation, does not deserve the implications of Nicodemism, hypocrisy and time-serving that elite Catholics and evangelicals alike imputed to it. From the perspective of theologians, of course, no other explanation was possible for the serial apostasies of people who 'change their doctrine at men's pleasure, as they see advantage and profit'.[9] Yet, from an historian's perspective, we need not be so incredulous that conscientious Christians could hold contradictory views simultaneously, nor that they could absorb the language, priorities and interpretive framework of evangelical religion without becoming Protestants *tout court*. The Henrician Reformation, after all, had been a fantastically precise dissector of

---

[5] This has been described most recently by Alec Ryrie, who stresses how disdain for carnal gospellers was linked to condemnations of 'lewd liberty': see Alec Ryrie, 'Counting Sheep, Counting Shepherds: The Problem of Allegiance in the English Reformation', in Peter Marshall and Alec Ryrie (eds.), *The Beginnings of English Protestantism, 1490–1558* (forthcoming). I would like to thank Dr. Ryrie for sharing this piece with me prior to publication.

[6] John Hooper, *A Declaration of the Ten Holy Commaundementes of Allmygthye God* (Zurich, 1549), p. 228.

[7] Hugh Latimer, *The Works of Hugh Latimer, Sometime Bishop of Worcester, Martyr, 1555*, ed. G. E. Corrie, 2 vols. (Cambridge, 1844–1845), II, p. 92.

[8] CCCC MS 102, pp. 463–9. Interestingly, Martyr was himself accused of just this sort of expedient dissimulation by the Catholic Richard Smith, who claimed that Martyr had defended the Real Presence when he first arrived in Oxford but then 'tipped and sang another song' when he 'came to court, and saw that that doctrine misliked them that might do him hurt in his living': Richard Smith, *A Confutation of a Certen Booke, Called a Defence of the True and Catholike Doctrine of the Sacrament* (Paris, 1550), sigs. A8v–B1r.

[9] Smith, *A Confutation of a Certen Booke*, sigs. A8v–B1r.

previously inseparable doctrines: purgatory was separated from intercessory prayer, vernacular Bibles were separated from Lollard sacramentarianism, and the unity of the Catholic Church was separated from unity with Rome. To the extent that, as Eamon Duffy has shown, 'medieval religion in England functioned as a comprehensive whole',[10] that holistic unity was shattered from the moment the Ten Articles denied 'that any saint doth serve for one thing more than another, or is patron of the same'.[11] It was thus perfectly natural for the English laity, trained in amateur casuistry in the crucible of the break with Rome, to break off pieces of the evangelical programme and put them to uses considerably different than those envisioned by preachers and politicians.

I want to suggest, then, that English people who embraced portions of the Edwardian Reformation did so for the same reason that people usually embrace new movements: because it seemed to offer something valuable to their lives. The fact that this 'something' was not always or even usually spiritual rebirth, and the fact that people sometimes embraced the Reformation reluctantly rather than enthusiastically, should not blind us to the importance of their choices. Active, popular engagement with the Edwardian Reformation was neither a mistake nor a last resort, but rather formed part of larger negotiations between government and people that offered some subjects an increased ability to influence the world in which they lived. In the peculiar circumstances of Edward VI's reign, the government appealed for popular support and was willing to make extraordinary bargains with those who would accept their terms. By relentlessly declaring that support for the Reformation was support for economic fairness and a genuinely responsive society of orders, the government in effect asked for, and in some sense got, a 'popular Reformation' – not a Reformation initiated from below or adopted by the majority of the population, but one with which many ordinary subjects could sympathise because it appealed to genuinely popular aspirations.

This notion of a Reformation negotiated between government and people suggests that the English Reformation was something more than an aggressive act of state and that historians have erred considerably in assuming an adversarial relationship between the people who enforced the Reformation and those upon whom it was enforced. This sort of polarisation may have developed in the later sixteenth century, as some historians have suggested, with a newly gentrified middle class enforcing a Protestantising 'reformation

---

[10] This eloquent summary of one of Duffy's central formulations is taken from Christopher Bradshaw, 'David or Josiah? Old Testament Kings as Exemplars in Edwardian Religious Polemic', in Bruce Gordon (ed.), *Protestant History and Identity in Sixteenth-Century Europe*, 2 vols. (Aldershot, 1996), II, p. 82.

[11] *Documents of the English Reformation*, ed. Gerald Bray (Minneapolis, 1994), p. 172.

of manners' upon the commonalty.[12] But, in Edward VI's reign, the people upon whom the government relied in propagating religious change – priests, churchwardens, constables, small landholders and so forth – were still very much members of the communities in which they lived. Thus, in the process of asserting royal power in the countryside, the Reformation offered new opportunities for members of the commonalty to co-opt and manipulate that power, just as we have been told they manipulated the law courts and other incipient state institutions, turning them into sites of cultural negotiation.[13] Popular political actors could *use* the Reformation in their local politics, often rendering disputes between neighbours virtually indistinguishable from disputes over religious change. These manipulations of the Reformation were not disingenuous (any more than people who sued their neighbours in royal courts were disingenuous just because at other times they resented the presence of those courts in their communities), but neither were they precisely Protestant. In practice, it was these manipulations from below, rather than 'enforcement' from above, that both guaranteed the success of the government's religious programme and firmly entrenched the Reformation in English society.

I

Before we can analyse popular engagement with the Reformation in Edward VI's reign, we need to examine the public face of that Reformation. For, as historians like Diarmaid MacCulloch have shown, the idea that the 'new learning' might offer significant advantages to the lower orders was not one

---

[12] This argument has been made most notably in Keith Wrightson and David Levine, *Poverty and Piety in an English Village: Terling, 1525–1700* (New York, 1979), and most recently in Steve Hindle, *The State and Social Change in Early Modern England, c. 1550–1640* (New York, 2000). Other historians, however, have noted many points of cultural contact between puritanism and 'the people'; see most notably Alexandra Walsham, *Providence in Early Modern England* (Oxford, 1999) and Peter Lake, 'Deeds against Nature: Cheap Print, Protestantism, and Murder in Early Seventeenth-Century England', in Kevin Sharpe and Peter Lake (eds.), *Culture and Politics in Early Stuart England* (Stanford, 1993). Patrick Collinson, who has argued both sides of this question as his ideas have evolved, recognised that English Protestantism in some senses 'regressed' after the mid sixteenth century, 'becoming less not more popular in character' as it moved from its initial association with 'novelty, youth, insubordination and iconoclasm (when indeed it was still a *protest*) to the period of its middle age, when it was more obviously associated with the maintenance of the *status quo*': Patrick Collinson, 'From Iconoclasm to Iconophobia: The Cultural Impact of the Second English Reformation', in Peter Marshall (ed.), *The Impact of the English Reformation 1500–1640* (London, 1997), p. 279. It is the grounds of this earlier 'popularity' that I am attempting to explore.
[13] On the royal courts as sites of cultural negotiation and appropriation, see Cynthia Herrup, *The Common Peace: Participation and the Criminal Law in Seventeenth-Century England* (Cambridge, 1987); Michael Braddick, *State Formation in Early Modern England c. 1550–1700* (Cambridge, 2000), ch. 4; Hindle, *The State and Social Change, passim*.

that they thought of by themselves, but rather was fed to them in a steady diet of evangelical propaganda.[14]

From the beginning of the Reformation, evangelicals had suggested that the liberation of the Gospel and the overthrow of papal tyranny would lead directly to economic prosperity and social harmony. This was, in most cases, not a political strategy so much as a hopeful *naïveté* typical of first-generation Protestants not yet jaded by harsh political realities. In England, this proposed relationship between godly Reformation and economic renewal had first been established by the 'commonwealth' writers patronised by Thomas Cromwell in the 1530s.[15] The radical reformer Clement Armstrong, for instance, expected that Henry VIII's break with Rome would lead to a national system of food redistribution to provide for the poor. He argued that the absence of a true Church in England had 'broken the link of charity' that should unite Englishmen, so that every man sought his living 'wheresoever he by any crafty means can get it from his neighbours'. Only once the king had 'led all men, elected and unelected, faithful and unfaithful, good and ill, all together to be saved from falling into outward works of sin' would England achieve economic success and be free of 'idle people without office or labour'.[16] More famously, Richard Morison's tracts against the Pilgrimage of Grace identified the avarice of monks as the root of England's economic woes. Morison argued that 'religion took a great fall' when riches had first corrupted monks' hearts, and given their bad example 'it is no marvel if a tapster or wine drawer reckon a penny or so more than his duty, when they see religious men so embrace money'.[17]

That this conception of evangelical economics survived the fall of Thomas Cromwell can be seen in a remarkable manuscript from the last years of Henry VIII's reign.[18] The author suggested that the English economy had collapsed because of clerical wealth, which distracted priests from their responsibility to provide a moral compass for the nation. He therefore offered

---

[14] MacCulloch, *The Boy King*, ch. 3; Ethan Shagan, 'Protector Somerset and the 1549 Rebellions: New Sources and New Perspectives', *EHR*, 114 (1999), 34–63.

[15] See G. R. Elton, *Reform and Renewal: Thomas Cromwell and the Common Weal* (Cambridge, 1973); Whitney Jones, *The Tudor Commonwealth, 1529–1559* (London, 1970); Paul Fideler and Thomas Mayer (eds.), *Political Thought and the Tudor Commonwealth: Deep Structure, Discourse, and Disguise* (London, 1992).

[16] PRO E 36/197, pp. 168–9, 193, 266–9. See Ethan Shagan, 'Clement Armstrong and the Godly Commonwealth: Radical Religion in Early Tudor England', in Peter Marshall and Alec Ryrie (eds.), *The Beginnings of English Protestantism, 1490–1558* (forthcoming).

[17] Richard Morison, *Humanist Scholarship and Public Order: Two Tracts against the Pilgrimage of Grace by Sir Richard Morison*, ed. D. S. Berkowitz (Washington, 1984), pp. 135–6.

[18] BL Royal MS 17 B. XXXV. This tract can be tentatively dated from an accusation that priests had 'driven the liberty to read the gospel into so few men's hands that now throughout all England (London only excepted) it is read of none': fol. 8r. This puts the tract between 1543 and 1547.

the radical proposal that all temporalities held by spiritual persons should be handed over to the king in exchange for 'benefices, or else ready made money out of the king's coffers'; in other words, the Church would be removed from the land-holding business altogether. This proposal was augmented by agrarian reform proposals, including the suggestion that all common lands 'now or at any time within twenty years last past enclosed . . . shall be either cast open or equally divided'. The link between the author's religious and economic proposals was made explicit in a diagram explaining how clerical corruption led to economic decay. It suggested that 'ignorance and non-residency of the clergy' led directly to a desire for 'private lucre'. This then had two effects, the 'enhancement of rents' and a 'plurality of farms'. These, in turn, led to the 'enclosure of tillage wastes and commons' and a 'universal dearth of all things necessary to life'.[19]

But it was in the reign of Edward VI that these connections between economic and religious reforms came to dominate public discourse through a resurgence of 'commonwealth' ideology. The 'commonwealth' in Tudor thought has usefully been described as a series of ideas, derived from classical republicanism and mediated through Christian humanism, implying 'the mutual interdependence of all subject within an organic social order' in which 'rulers and property owners were portrayed merely as temporary stewards, rather than absolute owners, of their estates'.[20] These ideas, and their concomitant defence of the poor from economic exploitation, immediately became central to the government's public persona when Protector Somerset came to power in early 1547, largely because Somerset pursued a strategy of 'popularity' politics to compensate for his structurally weak position as Lord Protector.[21] Early in Somerset's 'reign', anti-inflation bills regulating the production of leather, malt and steel were voted into law. Another bill concerning fraud in the manufacture of cloth collapsed in parliament, but Somerset, in a clear, public statement of the government's priorities, adopted the measure by proclamation. Price-rigging by victuallers and handicraft men was curtailed, as was the export of valuable commodities like bell metal. Compulsory purveyance was abolished, and the profits of town fee-farms were made available for poor relief and public works. A tax on sheep and woollen cloth was instituted, partially as a fiscal measure but partially to discourage the sort of large-scale pasturing that led to the enclosure of arable lands.[22] And perhaps most importantly, in 1548 and then

---

[19] BL Royal MS 17 B. XXXV, fols. 12r, 19v, 20r, 15v–16r.

[20] Hindle, *The State and Social Change*, p. 55.

[21] I have explored this political dynamic in Shagan, 'Protector Somerset and the 1549 Rebellions'; and Ethan Shagan, '"Popularity" and the 1549 Rebellions Revisited', *EHR*, 115 (2000), 121–33.

[22] Michael Bush, *The Government Policy of Protector Somerset* (London, 1975), pp. 48–53.

again in 1549, the government instituted 'enclosure commissions' to enforce the laws against enclosure and ensure that the commons were not preyed upon by avaricious landlords.

The Lord Protector also took action to curtail abuses of his own tenants and tenants of the Crown. In May 1548 the government disparked the Crown's chase at Hampton Court, explicitly citing as its rationale the complaints of 'many poor men of the area' that 'many households of the same parish be let fall down, the families decayed, and the king's liege people much diminished'.[23] Similarly, when Somerset started building a new country house in Wiltshire in November 1548, the plans included emparking nearly a square mile of waste; when it was learned that doing so would deprive tenants of their pasturing rights, the plan was revised to a much more modest level.[24] Somerset also passed a private bill in 1548 to provide greater security of tenure to some of his tenants, and in June 1549 he appointed a commission to dispark and disforest lands that had come to the Crown through the attainders of the Duke of Norfolk and Thomas Seymour, requiring the Crown's representatives to reapportion the lands locally and provide timber from those lands for local house-building and repairs.[25] All of this personal action was typical of Somerset's peculiar marriage of ideology with publicity; as he told the enclosure commissioners in July 1549, '[if you] for example's sake begin with the reformation of yourselves . . . you shall both have the better credit and may with the more boldness proceed to the redress of others.'[26]

The government's advocacy for the 'commonwealth', moreover, did not exist in a vacuum but rather was actively and unrelentingly linked to the causes of anti-popery and religious reform. This connection was far easier to make than historians have generally noticed, because the Edwardian spiritual campaign was itself heavily dependent upon the idea of a 'commonwealth'. The term 'commonwealth' in mid-Tudor parlance had three mutually reinforcing meanings, referring not only to the *respublica* and the 'common good' but also – much more mundanely – to the pot in which communities put their money to pool resources or aid the poor.[27] Thus, when the spiritual injunctions of 1547 required every parish to provide a 'strong chest . . . to the intent the parishioners should put into it their oblation and

---

[23] Ibid., pp. 43–4.

[24] W. K. Jordan, *Edward VI: The Young King. The Protectorship of the Duke of Somerset* (London, 1968), p. 499.

[25] Bush, *The Government Policy of Protector Somerset*, p. 55; Jordan, *Edward VI: The Young King*, p. 428.

[26] PRO SP 10/8, fol. 32r

[27] In 1541, for instance, the residents of Burford, Oxfordshire refused to pay their taxes as officially assessed and instead 'made a commonwealth', also referred to as a 'common purse' and 'common box', from which they would pay according to their own interpretation of equity: PRO STAC 2/7, fols. 51–71.

alms for their poor neighbours' rather than wasting that money on 'pardons, pilgrimages, trentals, [and] decking of images', the regime was precisely alleging an intrinsic connection between godly Reformation, economic reform and the strengthening of local communities.[28] The level to which this connection was internalised by committed evangelicals can be seen in Protector Somerset's 1549 draft instructions to the Lord President of the Council of the North, in which the need to 'inculcate' true religion and ensure conformity 'touching religion and the most godly service' led immediately to the need to ensure that 'the poor people be not oppressed' and that the Council 'grant the petition of the poorest man against the richest or greatest lord . . . as they should grant the same being lawfully asked against men of the meanest sort'.[29] There is evidence, furthermore, that the enormous practical potential of this rhetorical interconnection was well understood by the commons. Soon after the Duke of Norfolk's attainder in 1547, for instance, a group of twenty-six of his former serfs, now villeins of the Crown, petitioned for manumission. In attempting to win release from their servile (and somewhat anachronistic) condition, they not only appealed directly to Protector Somerset but also argued that freedom was due to them by 'the charity of Christ'.[30]

At the forefront of the public campaign to associate economic fairness with evangelical reform was Hugh Latimer, Bishop of Worcester. In Lent 1549, Latimer preached to the court on the subject of avarice, warning the young king not to tax his subjects unfairly and admonishing him to govern with a 'seasonable faith'. Latimer then launched into a remarkable assault on wealthy landlords whose avarice was destroying the kingdom, condemning them as 'unnatural lords' and 'hinderers of the king's honour' who had caused a 'monstrous and portentous dearth'. This tirade, so precisely in tune with the rhetoric of the riotous crowds in 1548–9, was structured explicitly around the thesis that God had elected Edward VI to deliver England 'from errors, and ignorance, and devilish antichrist the Pope of Rome'.[31]

Another renowned reformer, John Hooper, likewise lambasted landlords and even partially exonerated poaching, all in the context of evangelical proselytising. In his *Declaration of the Ten Holy Commaundementes of Allmygthye God* (1549), Hooper described the avarice of gentlemen as a species of theft. In particular, he attacked 'such as hath great forests or parks of deer, or conies that pasture and feed upon their neighbours' ground', and he rhetorically asked 'whether the keeping of such beasts be not against

---

[28] Bray (ed.), *Documents of the English Reformation*, p. 255.
[29] PRO SP 15/3, fols. 99r–101r.
[30] Diarmaid MacCulloch, 'Kett's Rebellion in Context', *P&P*, 84 (1979), 36–59, at pp. 55–6. The petition is undated but certainly is from 1547 to 1549.
[31] Corrie (ed.), *The Works of Hugh Latimer*, I, pp. 98–100, 100–2, 95, 84.

God's laws'. Most remarkably, he noted that the Justinian civil law only regarded animals as private property when they 'bide at home, or have a purpose to return home', and he thus suggested that the civil law was more righteous than the common law in determining 'whether those beasts be not as well the poor man's if he can take them in his pasture'. This tirade for tenants' rights formed the first half of Hooper's discussion on the eighth commandment, which focused on 'theft of such goods as appertain unto the body'. The second half of his discussion, however, attacked thieves of the soul, whom Hooper defined as ministers who 'preach man's laws and works not commanded in the Scripture'. Of these spiritual thefts, Hooper wrote, the most egregious was the misguided notion that 'the substantial body of Christ's humanity is present' in the sacrament.[32] Denial of the Real Presence and support for economic fairness, Hooper was arguing, were two sides of the same godly coin.

Perhaps the most important promoter of the link between godliness and the commonwealth was John Hales, designer of the enclosure commissions, chief commissioner in 1548, and commissioner for the Midlands in 1549. Hales was an extremely public figure, giving numerous speeches in which he promoted the government's economic reforms and glossed those reforms in explicitly evangelical fashion. He announced, for instance, that the goal of the government was:

> To remove the self-love that is in many men, to take away the inordinate desire of riches wherewith many be encumbered, to expel and quench the insatiable thirst of ungodly greediness wherewith they be diseased, and to plant brotherly love among us, to increase love and godly charity among us, to make us know and remember that we all, poor and rich, noble and ignoble, gentlemen and husbandmen, and all other of whatsoever state they be, be but members of one body mystical of our savior Christ.

Elsewhere he made explicit just what he meant by 'godly charity', telling the commons that the work of the enclosure commissioners would convince them to accept the new religion: 'When other people that hate God and His Word should perceive that we that have professed God's Word in the lips bring forth the fruit thereof, that is charity and mercy to our poor neighbours, they should no longer call us heretics, but should be forced to love and embrace God and His Word with us.'[33]

The same sorts of connections can be found in tracts not produced by the government but written as part of the same general programme. Robert Crowley's *Informacion and Peticion agaynst the Oppressours of the Pore Commons of this Realme* (1548), for instance, was blunt in its evangelism,

---

[32] Hooper, *A Declaration of the Ten Holy Commaundementes of Allmygthye God*, pp. 172 and 185–6.

[33] BL Lansdowne MS 238, fols. 312v and 323v.

looking forward to the day when preachers would prove to the commonalty 'that both they and their fathers were deceived and knew not how to worship God aright . . . And when they thought they had been most high in His favour, by doing Him such honour as they thought most acceptable in His sight, then committed they most detestable blasphemy and were abominable before Him'. But the main thrust of the tract was to tie these religious ideas to the economy and lament the covetousness that rendered the nation sinful in God's eyes. Crowley wrote that God had made 'possessioners but stewards of His riches' and declared that God would 'hold a straight account' with wealthy men at the day of judgment. Therefore he implored the rich to 'repent the violence done to the poor and needy members of the [realm], and become as hands ministering unto every member his necessaries'.[34] The same juxtaposition occurred in the anonymous *Pyers Plowmans exhortation unto the lordes, knightes and burgoysses of the parlyamenthouse*, published sometime between the dissolution of the chantries and the 1549 rebellions. The author rejoiced that 'we of this realm have expelled all vain traditions of men and received the true religion of Christ'. But again the main argument of the tract was economic, calling for trade barriers to protect English labourers and arguing that 'it is not agreeable with the Gospel that a few persons shall live in so great abundance of wealth and suffer so many [of] their Christian brothers to live in extreme poverty'.[35]

A much odder location for the rhetoric of godly commonwealth was the 1548 edition of Thomas Elyot's Latin–English dictionary, revised by the future Elizabethan bishop Thomas Cooper. Elyot had been an opponent of 'commonwealth' ideology in the 1530s, translating *respublica* as 'public weal' rather than 'common weal' in his *Book of the Governour* to avoid the implication 'that everything should be to all men in common'.[36] But Elyot had died in 1546, and Cooper's address to the king in the preface to the new edition explicitly linked the Reformation to the very movement his predecessor had despised:

We . . . by your most godly proceedings evidently perceive, how your grace willeth that your dear uncle and other most honourable counsellors and ministers should endeavour and apply themselves, first, to set up true religion to God's honour and glory, to abolish idolatry and superstition, and then consequently to proceed forth to the advancement of the commonweal, that is, truly to minister justice, to restrain extortion and oppression, to set up tillage and good husbandry whereby the people may increase and be maintained. Your godly heart would not have wild beasts

---

[34] Robert Crowley, *The Select Works of Robert Crowley*, ed. J. M. Cowper, EETS, extra series, 15 (London, 1882), pp. 154, 157–8 and 159–60.

[35] *Pyers Plowmans exhortation unto the lordes, knightes and burgoysses of the parlyamenthouse* (n.p., n.d.). This tract is unpaginated. W. K. Jordan dates the tract to early 1549: Jordan, *Edward VI: The Young King*, p. 420.

[36] Thomas Elyot, *The Governour*, ed. Foster Watson (London, 1907), pp. 1–2.

increase and men decay, ground so enclosed up that your people should lack food and sustenance, one man by shutting in of fields and pastures to be made and a hundred thereby to be destroyed.[37]

Similar examples could be repeated almost indefinitely. The point is not, of course, to resurrect the notion of a 'commonwealth party' so eloquently demolished by Geoffrey Elton, but to acknowledge the extent to which two ubiquitous discourses in mid Tudor politics – the language of the commonwealth and the language of evangelical Protestantism – became practically inseparable in the political environment of Edward VI's reign.[38] Certainly there was no *intrinsic* connection between these two discourses. But, even if the three-way relationship between Protestantism, the government and the 'commonwealth' was a constructed and contingent one, that relationship dominated the public persona of the Edwardian regime and helped to shape how the commons would respond to a newly energised, but still unambiguously state-sponsored, Reformation.[39]

II

The 'godly commonwealth' thus provided – like anticlericalism or the dissolution of the monasteries – a point of entry where Protestant ideas could be insinuated into popular culture, a rhetorical common ground to which both government and people might appeal in different ways in hopes of winning support from one another. The rest of this chapter, then, will explore a series of sites at which these negotiations occurred and, by connecting these sites together, construct a new narrative of the Edwardian Reformation.

The most obvious sites of popular engagement with the government's religious policies were the agrarian rebellions of 1549. When riots began in earnest in 1548 and early 1549, the commons imagined their opponents as the very same landlords and gentlemen whose avarice was condemned by the regime as the cause of economic decay. The rioters thus employed and co-opted much of the same commonwealth language that the government itself had been using, protesting against sheep-farming, inflation and the enclosure of land. They also demonstrated their political acumen by performing their

---

[37] Thomas Cooper, *Bibliotheca Eliotae* (London, 1548), sig. A1v. See David Weil Baker, *Divulging Utopia: Radical Humanism in Sixteenth-Century England* (Amherst, Mass., 1999), pp. 111–12.

[38] G. R. Elton, 'Reformation and the "Commonwealth-Men" of Edward VI's Reign', in Peter Clark, Alan G. R. Smith and Nicholas Tyacke (eds.), *The English Commonwealth 1547–1640: Essays in Politics and Society* (Leicester, 1979).

[39] Although the government's assertion of this three-way relationship waned after Protector Somerset's fall in 1549, it is important to note that it was asserted by groups among the commons for a considerable time afterwards, even (paradoxically) in the reign of Queen Mary: Shagan, 'Protector Somerset and the 1549 Rebellions', p. 51.

protests in ways which appealed directly to the government for aid. In May 1548, for instance, commons in Cheshunt, Hertfordshire, attacked rabbit warrens which had been built on their common lands. The rioters began their protest on a Monday, but they prorogued it for two days when they discovered that royal commissioners were not due to arrive in town (and hence would not be able hear their appeals) until the following Wednesday. At least one Cheshunt labourer ascribed this policy to 'trust [that] the king or his Council will not give away our common'.[40] Almost a year later at Frome, Somerset, two hundred men gathered to tear down fences and hedges. When confronted the next day by local justices, the men argued that they had acted lawfully, since they were only obeying a royal proclamation ordering the destruction of enclosures.[41] By 15 May 1549, Protector Somerset himself was aware that rioters were using his policies as a cloak for rebellion and had 'attempted to stir in great companies upon pretence of liberty by proclamations against enclosures'.[42]

There are hints that even in some of these early riots the commons understood that support for evangelical religion could play an important role in their dialogue with the government. In Cheshunt, for instance, even though the commons were not yet convinced of the Lord Protector's goodwill, they appealed particularly to two Justices of the Peace, Anthony Denny and John Gates. One witness confirmed, for instance, that 'he hath heard diverse of [the rioters] say and report [that] they found Mr Denny their especial good master and trusted that he and Mr Gates would do for them all that they could'.[43] The commons knew, of course, that Denny was a Privy Counsellor and had real influence with government. But it also could not have escaped their attention that Denny and Gates were the principal promoters of the Reformation in Hertfordshire and that appealing to those particular gentlemen was no more spiritually neutral than appealing to Cranmer or Latimer. Another example comes from Landbeach, Cambridgeshire, where in May 1549 the commons illegally impounded the livestock of a local gentleman. They appealed to their landlord, which happened to be Corpus Christi College, Cambridge, for support in the dispute, and in response they received suspiciously strong backing from the college's master Matthew Parker, who

---

[40] The bulk of Cheshunt material is in PRO STAC 10/16, fols. 133–200, PRO STAC 3/1/49 and PRO KB 9/980, fols. 21–2. This quote is on fol. 10r of a bundle labelled 'Cavendisshe v. Inhabitants of Cheshunte, North Mims, & Northam', in a folder labelled 'STAC 3: piece numbers not known', in the box with STAC 3/1/76–112. I owe many thanks to Amanda Jones for discussing the Cheshunt riots with me and providing me with copies of some of her notes.

[41] HMC Bath, vol. 4, pp. 109–10.

[42] R. C. Anderson (ed.), *Letters of the Fifteenth and Sixteenth Centuries, from the Archives of Southampton* (Southampton, 1921), p. 66.

[43] PRO STAC 10/16, fol. 171v.

also happened to be vice-chancellor of the university, a future archbishop and a close associate of Somerset and Cranmer.[44]

This was the political context, then, into which Somerset's government thrust the *Book of Common Prayer*, the Church of England's first full-scale, English language liturgy, delivered to the parishes in May 1549 and ordered to be put into exclusive use by 9 June. The Prayer Book must be seen, despite its conciliatory language, as bringing radical spiritual alterations: the heart of Christian worship had been stripped of its ancient mysteries and brought, warts and all, into the plain view of the commons. In the West Country, of course, and in parts of Oxfordshire, Buckinghamshire and Hampshire, the new English liturgy provoked riot and rebellion. In much of the Midlands and southeast, however, where rioters had been busily appealing to the Somerset government for aid against avaricious local landlords, the public response was very different. Since they regarded the government as a potential ally and were well aware of the government's argument that evangelical religion and economic reform went hand in hand, the rebellious commons not only used the new Prayer Book but ostentatiously demonstrated their commitment to the new religion.[45]

So, for instance, one letter to the government written on behalf of Essex rioters was so loaded with godly rhetoric that Protector Somerset could write in reply, 'We be glad to perceive by the allegation of sundry texts of scripture that ye do acknowledge the Gospel [for] which ye say ye greatly hunger.' In a reply to rebels in Suffolk, Somerset wrote that he was glad to see them 'professing Christ's doctrine in words' but was disappointed that by their deeds they showed 'the contrary fruit'. In a letter to the Norfolk commons, Somerset was sufficiently confident of their commitment to reform that he tried to dissuade them from rebellion on the grounds that they had been misled by 'naughty papist priests that seek to bring in the old abuses and bloody laws whereof this realm is by God's sufferance well delivered'.[46] Even in the act of surrendering and accepting the king's pardon, rebels in Suffolk, Essex and Kent not only confessed their faults but also 'for religion declared themselves'.[47] At Mousehold, one Thomas Coniers, minister of St Martin's on the Palace Plain in Norwich, was appointed by the rebels to perform the

---

[44] J. R. Ravensdale, 'Landbeach in 1549: Ket's Rebellion in Miniature', in Lionel Munby (ed.), *East Anglian Studies* (Cambridge, 1968).

[45] It is worth noting that the Prayer Book justified itself on 'commonwealth' grounds, stating in the preface that 'curates shall need none other books for their public service but this book and the Bible, by the mean whereof the people shall not be at so great charge for books as in time past they have been': *The First and Second Prayer Books of Edward VI*, ed. E. C. Ratcliff (London, 1910), p. 4.

[46] Shagan, 'Protector Somerset and the 1549 Rebellions', pp. 62, 58–9, 56.

[47] *Troubles Connected with the Prayer Book of 1549*, ed. Nicholas Pocock, Camden Society, new series, 37 (London, 1884), p. 24.

morning and evening prayer services from the new *Book of Common Prayer* every day, and on at least one occasion choristers from Norwich Cathedral sang the *Te Deum* in English for the rebels.[48] Archbishop Cranmer, at the height of the risings, noted with alarm that 'there be many among these unlawful assemblies that pretend knowledge of the Gospel and will needs be called gospellers'.[49]

The rebels also invited evangelical preachers into their camps. At Canterbury, for instance, Archbishop Cranmer's protégé Richard Turner preached twice to the assembled commons; we may plausibly see this overture by the rebels to the evangelical establishment as related to Protector Somerset's remarkable payrolling of the rebel leader John Latimer, known as 'the Commonwealth of Kent', as a government agent to negotiate with the Kentish commons.[50] At Mousehold outside Norwich, the rebels heard sermons from Cambridge vice-chancellor and future archbishop Matthew Parker, as well as from the popular evangelical preacher of Norwich Cathedral, John Barret; Parker infuriated the rebels by mixing rebukes for their disobedience with his theology and was run out of town on a rail. Furthermore, among the citizens of Norwich chosen by the rebels as figureheads and nominal captains of the revolt was not only the mayor but also Robert Watson, an evangelical protégé of Cranmer's, who had in June 1549 been granted a prebend in Norwich Cathedral despite not being a priest and even being 'twice married'.[51]

These appeals to the Reformation were certainly politically savvy, but they were also more than merely expedient; in their demands to the government, the rebels adopted evangelical principles in ways which demonstrated how aspects of the new religion could be made to reinforce their own desires and beliefs. Much like the German rebels of 1525, the English rebels of 1549 selectively filtered Protestant theology and adapted those elements of the evangelical programme that seemed empowering or emancipatory. For instance, in the rebels' Articles of grievance drawn up at Mousehold, Article 4 demanded that 'priests from henceforth shall purchase no lands' and that the 'lands that they have in their possession be letten to temporal men, as they were in the first year of the reign of King Henry VII'.[52] This amounted to a serious assault on the temporal status of the clergy, reflecting that part of

---

[48] Julian Cornwall, *The Revolt of the Peasantry 1549* (London, 1977), pp. 149–51.

[49] Nicholas Tyacke, 'Introduction: Re-Thinking the "English Reformation"', in Nicholas Tyacke (ed.), *England's Long Reformation 1500–1800* (London, 1998), pp. 14–15.

[50] Diarmaid MacCulloch, *Thomas Cranmer: A Life* (New Haven, Conn. 1996), pp. 432–3; J. D. Alsop, 'Latimer, the "Commonwealth of Kent" and the 1549 Rebellions', *HJ*, 28 (1985), 379–83.

[51] MacCulloch, *Thomas Cranmer*, p. 433.

[52] The Mousehold Articles cited here and in the following paragraphs are printed in Anthony Fletcher and Diarmaid MacCulloch, *Tudor Rebellions*, 4th edn (London, 1997), pp. 144–6.

the Protestant programme that dovetailed with lay concerns about clerical property. Article 8 likewise demanded 'that priests or vicars that be not able to preach and set forth the Word of God to his parishioners may be thereby put from his benefice, and the parishioners there to choose another or else the patron or lord of the town'. Besides echoing the Memmingen Articles of 1525, this was a remarkable blending of traditional anticlericalism with evangelical ideology: the laity claimed the right to charge and discharge their own priests, as they had for decades (see chapter 4 above), but now their stated rationale for removing priests was that they could not adequately perform the central duty of the Protestant ministry, the preaching of the Word.

Article 15 of the Mousehold demands sought to insure that parishioners were properly 'instructed with the laws of God' by requiring that priests not become pluralists by taking up private employment with 'any man of honour or worship'. This was not necessarily a Protestantising demand, but it drew an explicit connection between clerical abuses and the corruption of the social elite that dovetailed perfectly with Hugh Latimer's claim that avaricious landlords would 'make the yeomanry slavery, and the clergy shavery'.[53] Article 20 required priests with benefices of £10 or more to 'teach poor men's children of their parish the book called the catechism or the primer'. Again this was not necessarily a Protestantising demand, but it echoed a 'commonwealth' understanding of the link between clerical inadequacy and a perceived decline in education that was a favourite rallying cry of evangelicals.[54] More intriguingly, it also precisely mirrored for a humbler social stratum the government's own requirement, first included in the injunctions of 1536 and then repeated in the injunctions of 1547, that priests with benefices of £100 or more provide livings for Oxford or Cambridge scholars.[55] And Article 16, by far the most famous of the Mousehold Articles, demanded 'that all bond men may be made free, for God made all free with His precious bloodshedding'. As Diarmaid MacCulloch has shown, this article had somewhat mundane roots in the economic peculiarities of East Anglia.[56] Yet, by appealing to the Great Manumission of Calvary, the rebels once again echoed the strategies of the German peasants of 1525, mapping the aspirations of agrarian society onto the spiritual imperatives of evangelical religion.[57]

These appeals to religious reform were evidently popular enough that they did not inhibit widespread support for the rebels, even from parish

[53] Corrie (ed.), *The Works of Hugh Latimer*, I, p. 100.
[54] This is an especially prominent theme in BL Royal MS 17 B. XXXV, cited above.
[55] Bray (ed.), *Documents of the English Reformation*, pp. 178 and 252.
[56] Diarmaid MacCulloch, *Suffolk and the Tudors: Politics and Religion in an English County 1500–1600* (Oxford, 1986), pp. 75 and 308.
[57] For a discussion of the connections between the Mousehold articles of 1549 and the Memmingen articles of 1525, see Tyacke, 'Introduction: Re-Thinking the "English Reformation"', p. 14.

churches. Churchwardens from Carlton Colville, Suffolk, for instance, collected unpaid parish funds to support the insurgents, dutifully providing a receipt to one parishioner who paid after the churchwardens threatened to 'carry her up to the oak at Mousehold'.[58] Church officers in North Elmham, Norfolk made payments to the rebels out of parish coffers and recorded them in ordinary fashion in the parish disbursement book.[59] Churchwardens in Lavendon, Buckinghamshire, approved the use of a church house 'for the laying and keeping of harness and other weapons of war for the execution of the said rebellion'.[60] Clearly the ideals of the Mousehold Articles, so profoundly influenced by the Reformation, were not only 'popular' but also associated in people's minds with parish duty. Here, then, we seem to have just the opposite scenario to what Eamon Duffy found in Devon, where the parish of Morebath used church funds to support the Catholic 'Prayer Book Rebellion' and dutifully recorded those transactions in the churchwarden's account book.[61] Yet, as Duffy rightly reminds us, 'the notion that rural Norfolk and Suffolk by 1549 were populated by tens of thousands of peasant Protestants contradicts almost everything else we know about the religion of the region in the 1540s'.[62] How, then, can we account for the evangelical rhetoric of the eastern and midland commons?

For Duffy, of course, this paradox can only be resolved by concluding that the 1549 rebels were not *really* Protestants at all. Yet, if we shift our frame of reference, looking not for a process of national conversion but for a process of political engagement with the Reformation, the significance of the rebels' behaviour suddenly snaps into focus. In fact, their behaviour was wholly consistent with *other* ways that the commons of 1549 attempted to negotiate favourable terms by appealing to the perceived priorities of the Edwardian regime. In demanding that the government lower the price of wool, for instance, the commons were responding to numerous attempts by Protector Somerset to do just that; this allowed the government to grant the request while plausibly arguing that they were not capitulating to rebel demands but merely putting teeth into their own policies.[63] Similarly, when the Thetford rebels demanded the right to choose their own enclosure commissioners, they were ostensibly working *within* the structures of law enforcement established by the government, claiming only that those structures had been hijacked by avaricious gentlemen; again this allowed the government

---

[58] PRO C 1/1264, fol. 62.

[59] F. W. Russell, *Kett's Rebellion in Norfolk* (London, 1859), pp. 181–4.

[60] PRO C 1/1225, fols. 21–2.

[61] Eamon Duffy, *The Voices of Morebath: Reformation and Rebellion in an English Village* (New Haven, Conn., 2001), pp. 127–51.

[62] Ibid., p. 130.

[63] Shagan, 'Protector Somerset and the 1549 Rebellions', p. 44; Shagan, '"Popularity" and the 1549 Rebellions Revisited', p. 127.

to accept a remarkably radical demand while maintaining that they were only buttressing pre-existing policies.[64] Given this wider political strategy, it makes sense to imagine the evangelical rhetoric of the rebels as part of an effort to tailor their negotiations around the perceived priorities of the regime, an effort which, at least in the short run, was spectacularly successful in winning government concessions. This is not to say, of course, that the 1549 rebels were disingenuous in their support for the Reformation, any more than they were disingenuous in their support for lower wool prices. The point instead is that support for the new religion could fit within a variety of paradigms other than evangelical conversion. The fact that the 'gospel of liberty' had been integrated into the commons' mentalities in 1549 did not mean that they necessarily supported the concomitant doctrines of *sola fide*, *sola scriptura* and *sola gratia*. What it did mean, however, was that these more formal doctrines had a crucial point of entry into English society that was resonant with rather than antithetical to 'popular' interests.

III

The rebels of 1549 were in the end defeated by the very government in whom they placed their trust. This defeat, however, does not mean that attempts to assert political agency through collaboration with evangelical policies was intrinsically misguided, but only that in certain times and places those attempts were pushed too far. To get a more balanced sense of popular political strategies – and to see how those strategies could continue even after the fall of Protector Somerset – we need to look at more quotidian examples of popular engagement with the Reformation. One such site can be found, paradoxically, in the very process which historians have seen as the epitome of conflict between government and people: the Edwardian government's multifaceted attack on parish churches, from the confiscation of church plate to the burning of Latin service books to the destruction of stone altars.[65] To assert any element of 'popularity' in this process is tantamount to historiographical heresy, so I want to be very careful to explain what I mean. Scholars have sometimes stressed the Edwardian regime's success in securing conformity with its assault on parish churches, while at other times they have stressed the resistance the regime encountered, but they have almost unanimously imagined parish communities as essentially *unified* bodies, either passively accepting or actively resisting an *external* threat. In reality, however, even

[64] Shagan, 'Protector Somerset and the 1549 Rebellions', pp. 43–4.
[65] The impact of the Edwardian Reformation on parish churches has been described most thoroughly in Duffy, *The Voices of Morebath*. See also Beat Kümin, *The Shaping of a Community: The Rise and Reformation of the English Parish, c. 1400–1560* (Aldershot, 1996); Duffy, *Stripping of the Altars*.

theologically conservative communities were far from united, because, in any assault on parish *property*, religious conservatism was necessarily adulterated by issues of wealth, social relations and the complex relationships between individuals, the parish and the state. In this environment, many people found that they could use aspects of the Reformation to their advantage, constructing responses to government policies that enriched themselves or enhanced their social position at the expense of their local enemies.

A useful introduction to this process is the unprecedented wave of thefts from parish churches that began early in Edward's reign; theft, after all, was the epitome of a self-promoting response to the Reformation which, while often reflecting theological considerations, was certainly not bound by them. A survey of church goods from Warwickshire, for instance, shows that, out of 184 parish churches examined, 43 suffered significant thefts of valuables between 1548 and 1552. A survey from Huntingdonshire likewise revealed significant thefts in 18 churches of the 49 examined.[66] While some of these thefts may have been pious attempts to protect church property, and some were continuations of a longstanding medieval undercurrent of thefts from churches, there can be no doubt that, as Duffy has written, this huge wave of thefts resulted directly from 'the polemic of the reformers against the very notion of sacred objects'.[67] Thieves thus acted as de facto collaborators with the regime's spiritual programme – a fifth column within English communities, energised by the government's own ethos of desacralisation – despite the patently unauthorised and illegal nature of their activities. Even Duffy's hyper-conservative parish of Morebath was not immune to this enemy within: it cannot have been a spiritually insignificant coincidence that a thief picked St George's Day, the patronal feast day of the parish, to break through a church window and steal the parish's best surplice.[68]

To demonstrate that many Edwardian thefts reflected an ethos of desacralisation, it is useful to look at cases where the theft of devotional objects rendered traditional observance impossible in a particular church. So, for instance, at Arley, Warwickshire, thieves removed two brass censers, a cross, two handbells and a pyx; only the bells were expendable, since the church possessed no other censers, crosses or pyxes with which to perform divine service. At Hatton, Warwickshire, the churchwardens likewise reported that 'since the last survey their church was robbed and all that was worth the carriage away was stolen'.[69] While we can imagine circumstances in which traditionalist Catholics could steal chalices and pyxes without too much damage to conscience, those circumstances do not extend to cases where

---

[66] PRO E 315/513; *The Edwardian Inventories for Huntingdonshire*, ed. S. C. Lomas Alcuin Club Collections, 7 (London, 1906).
[67] Duffy, *Stripping of the Altars*, p. 487.   [68] Duffy, *The Voices of Morebath*, p. 127.
[69] PRO E 315/513.

the church possessed no other ornaments with which to perform mass the following Sunday. The point of these examples is not that the thieves were in any meaningful sense Protestants, but rather that the government's spiritual campaign was substantially aided by men and women in the countryside who, despite their violations of the law, chose to internalise evangelical ideas and benefit from the new dispensation at the expense of their neighbours.

In some cases, the local conflict engendered by these thefts can be perceived directly. In Tollesbury, Essex, for instance, a thief stole 'a cross of silver and partial gilt weighing 45 ounces, and two broken chalices, and a pyx, and a chrismatory'. It cannot be coincidental that this thief stole exactly those objects of Catholic devotion at the centre of evangelical critiques, and in this case further evidence shows the deep animosities that defined the local meanings of his crime. The churchwardens apparently knew who had stolen their goods, and they thus paid 30s 4d 'for pursuing the felon that did steal the church plate and for the suit of the law to recover our plate again'. By the time the devotional objects were recovered, however, they had been 'mangled and broken', leading us to conclude that destroying the objects was a motivation at least equal to profit in the thief's mind.[70] For another example, when 'goods, jewels, and ornaments' were stolen from a church in Holbeach, Lincolnshire, churchwardens sought the advice of a cunning man, who accused one John Partriche of the crime. We cannot know whether Partriche was really guilty or what local tensions led to him being accused, but it is clear that Partriche belonged to a very different spiritual world than his accusers, since he denounced the cunning man's work as an 'illusion of [the] devil' and had his accusers indicted for unlawful assembly. Partriche may or may not have been an evangelical, but clearly thefts from the parish church unleashed significant local dispute over the legitimacy of traditional religion.[71]

These sorts of thefts were fairly straightforward: people broke into churches and stole the stuff. Much more interesting, however, were cases of what we might call 'embezzlement': the unauthorised removal of church wealth for the purpose of preventing government confiscation. This ubiquitous practice has been widely seen, like the concealment of chantry property, as a form of resistance to the Reformation, and no doubt in some cases it was. Yet, in practice, embezzlement was rarely the work of unified parish communities protecting their wealth from outside predation, but rather reflected local conflicts about how people might legitimately respond to the government-sponsored Reformation. These conflicts exacerbated local

---

[70] 'Inventories of Church Goods, 6th Edw. VI', ed. H. W. King, *Transactions of the Essex Archaeological Society*, 5 (1873), 219–42, at p. 276.
[71] PRO STAC 3/3/34 and PRO STAC 3/7/90.

disputes over wealth and power and provided incentive for one or more parties to pursue advantage through collaboration.

The danger of imagining embezzlements from churches as purely 'conservative' can be seen in the case of William Gostwick, which Eamon Duffy has used as evidence that embezzlements were often 'far more respectable than they appeared'.[72] Duffy noted correctly that, even though Gostwick was accused in Edward's reign of embezzling ornaments from the parish of Willington, Bedfordshire, Marian authorities later discovered that he had actually owned the ornaments in question, having inherited them from his brother Sir John Gostwick, who had merely loaned them to the parish. Yet this does not mean, as Duffy implied, that Willington was a unified parish community, nor that Gostwick's actions were without repercussions for the local reception of the Reformation. Rather, to understand the local meanings of this case, we must consider how and why a wrongful accusation of embezzlement arose in the first place. In fact, the case came to the government's attention because Thomas Verney, a relative by marriage who had inherited the ornaments from William Gostwick when he died, was denounced to the authorities out of 'malice' by the 'late vicar there'. This malicious accusation turned out to be the result of earlier, far less 'respectable' raids on the parish church. In Edward's reign two parish clerks, William Nyxe and John Dawes, had allegedly embezzled 'certain vestments and ornaments . . . to the value of four pounds' with the complicity of at least one churchwarden. Afterwards Sir John Gostwick, concerned about the ornaments he had loaned to the church, stirred resentment among his neighbours by forcing the clerks and churchwardens to keep inventories of the parish's possessions and report directly to him in case of any discrepancies. Evidently, then, anger against Sir John Gostwick and his heirs found an outlet in accusations of disloyalty to the Reformation. Moreover, the 'malicious' vicar who denounced Thomas Verney to the authorities was also named 'John Gostwick', presumably a relative of the now-deceased original owner of the ornaments. So here, apparently, there was not only a bitter parish dispute over the disposition of church ornaments but also a bitter family dispute over the inheritance of property. None of these people were necessarily evangelicals, but clearly the parish was divided over the fate of their local treasures, and at least some people preferred those treasures to fall into the hands of the Crown than the hands of their local enemies.[73]

More evidence for the impious nature of many embezzlements comes from Mary's reign, when the queen had great difficulty convincing parishioners to return stolen objects despite her commitment to put them back to traditional use. As late as May 1557, for instance, commissioners in the diocese of Ely

---

[72] Duffy, *Stripping of the Altars*, p. 489.   [73] PRO E 117/14/2.

compiled an impressive list of people who were known to withhold church goods. A variety of men from Swaffham and March refused to give up their copes and were threatened with £10 fines, while John Cocke was 'enjoined' to pay 3s 4d for altar cloths. William Bradley of Little Saint Mary in Cambridge was likewise ordered to 'pay unto the said church 40s in recompense of a latten candlestick with five branches'.[74] Another list compiled in the same month in Hampshire accused one man of retaining in his possession 'three brass pots', another of retaining two bells, and so forth.[75] In Mondon, Essex, the parish engaged in a typical subterfuge in Edward's reign to save their best chalice from confiscation: a gentleman named William Harris borrowed it and 'promised to recompense the church a chalice as good in value for it' at some later date. Yet, when Harris died in 1556, he still listed the chalice in his will, so either the parish was mislead about his intentions or he changed his mind about the role of chalices in Christian worship.[76]

Even more extreme is a case from the parish of Radwell, Hertfordshire.[77] There a churchwarden named William Plomer 'heard tell that the king would have an inventory of all the church goods' and in response 'carried away out of the church a cope and a vestment that was bought about 27 years last past and then cost £16'. This would seem to be a case of a pious church officer protecting the fabric of traditional worship, but it turns out that Plomer was no religious conservative, since early in Mary's reign he not only refused to return the vestments but also 'vilely pulled down the sacrament of the altar, railing upon it, and called it idol, and broke the pyx in pieces'. His accuser, moreover, was the same parson of Radwell who twenty years before (in the midst of the Pilgrimage of Grace) had been shopped to Thomas Cromwell for telling his parishioners that 'they that pull down abbeys and churches... without the great mercy of God they shall be damned'.[78] There is a delicious irony in a traditionalist Catholic priest accusing a Protestant churchwarden of concealing church goods from the Edwardian commissioners.

In sum, then, while theft or embezzlement of church goods could sometimes function as resistance to the regime's confiscations, at other times it could function very effectively as collaboration with the regime's spiritual priorities. Whenever the government's religious injunctions cut through the mire of local politics and economics, individuals or groups emerged whose interests were served by supporting aspects of the government's programme,

---

[74] CUL EDR D2/4, fols. 3r–8v.
[75] PRO E 117/15/2. This manuscript does not say where these concealments took place, but the privy seals it lists were delivered to 'Mr White of Southwick', so presumably the manuscript refers to Hampshire.
[76] King (ed.), 'Inventories of Church Goods, 6th Edw. VI', 223 and 238.
[77] PRO C 1/1379, fols. 16–17.
[78] PRO SP 1/116, fol. 192r [*LP* XII, i, 572]. See ch. 5 above.

even if that support consisted merely of internalising iconoclastic disdain for church goods. In these circumstances, it was very often 'the people' – or at least an ever-shifting minority of those people – who brought the Reformation home to their own communities.

IV

Many different factors contributed to this sort of collaboration, but one key element was the interconnection between the languages of religious and economic reform that we saw so prominently in the 1549 rebellions. Supporting the government's religious policies often allowed people to assert themselves more effectively in disputes over 'commonwealth' issues with rapacious neighbours. Nor was this necessarily mere time-serving: embezzlement from churches by wealthy priests or landlords might seem to provide palpable evidence for the government's oft-repeated link between greed, religious traditionalism and political disobedience.

One case involving not parish ornaments but guild ornaments can usefully illustrate this dynamic, although it occurred on a very affluent scale. In Boston, Lincolnshire, one John Brown sued out a bill in Star Chamber, not coincidentally addressed to Protector Somerset, in which he accused a number of aldermen and guildsmen of embezzling 'all the plate, jewels, and moveable goods' of the town's guilds, worth the enormous sum of £1,000. His particular concern, however, was not simply that goods rightfully belonging to the Crown had been stolen, but that the money had been spent 'about such vain devices and expenses as was thought good by the said mayor and burgesses, and to no commonwealth and profit of the poor inhabitants of the same town'.[79] This language, so clearly designed (like the language of the 1549 rebels) to appeal to the government's predilections, shows the sorts of rhetoric and rationales available in disputes over ecclesiastical property.

This model can also be seen in the parish of Great Sherston, Wiltshire. Late in Queen Mary's reign, the churchwardens alleged that either late in Henry VIII's reign or early in Edward VI's reign one Thomas Hayes had stolen from the church 'a great ledger book ... [of] what taxes, payments, and sums of money or other things every householder dwelling within the said parish should yearly content and pay out ... towards the supportation, maintenance, and reparation of the said parish church of Sherston Magna aforesaid and of the ornaments of the same'. When accused of hiding this ledger from the churchwardens, however, Hayes told a very different story. According to him, the ledger had contained not only financial information but also 'diverse other things ... that for great offence and danger of laws then

[79] PRO STAC 3/5/11.

being was not allowable', in other words writings against the Reformation. As a result, he dutifully took the ledger to the Dean of Gloucester, who confiscated the book. Here, then, was an almost ideal illustration of the government's claim that the onerous financial exactions of the medieval Church went hand in hand with both superstition and disobedience to civil authority. It is all the more significant, then, that, even according to Hayes's traditionalist accusers, his pernicious example had led 'other of the said parishioners' likewise to 'refuse to pay such payments... whereby the said church is almost decayed and the ornaments thereof are now become very slender for due administration within the said church according to the laws of God and of Holy Church'.[80]

A much more complicated case, worth recounting in detail, comes from the town of Watford, Hertfordshire, where disputes over the local enforcement of the 1547 injunctions became intimately intertwined with commonwealth ideology and the 1549 rebellions.[81] The dispute began when Henry Heydon, a substantial gentleman and landlord, attempted to evict one of his tenants, John Warren. According to witnesses on the landlord's behalf, Warren was a detested local bully who 'much troubled and disquieted his neighbours for very light matters'. Heydon thus warned Warren that if he did not 'live in quiet among his neighbours... he should not tarry in his farm', and in late 1547, after more than a year of negotiation, Warren and his family were finally evicted. When Warren refused to leave 'peaceably', constables were called in to remove the family from their house and nail the doors shut. From the perspective of Warren and his witnesses, however, events looked very different. On this view, Heydon had illegally threatened to evict Warren in 1546 but then withdrawn his threat and ostensibly made peace. It thus came as a complete surprise to Warren when in December 1547 Heydon 'thrust the said Warren, his wife, and all his family out of the said farm and house, the said Warren being at that time unprovided of any other dwelling'. When Warren suggested that their dispute should be arbitrated by local notables, Heydon refused to accept any outcome except the total confiscation of Warren's goods, and, as the dispute escalated in the following months, Heydon had Warren thrown in jail.

None of this was necessarily unusual: disputes between landlords and tenants were commonplace, and landlords often used muscle when negotiations failed. But, in the late 1540s, relations between landlords and tenants were a hot topic in English politics, and the Warrens seem to have been well connected enough to make a very substantial fuss. Warren's wife complained in writing 'to my Lord of Somerset and to other of the king's majesty's Council',

80 PRO C 1/1363, fols. 9–11.
81 This case is in PRO STAC 3/7/53 and PRO REQ 2/15/93.

while Warren himself 'rode unto Sheen, unto my Lord of Somerset, unto whom he made his complaint'. According to witnesses for Warren, these appeals produced immediate results: the Council 'took order that the said Heydon should deliver unto the said Warren his goods'. Here, then, we have another example of Somerset's reputation for beneficence being brought to bear in local politics, with a tenant (albeit obviously a very substantial one) gaining advantage against his landlord in a dispute over 'commonwealth' issues through the Lord Protector's direct intervention.

The next stage in the dispute occurred in July 1549, when it became intertwined with the rebellion in and around St Albans. Henry Heydon was charged by the government with maintaining law and order in Watford during the risings, which he attempted to do by using the village constable as a deputy. Yet law and order proved difficult to achieve, and the constable whom Heydon had deputised was twice 'arrested' by rebel sympathisers. The constable alleged that these arrests were arranged 'through the procurement' of John Warren, who was subsequently arrested at Heydon's request for mistreating 'the king's officers in that busy time'. Once again, however, Warren's wife appealed the case directly to Protector Somerset, and once again her appeal produced action, apparently resulting in Warren's immediate release.

The importance of this story for our purposes, however, is that the government's zeal in helping John Warren was due not merely to Somerset's antagonism towards avaricious landlords but also to Warren's stance on religious issues, particularly his enforcement of the 1547 injunctions for the removal of idolatrous images. Warren claimed that he played a vigorous role in pulling down images in Watford church 'as was given him in commandment by the king's commissioners'. Just as importantly, he also claimed that Henry Heydon was an opponent of the king's injunctions who tried to save idolatrous images from destruction. It was therefore allegedly over this issue that Heydon had decided to evict the Warrens in December 1547 despite his earlier decision to let them stay. One witness on Warren's behalf, for instance, reported that Warren was evicted because he 'was an earnest man in helping to the pulling down of the images in the church'. Another witness reported that Warren had been evicted because he 'took down an image of St John which stood in the new aisle in the church of Watford'. The most interesting version of this story came from a Watford man named John Pratt:

The images then standing in Watford church were shortly after plucked down by the said Warren and this deponent and other honest men of the town. Whereupon certain persons were offended therewith and went unto London and complained to Mr Heydon thereof, he then being at London. And upon their complaint the said Mr Heydon ... sent for the said Warren for that matter ... and after certain communication had concerning the pulling down of images between the said Heydon and the said Warren, the said Heydon charged the said Warren, Gyles, Brown, and Fletcher to appear before the Lord Paget. And so this deponent came before my Lord Paget where also was Mr Heydon, and the said Lord Paget asked them what images they had pulled down. And the said Warren answered the said Lord Paget that they had plucked down four tabernacles. 'Yea, sir', [said] the said Mr Heydon, 'and the Trinity also'. To whom my lord made answer that that was the closest thing that ought to be plucked down ... [Afterwards] walking together talking in the palace at Westminster the said Heydon said, 'I am sorry that I have such tenants.' And the said Warren said again unto the said Heydon that he was sorry that he had such a landlord.

John Warren's subsequent suit against Henry Heydon in the Court of Requests was thus an example of the Reformation being put to political use, with a man claiming to be a vigorous reformer arguing before the royal courts that his local enemy was dangerously conservative. Depositions taken on behalf of Heydon, however, present the conflict in a very different light. Heydon's witnesses claimed that it was *he* who had supervised the removal of images according to the king's injunctions, while *Warren* 'was much against the pulling down of [images]'. Indeed, according to one witness, 'the said Warren took such a displeasure and conceived such a malice and rancour in his stomach against the said Heydon that he complained upon the said Heydon to the king's Council, laying ... the charge that he would not suffer the king's proceedings to go forward, where before the said Warren was most of any man against them that this deponent knew'.

The question is thus raised whether John Warren was a 'carnal gospeller'. He certainly enhanced his local standing and profited from his willingness to embrace the regime's well-publicised connection between the commonwealth and godly reform. But was it 'counterfeit godliness' as Heydon suggested, or was Warren truly a zealous reformer? A possible answer can be gleaned from depositions taken in 1552, after Warren's wife, who was herself so active in these proceedings, had died. According to numerous witnesses, on her deathbed Warren's wife had begged forgiveness from Heydon for 'such words as she had falsely spoken against him', desiring absolution for 'the false, scandalous reports' she had made against him. She even 'took her tongue by the end and said, "I am afraid that this hath perished my soul."' If true, these accounts suggest that Warren and his wife were not zealous reformers wronged by their landlord, but rather had invented charges of religious conservatism to score points in a dispute over property. It seems likely, then, that Warren was not an evangelical but belatedly joined the iconoclastic bandwagon when it became clear that Heydon, in the act of preventing over-aggressive acts of desecration, had left himself open to exactly the sorts of charges that would be most appealing to the Somerset government. Yet, even if Warren 'counterfeited' his faith, we cannot separate him from the process of Reformation and conclude that his expedient iconoclasm was somehow less meaningful than the iconoclasm of the godly. John Warren – and the many men and women who acted as witnesses on his behalf – agreed to a bargain in which they acquired real power against their landlord in exchange for the vigorous local enforcement of the Reformation. They thus came to see the new religion in something like the terms it was presented to them: godly social reform could only follow after the walls of Watford church were stripped bare.

v

Another whole class of responses to the Edwardian assault on parish churches was the sale of church goods to forestall confiscation. Since medieval parishes had always sold church plate to pay for necessary parish expenditures, the line was never entirely clear in Edward's reign between traditional, legitimate sales and illegitimate embezzlements intended to pre-empt royal predations. Even the instructions to royal commissioners making inventories of church goods in 1552 were ambiguous, requiring them to investigate the sale of church goods whenever the profits from those sales had not been 'employed or converted to the godly and lawful uses of the said churches'.[82] This ambiguity meant that for parishes to remain on the right side of the law, they had to appeal to the perceived priorities of the regime, interpreting the phrase 'godly and lawful uses' in ways the government would approve. Here, then, was a potential point of contact where room for negotiation between government and people became available. In leaving a loophole which allowed parishes to retain their wealth, but shaping that loophole around evangelical priorities, the government created both incentive for collaboration and a series of bitter conflicts within parishes over the meanings of these highly charged manoeuvres.

To illustrate this process, it is best to begin with the least controversial examples: places where parishioners legitimised sales of ornaments by appealing to the government but did not collaborate specifically with the Reformation. In the parish of Sparham, Norfolk, for instance, churchwardens sold a chalice and other plate that would have been forfeit to the king and, when later questioned about their actions, claimed that they had used the proceeds to buy 'harness to serve the king's majesty in his wars'.[83] In a similar manoeuvre, the parish of Longhope, Gloucestershire, sold a chalice, a pyx and a cross in the spring of 1548 and used the proceeds 'for the furniture of soldiers now into Scotland or into some other place of the king's

[82] *Inventory of Furniture and Ornaments Remaining in All the Parish Churches of Hertfordshire in the Last Year of the Reign of King Edward the Sixth*, ed. J. E. Cussans (Oxford, 1873), p. 6.
[83] PRO E 315/500, fol. 59r.

majesty's use and also for the amending of the highway'.[84] Here loyalty to
the king was publicly paraded, even in the act of defrauding the government.
Through a clever book-keeping trick, essentially spending the king's money
for the king, parishioners could claim that they had done no more than
eliminate the middle man. This was disingenuous, of course, since they were
technically required to provide arms for the king *and* surrender their church
plate. But, by effectively carrying out the spirit of both requirements, these
people sought to shield themselves from charges of embezzlement. Here,
then, parishioners appealed to the government's willingness to make deals:
they offered ostentatious loyalty to a self-consciously weak regime in return
for some measure of autonomy and financial stability.

This strategy was considerably expanded in the town of Nuneaton,
Warwickshire. Here the parish sold copes, vestments and crosses, and then
claimed that they had used the proceeds for 'reparation of highways', for 'a
free school there which is now established by our said sovereign', and for
'alteration of their church'.[85] This language is striking because not only was
the foundation of schools a priority of the government after the dissolution
of the chantries, but the 'alteration' of the church (unlike the 'reparation' of
churches which so many churchwardens reported) was clearly a euphemism
for compliance with the 1547 injunctions. Once again, loyalty to the regime
was elaborately performed, but now that loyalty was not merely to the person
of the king but also to the government's religious policies.

This sort of negotiation reached its apex in a series of parishes which
agreed to rid their churches of images and ostentatiously collaborate with the
Reformation if they could keep the proceeds from the sale of church plate. In
the village of Foulsham, Norfolk, for instance, the parish sold £40 worth of
plate and used the proceeds to replace the glass in church windows, to 'white
our church', and to create 'an alms in bread to be dealt every Sunday throughout the year'. The 'whiting' of churches was of course a crucial evangelical
programme, as was the establishment of poor relief outside the traditional
structure of intercessions. But, most interestingly, the replacement of windows, presumably providing clear glass instead of stained glass, represented
a particularly radical interpretation of the 1547 injunctions against idolatry.
Images in stained glass windows had never been objects of veneration and
thus technically should have been allowed to stand, but the government had
made clear its preferences through the wholesale destruction of stained glass
in Westminster, which Diarmaid MacCulloch has described as 'a high-profile
venue no doubt deliberately chosen to set fashions elsewhere'.[86] Evidently
the parishioners of Foulsham were paying attention. Another Norfolk parish

---

[84] GRO MS GDR 4, pp. 48–9.   [85] PRO E 315/513, fol. 17v.
[86] MacCulloch, *The Boy King*, p. 71. See also Duffy, *Stripping of the Altars*, p. 451.

likewise sold church plate to pay for 'the whiting of the church and other necessary things to be done according to the king's injunction'. More bluntly, another Norfolk parish used funds from its sale of church plate to pay for 'taking down of images and tabernacles, whiting of the church, and other necessary things to be done'.[87] Yet another Norfolk parish, eager to prove their reformist credentials, sold their plate and with the proceeds purchased a new Bible and built a new pulpit.[88]

Other parishes used the proceeds from sales of church plate to remake the interior of their churches in explicitly evangelical fashion. The church-wardens of Ramsey, Huntingdonshire, for instance, sold 'one coverlet for 7s [and] one old painted cloth for 4s' and used the proceeds 'in writing of scrip-tures about the Church there'. These scriptural passages were of course taken from the same Protestant translations of the Bible that Marian ecclesiasti-cal visitors would soon begin removing from parish churches.[89] The nearby parish of Aukenburie likewise sold its chalice for the considerable sum of £5 6d, which was then used 'in whiting and scripturing their church'.[90] Since it is implausible that painting the church could really have cost so much, it seems likely that someone was skimming funds off the top; but again, while the government may have lost money on this transaction, they did so by providing incentive for yet another parish to reform itself.

Elsewhere, liturgical accoutrements were altered and reused for evangelical purposes to prevent their confiscation. The wealthy parish of Dartford, Kent, for instance, declared in 1552 that they had failed to present a red silk canopy cloth and other valuable altar cloths to the government because those cloths had been 'altered for to make a cover for the table to receive the communion on'.[91] This is clearly a significant transformation: even if the persistence of the old cloths allowed parishioners more easily to imagine the new communion service as an 'English mass', it also allowed them more easily to accept the legitimacy of the new service. An equally significant transaction involving liturgical 'fabric' occurred in the Huntingdonshire parish of Somersham, where churchwardens 'did give to the poor 7 towels of plain cloth, 6 of diaper, 2 pair of old sheets, a veil for Lent, one old surplice, and one rochet'.[92] At Lachingdon, Essex, the parish likewise gave three albs and other ecclesiastical cloth to the poor, while at Lawling, Essex, the parish gave 'an old surplice and an old vestment to the poor'.[93] Here ecclesiastical linen and cloth was

---

[87] PRO E 315/500, fols. 56r–v, 69r, 76r.   [88] PRO E 117/14/65.

[89] Lomas (ed.), *The Edwardian Inventories for Huntingdonshire*, p. 31.

[90] Ibid., pp. 34–5.

[91] 'Inventories of Parish Church Goods in Kent, A.D. 1552', ed. M. E. C. Walcott *et al.*, *Archaeologia Cantiana*, 8 (1872), 74–163, at p. 141.

[92] Lomas (ed.), *The Edwardian Inventories for Huntingdonshire*, p. 33.

[93] King (ed.), 'Inventories of Church Goods, 6th Edw. VI', pp. 225–6.

actively desacralised, transmuting the goods of the Church into the goods
of the poor according to the spirit of the Edwardian injunctions. Certainly
there was nothing unequivocally Protestant about these transactions, but
the parishes could just as well have *sold* the cloths and then given away the
proceeds; we should not underestimate the spiritual significance of seeing
the local poor sleeping in the streets under albs and altar cloths.[94]

So in other words, by ostentatiously using the proceeds of embezzlements
to support the government's religious programme, these communities made
it hard for the regime to complain. In collaborating so visibly in evangelical
pursuits, these parishes publicly established themselves as complicit with the
Reformation, and in doing so they won themselves considerable immunity
from government interference. We have no evidence that anyone in these
parishes had converted to Protestantism, but they certainly understood the
priorities of a Protestant regime, and if it allowed them to keep ecclesiastical
wealth within the community, at least some parishioners were happy to
cooperate.

It might be argued that these sorts of negotiations and transactions were
without spiritual significance. Faced with an untenable situation, parishes
might have held their collective noses and done whatever it took to maintain
their viability while waiting for the day (in fact only a few years away) when
traditional worship would be legalised again. But this argument is belied
by the bitter controversies that sales of church ornaments often engendered,
suggesting that at least some people thought that these transactions were significant indeed. In the traditionalist parish of Morebath studied by Eamon
Duffy, for instance, the essentially secular goods of the church house (tables,
pots, dishes and so forth) were sold 'by the consent of the whole parish'
to pay for the *Paraphrases* of Erasmus and other required alterations. But
when churchwarden Lucy Scely sold the Lent cloth, painted hangings for the
Easter Sepulchre, and other explicitly *spiritual* furnishings, she did so 'without commission' and provoked the fury of many of her neighbours.[95] In the
village of Lansdown, Somerset, the conflict was between the churchwardens
and the parish clerk. The churchwardens claimed that they had accumulated
'diverse barres of iron, boards, and other timber to the value of £4...for
the necessary reparation and amending of the said parish church', and they
accused the clerk of stealing that iron and timber for his own use, leaving the
parish unable to provide for its needs. The clerk answered by claiming that

[94] Fifteen years before, in the context of the Pilgrimage of Grace, the Yorkshire priest John
Dakyn was horrified when he heard at the rebel convocation that servants of men who had
suppressed abbeys had made 'apparel (yea, and saddle cloths as I heard say) of vestments
and other ornaments of abbeys': PRO SP 1/117, fol. 202v [*LP* XII, i, 786(2)].
[95] Duffy, *The Voices of Morebath*, pp. 124–5.

it had been his job to collect money for the purchase of 'the new Homily, as also for every other books as they were commanded to have', and he suggested that the churchwardens' malicious accusation resulted only from his willingness to obey the king's injunctions.[96] A similar controversy struck the parish of South Lynn in Norfolk, where after Mary's accession a number of parishioners sued the former churchwardens, alleging that they had embezzled crucifixes, candlesticks, pyxes and other ornaments 'without the assent or agreement of the said parishioners'. The churchwardens, however, responded that they had sold those items with the full consent of the parish. Part of the money had been used 'upon the reparations of the said church and other thing wherewith the parishioners of the same church were charged', while the rest had been 'put into the common hutch, there safely to be kept to the use of the same parishioners'. Here we cannot tell who, if anyone, was telling the truth, but it is at least clear that the disposition of parish ornaments was an issue of serious local disagreement.[97]

Even when the sale of church goods did not divide communities in any outward way, the spiritual repercussions could still be traumatic, and at least one parish found itself busily apologising for such transactions in Mary's reign. Parishioners of Skidbrooke on Saltfleet Haven, Lincolnshire, had sold their church bells in Edward's reign, and the Marian regime, eager to reinvest churches with their former wealth, demanded £20 in reparations. The parishioners responded with a petition to the Crown, begging the queen's pardon for the fact that in May 1552 the community 'of one assent and consent... considering the universal talk of people then bruited abroad and the open preachings of many lewd and fantastical preachers openly preaching against bells and other laudable ceremonies of the church, then affirming the use of them to be superstitious and abominable, directly against God's laws, sold two bells then being in their parish church'.[98] This was as close to an admission as we are ever likely to see that some members of the community had accepted at least the basic intellectual categories of the Edwardian Reformation and used them as a basis for action. It was in cases like this that we can see the zone of intersection between political collaboration and spiritual Reformation.

VI

Popular engagement and collaboration can even be found in the programme that Eamon Duffy chose as his metaphor for the whole destructive force of

---

[96] PRO C 1/1217, fols. 60–1. This location is spelled 'Langyston,' in the MS, so it is probably Lansdown rather than Long Sutton.
[97] PRO C 1/1394, fols. 62–3.   [98] PRO E 117/14/50(1) and E 117/14/50(2).

the Reformation: the stripping of the altars.[99] The Edwardian altar policy was the most theologically aggressive aspect of the government's attack on parish churches. Altars were places of sacrifice; to remove them or replace them with more mundane objects was to assert that the sacrament of Christ's body and blood was no sacrifice at all. As such, even many loyal Henrician conservatives balked at the idea of divine service without altars. Bishop George Day of Chichester put the matter most succinctly in 1550, writing from prison after his deprivation:

I sticked not at the alteration either of the matter (as stone or wood) whereof the altar was made, but I then took, as I now take, those things to be indifferent, and to be ordered by them that have authority. But the commandment which was given to me to take down all altars within my diocese, and in the lieu of them to set up a table, implying in itself (as I take it) a plain abolishment of the altar (both the name and the thing) from the use and ministration of the holy communion, I could not with my conscience then execute.[100]

Less outspoken Catholics than Bishop Day scrambled for ways to avoid the government's requirements. The vicar of Blean in Kent was presented in diocesan court for erecting in his church a table that *resembled* an altar, telling his parishioners that his conscience was not violated since there was no difference between the table and an altar 'saving the one was stone and the other wood'. This was more resistance than most priests managed. Two Kentish clergymen who originally refused to comply with the removal of altars, for instance, were excommunicated and then quickly petitioned to be relieved of their sentence on the condition that they certified that all altars in their churches were destroyed within one week. One of these failed resistors who gave certification to Cranmer's court was none other than Richard Master, the parson of Aldington, who more than twenty years before had been a conspirator with the maid of Kent. Conservatism had truly fallen on hard times.[101]

Yet, even this most controversial of programmes could be finessed and negotiated when the government's altar policy intersected with the politics and economics of local communities. One fascinating case comes from the Wiltshire parish of Highworth, where trouble arose from the king's order 'that throughout all the diocese of Sarum all the altars in every church or chapel . . . should be taken down and in lieu of them a table set up in some

[99] Duffy was, of course, being subtle and ironic in his choice of a title; the 'stripping of the altars' is not only an apt description of mid Tudor sacrilege but also a solemn Catholic rite. My argument that ordinary parishioners could involve themselves in the 'stripping' process, while disagreeing with Duffy's interpretation of the Reformation, may perhaps tend to strengthen the irony that his title was intended to invoke.

[100] *Original Letters*, 3rd series, III, p. 303.

[101] 'Extracts from Original Documents Illustrating the Progress of the Reformation in Kent', ed. C. E. Woodruff, *Archaeologia Cantiana*, 31 (1915), 92–120, at pp. 103–4.

convenient part of the chancel ... to serve for the ministration of the blessed communion'. The Highworth dispute first came to the Privy Council's attention in the form of a Star Chamber bill, and it is typical of the way local communities tried to play to the government's perceived predilections that the first draft of the bill referred to the 'ministration of the blessed *sacrament*', but then the word 'sacrament' was crossed out and replaced with 'communion'. Evangelicals in the government in fact would not have been troubled by the word 'sacrament', but the writers of this most godly of bills (perhaps not actually evangelicals themselves) were taking no chances, and 'communion' was the word used in the Prayer Book.[102]

On 12 December 1550, according to the Star Chamber bill, William Willcockson and William Edwards, churchwardens of Highworth, 'peaceably and with quiet means did take down all the altars being in the said parish church of Highworth and did set up a table according to the tenor, form, and effect of the ... decree and commandment'. In the course of their business, however, one John Boller, 'in contempt of your highness, vituperating and resisting your grace's holy proceedings, ordinances, and decrees', said to William Willcockson: 'Wherefore do you pull down these altars? A dog commanded thee to do this and thou hast no more authority to do this than hath a dog.' If these words were really spoken, they amounted to serious sedition, and the two churchwardens took their story to Sir Anthony Hungerford, Justice of the Peace for Wiltshire. Yet, according to the bill:

Sir Anthony, forgetting his duty towards God and your highness, for the blind affection he bare to Sir John Bridges, being a man much addicted in the old ignorance of religion and little favouring your majesty's most godly proceedings, opened his mind to the said Willcockson and said that forasmuch as the said Boller was friend unto his cousin Sir John Bridges ... he had rather spend £100 than any displeasure should grow to the said Sir John Bridges or to any of his friends and adherents if he might help the matter by any means.

Hungerford therefore ordered the churchwardens 'to speak no further in the premises' and afterwards 'concealed, coloured, and cloaked the said offences without any manner of reproach or punishment of the said Boller'. Thus the target of this Star Chamber bill was not Boller, the yeoman who had allegedly spoken the offensive words and resisted the stripping of the altars, but Hungerford, the powerful gentleman who had protected him.

The story grows more complex, however, when we look at Hungerford's reply. Hungerford admitted that the churchwardens had appeared before him, but he added that he had also taken testimony from an eyewitness,

---

[102] This case is in PRO STAC 3/5/77. It is printed, along with related cases, in *Star Chamber Suits of John and Thomas Warneford*, ed. F. E. Warneford, Wiltshire Record Society, 48 (Trowbridge, 1993). I would like to thank Amanda Jones for discussing this case with me.

a 'vitteler' named William Yate. When Hungerford administered to Yate 'a corporal oath' requiring him to tell the truth on pain of his soul, Yate thought better of repeating the churchwardens' version and instead told a very different story:

At or about the day mentioned in the said information, he was in the church of Highworth [where] he saw the said Willcockson and the said Edwards . . . and diverse others pulling down the altar in the chancel there. And the said Yate departing thence in the churchyard met the said Boller with a bar of iron on his neck and asked the same Boller whither he went, who answered that he went to pull down the high altar. And the said Yate told him the altar was then down already, and the said Boller said, 'Then so much labour was saved.' And thereupon the said Yate and Boller came into the said church and the said Boller asked the said Willcockson and others why and to what purpose they carried away the stones of the said altar, and they answered and said, 'to the use of the parish'. And the said Boller said that if the parish ought to have them they should have them, but if they belong to the parsonage or vicarage then they belong to me that hath the parsonage and vicarage in farm. And then thou hast no more to do therein than a dog.[103]

According to this version, then, Boller was no religious conservative but merely the farmer of the vicarage who believed that he had a legal right to the valuable stones of the altar. This claim infuriated his neighbours, who wanted the stones for themselves, which is presumably why they were so eager to see Boller arrested. And, indeed, there is independent confirmation that John Boller was no conservative resistor to the Reformation. At the accession of Queen Mary, the vicar of Highworth was removed from his office for marriage. Just before losing his office he did what many priests did before their deprivations, leasing his income to a lay ally who would presumably funnel the profits back into his own pocket. In this case, the layman who conspired with the married vicar to defraud the newly appointed Marian priest was none other than John Boller.[104]

In Highworth, then, there was no confessional dispute in the parish; everyone accepted the stripping of the altars, with the only dispute being over who was entitled to the economic benefits of doing that stripping themselves. Everyone in this case seems to have imagined the implementation of the Reformation as an opportunity rather than a crisis of conscience. The churchwardens and the farmer of the vicarage squabbled over the spoils, with a wide array of village allies on both sides giving depositions to the courts: husbandmen, bakers, carpenters, and so on. Both sides also found elite backing, with two prominent gentlemen using the case as a battleground for their own disputes: the bill against Hungerford was ostensibly written

---

[103] The Wiltshire Record Society transcription of this quotation is erroneous in key respects. I would like to thank Simon Healy for checking the manuscript for me at the eleventh hour to confirm that my transcription was, in fact, correct.

[104] PRO C 1/1377, fol. 34r.

by the Wiltshire gentleman John Warneford on behalf of the churchwardens who were presumably his clients.[105] Moreover, the opposing parties both professed support for the Reformation while accusing their opponents of disloyalty and opposition to religious change. It is not clear, of course, whether any of these men were theologically Protestant. But, at Highworth, acceptance of and collaboration with the Reformation became not a position in local conflicts but the ground upon which all the different positions were constructed.

VII

This chapter has traced some of the contours of a Reformation in mid Tudor England that does not fit established models. It was not a Reformation loosed by the Holy Spirit, since only a minority of its proponents were in any coherent, theological sense Protestants. It was not a 'Revolution of the common man', as Peter Blickle has outlined for Germany, since it was created in explicit dialogue with the state. It was not a 'political reformation' in Christopher Haigh's terms, since it cannot be divorced from the evangelical ideas at its heart. And it was not a 'Reformation from above' as described by Eamon Duffy and J. J. Scarisbrick, since it would have been inconceivable without active, popular engagement and collaboration.

It was instead a Reformation of strange bedfellows and nitty-gritty practicalities, negotiated and finessed rather than won. That the English Reformation *might* have followed this path was made possible by the politically adulterated nature of the state-sponsored Reformation itself and the government's saturation of its religious policies with economic rhetoric and appeals for popular support; that it *did* follow this path depended upon the abilities of ordinary English subjects to respond actively and creatively to what they were told. English people did not merely obey the commands of their government but also shaped the meanings of those commands, investing their reactions to the Reformation with significance for their own economic, social and political lives. Just as Luther proved incapable of maintaining the coherence of his movement as it filtered out of Wittenberg, so the English Reformation acquired a multiplicity of local, contingent, and contested meanings as government policy filtered through Tudor society. Sometimes, as in much of Devon and Cornwall in 1549, the result was an explosion of discontent, but at other times, as this chapter has shown, this multivalent Reformation could become a powerful new weapon for those who attempted to shape and define it in their favour.

---

[105] Warneford's bill also accused Hungerford of concealing or ignoring a wide range of crimes, so it seems likely that the dispute between the two gentlemen was only peripherally related to the dispute over the altar stones at Highworth.

Whether the Reformation co-opted popular politics or popular politics co-opted the Reformation thus depends on one's point of view. But there is no question that the Reformation was accepted, employed and embraced by large numbers of people who otherwise would have had little time for formal theological debate. In the English Reformation, then, spiritual transformation often followed political positioning rather than preceding it. In this sense, English Protestantism, like E. P. Thompson's working class, 'did not rise like the sun at an appointed time. It was present at its own making.'[106]

[106] E. P. Thompson, *The Making of the English Working Class* (New York, 1966), p. 9.

Conclusion

In the reign of Mary Tudor, with Roman Catholicism restored and heretics fleeing for their lives, Catholic writers penned a series of what they assumed were post-mortems on England's brief Protestant experiment. Yet, despite the mercy that God had shown by providing a Catholic queen, the tone of these retrospective accounts was not self-congratulatory but rather betrayed a sense of deep frustration that so many English subjects, especially among the common people, had wandered off the True Path. John Bullingham, for instance, wrote that 'thousands of men (alas for pity) having their hearts clean void of charity, being corrupt in conscience, and flattering themselves with their counterfeit faith, have not only been turned into jangling and babbling, but at the last have fallen into great and horrible blasphemies'. As a result, he wrote: 'There is a plague and pestilence throughout England [and] the air is infected. Where corrupt hearts and minds are, there cannot be pure and lively faith. And where pure faith is not found, there is a commodious place for errors and heresies to dwell in.'[1] John Standish agreed that 'manifold, damnable heresies have caused most miserable schism among the rude people, being hauled from the truth and tossed from post to pillar on every side, even like as it was in the Arians' time, when the heretics used most commonly both to say and do many things well to obtain thereby credit among the simple and the weak, that so much more freely they might sow their heresies and pluck down the churches'.[2] The author of *A Plaine and Godlye Treatise Concernynge the Masse* likewise wrote: 'In my judgment, neither the malicious device of the devil, [nor] the cursed and pestilent malice of the heretics, seemed not much readier in their devilish drifts and pestilent persuasions, than did the frail folly and fond madness of such beetle-blind people that so readily and so fondly would

---

[1] Bullingham made these statements in the preface to John Venaeus, *A Notable Oration, Made by John Venaeus, a Parisien, in the Defence of the Sacrament of the Aultare* (London, 1554), sigs. A3r and A5r.

[2] John Standish, *The Triall of the Supremacy* (London, 1556), sigs. A3v–A4r.

believe and credit in so weighty matters of the faith such a rude, railing rabblement.'[3]

Certainly we should not take these accounts at face value; each was written for its own pastoral or polemical purpose. But it is none the less remarkable how far removed these descriptions are from recent historical accounts of the English Reformation, which have stressed the inherent conservatism of the common people. How, then, can we account for the expectations of these Catholic writers that their audience would recognise and respond to a version of English Reformation history that modern historians have dismissed as a mere fable propagated by anti-Catholic bigotry? The answer is that we must turn down the volume of our own historiographical din and listen carefully to what these sources are telling us. They describe the first quarter century of the English Reformation as an era of spiritual crisis when the 'beetle-blind people' were corrupted by a 'counterfeit faith' and reduced to 'great and horrible blasphemies'. Certainly this represents a significant departure from Eamon Duffy's 'traditional religion', but it is also a far cry from the triumphalist Protestant narrative of A. G. Dickens; arguing that the masses *responded* to heretics and *acted* like heretics, after all, is subtly but crucially different from arguing that they *became* heretics. These Marian authors in fact seem to be noting what this book has argued all along: that the Reformation was a muddled process in which action often preceded self-conscious theologising or identity formation. It required neither improbable feats of state power nor vast waves of religious conversions to undermine traditional religion; all it took was for 'the simple and the weak' to give 'credit' to the 'rude, railing rabblement' of heretics who offered them seductive incentives to help 'pluck down the churches'.

The goal of this book has been to explore this process by which the Reformation entered English culture through the back door, not dependent upon spectacular epiphanies but rather exploiting the mundane realities of political allegiance, financial investment and local conflict. Of course, I have not denied that spectacular epiphanies could and did occur, nor that the minority who converted to the new religion exercised an influence far outweighing their numbers. Nor have I denied, as have some recent historians, that there was a powerful minority of Catholics who utterly refused to compromise and

---

[3] *A Plaine and Godlye Treatise Concernynge the Masse* (London, 1555), sig. A5v. For an analysis of Marian writings on the English Reformation, see Thomas Betteridge, *Tudor Histories of the English Reformations, 1530–83* (Aldershot, 1999), ch. 3. Many more examples of pessimistic accounts by Marian Catholics can be found in Alec Ryrie, 'Counting Sheep, Counting Shepherds: The Problem of Allegiance in the English Reformation', in Peter Marshall and Alec Ryrie (eds.), *The Beginnings of English Protestantism, 1490–1558* (forthcoming). I would like to thank Dr Ryrie for sharing this piece with me prior to publication.

would rather risk death than walk through any Reformation door, whether front or back.[4] Both of these were crucial interest-groups who helped define what sort of Reformation occurred in England. But I have argued that no amount of study of radical reformers and radical resistors can help us to understand the majority who were neither. To appreciate *these* English subjects as more than hapless recipients of religious change – the two-dimensional stick-figures who so often appear in churchwardens' accounts and wills – I have perforce focused on sources where ordinary people can be observed playing an active role in the drama of Reformation, imprinting that drama with their own perspectives. The result is a narrative which acknowledges for the first time that the Reformation was necessarily based, like all aspects of Tudor government, on the collaboration of the governed. This collaboration was the result, in different times and places, of varying combinations of loyalism, greed, strategy and conviction. But, regardless of the precise blend, the Reformation thus created owed as much to the dynamics of popular engagement as to the dynamics of elite enforcement.

One response to this argument might be that a Reformation so reliant upon political expediency was a house built on shifting sands; when Mary took the throne and Catholicism again became politically advantageous, people would inevitably shift their opinions once more. In some sense this is absolutely true and is a necessary corollary to my argument that religious change in an environment of state-sponsored Reformation could only with great difficulty be divorced from politics. Yet, even if we assume that the commons negotiated the Marian Counter-Reformation with the same aplomb that they negotiated the Edwardian Reformation, that still does not mean – and indeed it largely denies – that Mary could have restored 'traditional religion' in England. Exactly because the changes of the Reformation resulted from the interaction of popular and elite politics rather than mere enforcement from above, those changes proved hard to erase and impossible to reverse. This is, in a sense, what sociologists call 'path dependency': the results of the early Reformation were no more solid (and in some ways considerably less so) than the system they replaced, but they still provided the new ground and context from which Mary would have to proceed with her own negotiations. Catholicism might be restored through the same laborious cultural process that had planted the Reformation on English soil, but 'traditionalism' was dead and buried, as Reginald Pole would soon discover when he asked English subjects to return the spoils of the Henrician and Edwardian Reformations. This was a lesson that would only be learned fully by English Catholics decades later, when men like Robert Parsons and

---

[4] Cf. Lucy Wooding, *Rethinking Catholicism in Early Modern England* (Oxford, 2000).

William Allen began the process of building a new and vital Catholic Church on the ruins of the old.[5]

In 1553, then, at the end of one attempt to remake the English Church and the beginning of another, there is no doubt that the effects of a quarter century of revolution had been enormous. As this book has shown, these effects cannot be measured simply by counting the number of people who, like Martin Luther in his 'tower experience', felt that they were 'altogether born again and had entered paradise'.[6] Instead, we can find the Reformation's footprint in the vastly different ways that English people came to imagine the Church, the relationship between Church and state, and their own complex relationship to those institutions. Religious change occurred not simply in the adoption of new doctrines, but in the acceptance of new political partnerships between traditionalists and heretics; in the creation of links between evangelical theology and agrarian grievances; in the financial 'investment' by even humble peasants and artisans in the dissolutions of monasteries and chantries; in the growing acceptance of religious division rather than religious unity as the foundation of the political order; and in the willingness of English subjects to admit new and frightening ideas into their symbolic vocabulary, even if they did not always follow those ideas to their radical conclusions.

It has recently been suggested that the 'Reformations' of the sixteenth century, for all their drama and ideological fervour, had little effect on ordinary people's lives:

While politicians were having their hesitant Reformations, while Protestants were preaching their evangelical reform, parish congregations went to church: they prayed again to their God, learned again how to be good, and went off home once more. That was how it had been in 1530; that was how it was in 1590. Some Reformations.[7]

Yet, as we have seen, this conception seriously misjudges the relationship between Protestants, politicians and the people. Parishioners did not simply go to church; they also participated in the political lives of their communities, where they engaged with the Reformation every day as it was filtered through the agendas of the petty civil and ecclesiastical officials charged with

---

[5] John Bossy, *The English Catholic Community 1570–1850* (London, 1975). A very different view can be found in Christopher Haigh, 'The Continuity of Catholicism in the English Reformation', in Christopher Haigh (ed.), *The English Reformation Revised* (Cambridge, 1987); Christopher Haigh, 'The Church of England, the Catholics, and the People', in Christopher Haigh (ed.), *The Reign of Elizabeth I* (Basingstoke, 1984); Christopher Haigh, 'The Fall of a Church or the Rise of a Sect? Post-Reformation Catholicism in England', *HJ*, 21 (1978), 182–6; Christopher Haigh, 'From Monopoly to Minority: Catholicism in Early Modern England', *TRHS*, fifth series, 31 (1981), 129–47.

[6] Cited in Steven Ozment, *The Age of Reform 1250–1550* (New Haven, Conn., 1980), p. 230.

[7] Christopher Haigh, *English Reformations: Religion, Politics, and Society under the Tudors* (Oxford, 1993), p. 295.

enforcing it. When those parishioners 'prayed to their God' in 1553 (much less in 1590!) they did so under a new dispensation, authorised by the heretical Tudor state. When they went to church, they not only 'learned how to be good' but also upon occasion tore down images or sold church plate. When they left church and 'went off home', sometimes they stopped along the way to put money in the parish poor box, read Bibles to each other in the churchyard, complain in an alehouse about their parish priest, or even tear down their landlords' fences, often justifying their actions with the new language of evangelical reform. This is not to say, of course, that these people became Protestants. But they did experience, internalise and contribute to a process of religious change that was not done *to* them, but rather was done *with* them in a dynamic process of engagement between government and people.

In the introduction to this book, I suggested that the archetypal conversion narratives of St Paul and St Augustine have provided influential models for analyses of the English Reformation, leading to inevitable confusion as historians have reduced complex cultural processes to debates over the success or failure of impossibly totalising revolutionary agendas. This book as a whole has suggested that other, more subtle models are available that might allow us to analyse the Reformation without remaining trapped forever within the interpretive categories and theological assumptions of its protagonists. So now, in conclusion, I want to borrow a very different literary image from the western canon that might serve in place of Paul and Augustine to represent the more ambivalent and contested model of change put forward here. In his *Portrait of the Artist as a Young Man*, James Joyce's alter ego Stephen Dedalus famously described his ambition to 'forge in the smithy of my soul the uncreated conscience of my race'.[8] The word 'forge' in this context was a typically Joycean pun: to create a conscience was necessarily to falsify, to make out of the world's corrupt and carnal matter that spark within the human soul that should be pure, intrinsic and uncreated. It is exactly this uneasy relationship between the internal experience of belief and the external environment in which beliefs are shaped and performed that this book has explored. Without ever denying that some English people may indeed have experienced the Reformation through the lens of a pre-existing and immaculate conscience, I have argued that in Tudor England most people 'forged' new consciences to navigate the unprecedented circumstances in which they found themselves. Their beliefs, like those of Stephen Dedalus, could be simultaneously conscientious and constructed, since they necessarily responded to new circumstances that were not assimilable to their prior selves. To a remarkable degree, as we have seen, people's shifting consciences

---

[8] James Joyce, *A Portrait of the Artist as a Young Man* (New York, 1976), p. 253.

could be made to incorporate theological novelties, but that does not mean that they necessarily did so. There had to be points of contact – sometimes spiritual but often relentlessly mundane – where those novelties bonded and resonated with pre-existing aspirations and experiences, creating the basis for action. This book has argued that it is only by exploring these locations – in other words by exploring popular politics – that we can begin to understand the English Reformation.

BIBLIOGRAPHY

MANUSCRIPT SOURCES

PUBLIC RECORD OFFICE, LONDON

C 1   Court of Chancery: Six Clerks' Office: Early Proceedings, Richard II to Philip and Mary
C 115   Chancery: Master Harvey's Exhibits: Duchess of Norfolk's Deeds
DL 1   Duchy of Lancaster: Court of Duchy Chamber: Pleadings
DL 42   Duchy of Lancaster: Cartularies, Enrolments, Surveys, and other Miscellaneous Books
DL 44   Duchy of Lancaster: Special Commissions and Returns
E 36   Exchequer: Treasury of the Receipt: Miscellaneous Books
E 117   Exchequer: Church Goods Inventories and Miscellanea
E 134   Exchequer: King's Remembrancer: Depositions Taken by Commission
E 178   Exchequer: King's Remembrancer: Special Commissions of Inquiry
E 179   Exchequer: King's Remembrancer: Particular of Accounts and Other Records Relating to Lay and Clerical Taxation
E 301   Court of Augmentations: Certificates of Colleges, Chantries and Similar Foundations
E 314   Court of Augmentations and Court of General Surveyors: Miscellanea
E 315   Court of Augmentations and Predecessors and Successors: Miscellaneous Books
E 321   Court of Augmentations and Court of General Surveyors: Legal Proceedings
E 323   Court of Augmentations: Treasurers' Accounts
KB 9   King's Bench: Crown Side: Indictment Files, Oyer and Terminer Files, and Informations Files
PROB 11 Prerogative Court of Canterbury and related Probate Jurisdictions: Will Registers
REQ 2   Court of Requests: Pleadings
SC 2   Special Collections: Court Rolls
SP 1   State Papers, Henry VIII: General Series
SP 2   State Papers, Henry VIII: Folios
SP 5   Exchequer: King's Remembrancer: Miscellanea relating to the Dissolution of the Monasteries and to the General Surveyors (formerly State Papers, Henry VIII: Suppression Papers)
SP 6   Theological Tracts: Henry VIII
SP 10   Secretaries of State: State Papers Domestic, Edward VI

STAC 2   Court of Star Chamber: Proceedings, Henry VIII
STAC 3   Court of Star Chamber: Proceedings, Edward VI
STAC 4   Court of Star Chamber: Proceedings, Philip and Mary
STAC 10   Star Chamber Miscellanea

BRITISH LIBRARY, LONDON

Additional MSS
Cotton MSS
  Caligula
  Cleopatra
  Titus
  Vespasian
Egerton MSS
Harleian MSS
Lansdowne MSS
Royal MSS
Stowe MSS

BODLEIAN LIBRARY, OXFORD

Tanner MSS
Hearne's Diaries MSS
Rawlinson MSS

CAMBRIDGE UNIVERSITY LIBRARY

EDR D2/4

DR. WILLIAMS LIBRARY, LONDON

Morice MS 31L/3

GLOUCESTERSHIRE RECORD OFFICE, GLOUCESTER

Wills
GDR 2
GDR 4
GDR 6
GDR D1/177

OXFORDSHIRE ARCHIVES, OXFORD

MS Oxf. Dioc. Papers

LICHFIELD RECORD OFFICE, LICHFIELD

B/A/1/12

LINCOLNSHIRE ARCHIVE OFFICE, LINCOLN
Episcopal Register XX

PARKER LIBRARY, CORPUS CHRISTI COLLEGE, CAMBRIDGE
MS 102
MS 128

SHAKESPEARE BIRTHPLACE TRUST RECORD OFFICE,
STRATFORD-UPON-AVON
MS DR 18/31/5

WORCESTERSHIRE RECORD OFFICE, WORCESTER
MS 802 BA 2764

PRINTED PRIMARY SOURCES

Acts of the Privy Council of England. Ed. J. R. Dasent. 32 vols. London, 1890–1907.
Aquinas, Thomas. *Summa Theologiae*. General Editor Thomas Gilby. 61 vols. Cambridge, 1964–1981.
Augustine, Saint. *St. Augustine's Confessions*. Ed. W. H. D. Rouse. 2 vols. Cambridge, Mass., 1912.
Bale, John. *A Mysterye of Inyquyte Contayned within the Heretycall Genealogye of Ponce Pantolabus*. London, 1545.
Ballads from Manuscripts. Ed. F. J. Furnivall. 2 vols. London, 1868–73.
Bunyan, John. *The Pilgrim's Progress*. Ed. Roger Sharrock. London, 1965.
Calendar of Letters, Despatches, and State Papers, Relating to the Negotiation between England and Spain. Ed. Martin A. S. Hume *et al*. 13 vols. London, 1862–1954.
Calendar of Patent Rolls Preserved in the Public Record Office. Edward VI. 6 vols. London, 1924–9.
Calendar of Somerset Chantry Grants, 1548–1603. Ed. G. H. Woodward. Somerset Record Society, vol. 77. Taunton, 1982.
Calendar of the Manuscripts of the Marquis of Bath, Preserved at Longleat, Wiltshire, 5 vols., Historical Manuscripts Commission. London, 1904–80.
Cooper, Thomas. *Bibliotheca Eliotae*. London, 1548.
Cranmer, Thomas. *The Remains of Thomas Cranmer, Archbishop of Canterbury*. Ed. Henry Jenkyns. 4 vols. Oxford, 1833.
The Works of Thomas Cranmer. Ed. J. E. Cox. 2 vols. Cambridge, 1846.
Crowley, Robert. *The Select Works of Robert Crowley*. Ed. J. M. Cowper. EETS, extra series, vol. 15. London, 1882.
Derby, Edward. *Correspondence of Edward, Third Earl of Derby*. Ed. T. N. Toller. Chetham Society, new series vol. 19. Manchester, 1890.
A Discourse of the Commonweal of the Realm of England. Ed. Mary Dewar. Charlottesville, 1969.
Documents of the English Reformation. Ed. Gerald Bray. Minneapolis, 1994.

The Edwardian Inventories for Huntingdonshire. Ed. S. C. Lomas. Alcuin Club Collections vol. 7. London, 1906.

Elyot, Thomas. *The Governour.* Ed. Foster Watson. London, 1907.

Erasmus, Desiderius. 'The Paraclesis'. In *Desiderius Erasmus: Christian Humanism and the Reformation.* Ed. John C. Olin. New York, 1965.

'Extracts from Original Documents Illustrating the Progress of the Reformation in Kent'. Ed. C. E. Woodruff. *Archaeologia Cantiana*, 31 (1915), 92–120.

Faculty Office Registers 1534–1549. Ed. D. S. Chambers. Oxford, 1966.

The First and Second Prayer Books of Edward VI. Ed. E. C. Ratcliff. London, 1910.

Foxe, John. *The Acts and Monuments of John Foxe.* Eds. G. Townshend and S. R. Cattley. 8 vols. London, 1837–41.

  Actes and Monuments. London, 1563.

Gardiner, Stephen. *The Letters of Stephen Gardiner.* Ed. James A. Muller. Westport, Conn., 1970.

  Obedience in Church and State: Three Political Tracts by Stephen Gardiner. Ed. Pierre Janelle. New York, 1968.

The Great Red Book of Bristol. Ed. E. W. W. Veale. Bristol Record Society, vol. 18. Bristol, 1953.

Hall, Edward. *The Triumphant Reigne of Kyng Henry the VIII.* Ed. C. Whibley. 2 vols. London, 1904.

  The Union of the Two Noble and Illustrate Famelies of Lancastre & Yorke. London, 1548.

Henry VIII. *Answere Made by the Kynges Hyghnes to Petitions of the Rebelles in Yorkeshire.* London, 1536.

  Answere to the Petitions of the Traytors and Rebelles in Lyncolnshyre. London, 1536.

Holme, Wilfrid. *The Fall and Evill Success of Rebellion.* London, 1572.

Hooper, John. *A Declaration of the Ten Holy Commaundementes of Allmygthye God.* Zurich, 1549.

The Institution of a Christen Man. London, 1537.

'Inventories of Church Goods, 6th Edw. VI'. Ed. H. W. King. *Transactions of the Essex Archaeological Society*, 5 (1873), 219–42.

'Inventories of Parish Church Goods in Kent, A.D. 1552'. Ed. M. E. C. Walcott *et al.* *Archaeologia Cantiana*, 8 (1872), 74–163.

Inventory of Furniture and Ornaments Remaining in All the Parish Churches of Hertfordshire in the Last Year of the Reign of King Edward the Sixth. Ed. J. E. Cussans. Oxford, 1873.

Joyce, James. *A Portrait of the Artist as a Young Man.* New York, 1976.

Lambarde, William. *A Perambulation of Kent: Conteining the description, Hystorie, and Customes of the Shyre.* London, 1576.

Latimer, Hugh. *The Works of Hugh Latimer, Sometime Bishop of Worcester, Martyr, 1555.* Ed. G. E. Corrie. 2 vols. Cambridge, 1844–5.

Latymer, William. 'William Latymer's Cronickille of Anne Boleyn'. Ed. Maria Dowling. Camden Society, 4th series vol. 39. London, 1990.

Letters and Papers, Foreign and Domestic, of the Reign of Henry VIII, 1509–47. Ed. J. S. Brewer *et al.* 21 vols. and 2 vols. addenda. London, 1862–1932.

Letters of the Fifteenth and Sixteenth Centuries, from the Archives of Southampton. Ed. R. C. Anderson. Southampton, 1921.

Lever, Thomas. *Sermons.* Ed. Edward Arber. London, 1871.

The Lisle Letters. Ed. Muriel St. Clare Byrne. 6 vols. Chicago, 1981.

A Little Treatise of Divers Miracles shown for the Portion of Christ's Blood in Hayles. N.p., n.d.

Matthewe, Symon. *A Sermon Made in the Cathedrall Churche of Saynt Paule at London, the XXVII. Day of June, Anno. 1535. by Symon Matthewe.* London, 1535.

More, Thomas. *The Correspondence of Sir Thomas More.* Ed. Elizabeth F. Rogers. Princeton, 1947.

    A dyaloge of syr Thomas More knyghte. London, 1529.

    The Supplycacyon of Soulys. London, 1529.

Morison, Richard. *Apomaxis Calumniarum Convitiorumque.* London, 1537.

    Humanist Scholarship and Public Order: Two Tracts against the Pilgrimage of Grace by Sir Richard Morison. Ed. D. S. Berkowitz. Washington, 1984.

Narratives of the Days of the Reformation, Chiefly from the Manuscripts of John Foxe the Martyrologist. Ed. J. G. Nichols. Camden Society, vol. 77. Westminster, 1859.

Nucius, Nicander. *The Second Book of the Travels of Nicander Nucius, of Corcyra.* Ed. J. A. Cramer. Camden Society, vol. 17. London, 1841.

Original Letters Illustrative of English History. Ed. Henry Ellis. 11 vols. in 3 series. London, 1824–46.

'The Pilgrimage of Grace and Aske's Examination'. Ed. Mary Bateson. *EHR*, 5 (1890), 330–48 and 550–78.

A Plaine and Godlye Treatise Concernynge the Masse. London, 1555.

Pole, Reginald. *Pole's Defense of the Unity of the Church.* Ed. Joseph E. Dwyer. Westminster, Md., 1965.

    Reginadi Poli Cardinalis Britanni, ad Henricum Octauum Britanniae Regem, pro Ecclesiasticae Unitatis Defensione. Rome, 1536.

Pyers Plowmans exhortation unto the lordes, knightes and burgoysses of the parlyamenthouse. N.p., n.d.

Records of the Reformation. Ed. Nicholas Pocock. 2 vols. Oxford, 1870.

Redman, John. *A Compendious Treatise Called the Complaint of Grace.* London, 1556.

The Registers of Thomas Wolsey . . . John Clerke . . . William Knyght . . . and Gilbert Bourne. Ed. Henry Maxwell-Lyte. Somerset Record Society vol. 55. Frome, 1940.

Ridley, Lancelot. *A Commentary in Englyshe upon Sayncte Paules Epystle to the Ephesyans.* London, 1540.

The Romance and Prophecies of Thomas of Erceldoune. Ed. James A. H. Murray. *EETS* vol. 61. London, 1875.

'The Sermon Against the Holy Maid of Kent and Her Adherents, Delivered at Paul's Cross, November the 23rd, 1533, and at Canterbury, December the 7th'. Ed. L. E. Whatmore. *EHR*, 58 (1943), 463–75.

Smith, Richard. *A Confutation of a Certen Booke, Called a Defence of the True and Catholike Doctrine of the Sacrament.* Paris, 1550.

Star Chamber Suits of John and Thomas Warneford. Ed. F. E. Warneford. Wiltshire Record Society, vol. 48. Trowbridge, 1993.

Starkey, Thomas. *Thomas Starkey's An Exhortation to the People Instructing Them to Unity and Obedience: A Critical Edition.* Ed. James M. Pictor. New York, 1988.

State Papers Published under the Authority of His Majesty's Commission, King Henry VIII. 11 vols. London, 1830–52.

The Statutes of the Realm. Ed. A. Luders *et al.* 11 vols. London, 1810–28.

Three Chapters of Letters Relating to the Suppression of Monasteries. Edited from the Originals in the British Museum. Ed. Thomas Wright. Camden Society, 1st series vol. 26. London, 1843.

Troubles Connected with the Prayer Book of 1549. Ed. Nicholas Pocock. Camden Society, new series, vol. 37. Westminster, 1884.

Tudor Royal Proclamations. Eds. Paul L. Hughes and James F. Larkin. 3 vols. New Haven, 1964–9.

Tudor Treatises. Ed. A. G. Dickens. Yorkshire Archaeological Record Series vol. 125. Wakefield, 1959.

Tyndale, William. *Doctrinal Treatises and Introductions to Different Portions of the Holy Scriptures by William Tyndale, Martyr, 1536.* Ed. Henry Walker. Parker Society vol. 42. Cambridge, 1848.

Valor Ecclesiasticus Temp. Henr. VIII. Ed. John Caley. 6 vols. London, 1810–25.

Venaeus, John. *A Notable Oration, Made by John Venaeus, a Parisien, in the Defence of the Sacrament of the Aultare.* London, 1554.

Wriothesley, Charles. *A Chronicle of England during the Reigns of the Tudors, A.D. 1485–1559. By Charles Wriothesley, Windsor Herald.* Ed. W. D. Hamilton. 2 vols. Camden Society, new series vols. 11 and 20. New York, 1965.

York Civic Records Vol. IV. Ed. Angelo Raine. Yorkshire Archaeological Society, Record Series vol. 108. Wakefield, 1945.

SECONDARY SOURCES

Aers, David. 'Altars of Power: Reflections on Eamon Duffy's *The Stripping of the Altars: Traditional Religion in England 1400–1580*'. *Literature and History*, third series, 3 (1994), 90–105.

Alsop, J. D. 'Latimer, the "Commonwealth of Kent" and the 1549 Rebellions'. *HJ*, 28 (1985), 379–83.

'Religious Preambles in Early Modern English Wills as Formulae'. *JEH*, 40 (1989), 19–27.

Arendt, Hannah. *Eichmann in Jerusalem: A Report on the Banality of Evil.* New York, 1963.

Aston, Margaret. *England's Iconoclasts: Volume I, Laws Against Images.* Oxford, 1988.

Atkyns, R. *The Ancient and Present State of Gloucestershire.* 2nd edn. London, 1768.

Baddeley, St Clair. 'The Holy Blood of Hayles'. *TBGAS*, 23 (1900), 276–84.

Baker, David Weil. *Divulging Utopia: Radical Humanism in Sixteenth-Century England.* Amherst, Mass., 1999.

Baskerville, G. 'The Dispossessed Religious of Gloucestershire'. *TBGAS*, 49 (1927), 63–122.

Beer, Barrett L. *Rebellion and Riot: Popular Disorder in England during the Reign of Edward VI.* Kent, Ohio, 1982.

Benedict, Philip. *Rouen During the Wars of Religion.* Cambridge, 1981.

'The St. Bartholomew's Day Massacre in the Provinces'. *HJ*, 21 (1978), 205–25.

Bennett, Rab. *Under the Shadow of the Swastika: The Moral Dilemmas of Resistance and Collaboration in Hitler's Europe.* Basingstoke, 1999.

Bernard, George. 'The Church of England c. 1529–c. 1642'. *History*, 75 (1990), 183–206.

'The Making of Religious Policy, 1533–1546: Henry VIII and the Search for the Middle Way'. *HJ*, 41 (1998), 321–49.

Betteridge, Thomas. *Tudor Histories of the English Reformations, 1530–83*. Aldershot, 1999.

Bindoff, S. T. *Ket's Rebellion 1549*. London, 1949.

Bindoff, S. T., ed. *The House of Commons, 1509–1558*. 3 vols. London, 1982.

Blench, J. W. *Preaching in England in the Late Fifteenth and Sixteenth Centuries: A Study of English Sermons, 1450–c. 1600*. Oxford, 1964.

Blickle, Peter. *The Revolution of 1525: The German Peasants' War from a New Perspective*. Trans. Thomas Brady and H. C. Erik Midelfort. Baltimore, 1981.

Bossy, John. *The English Catholic Community 1570–1850*. London, 1975.

Bowker, Margaret. *The Henrician Reformation: The Diocese of Lincoln Under John Longland 1521–1547*. Cambridge, 1981.

'Lincolnshire 1536: Heresy, Schism or Religious Discontent?' In Derek Baker, ed. *Schism, Heresy and Religious Protest*. Studies in Church History vol. 9. Cambridge, 1972.

Braddick, Michael. *State Formation in Early Modern England c. 1550–1700*. Cambridge, 2000.

Bradshaw, Christopher. 'David or Josiah? Old Testament Kings as Exemplars in Edwardian Religious Polemic'. In Bruce Gordon, ed. *Protestant History and Identity in Sixteenth-Century Europe*. 2 vols. Aldershot, 1996.

Brake, Wayne Te. *Shaping History: Ordinary People in European Politics, 1500–1700*. Berkeley, 1998.

Bridgett, T. E. *Life of Blessed John Fisher*. London, 1888.

Brigden, Susan. *London and the Reformation*. Oxford, 1989.

'Youth and the Reformation'. *P&P*, 95 (1982), 37–67.

Brock, E. P. Loftus. 'On the Cistercian Abbey of Hailes'. *Journal of the British Archaeological Association*, 32 (1876), 355–62.

Brown, Andrew. *Popular Piety in Late Medieval England: The Diocese of Salisbury, 1250–1550*. Oxford, 1995.

Burgess, Clive. ' "For the Increase of Divine Service": Chantries in the Parish in Late Medieval Bristol'. *JEH*, 36 (1985), 46–65.

Burnet, Gilbert. *The History of the Reformation of the Church of England*. Ed. Nicholas Pocock. 7 vols. Oxford, 1865.

Bush, Michael. *The Government Policy of Protector Somerset*. London, 1975.

The Pilgrimage of Grace: A Study of the Rebel Armies of October 1536. Manchester, 1996.

'Captain Poverty and the Pilgrimage of Grace'. *Historical Research*, 65 (1992), 17–36.

'"Enhancements and Importunate Charges": An Analysis of the Tax Complaints of October 1536'. *Albion*, 22 (1990), 403–19.

'The Richmondshire Uprising of 1536 and the Pilgrimage of Grace'. *Northern History*, 29 (1993), 64–98.

'Tax Reform and Rebellion in Early Tudor England'. *History*, 76 (1991), 379–400.

'"Up for the Commonweal": The Significance of Tax Grievances in the English Rebellions of 1536'. *EHR*, 106 (1991), 299–318.

Bush, Michael and David Bownes. *The Defeat of the Pilgrimage of Grace: A Study of the Postpardon Revolts of December 1536 to March 1537 and their Effect*. Hull, 1999.

Bynum, Caroline Walker. *Jesus as Mother: Studies in the Spirituality of the High Middle Ages.* Berkeley, 1982.

Carlson, Eric, ed. *Religion and the English People, 1500–1640: New Voices, New Perspectives.* Kirksville, Mo., 1998.

Cheney, A. Denton. 'The Holy Maid of Kent'. *TRHS*, new series 18 (1904), 107–29.

Clark, Peter. *English Provincial Society from the Reformation to the Revolution: Religion, Politics, and Society in Kent 1500–1640.* Hassocks, 1977.

Cohn, Henry. 'Anticlericalism in the German Peasants' War 1525'. *P&P*, 83 (1979), 3–31.

Collinson, Patrick. 'From Iconoclasm to Iconophobia: The Cultural Impact of the Second English Reformation'. In Peter Marshall, ed. *The Impact of the English Reformation 1500–1640.* London, 1997.

Cornwall, Julian. *The Revolt of the Peasantry 1549.* London, 1977.

Coulton, C. G. 'Priests and People before the Reformation'. In his *Ten Medieval Studies.* 3rd edition. Cambridge, 1930.

Crawford, Patricia. *Women and Religion in England 1500–1720.* London, 1993.

Crew, Phyllis Mack. *Calvinist Preaching and Iconoclasm in the Netherlands 1544–1569.* Cambridge, 1978.

Davies, C. S. L. 'The Pilgrimage of Grace Reconsidered'. *P&P*, 41 (1968), 54–75.
'Popular Religion and the Pilgrimage of Grace.' In A. Fletcher and J. Stevenson, eds. *Order and Disorder in Early Modern England.* Cambridge, 1985.

Davies, J. G. 'Pilgrimage and Crusade Literature'. In Barbara N. Sargent-Baur, ed. *Journeys Toward God: Pilgrimage and Crusade.* Kalamazoo, Mich., 1992.

Davis, N. Z. 'The Rites of Violence: Religious Riot in Sixteenth-Century France'. *P&P*, 59 (1973), 51–91.

Delumeau, Jean. *Catholicism Between Luther and Voltaire: A New View of the Counter-Reformation.* London, 1977.

Desan, Suzanne. 'Crowds, Community, and Ritual in the Work of E. P. Thompson and Natalie Davis'. In Lynn Hunt, ed. *The New Cultural History.* Berkeley, 1989.

Devereux, E. J. 'Elizabeth Barton and Tudor Censorship'. *Bulletin of the John Rylands Library,* 49 (1966–67), 91–106.

Dickens, A. G. *The English Reformation.* 2nd edition. London, 1989.
Late Monasticism and the Reformation. London, 1994.
Lollards and Protestants in the Diocese of York. London, 1982.
Reformation Studies. London, 1982.
'A Municipal Dissolution of Chantries at York, 1536'. *Yorkshire Archaeological Journal,* 36 (1945), 164–74.
'Secular and Religious Motivation in the Pilgrimage of Grace'. In G. J. Cumings, ed. *The Province of York.* Studies in Church History vol. 4. Leiden, 1967.
'Sedition and Conspiracy in Yorkshire During the Later Years of Henry VIII'. *Yorkshire Archeological Journal,* 34 (1939), 379–98.
'The Shape of Anti-Clericalism and the English Reformation'. In E. I. Kouri and T. Scott, eds. *Politics and Society in Reformation Europe.* Basingstoke, 1987.
'Some Popular Reactions to the Edwardian Reformation in Yorkshire'. *Yorkshire Archaeological Journal,* 34 (1939), 151–69.

Diefendorf, Barbara. *Beneath the Cross: Catholics and Huguenots in Sixteenth-Century Paris.* New York, 1991.

Dodds, Madeleine Hope. 'Political Prophecies in the Reign of Henry VIII'. *Modern Language Review,* 11 (1916), 276–84.

Dodds, Madeleine Hope and Ruth Dodds. *The Pilgrimage of Grace, 1536–7, and the Exeter Conspiracy, 1538.* 2 vols. Cambridge, 1915.

Duffy, Eamon. *The Stripping of the Altars: Traditional Religion in England 1400–1580.* New Haven, Conn., 1992.

The Voices of Morebath: Reformation and Rebellion in an English Village. New Haven, Conn., 2001.

'The Long Reformation'. In Nicholas Tyacke, ed. *England's Long Reformation 1500–1800.* London, 1998.

Duke, Alastair. 'Building Heaven in Hell's Despite: The Early History of the Reformation in the Towns of the Low Countries'. In his *Reformation and Revolt in the Low Countries.* London, 1990.

Dykema, Peter and Heiko Oberman, eds. *Anticlericalism in Late Medieval and Early Modern Europe.* Leiden, 1993.

Elton, G. R. 'The Good Duke'. In vol. 1 of his *Studies in Tudor and Stuart Politics and Government.* 4 vols. Cambridge, 1974–92.

Policy and Police: The Enforcement of the Reformation in the Age of Thomas Cromwell. Cambridge, 1972.

'Politics and the Pilgrimage of Grace'. In vol. 3 of his *Studies in Tudor and Stuart Politics and Government.* 4 vols. Cambridge, 1974–92.

Reform and Reformation: England 1509–1558. London, 1977.

Reform and Renewal: Thomas Cromwell and the Common Weal. Cambridge, 1973.

Star Chamber Stories. London, 1974.

'Tudor Government: The Points of Contact'. In vol. 3 of his *Studies in Tudor and Stuart Politics and Government.* 4 vols. Cambridge, 1974–92.

'Reformation and the "Commonwealth-Men" of Edward VI's Reign'. In Peter Clark, Alan G. R. Smith and Nicholas Tyacke, eds. *The English Commonwealth 1547–1640: Essays in Politics and Society.* Leicester, 1979.

Febvre, Lucien. 'Une Question Mal Posée: Les Origines de la Réforme Française et le Problème Général des Causes de la Réforme'. *Revue historique*, 161 (1929), 1–73.

Ferrell, Lori Anne and Peter McCullough, eds. *The English Sermon Revised: Religion, Literature and History 1600–1750.* Manchester, 2000.

Fideler, Paul and Thomas Mayer, eds. *Political Thought and the Tudor Commonwealth: Deep Structure, Discourse, and Disguise.* London, 1992.

Fitzpatrick, Sheila. *Everyday Stalinism: Ordinary Life in Extraordinary Times: Soviet Russia in the 1930s.* Oxford, 1999.

Fitzpatrick, Sheila and Robert Gellately, eds. *Accusatory Practices: Denunciation in Modern European History, 1789–1989.* Chicago, 1997.

Fletcher, Anthony and Diarmaid MacCulloch. *Tudor Rebellions.* 4th edition. London, 1997.

Fox, Adam. 'Ballads, Libels and Popular Ridicule in Jacobean England'. *P&P*, 145 (1994), 47–83.

'Custom, Memory, and the Authority of Writing'. In Paul Griffiths, eds. *The Experience of Authority in Early Modern England.* London, 1996.

Fox, Alistair. 'Prophecies and Politics in the Reign of Henry VIII'. In Alistair Fox and John Guy, eds. *Reassessing the Henrician Age: Humanism, Politics and Reform 1500–1550.* Oxford, 1986.

French, Katherine, L., Gary G. Gibbs and Beat A. Kümin, eds. *The Parish in English Life, 1400–1600.* Manchester, 1997.

Froude, J. A. *History of England: From the Fall of Wolsey to the Death of Elizabeth.* 12 vols. New York, 1873.

Gasquet, F. A. *Henry VIII and the English Monasteries.* London, 1906.

Green, Ian. *The Christian's ABC: Catechism and Catechizing in England c. 1530–1740.* Oxford, 1996.

Print and Protestantism in Early Modern England. Oxford, 2000.

Greenblatt, Stephen. *Hamlet in Purgatory.* Princeton, 2001.

Gregory, Jeremy. 'The Making of a Protestant Nation: "Success" and "Failure" in England's Long Reformation'. In Nicholas Tyacke, ed. *England's Long Reformation 1500–1800.* London, 1998.

Gross, Jan. 'A Note on the Nature of Soviet Totalitarianism'. *Soviet Studies,* 34 (1982), 367–76.

Gunn, Steven. *Charles Brandon, Duke of Suffolk, c. 1484–1545.* Oxford, 1988.

'Peers, Commons, and Gentry in the Lincolnshire Revolt of 1536'. *P&P,* 123 (1989), 52–79.

Haigh, Christopher. *English Reformations: Religion, Politics, and Society under the Tudors.* Oxford, 1993.

The Last Days of the Lancashire Monasteries and the Pilgrimage of Grace. Chetham Society, 3rd series vol. 17. Manchester, 1969.

Reformation and Resistance in Tudor Lancashire. London, 1975.

'Anticlericalism and the English Reformation'. In Christopher Haigh, ed. *The English Reformation Revised.* Cambridge, 1987.

'The Church of England, the Catholics, and the People'. In Christopher Haigh, ed. *The Reign of Elizabeth I.* Basingstoke, 1984.

'The Continuity of Catholicism in the English Reformation.' In Christopher Haigh, ed. *The English Reformation Revised.* Cambridge, 1987.

'The Fall of a Church or the Rise of a Sect? Post-Reformation Catholicism in England'. *HJ,* 21 (1978), 182–6.

'From Monopoly to Minority: Catholicism in Early Modern England'. *TRHS,* fifth series 31 (1981), 129–47.

'The Recent Historiography of the English Reformation'. In Christopher Haigh, ed. *The English Reformation Revised.* Cambridge, 1987.

Harris, Tim. *London Crowds in the Reign of Charles II: Propaganda and Politics from the Restoration until the Exclusion Crisis.* Cambridge, 1987.

Harris, Tim, ed. *The Politics of the Excluded, c.1500–1850.* Basingstoke, 2001.

Harrison, S. M. *The Pilgrimage of Grace and the Lake Counties, 1536–7.* London, 1981.

Harvey, I. M. W. *Jack Cade's Rebellion of 1450.* Oxford, 1991.

'Was there Popular Politics in Fifteenth-Century England?' In R. H. Britnell and A. J. Pollard, eds. *The McFarlane Legacy: Studies in Late Medieval Politics and Society.* New York, 1995.

Havel, Václav. 'The Power of the Powerless'. In his *Open Letters: Selected Writings 1965–1990.* Ed. Paul Wilson. New York, 1992.

Hazeley, William. 'The Abbey of St. Mary, Hayles'. *TBGAS,* 22 (1899), 257–71.

Herrup, Cynthia. *The Common Peace: Participation and the Criminal Law in Seventeenth-Century England.* Cambridge, 1987.

Hindle, Steve. *The State and Social Change in Early Modern England, c. 1550–1640.* Basingstoke, 2000.

Hoffman, Philip. *Church and Community in the Diocese of Lyon, 1500–1789.* New Haven, 1984.

Hogben, Brian. 'Preaching and the Reformation in Henrician Kent'. *Archæologia Cantiana*, 101 (1984), 169–85.

Holmes, Clive. 'Drainers and Fenmen: The Problem of Popular Political Consciousness in the Seventeenth Century'. In A. Fletcher and J. Stevenson, eds. *Order and Disorder in Early Modern England*. Cambridge, 1985.

Hope, W. H. St. John. 'Notes on the Holy Blood of Hayles'. *Archaeological Journal*, 68 (1911), 166–72.

House, Seymour Baker. 'Literature, Drama and Politics'. In Diarmaid MacCulloch, ed. *The Reign of Henry VIII: Politics, Policy and Piety*. New York, 1995.

Hoyle, Richard. *The Pilgrimage of Grace and the Politics of the 1530s*. Oxford, 2001.

'The Origins of the Dissolution of the Monasteries'. *HJ*, 38 (1995), 275–305.

'Thomas Master's Narrative of the Pilgrimage of Grace'. *Northern History*, 21 (1985), 53–79.

'War and Public Finance'. In Diarmaid MacCulloch, ed. *The Reign of Henry VIII: Politics, Policy and Piety*. New York, 1995.

Huber, Elaine C. *Women and the Authority of Inspiration: A Reexamination of Two Prophetic Movements from a Contemporary Feminist Perspective*. Lanham, Md., 1985.

Hutton, Ronald. *The Rise and Fall of Merry England: The Ritual Year, 1400–1700*. Oxford, 1994.

'The Local Impact of the Tudor Reformations'. In Christopher Haigh, ed. *The English Reformation Revised*. Cambridge, 1987.

Ives, E. W. *Anne Boleyn*. Oxford, 1986.

James, Mervyn. 'Obedience and Dissent in Henrician England: The Lincolnshire Rebellion, 1536'. *P&P*, 48 (1970), 3–78.

Jansen, Sharon L. *Dangerous Talk and Strange Behavior: Women and Popular Resistance to the Reforms of Henry VIII*. New York, 1996.

Political Protest and Prophecy under Henry VIII. Woodbridge, 1991.

Jansen Jaech, Sharon L. 'The "Prophisies of Rymour, Beid, Marlyng": Henry VIII and a Sixteenth-Century Political Prophecy'. *SCJ*, 16 (1985), 291–9.

Jones, Whitney. *The Tudor Commonwealth, 1529–1559*. London, 1970.

Jordan, W. K. *Edward VI: The Threshold of Power. The Dominance of the Duke of Northumberland*. London, 1970.

Edward VI: The Young King. The Protectorship of the Duke of Somerset. London, 1968.

Justice, Steven. *Writing and Rebellion: England in 1381*. Berkeley, 1994.

Kamen, Henry. *The Phoenix and the Flame: Catalonia and the Counter-Reformation*. New Haven, Conn., 1993.

Karant-Nunn, Susan. *Zwickau in Transition, 1500–1547: The Reformation as an Agent of Change*. Columbus, Ohio, 1987.

Kaufman, P. I. 'John Colet's Opus de Sacramentis and Clerical Anticlericalism: The Limitations of "Ordinary Wayes"'. *JBS*, 22 (1982), 1–22.

King, John N. *English Reformation Literature: The Tudor Origins of the Protestant Tradition*. Princeton, 1982.

Kishlansky, Mark. *Parliamentary Selection: Social and Political Choice in Early Modern England*. Cambridge, 1986.

Kitching, C. J. 'The Chantries of the East Riding of Yorkshire at the Dissolution'. *Yorkshire Archaeological Journal*, 44 (1972), 178–94.

'The Quest for Concealed Lands in the Reign of Elizabeth I'. *TRHS*, 24 (1974), 63–78.

Kleinberg, Aviad M. *Prophets in Their Own Country: Living Saints and the Making of Sainthood in the Later Middle Ages*. Chicago, 1992.

Knowles, David. *The Religious Orders in England*. 3 vols. Cambridge, 1950–9.

Knowles, W. H. 'Teddington Church, Worcestershire, in Which Are Structural Fragments from Hayles Abbey'. *TBGAS*, 52 (1930), 93–101.

Kotkin, Steven. *Magnetic Mountain: Stalinism as a Civilization*. Berkeley, 1995.

Kreider, Alan. *English Chantries: The Road to Dissolution*. Cambridge, Mass., 1979.

Kümin, Beat. *The Shaping of a Community: The Rise and Reformation of the English Parish c. 1400–1560*. Aldershot, 1996.

Lake, Peter. 'Deeds against Nature: Cheap Print, Protestantism, and Murder in Early Seventeenth-Century England'. In Kevin Sharpe and Peter Lake, eds. *Culture and Politics in Early Stuart England*. Stanford, 1993.

Le Goff, Jacques. *The Birth of Purgatory*. Trans. Arthur Goldhammer. Chicago, 1984.

Your Money or Your Life: Economy and Religion in the Middle Ages. Trans. P. Ranum. New York, 1990.

Lehmberg, Stanford. *The Reformation Parliament 1529–1536*. Cambridge, 1970.

Lingard, John. *A History of England, from the First Invasion by the Romans*. 2nd edition. 14 vols. London, 1823–31.

Litzenberger, Caroline. *The English Reformation and the Laity: Gloucestershire, 1540–1580*. Cambridge, 1997.

Longstaffe, W. H. D. 'The Connection of Scotland with the Pilgrimage of Grace'. *Archaeological Journal*, 14 (1857), 331–44.

McClendon, Muriel. *The Quiet Reformation: Magistrates and the Emergence of Protestantism in Tudor Norwich*. Stanford, 1999.

'"Against God's Word": Government, Religion and the Crisis of Authority in Early Reformation Norwich'. *SCJ*, 25 (1994), 353–69.

'A Moveable Feast: Saint George's Day Celebrations and Religious Change in Early Modern England'. *JBS*, 38 (1999), 1–27.

MacCulloch, Diarmaid. *The Boy King: Edward VI and the Protestant Reformation*. New York, 2001.

The Later Reformation in England 1547–1603. Basingstoke, 1990.

Suffolk and the Tudors: Politics and Religion in an English County 1500–1600. Oxford, 1986.

Thomas Cranmer: A Life. New Haven, Conn., 1996.

'Kett's Rebellion in Context'. *P&P*, 84 (1979), 36–59.

Macek, Ellen. *The Loyal Opposition: Tudor Traditionalist Polemics, 1535–1558*. New York, 1996.

McGrath, Alister. *The Intellectual Origins of the European Reformation*. Oxford, 1987.

McKee, J. R. *Dame Elizabeth Barton O.S.B. The Holy Maid of Kent*. London, 1925.

Mackie, J. D. *The Earlier Tudors 1485–1558*. Oxford, 1994.

Maltby, Judith. *Prayer Book and People in Elizabethan and Early Stuart England*. Cambridge, 1998.

Marsh, Christopher. *Popular Religion in Sixteenth Century England*. New York, 1998.

'In the Name of God? Will-Making and Faith in early Modern England.' In G. H. Martin and Peter Spufford, eds. *The Records of the Nation*. Woodbridge, 1990.

Marshall, Peter. *The Catholic Priesthood and the English Reformation*. Oxford, 1994.

'Mumpsimus and Sumpsimus: The Intellectual Origins of a Henrician *Bon Mot*'. *JEH*, 52 (2001), 512–20.

'Papist as Heretic: The Burning of John Forest, 1538'. *HJ*, 41 (1998), 351–74.

'The Rood of Boxley, the Blood of Hailes and the Defence of the Henrician Church'. *JEH*, 46 (October 1995), 689–96.

Mayer, Thomas. *Cardinal Pole in European Context: A Via Media in the Reformation*. Aldershot, 2000.

Reginald Pole: Prince and Prophet. Cambridge, 2000.

Moreau, Jean-Pierre. *Rome ou l'Angleterre? Les Reactions Politiques des Catholiques Anglais au Moment du Schisme, 1529–1553*. Paris, 1984.

Neame, Alan. *The Holy Maid of Kent: the Life of Elizabeth Barton, 1506–1534*. London, 1971.

Niccoli, Ottavia. *Prophecy and People in Renaissance Italy*. Trans. Lydia G. Cochrane. Princeton, 1990.

Ogier, D. M. *Reformation and Society in Guernsey*. Woodbridge, 1996.

O'Grady, Paul. *Henry VIII and the Conforming Catholics*. Collegeville, Minn., 1990.

Orme, Nicholas. 'The Dissolution of the Chantries in Devon, 1546–8'. *Report and Transactions of the Devonshire Association*, 3 (1979), 75–123.

Ozment, Steven. *The Age of Reform 1250–1550*. New Haven, 1980.

Page, William, C. R. Elrington and N. M. Helbert, eds. *A History of the County of Gloucester*. The Victoria History of the Counties of England. 11 vols. London, 1907– .

Palliser, D. M. 'Popular Reactions to the Reformation During the Years of Uncertainty 1530–70'. In Christopher Haigh, ed. *The English Reformation Revised*. Cambridge, 1987.

Parker, Geoffrey. *The Dutch Revolt*. Ithaca, 1977.

Paxton, Robert. *Vichy France: Old Guard and New Order 1940–1944*. New York, 1972.

Pollard, A. F. *Henry VIII*. London, 1913.

Thomas Cranmer and the English Reformation, 1489–1556. New York, 1904.

Questier, Michael C. *Conversion, Politics and Religion in England, 1580–1625*. Cambridge, 1996.

Ravensdale, J. R. 'Landbeach in 1549: Kett's Rebellion in Miniature'. In Lionel Munby, ed. *East Anglian Studies*. Cambridge, 1968.

Redworth, Glyn. *In Defence of the Church Catholic: The Life of Stephen Gardiner*. Cambridge, Mass., 1990.

Reid, R. R. *The King's Council in the North*. London, 1921.

Rex, Richard. *The Theology of John Fisher*. Cambridge, 1991.

'The Crisis of Obedience: God's Word and Henry's Reformation'. *HJ*, 39 (1996), 863–94.

'The Execution of the Holy Maid of Kent'. *Historical Research*, 64 (1991), 216–20.

'The New Learning'. *JEH*, 44 (1993), 26–44.

Rosenthal, Joel. *The Purchase of Paradise: The Social Function of Aristocratic Benevolence, 1307–1485*. London, 1972.

Rose-Troup, Frances. *The Western Rebellion of 1549*. London, 1913.

Rowse, A. L. *Tudor Cornwall*. New York, 1969.

Rudé, George. *The Crowd in History: A Study of Popular Disturbances in France and England 1730–1848*. New York, 1964.

Rule, John. 'Wrecking and Coastal Plunder'. In Douglas Hay, Peter Linebaugh, John G. Rule, E. P. Thompson and Cal Winslow, eds. *Albion's Fatal Tree: Crime and Society in Eighteenth-Century England*. New York, 1975.

Russell, F. W. *Kett's Rebellion in Norfolk*. London, 1859.

Sabean, David. *Power in the Blood: Popular Culture and Village Discourse in Early Modern Germany*. Cambridge, 1984.

Scarisbrick, J. J. *Henry VIII*. Berkeley, 1968.

The Reformation and the English People. Oxford, 1984.

Schwartz, W. *Principles and Problems of Biblical Translation: Some Reformation Controversies and the Background*. Cambridge, 1955.

Scott, James. *Domination and the Arts of Resistance: Hidden Transcripts*. New Haven, Conn., 1990.

Weapons of the Weak: Everyday Forms of Peasant Resistance. New Haven, Conn., 1985.

Scribner, Robert. *Popular Culture and Popular Movements in Reformation Germany*. London, 1987.

Shagan, Ethan H. '"Popularity" and the 1549 Rebellions Revisited'. *EHR*, 115 (2000), 121–33.

'Print, Orality, and Communications in the Maid of Kent Affair'. *JEH*, 52 (2001), 21–33.

'Protector Somerset and the 1549 Rebellions: New Sources and New Perspectives'. *EHR*, 114 (1999), 34–63.

'Rumours and Popular Politics in the Reign of Henry VIII'. In Tim Harris, ed. *The Politics of the Excluded, c. 1500–1850*. Basingstoke, 2001.

Shaw, Anthony. 'The Involvement of the Religious Orders in the Northern Risings of 1536/7: Compulsion or Desire?'. *Downside Review*, 117 (1999), 89–114.

'Papal Loyalism in 1530s England'. *Downside Review*, 117 (1999), 17–40.

Skeeters, Martha. *Community and Clergy: Bristol and the Reformation, c. 1530–c. 1570*. Oxford, 1993.

Smallwood, T. M. 'The Prophecy of the Six Kings'. *Speculum*, 60 (1985), 571–92.

Soergel, Philip M. *Wondrous in His Saints: Counter-Reformation Propaganda in Bavaria*. Berkeley, 1993.

Spufford, Margaret. 'The Scribes of Villagers' Wills in the Sixteenth and Seventeenth Centuries and their Influence'. *Local Population Studies*, 7 (1971), 28–43.

Spufford, Margaret, ed. *The World of Rural Dissenters 1520–1725*. Cambridge, 1995.

Strype, John. *Ecclesiastical Memorials*. 3 vols. Oxford, 1822.

Swanson, R. N. 'Problems of the Priesthood in Pre-Reformation England'. *EHR*, 105 (1990), 845–69.

Taylor, Rupert. *The Political Prophecy in England*. New York, 1911.

Thomas, Keith. *Religion and the Decline of Magic*. New York, 1971.

Thompson, E. P. *The Making of the English Working Class*. New York, 1966.

'The Moral Economy of the English Crowd in the Eighteenth Century'. *P&P*, 50 (1971), 76–136.

Tilly, Louise. 'The Food Riot as a Form of Political Conflict in France'. *Journal of Interdisciplinary History*, 2 (1971), 23–58.

Tyacke, Nicholas. 'Introduction: Re-Thinking the "English Reformation"'. In Nicholas Tyacke, ed. *England's Long Reformation 1500–1800*. London, 1998.

Tyerman, Christopher. *England and the Crusades, 1095–1588*. Chicago, 1988.

Underdown, David. *Revel, Riot and Rebellion: Popular Politics and Culture in England, 1603–1660*. Oxford, 1985.

Vogler, Günther. 'Imperial City Nuremberg, 1524–25: The Reform Movement in Transition'. In R. Po-Chia Hsia, ed. *The German People and the Reformation*. Ithaca, N.Y., 1988.

Wabuda, Susan. 'Equivocation and Recantation During the English Reformation: The "Subtle Shadows" of Dr Edward Crome'. *JEH*, 44 (1993), 224–42.

   'The Woman with the Rock: The Controversy on Women and Bible Reading'. In Susan Wabuda and Caroline Litzenberger, eds. *Belief and Practice in Reformation England: A Tribute to Patrick Collinson from His Students*. Aldershot, 1998.

Wall, Alison. *Power and Protest in England 1525–1640*. London, 2000.

Walsham, Alexandra. *Providence in Early Modern England*. Oxford, 1999.

Walter, John. 'Grain Riots and Popular Attitudes Towards the Law: Maldon and the Crisis of 1629'. In John Brewer and John Styles, eds. *An Ungovernable People: The English and Their Law in the Seventeenth and Eighteenth Centuries*. New Brunswick, N.J., 1980.

Warnicke, Retha. *Women of the English Renaissance and Reformation*. Westport, Conn., 1983.

Watt, Diane. *Secretaries of God: Women Prophets in Late Medieval and Early Modern England*. Cambridge, 1997.

   'The Posthumous Reputation of the Holy Maid of Kent'. *Recusant History*, 23 (1996), 148–58.

   'The Prophet at Home: Elizabeth Barton and the Influence of Bridget of Sweden and Catherine of Siena'. In R. Voaden, ed. *Prophets Abroad: The Reception of Continental Holy Women in Late-Medieval England*. Cambridge, 1996.

   'Reconstructing the Word: The Political Prophecies of Elizabeth Barton (1506–1534)'. *Renaissance Quarterly*, 1 (1997), 136–63.

Whiting, Robert. *Local Responses to the English Reformation*. New York, 1998.

   '"For the Health of my Soul": Prayers for the Dead in the Tudor South-West'. *Southern History*, 5 (1983), 68–94.

   The Blind Devotion of the People: Popular Religion and the English Reformation. Cambridge, 1989.

Williams, Glanmor. 'Prophecy, Poetry, and Politics in Medieval and Tudor Wales'. In H. Hearder and H. R. Lyon, eds. *British Government and Administration: Studies Presented to S. B. Chrimes*. Cardiff, 1974.

Wooding, Lucy. *Rethinking Catholicism in Reformation England*. Oxford, 2000.

Wood-Legh, K. L. *Perpetual Chantries in Britain*. Cambridge, 1965.

Woodward, Geoffrey. *The Dissolution of the Monasteries*. London, 1966.

   'The Destruction of the Catcott Chapel at the Reformation'. *Somerset Archaeology and Natural History*, 125 (1981), 67–71.

Wrightson, Keith. 'The Politics of the Parish in Early Modern England'. In Paul Griffiths, Adam Fox and Steve Hindle, eds. *The Experience of Authority in Early Modern England*. New York, 1996.

   'Two Concepts of Order: Justices, Constables and Jurymen in Seventeenth-Century England'. In John Brewer and John Styles, eds. *An Ungovernable People: The English and Their Law in the Seventeenth and Eighteenth Centuries*. New Brunswick, N.J., 1980.

Wrightson, Keith and David Levine. *Poverty and Piety in an English Village: Terling, 1525–1700*. New York, 1979.

Youings, Joyce. *The Dissolution of the Monasteries*. London, 1971.

Zarri, Gabriella. 'Living Saints: A Typology of Female Sanctity in the Early Sixteenth Century'. Trans. Margery J. Schneider. In Daniel Bornstein and Roberto Rusconi, eds. *Women and Religion in Medieval and Renaissance Italy*. Chicago, 1996.

'Ursula and Catherine: The Marriage of Virgins in the Sixteenth Century'. Trans. Anne Jacobson Schutte. In E. Ann Matter and John Coakley, eds. *Creative Women in Medieval and Early Modern Italy: A Religious and Artistic Renaissance*. Philadelphia, 1994.

Zell, M. L. 'The Personnel of the Clergy of Kent in the Reformation Period'. *EHR*, 89 (1974), 513–33.

'The Prebendaries' Plot of 1543: A Reconsideration'. *JEH*, 27 (1976), 241–53.

'The Use of Religious Preambles as a Measure of Religious Belief in the Sixteenth Century'. *BIHR*, 50 (1977), 246–9.

UNPUBLISHED THESES

Duggan, Christopher R. 'The Advent of Political Thought Control in England: Seditious and Treasonable Speech, 1485–1547'. Ph.D. dissertation, Northwestern University, 1993.

Zell, M. L. 'Church and Gentry in Reformation Kent'. Ph.D. dissertation, University of California Los Angeles, 1974.

INDEX

abbeys, purchase of dissolved 13–14
Abell, Thomas 85
Ackroyd, Sir Edmund 243
Act Extinguishing the Authority of the
  Bishop of Rome (1536) 52
Act of Six Articles (1539) 199, 204
Act of Supremacy (1534) 29, 31, 51–2
Acton, Sir Robert 175, 177, 180–1, 184–5,
  186
Adeson, John 85
Ager, Anthony 209
agrarian grievances, and the Pilgrimage of
  Grace 108–9
agrarian rebellions (1549) 24–5, 279, 280–6,
  291, 293
Aldington, and the maid of Kent affair 65–7,
  81
Aleyn, James 57
Aleyn, Thomas 57, 58
Allen, William 308
Amadas, Mrs 33
Ambler, Henry 249
Amicable Grant 19–20, 248
Amsterdam, religious divisions in 231
Andros, Richard 177, 180, 187
Anglicanism 30–1
anticlericalism 24, 131–61
  and the Axminster affair 147–52, 156
  and Catholicism 132, 133, 142, 152, 158
  and the confiscation of liturgical
    paraphernalia 137–8
  'displacing' of ministers by the community
    136, 140
  and evangelicals 133, 134, 140, 146–7,
    160–1
  and the Henrician Reformation 139,
    144–7, 157–9
  and heresy 134, 149, 151
  and the maid of Kent affair 80, 84
  and the Mousehold Articles 284

negative and destructive 134, 135
parliamentary actions against clerical
  abuses 140–1
and the Pawlett affair 131–2, 152–9
physical and verbal attacks on priests 131,
  133, 134, 136–7
positive, idealistic and religious 134
positive, idealistic and secular 134
and Protestantism 131–2, 158, 160
and revisionist historians 132–3, 159–60
and royal government 140–4
and royal supremacy 59, 133
Applygarthe, Robert 120
Aquinas, Thomas, and the blood of Hailes
  166–7, 169
Archibald of Faversham 206, 208
Arcles, Robert 54
Armstrong, Clement 274
Arte, Father 41–2
Arthur of Canterbury, Friar 35
Arthur, Jerym 153
Arundell, Sir Thomas 142
Arundell, Thomas (curate) 50
Ascue, Sir William 101
Asheton, Thomas 121
Ashlower, Gloucestershire, conformist
  Catholicism in 49–50
Aske, Christopher 104
Aske, Robert 20, 43, 92, 97–8, 100, 102,
  103–4, 105
  and the Doncaster agreement 111, 112–13,
    115, 116, 118
  and post-pardon revolts 121, 123
  and taxation 107, 108
Askew, Anne 246
Askew, Francis 246
Aston, Margaret 215
Audley, Thomas, Baron Audley of Walden
  124
Augustine, St 2–3, 42, 309

Bucer, Martin 195, 230
Bucker, Raymond 209
Buckingham, Duke of 71–2, 166
Bukbery, Henry 125
Bullinger, Heinrich 229
Bullingham, John 305
Bullock, John 264
Bulmer, Sir John 109
Bunyan, John 3
Burdon, Richard 54
Bures, Robert 260
Burges, John 177, 179–80
Burnley, Lancashire, spoilation of chapel at 265–6
Bush, Michael 115, 122
Butler, John 229
Butler, Robert 244
Butley Priory, Suffolk 87
Buxton, Derbyshire, chapel of St Anne at 267
Bynge, Sir Thomas, parson of Milton 202

Calvin, John 228, 230
Cambridgeshire, agrarian rebels in 281–2
Camerdaye, Richard 194
canon law
　and royal supremacy 45–6
　on schism and heresy 42–3
Canterbury *see* theological debate in Canterbury
Carden, Thomas 209, 218
Carew, Peter 149
Carew, Sir William 148–9, 150, 151
Carew, Thomas 151
Carthusian monks, execution of (1535) 35
Cartmel Priory, Lancashire 122
Cartwright, Thomas 17
Castelyn, Simon 209
Catherine of Aragon 29, 61, 70, 71, 83
Catholicism
　in Amsterdam 231
　and anticlericalism 132, 133, 142, 152, 158
　Catholic writers on the English Reformation 305–6
　and the dissolution of the chantries 268–9
　and the doctrine of purgatory 237–8, 240–1
　and the Doncaster agreement 116–17
　European 10
　fissures in 6
　in France 230–1
　and holy relics 166–7
　and the justice system 204
　and the maid of Kent affair 63, 70–1, 81, 87

　and the Marian Counter-Reformation 307–8
　and monastic plunder 163, 164
　and the Pilgrimage of Grace 91, 124, 127
　and 'popular piety' 8, 9
　and popular politics 220
　and the Prebendaries' Plot (1543) 198, 199
　and the purchase of dissolved abbeys 13–14
　and Queen Mary 23
　and religious practice 10–11
　and revisionism 4, 5
　and royal supremacy 23–4, 29, 30–2, 36–60
　　accusations of heresy 32–6
　　conformist views on 44–51, 54–5, 59, 72
　　nonconformist views on 36–44, 54–5, 59
　　and the Romanist movement 59–60
　and the spoilation of the Abbey of Hailes 187–9, 191–3, 195
　and theological debate
　　on confession and penance 207
　　on English prayers 212–13
　　on images and idolatry 216–17
　　on Lenten fasting 215
　　on salvation and the sacrifice of Christ 205, 206–7
　and wills 185
　see also Romanist Catholics
Cawdray, John 264–5
Celsay, Elizabeth 227
chalices
　confiscation of by laymen 138–9, 290
　selling of 295, 297
Chaloner, Robert 124
Chanseler, Margaret 48
chantries
　and chapels of ease 249–50, 262–3, 266–7
　concealment of chantry lands 251–3
　decline in lay bequests to 242–3
　dissolution of 24, 236, 243–69
　　and collaboration 257–69
　　resistance to 247–57
　economic value of chantry endowments 236–7
　embezzlement of chantry goods 250–1, 253–7, 261
　origins and numbers of 238–9
　priests 238–9, 245, 246–7, 248, 253
　purchase of ex-chantry lands from the Crown 259–61
　spoilation of chapels 262–5
Chantries Act (1545) 244

Cambridge Studies in Early Modern British History

Titles in the series

**Also published as a paperback*